Latin American Underdevelopment

Latin American Underdevelopment

A History of Perspectives in the United States, 1870–1965

James William Park

Louisiana State University Press

Baton Rouge and London

Copyright © 1995 by Louisiana State University Press
All rights reserved
Manufactured in the United States of America
First printing
04 03 02 01 00 99 98 97 96 95   5 4 3 2 1

Designer: Amanda McDonald Key
Typeface: Trump Mediaeval
Typesetter: Moran Printing, Inc.
Printer and binder: Thomson–Shore, Inc.

Library of Congress Cataloging-in-Publication Data
Park, James William.
    Latin American underdevelopment : a history of perspectives in the
  United States, 1870–1965 / James William Park.
      p.   cm.
    Includes bibliographical references and index.
    ISBN 0-8071-1969-5 (alk. paper)
      1. Latin America—Foreign public opinion, American—History.
  2. Public opinion—United States—History.   3. Latin America—
  Economic conditions—Public opinion—History.   4. Latin America—
  Social conditions—Public opinion—History.   5. Latin America—
  Politics and government—Public opinion—History.   I. Title.
  F1418.P357   1995
  980—dc20   94-37209
                                                                        CIP

Table 1 is from L. Ronald Scheman, "The Alliance for Progress: Concept and Creativity," in Scheman, ed., *The Alliance for Progress: A Retrospective*, page 15, copyright
© 1988 by Praeger Publishers, an imprint of Greenwood Publishing Group, Inc., Westport, CT. Reprinted with permission.

The paper in this book meets the guidelines for permanence and durability of the Committee on Production Guidelines for Book Longevity of the Council on Library Resources. ∞

To Cynthia, Hillary, and David

Contents

Illustrations

Acknowledgments

Nearly all of the research for this work was conducted in San Diego, California, an achievement made possible through the remarkable convenience of interlibrary loan. In particular, I relied most heavily on the facilities of the San Diego State University Library, whose staff members in interlibrary loan service as well as in the other divisions of the library were unfailingly courteous and helpful in answering my questions and responding to my many requests. I also wish to thank the staffs of the University of San Diego Library and the city library of San Diego for their assistance and their kindness. It is unlikely that this study would have been completed had it not been for the grant of a sabbatical leave in 1987 by the San Diego Community College District and for the support of Ray Ramirez in obtaining that leave. For this I remain indebted.

Foremost among the individual scholars I want to thank formally for making publication of this work possible is Roger L. Cunniff, who very carefully read an early version of it. He wrote a detailed critique, discussed some of the major strengths and weaknesses of the study, and offered ideas that greatly improved the final product. I also owe a special debt to Helen Delpar for her helpful, friendly suggestions and for her timely encouragement. Many other friends and colleagues read the manuscript and offered valuable advice, all of which was gratefully received and most of which was followed. Along with the solicited criticism and advice came invaluable words of encouragement and words of caution. I am particularly thankful to three scholars whose support and friendship date back to my days at the University of Kansas—Robert L. Gilmore, Donald R. McCoy, and Charles L. Stansifer. Another friend of even longer standing, Robert A. Naylor, provided buoyant enthusiasm and useful criticism gleaned from a careful reading of the manuscript. I also deeply appreciate the early support of Richard Griswold del Castillo and the perceptive commentary of

J. Leon Helguera and Simon Collier. In addition, I wish to thank the anonymous readers solicited by Louisiana State University Press for their contributions and insights. The selfless support of all these readers has sustained me in this endeavor, and their commentary has helped me avoid embarrassing errors of fact and interpretation. But the errors that inevitably adhere to a work such as this are solely my responsibility. Lastly, I thank Cynthia, whose patience, faith, and support have assured that this project was treated as a welcome guest in our home rather than an intrusive stranger.

Latin American Underdevelopment

Introduction

Within a few weeks of his January, 1961, inauguration as president of the United States, John F. Kennedy launched the Alliance for Progress, and at the end of the year he warned that if this U.S.-led effort to spur modernization in Latin America failed, "the heritage of centuries of Western Civilization will be consumed in a few months of violence." The growing U.S. concern of the late 1950s over Latin American problems changed to alarm in 1959 when Fidel Castro suddenly emerged as champion of the revolutionary path to hemispheric development. For a long moment in the late 1950s and early 1960s the Latin American terrain seemed fertile ground for cataclysmic upheaval. The resulting focus of attention directed to the region stimulated the sense of crisis that led Kennedy to early enactment of the Alliance for Progress. Enjoying broadly based, bipartisan support, the Alliance expressed the nation's prevailing optimism, its utopian vision of Latin America's future, and confidence in the ability of the U.S. to carry out the anticommunist mission of the postwar period by guiding Latin America toward modernization in the U.S. image. Before the end of the decade the Alliance was judged a failure, and the consensus that had produced it collapsed. The debate of the 1960s over Latin American underdevelopment continued into the next two decades, when it was conducted amidst an energy crisis, massive Latin American indebtedness, civil war and international conflict in Central America, a large influx of undocumented Latin Americans into the U.S., and the invasions of Grenada and Panama. The Alliance for Progress sprang from an interpretation of Latin American underdevelopment that is yet today expressed as a major voice in the ongoing debate in academic circles on hemispheric development and that rests on a perspective with very deep roots in the American past.

This study presents a history of how Americans explained Latin American underdevelopment from 1870 to implementation of the Alliance for Progress. It begins with the 1870 debate over the proposed treaty to annex the Dominican Republic, an event that provided an opportunity for extended commentary about Latin America without the distorting passions associated with the Mexican-American and

Spanish-American wars. The debate of 1870, a neutral midpoint between the wars, also provides a point of reference for American views as they existed before being influenced by the late-nineteenth-century surge of interest in Latin America. It concludes with the implementation of the Alliance for Progress in the early 1960s, a time representing the high-water mark of the post–World War II era in the formulation of a consensus of views on Latin American underdevelopment. Because the interpretation of the region's underdevelopment was only indirectly expressed as part of the general perspective on Latin America during much of this period, the study is necessarily set within the broader framework of a history of U.S. perceptions of Latin America. But it must be noted that an understanding of what is glibly referred to herein as "American perceptions" rests on samplings of the expressed views of that tiny segment of the educated public that had the occasion and desire to communicate an opinion on a subject of limited interest. As a history covering a century of American thought about Latin American developmental problems, it is placed within the context of the course of U.S. relations with its hemispheric neighbors, the U.S. rise to global preeminence, and the intellectual currents within the nation that shaped attitudes toward Latin America. This study thus provides the broad background essential for understanding the debate of the last two decades about Latin American underdevelopment.

The treaty debate of 1870 revealed that, at a time when Americans had little contact with, interest in, or solid information about Latin America, those who commented on the region held firm views about things Latin American, and they offered ready explanations for its failure to keep pace with the U.S. in achieving political stability within a democratic framework, balanced economic growth, and social integration. This set of shortcomings is broadly referred to herein as *underdevelopment*, a term that came to imply a willful failure to meet potential as opposed to *undeveloped*, the presumed starting position of every country. Until the post–World War II period, when the term *underdeveloped* became popularized, all of the Latin American nations were referred to as "backward" or "retarded" in contrast to the "forward," "progressive," or "advanced" countries, i.e., the U.S., Canada, and the countries of Western Europe. Underdeveloped gained acceptance as a less-pejorative term when large numbers of what are today commonly called Third World or lesser-developed countries were freed from colonial status during the two decades following World War II. The Latin American nations, though long independent, were usually categorized as underdeveloped along with these newly emerging nations. Such classification resulted primarily from the application of economic criteria such as per capita income, but other factors such as political maturity, size of the middle class, educational achievement, and technological progress were also important, otherwise an oil-rich country like Venezuela, with a relatively high per capita income, would not have been ranked in the postwar years as underdeveloped. Throughout the period studied, commentators generally perceived significant differences in the levels of development from country to country in Latin America, but they were so influenced by the relatively high degree of material prosperity in the United States and by such commonly observed Latin American characteristics as the gap between rich and poor, the lack of technological progress, and political instability that the entire region was considered underdeveloped. Significant economic growth in a few countries at certain times was often masked by a pervasive tone of pessimism and thus unnoted. The concept of underdevelopment, though essentially an economic one, is used here to include its political and social parameters, because much of the commentary implied this broader meaning and assumed that the economic, political, and social sectors were somehow linked so that progress in one would bring progress in the others. The U.S. example seemed to validate this assumption in most observers' minds.

Interpretation of Latin American underdevelopment by interested commentators of the post–Civil War generation sprang directly from inherited perceptions of people, culture, and environment. This collective wisdom held that Latin Americans were a racially inferior people handicapped by an authoritarian, medieval cultural legacy and by a tropical setting inimical to progress. Frequent retelling of the El Dorado myth of Latin America's untapped natural abundance emphasized the theme of failure as did an ever-widening chasm between a seemingly stagnant Latin America and a dynamic United States. In the decades between the conclusion of the Civil War and the onset of the Great Depression, the U.S. achieved national integration, impressive population and industrial growth, and world-power status. Amidst these transformations and in the ebb and flow of interest in Latin America, in the policy meanderings toward the region, and in the alternations between apathy and alarm about the state of U.S.–Latin American relations, perceptions of Latin America remained remarkably fixed, although interpretation of the region's developmental problems was largely a product of amateurish interest and idle curiosity. It emerged incidentally from the commentary of travelers, journalists, businessmen, statesmen, politicians, members of scientific expeditions, scholars, and oftentimes of essayists and editorialists who had never ventured south of the Rio Grande.

This study documents a notably consistent and enduring pattern of disdain toward the peoples and cultures of Latin America. Ignorance, misinformation, an ethnocentric perspective, and racial bias provided the basis for that attitude. It is well to note, however, that these patterns of misunderstanding should not be taken as uniquely American, for they were quite universal. Interpretation of Latin America's seeming failure to progress underwent some modification as a result of the entry of academic specialists into the discussion, which began approximately in the 1920s, as well as the internal crisis caused by depression during the 1930s and the depression-born appeal of the anti-industrial perspective. But it was not until after World War II that the traditional interpretation gave way to more-complex analyses.

Commentary on Latin American underdevelopment during the 1950s differed from that of earlier periods in that it focused directly rather than incidentally on the problem. The concept of underdevelopment became popularized by the postwar breakup of colonial empires and by the drama of dozens of new countries attempting to establish nationhood. The 1950s marked the beginning of a slowly growing sense of responsibility for Third World development that sharpened as the U.S. assumed ever-larger global responsibilities, as Cold War competition moved into Third World regions, and as those countries found voices to champion their cause in the United Nations and other international agencies. At the same time, U.S. understanding of the process of development grew in sophistication, and the study of underdevelopment became an academic fad. Scholars published several studies of the developmental process, some of which centered on Latin America, but by 1960 the scholarly analysis of underdevelopment was just gaining momentum. Simultaneously, the rise of Castro delivered a blow to U.S.–Latin American relations, and U.S. national interests appeared to be directly involved in the outcome of the Latin American effort to modernize. The case for active participation in that effort seemed compelling, and the result was the Alliance for Progress. The Alliance rested on a woefully inadequate interpretation of Latin America's developmental problems. As evidence for the failure of the Alliance mounted in the mid-1960s, questions about the validity of that interpretation sparked the ongoing debate over cause and cure for Latin American underdevelopment.

This study is based almost exclusively on familiar U.S. sources that have been examined from a fresh point of view. Exceptions are works by Latin Americans that influenced commentary within the United States such as Domingo F. Sarmiento's *Life in the Argentine Republic in the Days of the Tyrants* (1868), Francisco García Calderón's *Latin*

America: Its Rise and Progress (1913), and various writings of the 1950s by the Argentine economist Raúl Prebisch. During the research phase of this study it quickly became apparent that U.S. commentators on Latin America often presented their negative comments through the simple device of quoting Latin Americans, thus making the observations more authoritative while deflecting criticism from the more sensitive among the U.S. authors. It also became clear that a substantial literature of Latin American self-criticism has existed since independence, beginning with Simón Bolívar. That literature is only an incidental part of this study—it would surely require an additional volume—even though much of that self-criticism was inspired by the same currents of Western thought that influenced observers in the United States.

Much has been written in the last quarter century about the causes of Latin American underdevelopment, and it centers on conflicting theories of development, particularly the so-called modernization and dependency theories that are treated in the final chapters of this work. An excellent exposition of these theories and the recent evolution of thought on this theme is provided by Peter F. Klarén and Thomas J. Bossert, editors of *Promise of Development: Theories of Change in Latin America* (1986). But the large body of post-1960 literature, which for the most part is multidisciplinary, does not include a systematic effort to trace the history of the U.S. interpretation of Latin American underdevelopment before the 1960s. The origin, relative strength, duration, and course of the different interpretations remain largely unexamined. Lacking a major historical component, this literature does, however, generally recognize that many American observers had freely commented on their southern neighbors' lack of progress long before academicians took up the theme in the mid-twentieth century. Those earlier explanations were usually based on racial, cultural, and geographic factors, as shown by studies examining U.S. perceptions of Latin America, of which the most recent and most noteworthy is Fredrick B. Pike's *The United States and Latin America: Myths and Stereotypes of Civilization and Nature* (1992), a sweeping historical analysis of stereotypes held by Americans and Latin Americans of each other. Other important studies of U.S. perceptions include Philip Wayne Powell's *Tree of Hate: Propaganda and Prejudices Affecting United States Relations with the Hispanic World* (1971), Arthur G. Pettit's *Images of the Mexican American in Fiction and Film* (1980), and two works by John J. Johnson: *Latin America in Caricature* (1980) and *A Hemisphere Apart: The Foundations of United States Policy Toward Latin America* (1990). The latter book also tackles the more-complex issue of relating those perceptions to the formulation of U.S. policy toward newly independent Latin American nations in the early nineteenth century. The more-modest goal of this study is to identify the salient interpretations of Latin American underdevelopment, trace their evolution, and relate them to the emergence in the 1960s of conflicting theories of development.

1

United States Perspectives on Latin America to 1870

On January 10, 1870, President Ulysses S. Grant requested that the United States Senate ratify a treaty calling for annexation of the Dominican Republic. Immediate public reaction was subdued, but the issue, which Grant had "irresponsibly evoked from nowhere," provoked inflamed debate before the Senate killed the treaty six months later, thus inflicting on Grant, a man of great stubbornness, his first decisive defeat as president.[1] Debate on annexation offered one of the few opportunities between the 1840s and 1890s for Americans to give serious thought to any part of Latin America. The debate is also significant because it registered U.S. attitudes toward the Dominican Republic and the larger Latin American region at a time when foreign affairs aroused meager interest. Indeed, one striking feature of the debate was the revelation that attitudes toward the Dominican Republic and Latin America were well defined and vigorously espoused even though contacts with the region were irregular and knowledge was scant. In the post–Civil War years, foreign crises such as the Canadian fisheries dispute, Chinese immigration, and the *Virginius* affair arose sporadically, but they failed to generate a sustained interest in foreign affairs. One historian, specializing in the late nineteenth century, correctly noted that, when these infrequent crises erupted, Americans "did not halt and reflect afresh on the nature of a particular antagonist, for a complete characterization already existed. Americans automatically referred to a collective compendium of national images that assigned values to every overseas people."[2]

The collective compendium of Latin American images in the post–Civil War years was the product of varied, often contradictory influences that had operated for many decades before the Civil War. One favorable influence that sprang from the Enlightenment and persisted through much of the nineteenth century was the interest in all

1. Allan Nevins, *Hamilton Fish: The Inner History of the Grant Administration* (New York, 1936), 249.
2. Gerald F. Linderman, *The Mirror of War: American Society and the Spanish-American War* (Ann Arbor, 1974), 114.

aspects of Latin American culture by men of learning who participated in an inter-American book trade, sponsored Latin Americans to membership in learned societies, and supported scientific expeditions to the region.[3] During the 1850s several well-publicized, government-sponsored expeditions undertook scientific investigations in Latin America. These included explorations of the Isthmus of Darien to find an interoceanic canal route, others in the La Plata Basin to report on the area's natural resources and trade prospects, and still others in Chile and western Argentina supplementary to the work of the U.S. Astronomical Expedition to Chile. The most-fascinating expedition was the Navy-sponsored exploration in 1851–1852 of the Amazon River Basin, from the river's Andean sources in Peru and Bolivia, by Lieutenants William Lewis Herndon and Lardner Gibbon. Foreseeing a bright commercial future for the basin if the river were opened to free navigation, Herndon, the expedition leader, concluded that the basin was a land of "unrivalled fertility" capable of "yielding support, comfort, and luxury to many millions of civilized people. . . ." These various expeditions to Latin America attracted considerable interest, and the expedition leaders publicized their experiences and their observations of terrain and climate, people and customs, and economic and trade prospects in popular books, official reports, articles, and lectures.[4]

The more than two dozen artist-travelers from the United States who spent time in Central and South America during the middle decades of the nineteenth century constituted another influential group of visitors to Latin America. This group included such well-known American artists of the period as Frederic Church, Martin Heade, James McNeill Whistler, and Titian Peale. Most of them were attracted south by the same fascinating natural phenomena—the volcanoes, towering Andes, and pulsating tropics—that lured the scientists. In fact, several artists went to Latin America as draftsmen and illustrators attached to scientific expeditions. In a larger sense these artist-travelers were beckoned by "the frontier quality of tropical America" and by "its mythical identification with the terrestrial paradise and the land of El Dorado." Important exceptions to the artists at-

3. Harry Bernstein, "Free Minds in the Americas," in *Responsible Freedom in the Americas*, ed. Angel Del Río (Garden City, N.Y., 1955), 226–38.

4. Merle Curti and Kendall Birr, *Prelude to Point Four: American Technical Missions Overseas, 1838–1938* (Madison, Wis., 1954), 12–13; Vincent Ponko, Jr., *Ships, Seas, and Scientists: U.S. Naval Exploration and Discovery in the Nineteenth Century* (Annapolis, 1974), 89, 132, 174; Lieutenants William Lewis Herndon and Lardner Gibbon, *Exploration of the Valley of the Amazon, Made Under Direction of the Navy Department* (2 vols.; Washington, D.C., 1853), I, 367, 370.

tracted by the natural setting were those, such as Frederick Cather-
wood, who were intrigued by the mysteries surrounding ancient Indian ruins; another exception was the famous portraitist of North
American Indians, George Catlin, who spent five years observing and
painting the Indians of South America. The most famous work produced from this group of artists was Church's *Heart of the Andes,* an
expansive oil-on-canvas landscape exhibited in New York City in 1859
to "unprecedented acclaim." Exhibited subsequently to large crowds
in other cities, it was emulated, copied by fellow artists, and widely
circulated as an engraving. Aside from contributing significantly to
the development of North American landscape art, the artists' Latin
American experience added to the scanty amount of information available about the region through their correspondence and articles, pamphlets that accompanied their exhibitions, and the works of art themselves, which in turn excited curiosity about Latin America.[5]

Another positive influence was the appearance at midcentury of a
truly classic travel literature. Several venturesome travelers to Latin
America described exotic natural scenes, quaint social customs, and
unharried life-styles that attracted multitudes of homebound readers.
John Lloyd Stephens in *Incidents of Travel in Central America, Chi-
apas and Yucatan* (1841), a beautifully illustrated two-volume work,
wrote with enthusiasm and good humor about his strange adventures
and pioneer archaeological work in the Mayan ruins. In the same year,
Richard Henry Dana published *Two Years Before the Mast,* an account
of a young seaman's experiences sailing from Boston around Cape Horn
to California and back. Though Dana expressed some very critical
racial stereotypes about the residents of Mexican California, he was
enchanted with its missions and fandangos, and he found the region
"blessed with a climate, than which there can be no better in the
world." Two years later appeared Madame Calderón de la Barca's *Life
in Mexico during a Residence of Two Years in That Country,* a record
of life among the upper crust by a gifted writer who conveyed enthusiasm and fascination for the picturesque landscape and the "graceful
cordiality" of its people. Another notable travel account of the period
was *Notes on Central America* (1855) by E. George Squier; he registered great optimism for the future of Honduras and El Salvador, which
he described in scientific detail while surveying for a projected railroad route. These four classics introduced many readers to Latin American themes and aroused interest in the region through descriptions of

5. Katherine Emma Manthorne, *Tropical Renaissance: North American Artists
Exploring Latin America, 1839–1879* (Washington, D.C., 1989), 1–4, 26, 32, 55, 91–92,
104.

high adventure, ancient ruins, gracious living, and undeveloped wealth.[6]

The travel genre in the pre–Civil War decades also included books of lesser quality with smaller circulations, written by traders, whalers, missionaries, and people with varied experiences in Latin America. American merchant vessels regularly visited the ports of the West Indies, Rio de Janeiro, La Plata Basin, Valparaiso, and Callao for trade or for provisioning en route to China or the Pacific Northwest or California. Whalers hunting in the Pacific whaling grounds off the Chilean coast frequently called at Valparaiso. Beginning in 1849, travel to the California goldfields by way of the Isthmus of Panama, Nicaragua, or Cape Horn—the latter route often included provisioning stops in Latin American ports—inspired these argonauts to add to the mid-nineteenth-century travel literature their colorful descriptions of brief visits to Latin America.[7] A sailor's 1857 account of his experience in the U.S. Navy, merchant marine, and on whaling ships illustrates the commonly expressed sense of wonder evoked by even brief contact with the periphery of Latin America. Upon arrival in the harbor of Rio de Janeiro, he recorded: "All this variety . . . seemed so strange, and withal so beautiful, that even as I gazed I almost fancied myself transported into fairy land. . . ."[8]

Despite this travel literature, knowledge of Latin America at mid-century is best characterized by its lack of depth and substance. An article in the *North American Review* in 1849 aptly noted: "Spanish America at the present hour, looms up to us on the far horizon of the political world in a mist of lurid light, which veils her from the general gaze about as effectually as the darkness of her old estate."[9] The writer, a literary critic reviewing Spanish-American poetry, suggested that Latin America appeared in a "mist of lurid light" because of apathy, but factors of greater weight were the expense, hardship, and danger of travel there.[10] Sources that would provide more solid informa-

6. Richard Henry Dana, *Two Years Before the Mast* (1841; rpr. New York, 1946), 144; Stanley T. Williams, *The Spanish Background of American Literature* (New Haven, 1955), I, 86–90.

7. Samuel Eliot Morison, *The Maritime History of Massachusetts, 1783–1860* (Rev. ed.; Cambridge, Mass., 1961), 266, 271, 316.

8. Charles Nordhoff, *Nine Years a Sailor: Being Sketches of Personal Experience in the United States Naval Service, the American and British Merchant Marine, and the Whaling Service* (Cincinnati, 1857), 116.

9. W. H. Hulbert, "The Poetry of Spanish America," *North American Review*, LXVIII (January, 1849), 130–31.

10. Williams, *The Spanish Background*, I, 51–52, 84–85. Toward the end of the century it still took nearly six days to sail from New York to Venezuela. See Richard Harding Davis, "The Paris of South America," *Harper's New Monthly Magazine*, XCII (December, 1895), 108.

tion on the region by the end of the century, such as scientific descriptions, histories, and government reports, were rare at midcentury, and the few that did appear complained uniformly of limitations imposed by arduous travel conditions. The following summary of a study of U.S. government efforts to establish relations with Central America from 1825–1850 suggests the impediments to a reliable flow of information:

Of the eleven appointees [to Central America] before 1849, three died *en route*; another succumbed before he started on his mission; one escaped with his life by being dismissed before he embarked; another survived by contriving to draw his salary for more than a year without going near the Central American capital; and another traveled over the length and breadth of the country, unable to find a government to receive him. Though the remaining four reached their destination and were received, only one of these prolonged his stay beyond a few months, and he committed suicide soon after his return to the United States.[11]

While men of learning were seeking to establish a New World community of scholars and artists, and other travelers were imparting an alluring quality to Latin America, other more-powerful influences helped form the U.S. view. One such influence was growing contact with Mexico. During the colonial period Anglo-American expansion in North America had conflicted with Spanish interests in East and West Florida, along the Mississippi River, and at New Orleans over control of commerce. Those colonial rivalries were inherited by Mexico and the United States in the 1820s.[12] Because Mexico was the part of Latin America with which Americans had their most-direct and continuous contact, attitudes toward Mexico shaped predispositions toward the larger region. In a study of the attitudes of fifteen Americans who visited Mexico from 1821 to 1846, one historian found that the visitors uniformly regarded Mexicans as economically and politically backward, lacking in character and republican spirit, racially inferior, and oppressed by a Catholic church that maintained the people in a state of ignorance. Similar findings were reported for the 1840s in a detailed study subtitled *The Mexican War in the American Imagination,* in which the author noted that U.S. observers were deeply impressed by the contrast between Mexico's natural beauty and wealth and its ignorant, oppressed, mongrel population. Studies of Manifest Destiny have abundantly documented the orgy of anti-Mexican sen-

11. Joseph B. Lockey, "Diplomatic Futility," *Hispanic American Historical Review,* X (1930), 265.

12. Philip Wayne Powell, *Tree of Hate: Propaganda and Prejudices Affecting United States Relations with the Hispanic World* (New York, 1971), 117.

timent set off by the war with Mexico in the 1840s.[13] In addition, Arthur G. Pettit, in *Images of the Mexican American in Fiction and Film*, has convincingly shown that beginning in the aftermath of the Texas Revolution and continuing into the twentieth century, U.S. fiction set in the Southwest presented an overwhelmingly negative image of the Mexican and Mexican American as a dark, sinister "greaser bandido."[14] Following the Treaty of Guadalupe-Hidalgo ending the Mexican-American War, U.S. consciousness of Mexico faded—except in the Southwest—until the closing decades of the nineteenth century, but the attitudes formed in those earlier years persisted and largely contributed to the distorted generalizations about Latin America.

One factor that could still arouse sporadic interest in Mexico during the 1850s and, at the same time, provided a barometer of American sentiment toward its southern neighbor was the launching from U.S. territory of six major filibustering expeditions—four led by Americans and two by Frenchmen—against Sonora and Baja California. These expeditions, some of which attracted hundreds of volunteers, were motivated not only by a taste for adventure and quick wealth but also by a desire to bring enlightenment and progress to "an indolent and half civilized people."[15] Widely and favorably reported in the press, these filibustering enterprises were nourished by the decade's spirit of Manifest Destiny and expansionistic adventurism, and they were directed against a people whom many Americans regarded as inferior.[16] Shortly after the failure in 1853 of one such expedition, its leader, William Walker, captured the nation's headlines by directing his followers to Central America and seizing control of Nicaragua; from that base he struggled to bring the Central American republics under "the civilizing influence of the American people" until his capture and execution in 1860.[17] Through his book, *The War in Nicaragua*, which became a best-seller after its 1860 publication, and the extensive publicity surrounding his exploits, millions of Americans became con-

13. David Thomas Leary, "The Attitudes of Certain United States Citizens Toward Mexico, 1821–1846" (Ph.D. dissertation, University of Southern California, 1970), 234–42; Robert W. Johannsen, *To the Halls of the Montezumas: The Mexican War in the American Imagination* (New York, 1985), 21–25, 165–67, 289–93; Albert K. Weinberg, *Manifest Destiny: A Study of Nationalist Expansionism in American History* (Baltimore, 1935), 167–89; Frederick Merk, *Manifest Destiny and Mission in American History: A Reinterpretation* (New York, 1963), 121–28, 157–66.

14. Arthur G. Pettit, *Images of the Mexican American in Fiction and Film* (College Station, Tex., 1980), 22, 58–59.

15. Joseph Allen Stout, Jr., *The Liberators: Filibustering Expeditions into Mexico, 1848–1862, and the Last Thrust of Manifest Destiny* (Los Angeles, 1973), 92–93.

16. *Ibid.*, v, vii, 91, 185–86.

17. Albert Z. Carr, *The World and William Walker* (New York, 1963), vii, 151.

vinced that this "Man of Destiny" was a missionary for Americanism who sought to uplift a benighted people burdened with feudalism and restore a land "the Spaniards had cursed . . . with a mixed race" by securing control to the superior race.[18]

The war with Mexico, the filibustering raids, and many of the observations of U.S. visitors to Latin America reflected in their totality more than disdain toward the peoples and cultures of Latin America— they expressed elements of the "Black Legend." The Black Legend originated in anti-Spanish attitudes that had formed in the Old World by at least the sixteenth century and that were extended to Spanish America after the New World conquests and, to a lesser extent, Portugal and Brazil. Anti-Spanish attitudes were intensified by Spain's early imperial success overseas and by its refusal to be "reformed" in the religious revolution of the sixteenth and seventeenth centuries. In the main, the legend portrayed Spaniards as a treacherous, bigoted, and decadent people, thwarted in their progress by authoritarian government, political corruption, and indolence, and further stigmatized by descriptions of their New World conquests emphasizing the Spaniards' insatiable greed and brutal destruction of the indigenous peoples and cultures.[19] Generation after generation, these characterizations suffused Anglo-American accounts of the Dutch rebellion against Philip II, England's defeat of the Spanish Armada, the activities of the Spanish Inquisition, and the massacres of untold numbers of highly cultured Aztecs, Mayas, and Incas. Hatred of things Spanish was early carried from Europe to the North American colonies, particularly by English and Dutch settlers, because of such factors as religious rivalry, colonial conflict, and economic competition. At the end of the colonial period Thomas Jefferson wrote that, although the Spanish American colonies appeared headed for independence, "History, I believe, furnishes no example of a priest-ridden people maintaining a free civil government." Secretary of State John Quincy Adams noted in conversation with Henry Clay in 1821, on the eve of extending recogni-

18. William Walker, *The War in Nicaragua* (1860; rpr. Tucson, Ariz., 1985), 10, 259, 430; Carr, *The World and William Walker*, vii, 156, 175, 208.

19. Charles Gibson, ed., *The Black Legend: Anti-Spanish Attitudes in the Old World and the New* (New York, 1971), 18–27; Ruth Miller Elson, *Guardians of Tradition: American Schoolbooks of the Nineteenth Century* (Lincoln, Nebr., 1964), 75–76, 156–61; Lewis Hanke, *The Spanish Struggle for Justice in the Conquest of America* (Boston, 1965); Benjamin Keen, "The Black Legend Revisited: Assumptions and Realities," *Hispanic American Historical Review*, XLIX (1969), 703–19. For discussion of the transfer of Anglo-American negative perceptions about Old World Iberians to New World Creoles, see John J. Johnson, *A Hemisphere Apart: The Foundations of United States Policy Toward Latin America* (Baltimore, 1990), 56–58.

tion to the newly independent states of Latin America, that though he wished them well, he considered their prospects bleak: "They are not likely to promote the spirit either of freedom or order by their example. They have not the first elements of good or free government. Arbitrary power, military and ecclesiastical, is stamped upon their education, upon their habits, and upon all their institutions. Civil dissension is infused into all their seminal principles. War and mutual destruction are in every member of their organization, moral, political, and physical." [20] Latin America's uncertain and often bloody struggle to maintain free civil government in the decades after independence helped ensure that the Black Legend would remain embedded in U.S. culture and thus operate as a shaping influence on attitudes toward that region.

For fifty years during the mid-nineteenth century a powerfully influential group of New England historians published several substantial historical works that exhibited elements of the Black Legend, promoted its spirit, and thus molded American views toward Latin America. Their immediate predecessor and the nation's "first man of letters," Washington Irving, in his several histories on Spanish themes written in the 1820s and 1830s, displayed these same qualities while proving the popularity of the romantic epic drawn from Spain's past. Historians John Lothrop Motley, Francis Parkman, and George Bancroft wrote in the romantic tradition and expressed the basic assumptions that human progress "had proceeded westward, from the Middle East to North America." In their view the most-significant advances in history came about through victories won on behalf of Christianity, the Reformation, nationalism, and democracy; nations advanced through adherence to the progressive principle that expressed "the grand design of Providence." These historians believed in national character and that "the enduring progressive traits belong to Dutchmen, Englishmen, and Americans rather than to Frenchmen, Spaniards, or Italians." Spain, in particular, they regarded as an anti-progressive nation because of its absolutism and the influence of the Roman Catholic church on Spanish government and society. In addition, they portrayed Spaniards as "romantic, haughty, sometimes chivalrous, often cruel,

20. Williams, *The Spanish Background*, I, 3; Thomas Jefferson to Alexander von Humboldt, December 6, 1813, cited *ibid.*, I, 26; Adams's notation of conversation with Clay as cited in Samuel Flagg Bemis, *The Latin American Policy of the United States: An Historical Interpretation* (New York, 1943), 44. For a survey of the Black Legend in U.S. history and its influence on relations with Latin America in the colonial period and nineteenth century see Powell, *Tree of Hate*; for the role of schoolbooks and grammar school readers in perpetuating the Black Legend in the nineteenth century see Linderman, *The Mirror of War*, 115, and Elson, *Guardians of Tradition*, 75–76.

fanatical," while the Dutch and English were seen as "frank and manly, self-reliant, enterprising, vigorous." The United States emerged as the embodiment of human progress and the Spanish world as its antithesis in the works of these romantic historians, who set the standards for writing classical history in the U.S. from the mid-nineteenth until the early twentieth century.[21]

Separate mention must be made of William Hickling Prescott, who shared the romantic outlook of his fellow New England historians but who, at the same time, consciously strove to keep in check his regionally based, anti-Spanish prejudices. Two of his four great epic works, *History of the Conquest of Mexico* (1843) and *Conquest of Peru* (1847), enjoyed enormous popularity and helped, along with a high-quality travel literature and the war with Mexico, to turn that decade's attention toward Latin America. Both of these histories present the triumph of civilization over semicivilization, of Christianity—even in its Catholic form—over savage paganism. In describing these triumphs Prescott paid generous tribute to the steadfastness, daring, and valor of the conquerors, but he also detailed the vengeful acts of brutality taken against the Indians. These acts would become part of the Black Legend, but Prescott gave them religious justification. In concluding his discussion of Aztec religious practices, which included human sacrifice and cannibalism, he wrote that the rescue of the land from "brutish superstitions" had been "beneficiently ordered by Providence. . . . It is true, the conquerors brought along with them the Inquisition. But they also brought Christianity."[22]

The concept of race in the nineteenth century—a concept confused with culture, language, and nationality throughout the century—also had direct bearing on U.S. attitudes toward Latin America. The Enlightenment perceptions that humankind originally consisted of one race and that the environment was the cause of racial differences prevailed in Western thought until the early 1800s. From then until midcentury those views gradually lost adherents to the proposition of distinct races possessing innately different characteristics. As racial thinking evolved toward the view that racial differences were innate, the notion of a hierarchy of races—with Caucasians firmly po-

21. David Levin, *History as Romantic Art: Bancroft, Prescott, Motley, and Parkman* (Stanford, 1959), 27, 74, 93–94; Powell, *Tree of Hate,* 121–22. Levin includes Prescott in this group, but he is given separate treatment here for reasons presented in the following paragraph of the text.

22. Williams, *The Spanish Background,* I, 140, 142; II, 6–8, 94–95; Johannsen, *To the Halls of the Montezumas,* 245–48; William H. Prescott, *History of the Conquest of Mexico and History of the Conquest of Peru* (Modern Library ed., New York, n.d.), 51–52.

sitioned at the apex and racial mixtures at the bottom—also won general acceptance. These changing concepts of race in Western thought emerged in response to growing interest in racial differences, and in the United States this evolution was advanced by the work of scientists such as Samuel George Morton and Louis Agassiz and by amateur archaeologist E. George Squier.[23] Practical politics and everyday life in the U.S. also called forth these racial doctrines and moved discussion of them from scientific circles to popular forums. The slavery question occupied the center of American politics, Indian relations troubled national policymakers and disturbed the Western states, and the war with Mexico in the Southwest "thrust the Mexicans into American racial discussions." Racial thinking as it had evolved by midcentury markedly shaped attitudes toward Latin Americans, who were generally classified as mixed breeds. For example, the debate over annexation of Mexican territory in the 1840s was essentially "an argument not about territory but about Mexicans."[24]

The crisis of civil war interrupted the meager flow of information about Latin America, but the brief span between war's end and President Grant's 1870 proposal for annexing the Dominican Republic saw the recurrence of pre–Civil War themes and attitudes. They were echoed by an assortment of travelers to Latin America, including expatriates from the Confederacy, scientists, explorers, textbook authors, and missionaries, and the same views were occasionally presented by Latin Americans themselves.

In the immediate post–Civil War years at least eight to ten thousand Southerners, unable to confront their region's desperate plight, attempted to start new lives in Latin America. Their interest in it after the war was a natural continuation of interest from the antebellum years when, from the Southern viewpoint, the "fingers of 'manifest destiny' pointed southward as frequently as westward." Most emigrants went to Mexico and Brazil, which offered inducements such as travel subsidies, free land, and the promise of temporary exemptions from taxation and military service. Prominent ex-Confederate military and political officials lent their prestige to the colonizing enterprise, and colonization companies were established throughout the South to gather recruits, disseminate information, and send agents southward to select sites. But the project failed in both countries—abruptly in Mexico in 1867, when Napoleon III withdrew the French army and the forces of Benito Juárez captured and executed Maximil-

23. Reginald Horsman, *Race and Manifest Destiny: The Origins of American Racial Anglo-Saxonism* (Cambridge, Mass., 1981), 116, 125, 132–34.
24. *Ibid.*, 137–38, 156–57, 236.

ian, patron of American colonization, and more gradually in Brazil because of difficulties such as insufficient capital, transportation problems, isolation, and disease.[25]

The letters, pamphlets, newspaper articles, and books written by those involved with colonization reflect a wide range of opinions toward the host countries; such sources have obvious limitations because many were written by paid propagandists, recruiting agents, and colonists who suffered bitter personal losses. Some common themes stand out, nevertheless. One frequently stated view was that Mexico and Brazil enjoyed such a bounteous tropical abundance that a person could live well there with scant labor. An American adventurer-scholar who spent six months near a colony of ex-Confederates in Mexico proclaimed in his diary: "With a good government, what a paradise this would be!"[26] Another common view was that Mexico and Brazil were extremely backward and that American immigrants would bring quick progress. An American ship captain who observed the migration to Brazil in 1866 blamed Brazil's backwardness on its high degree of racial mixing. "But," he declared, "let the government, the custom-house, the post-office, and the courts be directed by North American intellects, the soil be cultivated by North American energy and machinery, down will go the tottering relics of barbarism. . . ."[27] Negative commentary on miscegenation by those associated with colonization was noteworthy, but other U.S. travelers to Latin America even more consistently and forcefully condemned the mixing of races.

In 1867 Louis Agassiz and his wife published *A Journey in Brazil*, which attracted considerable attention because of the scientific renown of Agassiz, who had arrived in the United States from his native Switzerland in 1846. A naturalist and geologist who established his reputation as an ichthyologist and expert on glaciers before accepting a Harvard University professorship in 1848, Agassiz revolutionized the study of natural history in his adopted country from that date until his death in 1873. In 1865 he and his wife Elizabeth—a well-known writer—six

25. Douglas Audenreid Grier, "Confederate Emigration to Brazil, 1865–1870" (Ph.D. dissertation, University of Michigan, 1968), 31, 78–79, 83, 109–12; Lawrence F. Hill, "The Confederate Exodus to Latin America," *Southwestern Historical Quarterly*, XXXIX (1935), 100–103; Lawrence F. Hill, "Confederate Exiles to Brazil," *Hispanic American Historical Review*, VII (1927), 193–97; George D. Harmon, "Confederate Migration to Mexico," *Hispanic American Historical Review*, XVII (1937), 458–59, 469, 486.

26. Ramón Eduardo Ruiz, ed., *An American in Maximilian's Mexico, 1865–1866: The Diaries of William Marshall Anderson* (San Marino, Calif., 1959), 29.

27. John Codman, *Ten Months in Brazil, with Incidents of Voyages and Travels, Descriptions of Scenery and Characters, Notices of Commerce and Productions, etc.* (Boston, 1867), 144.

scientific assistants, and several volunteers began a year's study of Brazilian fauna, focusing their investigations on fish in the Amazon River and its tributaries. The book that emerged was an informed travel account, with commentary on life in Brazil as well as on the scientific work of the expedition. It should be noted that the observations on Brazilian society may have been influenced by the attitudes of French and German exiles with whom the couple was in frequent contact.

The racial patterns of Brazil made a distinct impression on Agassiz and his wife, and they commented at length on the relationship between race and "the enfeebled character of the population." "It is not merely that the children are of every hue," but in Brazil "this mixture of races seems to have had a much more unfavorable influence on the physical development than in the United States. It is as if all clearness of type had been blurred, and the result is a vague compound lacking character and expression." [28] They invited any person who doubted "the evil of this mixture of races" to come to Brazil: "He cannot deny the deterioration consequent upon an amalgamation of races, more widespread here than in any other country in the world, and which is rapidly effacing the best qualities of the white man, the negro, and the Indian, leaving a mongrel nondescript type, deficient in physical and mental energy." [29]

Although Agassiz and his team traveled along the coast of Brazil, they spent most of the year in the Amazon Valley, which they regarded, like Alexander von Humboldt and countless other visitors before and since, as an emporium of potential wealth lacking only a sufficient population for proper development. "We long to see a vigorous emigration pour into this region so favored by Nature, so bare of inhabitants. But things go slowly in these latitudes; great cities do not spring up in half a century, as with us." But the authors had a particular quality of immigrant in mind, for they noted: "If also I miss among them [the Brazilians] something of the stronger and more persistent qualities of the Northern races, I do but recall a distinction which is as ancient as the tropical and temperate zones themselves." The authors also briefly discussed other factors they believed contributory to Brazil's apparent stagnation, but these are insignificant when contrasted to the attention given primarily to race and secondarily to climate. [30]

A synopsis of an account of a scientific expedition's travels through Ecuador and Brazil appeared nearly three years after the Agassiz book

28. Louis Agassiz and Elizabeth Cabot Cary Agassiz, *A Journey in Brazil* (Boston, 1895), 292.
29. *Ibid.*, 293.
30. *Ibid.*, 342, 517, 496–97, 504.

and just as the debate on Dominican annexation was getting under way. The article, published in *Harper's New Monthly Magazine*, was based on a book by the naturalist James Orton of Vassar College; his expedition was sponsored by the Smithsonian Institution in 1867. Like Agassiz, Orton stressed the enormous potential of the Amazon Valley, claiming that the climate was "temperate rather than tropical" and that, if fully populated, the valley could "feed four hundred millions."[31] Most striking about the article, however, is the drawing "At Home on the Amazon," which heads the article. The drawing belies the assertion of the Amazon Valley's temperate climate, and it conveys a powerful image of tropical indolence.

THE ANDES AND THE AMAZON

AT HOME ON THE AMAZON

"At Home on the Amazon"
Harper's New Monthly Magazine, XL (February, 1870), p. 344.

31. A. H. Guernsey, "The Andes and the Amazon," *Harper's New Monthly Magazine*, XL (February, 1870), 356–57.

In 1866, one year before the Agassiz study appeared, George Earl Church, a geographer and explorer with unusually wide experience in Latin America, published *Mexico, Its Revolutions: Are They Evidence of Retrogression or of Progress?* This extended essay was a revision of an article published in the New York *Herald* and was written with sympathy toward Mexico near the end of its struggle against Maximilian and the French. Church argued that the revolutionary turmoil common to Mexico and the other Spanish American republics since independence constituted essential first steps toward progress, because those struggles were waged to extirpate the iniquitous colonial heritage. According to Church, Mexico's plight derived from two factors—the colonial heritage and the influential role of a benighted clergy. He held that Mexico would not advance until "that great cloud of fifteenth century darkness . . . shall be swept away by the advancing sun of modern civilization, and her people freed from the incubus of a long night of bigoted religious misrule. . . . " In reference to Spanish America he asserted: "It is a sickening tale of horror to run through the three hundred years of sword, bullet, fagot, torture, and famine. . . ." Progress has inevitably been slow, Church reasoned, because the Creoles began the struggle for independence "with minds corrupted by their masters; with the most disgusting [political] vices . . . ; with the clergy pandering to every known vice of a corrupt education." Church, nevertheless, foresaw a bright future for Mexico because no country surpassed it in the blessings of climate and natural bounty.[32]

Benson John Lossing, a New York editor and author of more than twenty popular and school texts on U.S. history, published in 1867 a revised edition of a history that expressed an attitude toward the Spanish colonial period similar to that of Church. But Lossing's condemnation of the Spanish was directed toward their treatment of the Indians. He portrayed the Aztecs as "the most efficient instruments in the hands of Providence for spreading the light of dawning civilization over the whole Continent," but in the sweep of the Spanish conquest the Aztecs "were beaten into the dust of debasement by the falchion blows of avarice and bigotry." In the final paragraph of his account of Spanish colonization, Lossing drew a sharp contrast between the Spanish and English as colonizers, and he explained the disordered state of Spanish America on the basis of its colonial legacy.

[The Spanish] were impelled by no higher motive than the acquisition of gold, and treachery and violence were the instruments employed to obtain it. They

---

32. George Earl Church, *Mexico, Its Revolutions: Are They Evidence of Retrogression or of Progress?* (New York, 1866), 6, 10, 17, 5.

were not worthy to possess the magnificent country which they coveted only for its supposed wealth in precious metals; and it was reserved for others, who came afterward, with loftier aims, better hearts, and stronger hands, to cultivate the soil, and to establish an empire founded upon truth and justice. The Spaniards did finally become possessors of the southern portion of the Continent; and to this day the curse of moral, religious, and political despotism rests upon those regions.[33]

Two Protestant missionaries, whose experiences in Brazil spanned twenty years, authored a historical and descriptive survey of Brazil that went through several editions in the 1860s and 1870s. They wrote the book from a militantly evangelical perspective, and they boldly distributed religious tracts and the King James Version of the Bible in Portuguese translation in hopes that, over time, Brazil would abandon "the exclusiveness of Romanism."[34] These missionary-authors also summoned a vision of Brazil's unlimited bounty, and in answer to the question of why Brazil had failed to live up to its potential, they argued that had a people of similar faith, morals, and habits of industry to those of the North American Protestants "gained an abiding footing in so genial a climate and on a soil so exuberant, long ago the still unexplored and impenetrable wilderness of the interior would have bloomed and blossomed in civilization as the rose, and Brazil from the sea-coast to the Andes would have become one of the gardens of the world."[35]

On occasion during the nineteenth and twentieth centuries an authentic Latin American voice has captured the attention of the literate American public and presented an influential, firsthand perspective on the region. Such a voice in the mid-nineteenth century was that of Domingo F. Sarmiento, whose classic work *Civilization and Barbarism*, though written in 1845, first appeared in English translation in the U.S. in 1868 under the title *Life in the Argentine Republic in the Days of the Tyrants; or, Civilization and Barbarism.* Sarmiento was a journalist, philosopher, educational reformer, and vigorous opponent of Juan Manuel de Rosas, Argentine dictator from 1829 to 1852. During a brief visit to the United States in the 1840s, Sarmiento established a friendship with Horace Mann, the famous Massachusetts educator, and during his residence in the U.S. as Argentine minister from 1865–1868, he became well acquainted with members of the

33. Benson John Lossing, *A Pictorial History of the United States: From the Earliest Period to the Present Time* (Rev. ed.; New York, 1867), 10, 45.

34. James C. Fletcher and D. P. Kidder, *Brazil and the Brazilians Portrayed in Historical and Descriptive Sketches* (Boston, 1879), 140–41.

35. *Ibid.,* 59.

New England literati. Sarmiento's book was translated and introduced by Mary Mann, widow of the educator, and it auspiciously appeared within months of his 1868 election and inauguration to a six-year term as Argentine president. The book was well received not only because of the author's international reputation for his varied accomplishments but also because of his favorable biography, in Spanish, of Abraham Lincoln, his adoption of educational reform following the ideas of Horace Mann, and his advocacy of Argentine modernization through "North Americanization." [36]

On the surface, Sarmiento's book is a biography of a provincial caudillo, but in a deeper sense it indicted the pervasive barbarism of the Rosas regime and of the hinterland gaucho culture that sustained it. In opposition to the dark forces of barbarism, Sarmiento championed the cause of civilization with its base in European culture and city life. The book offered confirmation in this Argentine case of what many Americans already knew about Latin America. In the words of one reviewer, the book presented a "tale of barbaric intrigue, violence, and revolution which has always greeted us in the 'latest advices from South America.'" [37] Many themes in the book were familiar to Americans with some knowledge of the region. In her laudatory introduction, Mary Mann touched upon one familiar theme when she applauded Sarmiento for his unflagging efforts to arouse his countrymen "from the apathy inherent . . . in a Spanish and at the same time priest-ridden community." Sarmiento judged Argentina "a country unusually favored by nature" but overwhelmed by barbarism. This tragic condition existed because of a population, essentially homogeneous but made up of Spanish, Indian, and black elements, "characterized by love of idleness and incapacity for industry," except when uplifted through education. He concluded, "Pity and shame are excited by the comparison of one of the German or Scotch colonies in the southern part of Buenos Ayres and some towns of the interior of the Argentine Republic." The former were clean, well ordered, and prosperous-looking while the latter were dirty, wretched, and poverty-stricken. [38] The parallels between Sarmiento and U.S. observers in their explanations for Latin American developmental problems suggest that those views had a common origin in the greater Western cultural tradition.

36. For favorable reviews see New York *Times*, August 17, 1868; *Atlantic Monthly*, XXII (July–December, 1868), 374–77.

37. *Atlantic Monthly*, XXII (July–December, 1868), 374.

38. Mary Mann, "Preface," in Domingo F. Sarmiento, *Life in the Argentine Republic in the Days of the Tyrants; or, Civilization and Barbarism*, trans. Mary Mann (1868; rpr. New York, 1971), v; Sarmiento, *ibid.*, 3, 11.

During the half century following the securing of Latin American independence in the 1820s, a variety of sources led Americans to draw sharp distinctions between themselves and Latin Americans. Those distinctions were the result not only of the negative imagery of Latin Americans but also of a deeply rooted American sense of superiority. It is commonplace to recognize the powerful influence in this period—and indeed, throughout much of the nineteenth century— of the concepts of an American Manifest Destiny for continental dominion, a mission of world redemption, a self-image as a "chosen people," and the idea of inevitable progress. These concepts, intermingled and varying in strength, though not unchallenged, were in part rooted in Western tradition, in part based on religion, and in part expressions of a youthful and robust nationalism.[39] They gained nourishment from rapid territorial growth and westward expansion, a flattering level of immigration, vigorous economic activity, and the uprooting of slavery, all of which occurred within a settled democratic tradition. When prideful Americans contrasted their notable achievements with what they vaguely perceived as the disordered, unprogressive state of Latin America, the conclusions about their neighbors' reputed backwardness seemed inescapable.

In the post–Civil War years, the judgment that Latin America was backward was most clearly expressed, along with a discussion of the causes of its backwardness, by members of the U.S. Senate in 1870 after President Grant abruptly directed national attention toward the Dominican Republic by his proposal for annexation. Americans were little prepared for the ensuing debate. Following the turbulence of the Civil War, they found themselves distracted by the problems of Reconstruction and Indian relations and caught up in the opportunities and risks attendant upon westward expansion and industrialization. But participants in the treaty debate expressed themselves forcefully despite these more immediate concerns and despite their paucity of knowledge of the Dominican Republic.

Debate on the annexation treaty registered attitudes toward the Dominican Republic and Latin America in the absence of solid information and before the region entered the national consciousness in any sustained sense. Most of those attitudes survived into the twentieth century. They were the product of romance, legend, inherited animosities, and the war with Mexico; and the scanty knowledge available about Latin America was interpreted through the distortions im-

39. Robert Nisbet, *History of the Idea of Progress* (New York, 1980), 308; Ernest Lee Tuveson, *Redeemer Nation: The Idea of America's Millennial Role* (Chicago, 1968), 52, 91, 131.

posed by racism and ethnocentrism. The history of Grant's proposal and of the treaty debate thus offers an illuminating perspective on American attitudes toward Latin America in the early post–Civil War era and on interpretations of what was widely regarded to be its backward state.

The Dominican Republic, whose nineteenth-century history is perhaps more melancholy than that of any other Latin American nation, suffered a twenty-three-year delay in securing its independence. Within weeks of the Spanish forces' departure in 1821, Haitian armies invaded the country and remained in occupation until driven out in 1844. Much of Dominican history has been shaped by the quest for security from interference, military and otherwise, from Haiti, which comprises the western third of the tropical island of Hispaniola but whose population outnumbered the approximately 150,000 Spanish-speaking Dominicans by at least ten to one at midcentury. During the decade following the ouster of the Haitians, the Dominicans remained preoccupied with security problems posed by Haitian threats. Efforts were exerted to interest the governments of Spain, France, Great Britain, and the United States in guaranteeing Dominican independence through treaty or establishment of a protectorate. By the late 1850s the Dominicans decided to return the nation to Spanish control. The four-year period of restored Spanish governance corresponded not coincidentally with the U.S. Civil War, but it ended largely because of a widespread uprising of Dominicans against oppressive Spanish rule.[40]

Following the recovery of independence, the Dominican Republic was economically prostrate and cursed with a power struggle won in 1868 by an unprincipled caudillo, Buenaventura Baez. Faced with the same threats from Haiti as his predecessors had encountered, Baez also looked abroad for security, increasingly turning for protection to the U.S., which was known to want a harbor in the Caribbean. Samaná Bay on the northeast Dominican coast offered one of the finest natural sites. Almost immediately after the Spanish ouster in 1865, Dominican leaders began exploring the possibilities of an arrangement with Washington, and by mid-1868 Baez was trying to sell the peninsula and bay of Samaná to the U.S. for money, military support, and a guarantee of Dominican territorial integrity. He seemed unconcerned by the constitutional prohibition against alienation of territory.[41]

Changes in U.S. policy following the Civil War encouraged the Dominicans in their hopes for an understanding. The expansion-minded

40. Sumner Welles, *Naboth's Vineyard: The Dominican Republic, 1844–1924* (New York, 1928), I, 51–141, 192–211, 223–46, 278–98.

41. *Ibid.*, I, 67, 302, 341–56.

secretary of state from 1861 to 1869, William Seward, sought to reduce the European presence in the hemisphere, a goal necessarily postponed by the Civil War; following the war he hastened the departure of the French from Mexico and obtained Alaska from the Russians. As a result of experience during the war with Confederate blockade runners, he cast about the Caribbean for a suitable naval station. The choices narrowed to Samaná Bay and the Danish West Indies (Virgin Islands). A treaty was negotiated to purchase the latter, but the Senate failed to ratify it. Seward took a personal interest in the Dominican Republic, which he visited in early 1866 and to which he sent his son, the assistant secretary of state, the following year to negotiate the cession or lease of Samaná. Discord within the Dominican cabinet, however, rendered the discussions fruitless. President Andrew Johnson, during his final months in office, urged Congress to consider annexation of Hispaniola, but his proposal came so late that formulation of a Dominican policy was left to the incoming administration of Ulysses S. Grant.[42]

By the advent of the Grant administration, Baez and certain U.S. interests were fast approaching an understanding whereby the U.S. could look forward to a long-term lease of Samaná Peninsula and Bay or perhaps even annexation of the Dominican Republic itself. Much of the credit for bringing about a meeting of minds belongs to Joseph Warren Fabens and William L. Cazneau, adventurers and speculators, characterized by Allan Nevins in his study of the period as "full of schemes, avid of money, and devoid of scruples." Fabens and Cazneau had been involved in the Texas struggle for independence, obtained minor diplomatic assignments in the 1850s, and began their partnership in land speculation and other financial schemes in the Dominican Republic in 1859. By 1869 they had secured major land concessions with the connivance of Baez and had succeeded in interesting various U.S. banking, investing, and shipping interests in their plans. This pair of charlatans was thus positioned to reap windfall profits by cementing the U.S.-Dominican connection.[43]

42. *Ibid.*, I, 324–31; Ulysses S. Grant, "Fourth Annual Message," December 9, 1868, in *A Compilation of the Messages and Papers of the Presidents, 1789–1905*, comp. James D. Richardson (Washington, D.C., 1897–1907), VI, 689.

43. Nevins, *Hamilton Fish*, 254. The following offer the best accounts of the annexation struggle during the Grant administration: William S. McFeely, *Grant: A Biography* (New York, 1981), 332–55; Nevins, *Hamilton Fish*, 249–78, 309–34, 363–71, 497–501; Charles Callan Tansill, *The United States and Santo Domingo, 1789–1873: A Chapter in Caribbean Diplomacy* (Baltimore, 1938), 338–464; Welles, *Naboth's Vineyard*, I, 359–408.

Grant was fully committed to annexation by mid-1869. His early commitment, despite the attitude of his secretary of state, Hamilton Fish, who was lukewarm at best but loyally supportive, poses an intriguing question as to motivation. It appears that Grant was taken with the prospect of expansion, and he was always susceptible to the influence of men of money whom Fabens had involved in the scheme. Fabens operated quite comfortably in the tawdry atmosphere introduced into Washington upon Grant's inauguration, and he early obtained an introduction to the president. In addition, Grant may have been swayed by two of his close personal friends, Senator Cornelius Cole of California, who expressed the Pacific Coast interest in an isthmian canal and protection for its approaches, and Admiral Daniel Ammen, who voiced the navy's interest in acquiring a Caribbean base and coaling station. In addition, Grant counted several ardent imperialists among his friends and political allies.[44] He also affirmed in his memoirs that, following annexation, the Dominican Republic was to have served as an area where the nation's four million disillusioned former slaves would be encouraged to settle.[45]

Grant acted with little delay and dispatched General Orville E. Babcock, his youthful and ambitious secretary, to the Dominican Republic at midyear to obtain information. While there, Babcock came under the influence of Fabens and Cazneau and met with Baez. By September he was back in Washington with a signed protocol calling for purchase of Samaná Bay or annexation of the country and committing the U.S. immediately to provide cash and arms to the Baez government and military support against Haiti. Babcock's report strengthened Grant's determination for annexation, and, despite an unenthusiastic cabinet, he sent Babcock back to the Dominican Republic to obtain signatures on a treaty of annexation drafted by Fish. The treaty calling for annexation and ultimate statehood was to expire if not ratified by March 29, 1870, so an accompanying convention provided for a fifty-year lease of Samaná Bay and Peninsula for an annual rental of $150,000. After securing the necessary signatures, Babcock arranged for transfer to U.S. possession of the province of Samaná and turned over to Dominican officials the sum of $150,000, which Grant had improperly obtained from Secret Service funds. In deference to the U.S. desire for evidence that Dominican public opinion was favorable

44. Nevins, *Hamilton Fish*, 262–64, 275; Welles, *Naboth's Vineyard*, I, 370; Tansill, *The U.S. and Santo Domingo*, 351.

45. Ulysses S. Grant, *Personal Memoirs of U.S. Grant* (New York, 1885–1886), II, 550. See also Grant, "Second Annual Message," December 5, 1870, in *Messages and Papers*, comp. Richardson, VII, 99–100.

to annexation, Baez arranged, with four-days' notice, a wholly farcical plebiscite that produced the desired vote in February, 1870.[46]

The Grant administration had kept the treaty secret until it was presented to the Senate for ratification in January, 1870. Grant's failure to prepare public opinion is one indication of his rashness, as is his failure to line up Senate support before 1870. During his first year in office Grant had fared poorly in his dealings with Congress, so his failure to take key senators into his confidence was critical to the course of the debate. In that post-impeachment era Congress was riding high in open defiance of the president on several issues. It challenged him on foreign policy questions, it defied him on the tenure of office question and on Reconstruction, and it rejected the very capable Rockwood Hoar as a Supreme Court nominee.[47] Grant seemed strangely inattentive to the divisions within his own party, apparent both in the Senate and cabinet, which would widen to a chasm in the next presidential election.

In mid-March, 1870, the Foreign Relations Committee reported unfavorably on the treaty and convention, but two days later Grant suddenly appeared in the Capitol and proceeded to lobby senators. A week later he hosted another lobbying session for fifteen senators in the White House.[48] The deadline for ratification was then extended, and Grant agreed to minor modifications but rigidly opposed changing the treaty terms from annexation to establishment of a protectorate, a major modification urged by Fish. Grant next sent a message on the treaty to the Senate demanding ratification without further change. This curious message was filled with factual errors and ludicrous statements, such as the assertion that the Dominican Republic was "capable of supporting a population of ten million people in luxury." Furthermore, he argued that the Dominican Republic "possesses the richest soil, best and most capacious harbors, most salubrious climate, and the most valuable products of the forest, mine, and soil of any of the West India islands."[49] Grant also remained insistent on promising eventual statehood. Despite his extravagant use of patronage, the president's frantic efforts to rescue the treaty were unavailing. The final vote, 28 to 28, taken in June fell substantially short of the necessary two-thirds. Grant had suffered his first decisive defeat, "the most spec-

46. McFeely, *Grant*, 338; Nevins, *Hamilton Fish*, 268–69, 277–78, 310, 314–15, 501; Welles, *Naboth's Vineyard*, I, 380, 383–84, 387.

47. Nevins, *Hamilton Fish*, 279–308.

48. *Ibid.*, 316–17; McFeely, *Grant*, 342.

49. Nevins, *Hamilton Fish*, 323, 326–27; Grant, "To the Senate of the United States," May 31, 1870, in *Messages and Papers*, comp. Richardson, VII, 61–62.

tacular reverse of his Administration," in the opinion of Allan Nevins.[50]

This story has an epilogue, for Grant did not easily admit defeat. In his annual message at year-end he asked Congress to pass a joint resolution authorizing him to appoint a commission to negotiate a new treaty of annexation. Heated opposition led instead to appointment of a commission whose task was simply to make a visit of inquiry to the Dominican Republic. The three-member commission departed in January and returned in five weeks with a report favorable to annexation. Grant then forwarded the report to Congress, where the entire issue was soon forgotten.[51]

During the debate on annexation, opponents directed much of their attack against the unscrupulous methods of the treaty proponents. The phony plebiscite attracted criticism as did the financial speculations of Fabens and Cazneau. Within the Dominican Republic, enemies of Baez, whose hold on the presidency was never secure, used the annexation scheme to rally opposition and unify their revolutionary efforts, and their objections were highlighted by treaty opponents in the United States. Anti-annexationists also counted among their ranks those who had followed Cuba's struggle against Spain in the early stages of the Ten Years' War and who professed to see in the annexation project a mere diversion designed to sidetrack their ambitious plans for a Cuban adventure. Treaty opponents also pointed to the recent bloody struggle against Spain as evidence of a true desire for independence among Dominicans, and they argued that annexation would require an increase in size of the army and navy. Much of the debate also concerned the procedural questions of whether to annex by treaty or joint resolution and whether to bring the Dominican Republic in as a territory or state.[52] None of these arguments, however, was central to the final outcome, which hinged on opposition to expansion into noncontiguous territory and on the highly negative view taken of the Dominican people.

When the debate began, public opinion showed little appetite for the acquisition of Caribbean territory, and the public seemed largely inattentive to the issues. During the whole of 1870 only three editorials on the subject appeared in *Harper's Weekly*, much less interest than shown in either the Cuban insurrection or the Paraguayan War. In early 1870 Secretary Fish privately wrote that many people had doubts about a general policy of "acquiring insular possessions, and

50. Nevins, *Hamilton Fish*, 329, 365–68, 371, 250.

51. *Ibid.*, 497–98; Welles, *Naboth's Vineyard*, I, 396–98.

52. *Nation*, X (February 3, 1870), 68; Welles, *Naboth's Vineyard*, I, 361–64; Nevins, *Hamilton Fish*, 318–20.

of the effect of the tropical climate upon the race who inhabit them.
. . . ." A New England editor wrote to Senator Charles Sumner, "We
don't want any of those islands just yet, with their mongrel cutthroat
races and foreign language and religion."[53] A *Harper's Weekly* editorial in early 1870 focused its objections on the Dominican population,
which it characterized as a "radically alien and essentially perilous element." It then suggested reviving the moribund treaty with Denmark: "If we wish a naval station in the West Indies, we have agreed
in honor to take St. Thomas, and the taking involves no hatred, no barbarism, and nothing but the addition of a few thousands of peaceful
Danes to the population." Six months later the same journal noted,
"If annexation be our policy, we should seek it northward, not
southward," a reference to the century-long desire for incorporation
of Canada.[54]

Senators Allen G. Thurman of Ohio and Thomas F. Bayard of Del-
aware assumed leadership for the Democratic party's firm opposition
to Grant's treaty, and both directed attention to the quality of the population. Thurman expressed his opposition as follows: "The question
is, are you prepared to bring in as one of the States of this Union one
hundred and twenty thousand people, not one hundred of whom can
speak the English language; not one hundred of whom are white; not
one out of ten thousand of whom, perhaps, can read in any language
or ever had any education that could be called education at all?" Thurman characterized the Dominican Republic as "a land of throes and
convulsions . . . a volcano of human passions and a river of human
blood."[55]

Bayard, who would become secretary of state in the 1880s, spoke
out forcefully against the notion of attempting to absorb a "population of black cut-throats," a "semi-barbarous population, this chaotic
mass of crime and degradation." He warned that "the fiat of nature
has declared that we are unable to elevate such a race as inhabit that
island to the level of our own. If a level is to be achieved at all it will
only be by dragging us down, and not by bringing them up." Stressing
the vast differences between the American and Dominican people and
institutions he declared that the resolution called for the incorporation of "a semi-barbarous race, the descendants of African slaves, whose

53. Hamilton Fish to George Bancroft, February 9, 1870, cited in Nevins, *Hamilton Fish*, 313; General J. R. Hawley to Charles Sumner, n.d., cited *ibid.*, 318.

54. *Harper's Weekly*, XIV (February 19, 1870), 115; *ibid.* (July 16, 1870), 451.

55. Remarks of Allen G. Thurman, *Congressional Globe*, Senate, 41st Cong., 3rd Sess., Pt. 1, p. 249. Senator Justin S. Morrill of Vermont also expressed opposition to annexation because of the nature of the population; see *ibid.*, 197.

attempts at self-government, continued for upward of half a century, have been but a series of blood-stained failures. . . . Their institutions are mere mockeries, bloody travesties of political government, and to them the presence of a strong-handed and just-minded white ruler would be the greatest blessing that Heaven could bestow."[56]

Anti-annexationists within the Republican party were led by Charles Sumner of Massachusetts, chairman of the Foreign Relations Committee, a humorless idealist generally recognized as his party's conscience, and leader of the Radical Republicans. Sumner's opposition stemmed from complex motives, but it was primarily based on his extreme solicitude for the black race, a stance that went back to his leadership in the abolitionist cause. Sumner feared that annexation of the Dominican Republic would inevitably lead to annexation of Haiti, thus extinguishing a noble experiment—the African race's "first effort at Independence." Sumner invoked respect for natural law and argued that "by a higher statute is that island set apart to the colored race. It is theirs by right of possession; by their sweat and blood mingling with the soil; by tropical position; by its burning sun, and by unalterable laws of climate."[57] Sumner thus held that the island's tropical setting destined it for occupation by non-Caucasians. One of Sumner's supporters on the Foreign Relations Committee, Eugene Casserly of California, asserted that the political instability of the Dominican Republic was typical of Latin America. He argued that entanglements with the Dominican Republic should be avoided because that nation "shares the general revolutionary condition of so many of the States and republics in that part of the world, in the West Indies and in Central America."[58]

Sumner's chief ally on the Foreign Relations Committee and in Senate debate was Carl Schurz, freshman senator from Missouri, who obtained a vacant seat on Sumner's committee at the chairman's insistence. Schurz had immigrated from Germany in 1852, became an abolitionist, and joined the new Republican party. As a champion of Radical Reconstruction and reform causes he would break with the Grant administration and become a chief organizer of the Liberal Republican party in 1872. The central thesis of Schurz's lengthy argument during debate on authorizing the commission of inquiry was that the Dominican Republic was condemned to hopeless stagnation because of its tropical setting. Urging his auditors to read the

56. Remarks of Thomas F. Bayard, *Congressional Globe*, Senate, 41st Cong., 3rd Sess., Pt. 1, p. 225.
57. Remarks of Charles Sumner, *ibid.*, 231.
58. Remarks of Eugene Casserly, *ibid.*, 269.

history of that nation and of all other tropical countries, he challenged them to show him a single example of the successful establishment and maintenance of democratically based republican institutions in a tropical climate. "There is none," he averred. "But, more than that, show me a single instance in any tropical country where labor when it was left free did not exhibit a strong tendency to run into a shiftlessness, and where practical attempts to organize labor did not run in the direction of slavery. . . . You find none."[59]

Schurz lucidly expounded geographical determinism and applied it to the Dominican case:

Whenever man has to struggle with nature, with an encouraging promise of reward, there he grows great. Wherever that reward is denied him, or wherever nature is so bountiful as to render constant labor superfluous, there man has, as far as our observations go, always degenerated. While the temperate climate stimulates the exercise of reason and the sense of order, the tropical sun inflames the imagination to inordinate activity and develops the government of the passions. The consequences are natural: there is a tendency to government by force instead of by argument; revolutions are of chronic occurrence, like volcanic outbreaks, and you will find political life continually oscillating between two extremes—liberty which there means anarchy, and order which there means despotism.

Schurz excluded race as a cause of anarchy and despotism in the Dominican Republic. Insisting that the tropical setting was the single most important factor, he asserted that "the Anglo-Saxons have been tried under the tropical sun and have, in the main points, failed in every instance."[60]

Like Casserly, Schurz generalized his explanation of Dominican problems to Latin America, thus lending additional significance to his hypothesis. He labored under the misconception that most Latin Americans resided in the tropics and that their disordered condition stemmed from the same cause as the Dominican disorder—their tropical environment. Schurz stated his position in the following rhetorical questions concerning Latin Americans: "Is there any foreign Power that holds them under coercion? Is not every man there a freeman? . . . What is it that prevents them from building up a stable political system, resting upon the basis of self-government, like ours?" The answer was that they were "laboring under natural diffi-

59. Senate speech of January 11, 1871, in *Speeches, Correspondence and Political Papers of Carl Schurz*, ed. Frederic Bancroft (New York, 1913), II, 78.
60. *Ibid.*, II, 82–84. This doctrine of the perpetual backwardness of the tropics was rejected by Senator Henry Wilson of Massachusetts; see *Congressional Globe*, Senate, 41st Cong., 3rd Sess., Pt. 1, p. 430.

culties" in the form of their tropical climate.[61] Schurz considered any attempt to assimilate people from the West Indies to be utterly futile because such people had "nothing in common with us; neither language, nor habits, nor institutions, nor traditions, nor opinions nor ways of thinking; nay, not even a code of morals—people who cannot even be reached by our teachings, for they will not understand or appreciate them; all the good lessons we may try to impart to them will evaporate into nothing under the hot rays of the tropical sun." Furthermore, if the Anglo-Saxon tried to populate the tropics the result would be degeneration, loss of Anglo-Saxon vigor, and "assimilation downward."[62] In his peroration Schurz warned: "Incorporate the tropics, with their population, with their natural influences, in our political system, and you introduce a poison into it which may become fatal to the very life of this Republic."[63]

The principal factors adduced by treaty opponents to explain the deplorable condition of the Dominican Republic were its tropical setting, its black and racially mixed population, and the cultural patterns inherited from Spain that left a largely uneducated populace groping for order and progress under unviable political institutions. The retrogressive influence of the Catholic church noted by so many travelers to Latin America received relatively slight attention in this public forum. The major factors of climate, race, and cultural heritage were often examined within the context of a description of the Dominican Republic as a land of substantial potential wealth, a theme most often championed by treaty defenders but unchallenged by its opponents. It is also noteworthy that this negatively portrayed Dominican Republic was seen to be representative of Latin America.

A consensus in views about Latin America prevailed in the immediate post–Civil War years to 1870, and those views were consistent with the attitudes of the previous half century. Whether interest in Latin American themes was moderate, as during the 1870 annexation debate when serious men gave serious thought to Latin America, or low, as during the previous two decades when much of the information on the region came from travelers' casual comments, the perceptions varied little. They emerged from a highly ethnocentric context and were formed in the absence of solid information about the nations to the south. Contacts with those countries were irregu-

61. Senate speech of January 11, 1871, in *Speeches of Schurz*, ed. Bancroft, II, 84.
62. *Ibid.*, II, 93–95.
63. *Ibid.*, II, 117. For a discussion of the debate in terms of economic considerations, party and sectional divisions, and the influence of European thought, see Ernest R. May, *American Imperialism: A Speculative Essay* (New York, 1967–1968), 100–115.

lar and infrequent, and Americans exhibited little desire to change that condition. Few people knew about Latin America and few cared to know, despite alluring depictions of a quaint, charming culture. Such depictions could not overcome the overwhelmingly negative evaluation of things Latin American, and the two images often existed side by side. In any case, the nation's attention was too much absorbed by internal matters to permit more than passing interest in its hemispheric neighbors.

The inherited images of the past suffused the few things uttered or written about Latin America. The Black Legend undergirded the common portrait of a slothful, priest-ridden population of inferior, mixed breeds perpetuating the nonproductive ways of the colonial era and stagnating in tropical languor amid undeveloped abundance. With noticeable agreement, most informed Americans knew that Latin America was backward, and they concurred on the reasons for that state of affairs—climate, the colonial legacy, and race. Having ascribed such fundamental causes to the problems of the region, it is not surprising that commentary on the Latin American condition was largely nonprescriptive, aside, that is, from suggestions to root out the Hispanic heritage or encourage European immigration, indicating that the problems were judged so elemental that no solutions were possible short of starting over with a new continent, a new past, and a new people. As the United States approached the status of a world power in the next few decades, information about Latin America and interest in the region would grow, but the accompanying attitudes seemed stubbornly resistant to change.

2

Growing Interest, Lagging Knowledge, 1870–1900

The closing years of the nineteenth century marked a fundamental shift in United States policy toward Latin America, but this shift was not ushered in by equally significant changes in perceptions of the region. Through the acquisition of Puerto Rico and the establishment of a protectorate over Cuba—consequences of the defeat of Spain in 1898—the U.S. became a major power within Latin America, thereby climaxing an accelerating trend discernible in the early 1880s toward increasing contact, diplomatic assertion, and commercial and financial penetration. Despite the evidence of heightened interest in Latin America, a genuine understanding of its civilization was still absent at the turn of the century. By and large, the perceptions that had shaped U.S. thinking about the region in the early post–Civil War years yet prevailed in 1900.

Aside from disorders along the Mexican border and Cuba's abortive Ten Years' War for independence, 1868–1878, developments during the decade following the debate on Dominican annexation gave Americans few reasons to pay attention to the states south of the border, but the decade of the 1880s witnessed a notable elevation of interest in Latin America. In Mexico, establishment of internal peace and security, construction of railroads and other travel accommodations, and encouragement of foreign investment brought larger numbers of visitors than ever before and attracted U.S. capital and its agents, who included such prominent Americans as Ulysses S. Grant in the ranks of these Mexico boosters.[1] Guidebooks for the Mexico-bound tourist began appearing in the 1880s, and they painted a picture of an exotic land in which travel promised more high adventure than real danger. *Appletons' Guide to Mexico* advised in 1883 that travel in Mexico was as safe as in the western United States. "There are no brigands on the stage-roads any longer, except in the States of Jalisco and Sinaloa. It is well, however, to go armed, and to keep your fire-arms in sight."[2]

1. David M. Pletcher, *Rails, Mines and Progress: Seven American Promoters in Mexico, 1867–1911* (Ithaca, 1958), 27–30; letter from Ulysses S. Grant, December 3, 1883, as frontispiece of Alfred R. Conkling, *Appletons' Guide to Mexico Including a Chapter on Guatemala, and a Complete English-Spanish Vocabulary* (New York, 1884).
2. Conkling, *Appletons' Guide to Mexico*, 1.

Mexico and Cuba led other Latin American areas in appealing to various types of travelers such as businessmen, journalists, engineers, scientists, and tourists, but the many attractions of the larger region exerted an only somewhat lesser appeal. The Amazon enticed several naturalists—mostly from Europe—and by the 1880s more than a dozen books on South American flora and fauna had been published, beginning with the classic work of Alexander von Humboldt at the turn of the century and including Charles Darwin's well-known account of the voyage of the *Beagle* in the 1830s and the highly respected studies of Amazonian natural life by Alfred Russel Wallace and Henry Walter Bates in the 1850s and 1860s.[3] Also, a bibliography of nineteenth-century English-language travel books on Latin America shows that more appeared in the 1880s than in any other decade.[4] In 1889 a noted interpreter of Latin America observed, "More has been written and published in the United States concerning the countries south of us during the last four years than in a quarter of a century previous. . . ."[5]

At an official and semiofficial level, Latin America also began attracting increasing attention in the 1880s. Ferdinand de Lesseps, builder of the Suez Canal, arrived in the U.S. in 1880 after having announced plans for construction by his French company of a sea-level isthmian canal across the Colombian state of Panama. The announcement caused alarm because it had long been assumed that the future canal would be solely a U.S. enterprise; his promotional and fund-raising tour of the country pushed dormant U.S. interests toward laying the groundwork for rival canal projects.[6] Other factors that quickened interest in Latin America included border disputes involving several Latin American states and the War of the Pacific, 1879–1883—the result of Chile's aggression against Peru and Bolivia for control of the mineral-rich Atacama Desert. Bungled efforts by Secretary of State

3. Williams, *The Spanish Background,* I, 93; Clinton Harvey Gardiner, "Foreign Travelers' Accounts of Mexico, 1810–1910," *The Americas,* VIII (1952), 324–25; Paul Russell Cutright, *The Great Naturalists Explore South America* (1940; rpr. Freeport, N.Y., 1968), 3–40.

4. Graph entitled "Number of Books Published in the United States Each Year in English, Dealing with Latin America, 1840–1900," p. 156 in A. Curtis Wilgus, *Latin America in the Nineteenth Century: A Selected Bibliography of Books of Travel and Description Published in English* (Metuchen, N.J., 1973); Garold Cole, *American Travelers to Mexico, 1821–1972: A Descriptive Bibliography* (Troy, N.Y., 1978).

5. William Eleroy Curtis, "Friends in South America," *North American Review,* CXLIX (September, 1889), 378.

6. David McCullough, *The Path Between the Seas: The Creation of the Panama Canal, 1870–1914* (New York, 1977), 118–22; David M. Pletcher, *The Awkward Years: American Foreign Relations Under Garfield and Arthur* (Columbia, Mo., 1962), 7–8, 22–26, 270–83.

James G. Blaine to mediate two of these disputes involved the U.S. in explosive issues and yielded considerable ill will.[7]

A desire for expanded trade with Latin America grew noticeably during the 1880s as a result of the gradual decline of the U.S. economy toward depression from 1882 to mid-decade. Though less severe than the depression of the 1870s, its occurrence so soon after recovery led some journals, businessmen, and politicians to conclude that over-production was the culprit and that expansion of overseas markets offered a solution. But an effort to increase exports faced formidable obstacles. Foreign trade represented a minor portion of the U.S. economy, so only a limited number of special interests worked to promote it. A spectacular array of protective tariffs posed serious barriers to trade expansion, as did the condition of the merchant marine and the navy—both of which had deteriorated markedly after the Civil War.[8] A detailed study of U.S. trade with Latin America prepared by the House Committee on Foreign Affairs in 1883 documented the nation's weak trade position in the region in relation to that of its European rivals. The report showed that the U.S. conducted only 18.9 percent of Latin America's foreign trade, and with only four countries did it handle more than 30 percent of the foreign trade. Even worse, U.S. exports to Latin America lagged substantially behind imports.[9] In a period when European powers were actively competing for colonies and overseas markets and granting generous subsidies to their merchant marines, there was growing concern and some alarm over European commercial and financial penetration into Latin America. Trade expansionists thus represented Latin America as one of the target areas where export promotion seemed likely to pay dividends.[10]

7. Russell H. Bastert, "A New Approach to the Origins of Blaine's Pan-American Policy," *Hispanic American Historical Review,* XXXIX (1959), 376, 380–88; Russell H. Bastert, "Diplomatic Reversal: Frelinghuysen's Opposition to Blaine's Pan-American Policy in 1882," *Mississippi Valley Historical Review,* XLII (1956), 660–63, 670; Allan Peskin, "Blaine, Garfield and Latin America: A New Look," *The Americas,* XXXVI (1979), 79.

8. Samuel Rezneck, "Patterns of Thought and Action in an American Depression, 1882–1886," *American Historical Review,* LXI (1956), 284; Justus D. Doenecke, *The Presidencies of James A. Garfield and Chester A. Arthur* (Lawrence, Kans., 1981), 167; Pletcher, *The Awkward Years,* 147; David M. Pletcher, "Inter-American Shipping in the 1880's: A Loosening Tie," *Inter-American Economic Affairs,* X (1956), 14, 37–38; Thomas C. Reeves, *Gentleman Boss: The Life of Chester Alan Arthur* (New York, 1975), 397; Walter LaFeber, *The New Empire: An Interpretation of American Expansion, 1860–1898* (Ithaca, 1963), 58–59.

9. *House Reports,* 48th Cong., 1st Sess., No. 1445, p. 3; Pletcher, "Inter-American Shipping," 16, 24; Milton Plesur, *America's Outward Thrust: Approaches to Foreign Affairs, 1865–1890* (DeKalb, Ill., 1971), 94.

10. Pletcher, *The Awkward Years,* 178; Pletcher, "Inter-American Shipping," 38;

To facilitate exports, Blaine's successor as secretary of state negotiated bilateral reciprocity treaties with six Latin American nations. Political opposition blocked their implementation, but the struggle to reverse the decline of the navy was more successful. In 1883 Congress laid the foundations for a modern navy when it appropriated funds for construction of four steel ships.[11] One hopeful gesture of the expiring Republican administration toward a larger Latin American policy was the appointment in 1884 of a three-member commission to travel to Latin America to find "the best modes of securing more intimate international and commercial relations" in the hemisphere and to determine the level of interest in holding an inter-American conference.[12]

The commissioners undertook their mission in late 1884, traveling to Mexico City where they were on hand for the inauguration of Porfirio Díaz. In January they departed from New Orleans and spent the next three months in Venezuela, Costa Rica, and Guatemala, after which only two commissioners continued on to make a rapid tour of six South American nations. The final report had more to say about shipping than anything else, although it included several recommendations such as the convening of an inter-American conference, agreement on a common silver coin for the hemisphere, and an improved official representation in Latin America. Because the report centered on the need to provide regular steamship service between the U.S. and Latin America, it was quickly injected into the highly partisan and inconclusive debate between Republicans who generally favored protectionism and shipping subsidies and Democrats who argued that shipping would not need subsidies if tariffs were lowered.[13]

Despite the commission's lack of concrete results and the apathy that greeted its final report, it had one unforeseen but important consequence—the quick elevation of its most-junior member from the ranks of a workaday Chicago journalist with a bent toward foreign reporting to the status of an authoritative spokesman on Latin Amer-

John A.S. Grenville and George Berkeley Young, *Politics, Strategy, and American Diplomacy: Studies in Foreign Policy, 1873–1917* (New Haven, 1966), 76, 83.

11. Pletcher, *The Awkward Years*, 284–307; LaFeber, *The New Empire*, 59–60.

12. Frederick Frelinghuysen to Thomas C. Reynolds, Solon O. Thacher, and George H. Sharpe, August 27, 1884, in *House Executive Documents*, 49th Cong., 1st Sess., No. 50, pp. 5–7, 11.

13. James Floyd Vivian, "The South American Commission to the Three Americas Movement: The Politics of Pan Americanism, 1884–1890" (Ph.D. dissertation, American University, 1971), 26, 52–53, 60, 72, 92, 100, 105, 110, 127, 132, 143, 147, 151–59, 176–79, 204, 338–44.

ican affairs. Shortly before the commission's departure, President Chester A. Arthur had rewarded William Eleroy Curtis for political favors by naming him secretary to the commission, and later in the year the president named him a commissioner to replace one of the original appointees. At the age of thirty-four Curtis was the most-dynamic member of the commission and one of the two members to stick with the tour to its conclusion. After co-authoring the final report, he solidified his reputation as an interpreter of foreign cultures by accepting appointments as an agent for the Department of State to prepare for the Pan American Conference of 1889 and as first director of the Bureau of the American Republics in 1891, and by authoring several travel articles and books and a daily column in the Chicago *Record-Herald*. Curtis wrote *The Capitals of Spanish America* (1888), an account of observations made while traveling through Latin America as a commissioner. Largely a compilation of articles written during the commission's tour, this well-received book became one of the major works on Latin America to appear in this period. During the last fifteen years of the century, Curtis thus served as one of the nation's foremost interpreters of Latin America.[14]

Because of its scope, detail, and semiofficial character, *The Capitals of Spanish America* provides insight into the way Latin America was interpreted in this period. Curtis displayed a superficial understanding of the region throughout this lengthy book, and he strengthened existing stereotypes. For example, he referred to the colonial era as a "carnival of murder and plunder" without attempting serious analysis of the period.[15] A major theme of the book is that Latin America was cursed by the bane of Roman Catholic influence. Curtis portrayed Mexican history as a struggle between "antiquated, bigoted, and despotic Romanism, allied with the ancient aristocracy . . . on the one hand, and the spirit of intellectual, industrial, commercial, and social progress on the other." He asserted that "the social and political condition of Ecuador presents a picture of the dark ages," and that "until the influence of the Romish Church is destroyed, until immigration is invited and secured, Ecuador will be a desert rich in undeveloped resources."[16]

Curtis was also much impressed by the potential abundance of Latin

14. *Ibid.*, 31–40, 60, 117–18, 206; Allen Johnson and Dumas Malone, eds., *Dictionary of American Biography* (New York, 1928–1958), II, 620–21; "Prominent in Pan American Affairs," *Bulletin of the Pan American Union*, XXXIII (October, 1911), 785–87.

15. William Eleroy Curtis, *The Capitals of Spanish America* (New York, 1888), 82, 196.

16. *Ibid.*, 3, 317, 337, 82.

America but at the same time by the prevalence of deep poverty. He wrote of "the vast resources" of Honduras, that Ecuador has "plenty of natural wealth," and that Venezuela "could sustain a population of 100,000,000." Just as regularly, Curtis emphasized the widespread poverty that, in his view, stemmed from laziness.[17] He concluded that this indolence was a product of geography as well as a manifestation of defective character. Curtis reasoned that the tropical setting, which in his mind was characteristic of most of populated Latin America, was debilitating both to natives and to immigrants from temperate zones. In commenting on Brazil—an odd inclusion in a book on Spanish America—he noted that many Germans had come to Brazil "but the climate is so enervating that after an experience of two years the German colonist will be found by his Portuguese predecessor sitting in the shade of the fig tree and hiring a negro to do his work." There seemed no possibility of escaping this enervating influence by moving to higher elevations, for on his visit to Bogotá, situated in Colombia's mountainous interior, he wrote that a man accustomed to eight hours' daily labor in New York "will here find it impossible to apply himself closely for more than five hours each day. If he exceeds that limit ominous symptoms of nervous prostration will be almost sure to follow." Curtis was struck by the progressive spirit he discerned among the people of Chile and Argentina, and he attributed their advances to a temperate climate and a European-based population.[18]

Despite the increasing level of interest, official and unofficial, in Latin America in the 1880s, the information available to the reading public was scant, and much of it remained highly distorted. An important exception to these deficiencies was the appearance during the 1880s of a large chunk of Hubert Howe Bancroft's massive thirty-nine-volume history of western America—his three-volume *History of Central America* and six-volume *History of Mexico.* These weighty tomes are evenhanded in their treatment of the Spanish in America, but they are so encyclopedic in detail and so heavily footnoted that they had limited impact on the general public except for use as reference books. For historians, however, Bancroft's published works and his vast collection of historical material on western America constituted an invaluable resource for the study of Spain in Central and North America. Toward the end of the decade and on the eve of the first Inter-American Conference, novelist and critic William Dean Howells could still write that the Spanish-American republics were "almost as strange to us as

17. *Ibid.*, 116, 337, 266, 124, 150.
18. *Ibid.*, 706, 244–45.

so many imaginable commonwealths in the planet Mars."[19] The struggle for a more-active Latin American policy often provoked editorial comment marked by sweeping generalizations born of half-truths. Such is the following protest against the Nicaraguan Canal Treaty negotiated at mid-decade:

All the countries now lying between us and the canal contain a population of about 15,000,000, whom it is no exaggeration to describe as slightly Catholicized savages, who are still ruled by chiefs and priests under a simulacrum of constitutional government, and whose favorite pastime is rebellion. In fact, rebellion in those regions occupies very much the place in the national life which is occupied by base-ball, trotting matches, and going to the circus in ours. The Nicaraguan, Guatemalan, or Honduran gentleman rebels for the pure love of amusement, and the Indians, to whom the Spaniards have given a slight Catholic varnish, follow him readily to a three or four days' war, which pleasantly varies the dulness of tropical life.[20]

This decade of growing attention to Latin America fittingly concluded with the convening of the first Inter-American Conference, which came less in response to recommendations of the commission to Central and South America than to a movement to commemorate the U.S. Constitution's centennial in 1889 and the quadricentennial three years later of Columbus's discovery of America.[21] All the Latin American states except the Dominican Republic were in attendance when the conference opened in October, 1889, at the White House.[22] President Benjamin Harrison appointed a ten-member, bipartisan U.S. delegation headed by Andrew Carnegie, and he named William Eleroy Curtis to take charge of preparations for the conference. The day after the opening session the delegates embarked by luxury train on a six-week, 5,400-mile tour, arranged by Curtis, of the Northeast and Midwest. The purposes of the exhausting tour were to arouse American business interests to the possibilities of the Latin American market and to impress the delegates with the nation's agricultural and in-

19. John Walton Caughey, *Hubert Howe Bancroft: Historian of the West* (Berkeley, 1946), 157–81; Howard F. Cline, "Latin American History: Development of Its Study and Teaching in the United States Since 1898," in *Latin American History: Essays on Its Study and Teaching, 1898–1965,* ed. Howard F. Cline (Austin, Tex., 1967), I, 7; William Dean Howells, "Editor's Study," *Harper's New Monthly Magazine,* LXXVII (October, 1888), 804.

20. *Nation,* XXXIX (December 25, 1884), 538.

21. A. Curtis Wilgus, "James G. Blaine and the Pan American Movement," *Hispanic American Historical Review,* V (1922), 685–91.

22. Harry J. Sievers, *Benjamin Harrison, Hoosier President* (Indianapolis, 1960–1968), III, 104; J. Lloyd Mecham, *The United States and Inter-American Security, 1889–1960* (Austin, Tex., 1961), 51–52.

dustrial capacity. Back in Washington the reassembled delegates remained in session until April, 1890. The conference had few concrete accomplishments, although it marked the beginning of the Pan American movement. It also recommended reciprocity treaties and established the Commercial Bureau of the American Republics, which became the permanent secretariat of the conferences.[23]

Through intense efforts the Harrison administration obtained a tariff bill from Congess in 1890 with a reciprocity provision, and reciprocity treaties were subsequently negotiated with all but three Latin American states. The tariff struggle, renewed three years later during the second administration of Democrat Grover Cleveland, led to enactment of the 1894 tariff that produced a modest downward revision but repealed reciprocity. The Harrison administration also obtained appropriations for construction of ships that would form the nucleus of a modern battleship navy and secured a bill from Congress granting modest mail subsidies to domestic steamship companies. One sour note in U.S.–Latin American relations during Harrison's presidency was a crisis with Chile, which ended only slightly short of war, thus halting momentum toward improved relations with the region.[24]

The panic of 1893 and the succeeding four-year depression shaped the agenda of the second administration of Grover Cleveland, elected in 1892 to succeed Harrison. Depression gave rise to the period's most important social-political trends, namely, labor unrest that climaxed in the violent Pullman strike of 1894, the Populist movement that peaked during the political conventions and campaigns of 1896, and the debate between silverites and goldbugs. The 1890s' depression holds a similar relation to the growing attention paid to Latin America as did the depression of the 1880s; the Cleveland administration argued that the depression was caused by overproduction, not the lack of money, and that the solution was expanded foreign markets, not bimetalism. Differences between the 1880s and 1890s, however, that resulted in a more-serious and sustained interest in Latin America in the latter decade, were that the downturn of the 1890s was deeper and the accompanying unrest more threatening; in addition, the proportion of manufactured goods in the nation's exports had grown, thus highlighting the importance of export expansion to nonindustrial regions of Asia and Latin America. During the 1880s

23. Sievers, *Harrison*, III, 111–14; Mecham, *The U.S. and Inter-American Security*, 57–58; LaFeber, *The New Empire*, 113.

24. LaFeber, *The New Empire*, 114–36, 171, 109; Sievers, *Harrison*, III, 191–97; Fredrick B. Pike, *Chile and the United States, 1880–1962: The Emergence of Chile's Social Crisis and the Challenge to United States Diplomacy* (Notre Dame, 1963), 71–81.

the manufacturers' share of exports showed a modest increase, but from 1890 to 1900 that share rose from 17.9 percent to 31.7 percent. Also, the business community largely concurred with the Cleveland administration's analysis of the cause of depression in the 1890s and its solution. Historian Walter LaFeber has shown that after 1893, American business interests gave more and more attention to Latin America, American investment capital flowed into Latin America in substantial quantities, and steamship companies expanded their fleets and routes to Latin America.[25]

Although, as noted above, the reciprocity provision was abandoned in the 1894 tariff, the Cleveland administration pursued with success the policy of naval expansion initiated in 1883. Several factors contributed toward acceleration of this program, but probably none was more important than the influence of naval historian-philosopher Alfred T. Mahan, who through his books, articles, and lectures cultivated a coterie of influential followers within the navy and in government toward the view that sea power was essential for prosperity and world-power status. Other factors that led to authorization to construct five battleships during the Cleveland administration were the desire to create jobs during the depression and the need to protect overseas markets for U.S. exports.[26] The advantage of a U.S. naval presence in Latin American waters was clearly demonstrated during the crisis with Chile and again in the harbor of Rio de Janeiro in 1893–1894, when U.S. warships acted to uphold the Brazilian government against revolutionary forces; these were aided by the British who sought to undermine U.S. commercial penetration into that country. Also, in Nicaraguan waters in 1894–1896, the navy helped the U.S. displace the British as the principal political and commercial power along the Mosquito Coast and support the primacy of U.S. interests in a future Nicaraguan canal.[27]

By the mid-1890s U.S. public opinion was becoming fully alive to the nation's Latin American interests. A single issue sharply spurred trends that had been underway since the early 1880s toward increas-

25. Albert K. Steigerwalt, *The National Association of Manufacturers, 1895–1914: A Study in Business Leadership* (Grand Rapids, Mich., 1964), 12–14, 21–24, 50–54, 69–72; LaFeber, *The New Empire*, 154–56, 184, 187–89; Emily S. Rosenberg, *Spreading the American Dream: American Economic and Cultural Expansion, 1890–1945* (New York, 1982), 39–40; Theodore C. Search, "Our Trade with South America," *North American Review*, CLXIII (December, 1896), 716–17.

26. Sievers, *Harrison, III*, 135, 277; LaFeber, *The New Empire*, 85–94, 229–41; Ralph Dewar Bald, Jr., "The Development of Expansionist Sentiment in the United States, 1885–1895, as Reflected in Periodical Literature" (Ph.D. dissertation, University of Pittsburgh, 1953), 202.

27. LaFeber, *The New Empire*, 210–29.

ing attention to Latin America, higher levels of trade and investment, a more-conspicuous naval presence, and a more-acute wariness about European intentions in the region. That issue was the Venezuelan border crisis with Great Britain in 1895–1896.

Dispute over the location of the border between Venezuela and the British colony of Guiana had gone on since 1841, but after the British expanded their claims in the 1880s to include a gold-mining district and the mouth of the Orinoco River, Venezuela ended diplomatic relations with Great Britain and pressed the U.S. for support. Cleveland responded with a bold assertion of the Monroe Doctrine and a demand that the British agree to arbitration.[28] Prior to British acceptance of the U.S. position in early 1896, commentary on the issue demonstrated that Cleveland's surprisingly forceful posture in expanding the purview of the Monroe Doctrine rested solidly on public sentiment. On the whole, informed opinion in the country saw the dispute, particularly in its latter stages, as a conflict between Great Britain and the U.S. over application of the Monroe Doctrine and accepted the argument that U.S. economic interests in the Caribbean required this challenge to British assertion. Little pretense was made that the U.S. was acting primarily in defense of a helpless sister republic, and some observers even blamed the crisis on Venezuelan negligence and misgovernment.[29]

In early 1895, a year before resolution of the Venezuelan crisis, Cuban revolutionaries began a desperate struggle for independence from Spain, and in little more than three years it would lead to the period's climactic event in U.S.–Latin American relations—the Spanish-American War. Events leading up to the war and the war itself have been recounted in detail elsewhere, but one part of the story that bears directly on this study concerns U.S. perceptions of Cubans.[30]

28. Allan Nevins, *Grover Cleveland: A Study in Courage* (New York, 1932), 630–48; LaFeber, *The New Empire*, 242–70, 276–83.

29. Henry Cabot Lodge, "England, Venezuela, and the Monroe Doctrine," *North American Review*, CLX (June, 1895), 651–58; Joseph Wheller and Charles H. Grosvenor, "Our Duty in the Venezuelan Crisis," *North American Review*, CLXI (November, 1895), 628–33; Mayo W. Hazeltine, "The Work of the Next Congress," *North American Review*, CLXI (December, 1895), 641–49; Richard Harding Davis, "The Paris of South America," *Harper's New Monthly Magazine*, XCII (December, 1895), 114–15; "The Progress of the World," *Review of Reviews*, XII (December, 1895), 644–46; William Eleroy Curtis, "Venezuela: Her Government, People, and Boundary," *National Geographic Magazine*, VII (February, 1896), 57; "The Venezuelan Question," *North American Review*, CLXII (February, 1896), 141.

30. David F. Trask, *The War with Spain in 1898* (New York, 1981), 1–29; Nevins, *Cleveland*, 713–19; David F. Healy, *The United States in Cuba, 1898–1902: Generals, Politicians, and the Search for Policy* (Madison, Wis., 1963), 8–13, 17; Ernest R. May,

Evolution of the American image of the Cuban from the beginning of the struggle until the declaration of war in April, 1898, was truly remarkable. When the insurrection began, little distinction was made between Spaniard and Cuban, but by April, 1898, Americans had stamped the two with opposite traits. The already negative image of the Spaniard was never more negative than in 1898. The few positive characteristics accorded him at midcentury—dignity, courtesy, and honor—had been withdrawn by the 1890s as Spanish power waned. Sensationalized accounts of the Spanish reconcentration policy and the destruction of the *Maine* merely confirmed the characterization Americans had of the Spaniard as cruel, malevolent, and greedy. While the image of the Spaniard became ever-more sinister, that of his Cuban "victim" tended toward that of a freedom fighter valiantly struggling for republicanism, democracy, free enterprise—all U.S. ideals. Americans envisioned the Cuban revolutionary army as a thoroughly conventional, uniformed, and mounted force, not unlike Spanish units, and Americans had little grasp of the messy, dirty guerrilla campaign the Cubans were actually waging. Propaganda and press reports exhibited a noted tendency to instill Anglo-Saxon traits in the Cuban and to bleach him. Various accounts described the Cuban as almost entirely white, as often "light or blond," or as "fully nine-tenths" white. There were, of course, Americans who disparaged the Cubans throughout this period; Grover Cleveland privately described them at the beginning of the war as "the most inhuman and barbarious cutthroats in the world." But this was not the majority view. By 1898 the Cuban had become a whitened, Americanized, worthy ally in the struggle against a ruthless tyrant, images actively promoted by the New York-based Cuban junta and happily accepted by most Americans.[31]

Little time elapsed between the arrival of U.S. troops in Cuba and the rapid reversal of this image. Theodore Roosevelt's reaction to the Cuban troops upon landing near Santiago was typical of the disillusionment of many U.S. soldiers:

The Cuban soldiers were almost all blacks and mulattoes and were clothed in rags and armed with every kind of old rifle. They were utterly unable to make a serious fight, or to stand against even a very inferior number of Spanish troops, but we hoped they might be of use as scouts and skirmishers. For various reasons this proved not to be the case, and so far as the Santiago

---

Imperial Democracy: The Emergence of America as a Great Power (New York, 1961), 69–93, 112–47.

31. Linderman, *The Mirror of War*, 120–36. Cleveland is cited by Philip S. Foner, *The Spanish-Cuban-American War and the Birth of American Imperialism, 1895–1902* (New York, 1972), I, 181.

campaign was concerned, we should have been better off if there had not been a single Cuban with the army. They accomplished literally nothing, while they were a source of trouble and embarrassment, and consumed much provisions.[32]

On-the-scene accounts by the large number of correspondents in Cuba and letters from soldiers published in hometown newspapers quickly spread the dismay. Carl Schurz was reported to have said in August, 1898: "There are multitudes of Americans who say now that if they had known what a sorry lot the Cubans are, we would never have gone to war on their behalf." A U.S. officer with ten years' experience in dealing with Cubans wrote at the end of the war how pained he was to see "on the part of some of our public journals and many private citizens, a disposition to alienate the Cuban patriots."[33]

The Cubans were indicted for their ingratitude, laziness, unreliability, lack of fighting spirit, their desperate and unseemly scramble for U.S. provisions, and their ruthless reprisals against the Spanish. Americans failed to understand the Cuban style of guerrilla warfare, and the Cubans resented being assigned duties as a labor force and as scouts and guides. Upon the defeat of Spanish forces in Santiago, Cubans were not allowed to participate in the surrender negotiations, share in control of the city following its surrender, nor hold a victory parade to celebrate the departure of Spanish forces. Because the U.S. refused to recognize the Cuban revolutionary government, official relations with the Cubans were tense during the war and throughout the first part of the occupation period. The bitterness between wartime allies was deep as U.S. occupation forces settled in.[34] In a history of his military unit compiled immediately after the war, an officer wrote an evaluation of the Cuban that provides a measure of the sudden and remarkable reversal of the U.S. image of the Cuban: "[He] is a treacherous, lying, cowardly, thieving, worthless, half-breed mongrel; born of a mongrel spawn of Europe, crossed upon the fetiches of darkest Africa and aboriginal America. He is no more capable of self-government than the Hottentots that roam the wilds of Africa or the Bushmen of Australia."[35]

---

32. Theodore Roosevelt, "The Fifth Corps at Santiago," in *The Works of Theodore Roosevelt* (New York, 1923), XIII, 221–22.

33. Linderman, *The Mirror of War*, 142–43; New York *Evening Post*, August 19, 1898, cited by Healy, *The U.S. in Cuba*, 38; O. O. Howard, "The Conduct of the Cubans in the Late War," *Forum*, XXVI (October, 1898), 155.

34. Trask, *The War with Spain*, 209–12; Linderman, *The Mirror of War*, 127–44; Healy, *The U.S. in Cuba*, 32–38, 67–80.

35. John H. Parker, *History of the Gatling Gun Detachment Fifth Corps at Santiago* (Kansas City, Mo., 1898), 78, cited by Trask, *The War with Spain*, 210.

By the end of the century Cubans were no longer confused in the American mind with Spaniards but were given a distinct identity as Cubans and as Latin Americans.[36] The negative image of the Cuban was a direct product of the war and the occupation, but it was not incompatible with the nineteenth-century image of the Latin American. The Cuban of 1900 fit comfortably within the outlines of a general Latin American image.

That image grew out of an intellectual context that consisted of prideful awareness of territorial and economic expansion together with rising nationalism, Anglo-Saxon "racial" pride, Social Darwinism, and a sense of mission and destiny. These concepts were most actively promoted and popularized in books, essays, and lectures by Josiah Strong, John Fiske, and John W. Burgess, but other figures less closely identified with the concepts also expressed them. In an essay of 1897 William Dean Howells wrote that much of the recent self-criticism related to agrarian discontent, labor unrest, political radicalism, depression, and the closing of the frontier was "an effect of the unfathomable confidence we have in our destiny, which is one with our duty as well as our glory."[37]

From the American perspective of the late-nineteenth century, Latin Americans were a decidedly unfit people. Avowedly racist interpretations were an inevitable outcome of the period's "full flowering of racism" in the U.S.—a vicious current evidenced by the record high 162 lynchings of blacks in 1892. Historian John J. Johnson has shown that editorial cartoonists began in the 1890s to depict Latin Americans, particularly of the Caribbean nations, in overwhelmingly pejorative black stereotype, a finding consistent with the image given the Cuban by the end of the Spanish-American War.[38] Commentary was also filled with remarks about the legendary stupidity and laziness of the Indians, but the most-frequent attacks were directed against Latin America's racially mixed population. In 1884 the secretary of the U.S. legation in Brazil noted in a dispatch that the Brazilian was a mixture of Portuguese, Negro, and Indian, and, although this mixture had produced men remarkable in public affairs and letters, "every one

36. Linderman, *The Mirror of War*, 144–47.

37. William Dean Howells, "The Modern American Mood," *Harper's New Monthly Magazine*, XCV (July, 1897), 203; Josiah Strong, *Our Country* (1885; rpr. Cambridge, Mass., 1891), 213; Josiah Strong, *The New Era or the Coming Kingdom* (New York, 1893), 56; Josiah Strong, *Expansion Under New World-Conditions* (New York, 1900), 213; see also R. S. Storrs, "Sources and Guarantees of National Progress," *Magazine of American History*, XXIV (October, 1890), 262.

38. John J. Johnson, *Latin America in Caricature* (Austin, Tex., 1980), 157–65.

knows this *metissage* has not formed a people of steady, economical workers."[39] A similar message came from an 1886 book based on an extensive excursion by rail through well-traveled parts of Mexico by the highly regarded economist, David A. Wells. After rejecting the common notion that Mexico "is a rich prize," he concluded that it "is one of the very poorest and most wretched of all countries." A major reason Wells forecast a dim future for Mexico was that a large element within the ranks of the mestizos—the bulk of the population—was "among the lowest and vilest specimens of humanity in existence; a class exhibiting every vice, with hardly the possession of a single virtue."[40] A newspaper editor who spent two months traveling through Mexico in 1887 was favorably impressed with the country's natural beauty, marvelous climate, and the graciousness of its people, but he was depressed by the widespread miscegenation: "the black hybrids, yellow hybrids, Spanish types, Indian types . . . and dandies of the city, slender-legged, effeminate young milksops, the fag-end of a decayed civilization, without virility or purpose." And everywhere were swarms of children. "And the sad pity of it, to think that they will all grow up and become Mexicans!" Another perspective on Mexicans comes through the eyes of Mormons who migrated from Utah to northern Mexico from the mid-1870s through the 1880s as missionaries, communal colonists, and refugees from federal prosecution of polygamists. One sympathetic study of these colonists noted that they harbored "Anglo-American condescension" toward Mexicans and felt that Mexicans were poverty stricken because they chose to live "in a manner not in accord with the Mormon idea of industry and thrift."[41]

A grammar school geography of 1900 characterized Latin American "half-breeds" as "ignorant" and "backward" and argued that one reason "the Spaniards have not developed is found in their relation to the Indians. Although robbing and enslaving them, they at the same time married them freely, so that, in time, half-breeds have come to make up more than half the population." The author of an 1897 school history text expressed gratitude that Indians in the U.S. had rejected civilization, thus allowing the nation to escape Mexico's problem of a proliferation of "shiftless half-breeds." Similar senti-

39. U.S. Department of State, Diplomatic Dispatches, Brazil, Vol. XLVI, Charles B. Trail, U.S. Secretary of Legation, Rio de Janeiro, September 16, 1884, to Secretary of State Frederick T. Frelinghuysen, Record Group 59.

40. David A. Wells, *A Study of Mexico* (New York, 1886), 39, 93–94, 38–44.

41. Charles Dudley Warner, "Mexican Notes," *Harper's New Monthly Magazine,* LXXV (June, July, August, 1887), 27, 287, 452; F. LaMond Tullis, *Mormons in Mexico: The Dynamics of Faith and Culture* (Logan, Utah, 1987), 53–57, 63.

ments were written privately by Senator Henry Cabot Lodge who argued that Puerto Rico and Hawaii should be maintained as territories rather than elevated to statehood status for the same reason New Mexico had been kept for so long as a territory, though entitled to statehood—"simply because we do not like the character of the population."[42]

While most critics of the Latin American population directed their attacks on the racially mixed elements, the Spanish and Portuguese Creoles did not escape condemnation. In an article on Peru, one author noted that in all the South American republics "the old creole population . . . is useless for progress; [its members are] in most cases nothing better than national parasites." The U.S. minister to Central America charged that less than 20 percent of the whites "are familiar with, and know how to appreciate the present civilization of the Anglo-Saxon race." He argued that the Central American elites, in contrast to the early American colonists, were sadly inferior because they "have never undergone that development of mind and body, which a hard struggle for subsistence and place in the world, invariably brings." One of the better travel books on Latin America to appear in the period was *Tropical America* by Isaac N. Ford, a New York journalist who spent about one year traveling in nearly all the Latin American countries between 1889 and 1891. Like many such books of the time, its observations are flawed by the author's inability to speak Spanish or Portuguese and by an itinerary that carried him along the periphery of the continent. Ford favored the people of Chile and Argentina, noting that they possessed qualities absent in all other Latin Americans, "something of the Anglo-Saxon energy and reserve of power," but he declared that they lacked "both the practical judgment and moral qualities of the New England stock."[43]

Closely related to the commentary on race, though mentioned with less frequency and given less prominence as a cause of underdevelopment, was Latin America's small population base. Several observers

42. Ralph S. Tarr and Frank M. McMurry, *Tarr and McMurry Geographies. Second Book: North America* (New York, 1900), 100–101; D. H. Montgomery, *The Student's American History* (Boston, 1897), 20; "A Specimen Spanish-American Republic," *Nation*, LXII (February 20, 1896), 153; Henry Cabot Lodge to George Lyman, June 15, 1898, quoted in John A. Garraty, *Henry Cabot Lodge: A Biography* (New York, 1965), 195.

43. Theodore Child, "Impressions of Peru," *Harper's New Monthly Magazine*, LXXXII (January, 1891), 274; Department of State, Diplomatic Dispatches, Central America, Vol. XVII, Cornelius A. Logan, U.S. Minister to Central America, Guatemala City, June 15, 1881, to Secretary of State James G. Blaine, Record Group 59; Isaac N. Ford, *Tropical America* (New York, 1893), 98, 120.

noted the region's vast, empty territories and argued that progress would occur only when those vacant lands were filled with immigrants. William Eleroy Curtis commented on the scant population in several countries and concluded that the enterprise and capital needed for progress could only be secured through immigration. At the same time, he explained the rapid development of Argentina on the basis of its natural resources, temperate climate, industrious population, and heavy European immigration. The U.S. minister to Mexico reported that he had pointed out many times to the host government the great need for "an enlightened encouragement of immigration," and his counterpart in Brazil noted that it would become a great nation "if the colonization of skilled farm labor can be accomplished."[44] U.S. railroad entrepreneurs Henry Meiggs and Minor C. Keith complained that among the difficulties they faced in carrying out their projects in Peru and Costa Rica were the lack of skilled labor such as carpenters and machinists and the severe shortage of unskilled manpower, a deficit that Meiggs remedied by importing workers into Peru from China, Chile, and Bolivia.[45] Though the emphasis in the commentary on population centered on race and character, many observers were struck by the region's small population base and its large, unpopulated hinterland and argued that the labor deficiency hindered exploitation of natural resources, launching of major transportation projects, and formation of national markets, all of which were considered essential for development. It is worth noting that throughout the nineteenth century these arguments were shared by Latin American leaders, who showed a keen sensitivity to the importance of immigration by sponsoring numerous colonization projects into their countries.

The role of climate as a factor shaping national development ranks with race as a major theme in the literature of the period. It loomed large in Reverend Josiah Strong's vision of the future, for he argued that Americans were distinguished by their "intense and persistent energy," which he attributed primarily to "our climate, which acts as a constant stimulus." He held that the tropics were disadvantaged not

44. Curtis, *The Capitals of Spanish America*, 149, 223, 266, 579–81; Department of State, Diplomatic Dispatches, Mexico, Vol. LXXIII, Philip H. Morgan, U.S. Minister, Mexico City, August 13, 1881, to Secretary of State James G. Blaine, Record Group 59; Department of State, Diplomatic Dispatches, Brazil, Vol. XLIII, John C. White, U.S. Minister, Rio de Janeiro, February 27, 1879, to Secretary of State William Evarts, Record Group 59.

45. Watt Stewart, *Henry Meiggs, Yankee Pizarro* (1946; rpr. New York, 1968), 111, 203; Watt Stewart, *Keith and Costa Rica: A Biographical Study of Minor Cooper Keith* (Albuquerque, N.M., 1964), 64, 81.

only in the lack of a stimulating climate but also in the inevitable failure of manufacturing, which would never succeed because the high humidity would destroy machinery and because "tropical races are deficient in mechanical ability." Interest in tropical regions and in the nation's relationship with them is suggested by the popularity of a book-length essay by British sociologist Benjamin Kidd that appeared in the U.S. at the end of the century. In *The Control of the Tropics* Kidd argued that in the future the tropics would supply an ever-increasing proportion of the world's food and resources, but that to ensure proper development of those resources, the tropics would have to be administered from abroad by whites who would find it impossible to acclimatize to tropical conditions.[46]

An emphasis on climate as a prime cause of Latin America's lack of progress was a theme common to much of the travel literature. A much-traveled Protestant minister, who wrote a short description in 1878 of his journeys by rail from Veracruz to Mexico City and back, was much taken by Mexico's natural wealth and beauty. But an afternoon walk in the city of Orizaba left him "with impressions as sad of its humanity as they are fascinating of its site and scenery." While visiting a market in the capital, he expressed a dislike for the country's varied tropical fruits and a "preference for a good peach or apple to all their luxuriant insipidity. And so it is with almost all things tropical; for character and strength you must go to the sterner, severer North—and thus we have much of the moral of history!" In an article describing Peru, a seasoned traveler painted Lima as a city filled with people living "in an indigent, primitive, and thoroughly unhygienic manner, which would be unendurable were it not for the clemency of the climate, which enervates and conduces to a languid and indolent state, comparable in some respects to the fatalism of the Turk."[47] In his travel book, journalist Isaac N. Ford noted that Brazilians exhibited "a national habit of deliberation and procrastination formed under the influence of an enervating climate," and in Peru the problem was not the tropical heat but the debilitating effect of the constancy of the climate. William Eleroy Curtis shared these views on climate, which he expressed in 1900 in his third book on Latin America. He explained the differences between "primitive" Peru and Ecuador

46. Strong, *Our Country*, 212–13; Strong, *Expansion*, 35; Benjamin Kidd, *The Control of the Tropics* (New York, 1898), 3, 30, 48, 51–52, 96–97.

47. Albert Zabriskie Gray, *Mexico As It Is, Being Notes of a Recent Tour in That Country* (New York, 1878), 10, 85, 33, 63, 129, 45–46, 55; Child, "Impressions of Peru," 260. See also Martha J. Lamb, "Our South American Neighbors," *Magazine of American History*, XXIII (April, 1890), 265.

and the more-civilized Chile on the basis of climate. "As you approach the temperate zones nature exacts more labor as the price of existence. A higher value is placed upon human life, and more energy and intelligence are applied to its development."[48]

In a dispatch from Guatemala City in 1881, the U.S. minister described Central America's Indian masses as people with "the fewest possible wants, which nature alone, almost supplies in these tropical countries." Their requirements for clothing and shelter are minimal, corn and beans can be grown with little labor, and the banana "grows almost spontaneously. It would be the making of a new civilization for all the people of Central America, could every banana tree be blighted forever, in a single night." A 1900 grammar school geography touched upon the same theme in analyzing the reasons the English colonies in the New World had developed such a dynamic, progressive culture while the Spanish ones had not. The authors focused on two factors, climate and race, and argued that in the warm countries settled by the Spanish,

So little energy is required to find sufficient food that the people do not need to exert themselves, and hence do not. By taking a few steps, the Central American can find bananas and other nourishing food at almost any season of the year; why then should he work? The people, therefore, lose the inclination to bestir themselves. . . .

As for the English, the temperate climate of their section is the best in the world for the development of energy. The warm summers allowed abundant harvests; but the long, cold winters forced the settlers to exert themselves to store supplies for the cold season.[49]

Because of the heavy emphasis on tropical climate as a handicap to development, one would expect observers to have attached similar importance to the high incidence of tropical disease in nineteenth-century Latin America. Surprisingly, this explanation received minor attention. It was most often mentioned as a factor contributing to the failure of the de Lesseps canal project and to delays in completing various railroad projects; it was also listed as a hindrance to development in some travel accounts and diplomatic dispatches. But it did not re-

48. Ford, *Tropical America,* 2, 138, 72, 204; William Eleroy Curtis, *Between the Andes and the Ocean: An Account of an Interesting Journey Down the West Coast of South America from the Isthmus of Panama to the Straits of Magellan* (Chicago, 1900), 386.

49. Department of State, Diplomatic Dispatches, Central America, Vol. XVII, Cornelius A. Logan, U.S. Minister to Central America, Guatemala City, June 15, 1881, to Secretary of State James G. Blaine, Record Group 59; Tarr and McMurry, *Geographies,* 100–101.

ceive the consistent, elevated attention given race and climate. Typical of the attitude toward disease was Curtis's book, *The Capitals of Spanish America,* in which he described several well-provisioned hospitals of Mexico City but did not discuss disease; he described a funeral procession in San José, Costa Rica, and he deplored the filth and dirt of Guayaquil, Ecuador, but did not mention disease. The closest he came to assigning to tropical disease the importance it deserved was when he noted that in Rio de Janeiro "yellow-fever and other epidemics carry off a large percentage of the population every summer, but the increase from natural causes more than keeps pace with the mortality."[50] This insouciant attitude toward disease would change in the early twentieth century as a result of the large-scale U.S. presence in Cuba and Panama.

Geographical factors such as resources, terrain, and rainfall also received attention from observers who pondered the factors governing development, but they received less attention than climate. Portrayal of Latin America as an El Dorado of undeveloped abundance was widespread and has been noted in the debate on Dominican annexation and in the observations of William Eleroy Curtis and other travelers. One exception to this pattern is the travel book on Mexico by economist David A. Wells who considered the usual estimates of Mexico's potential wealth to be grossly inflated and who argued that the mountainous terrain and shortages of fuel and water constituted severe impediments to development. A traveler to Brazil also held that its resources, though imposing, "are yet inferior to what is commonly supposed." But the great majority of commentators wrote of "matchless resources, mineral and agricultural."[51] The emphasis on poverty amidst neglected wealth resembles the charge of poor stewardship of the land and improper use of the soil leveled against American Indians, and it presented a stark contrast to how most Americans perceived the course of their own development.

Americans had always been certain of the superior state of their civilization compared to Latin America's, and they had often spoken of that superiority in terms of the advance of democracy, the spread of freedom, and the growth of free institutions while criticizing Latin America's religious practices, political system, social structure, and

50. Stewart, *Henry Meiggs,* 203; Stewart, *Keith and Costa Rica,* 81–85; Curtis, *The Capitals of Spanish America,* 56, 220, 312, 258, 697.

51. Wells, *A Study of Mexico,* 133; Christopher C. Andrews, *Brazil: Its Condition and Prospects* (New York, 1887), 287; Department of State, Diplomatic Dispatches, Mexico, Vol. LXXIII, Philip H. Morgan, U.S. Minister to Mexico, Mexico City, August 13, 1881, to Secretary of State James G. Blaine, Record Group 59.

pattern of land tenure. But beginning in the late decades of the nineteenth century the evidence of superiority seemed more and more to rest on the tangible symbols of material progress. Highly conscious of the nation's rapid industrial development and enthralled with the advance of science and technology, Americans pointed to the increasing number of new inventions, growing coal and steel output, and expanding railway mileage as solid evidence of national progress.[52] Because the idea of progress acquired this pronounced material dimension, Americans became more sensitive to Latin America's technological deficiencies, and their observations in this period are replete with accounts of "prehistoric backwardness."[53] The following report from an 1881 diplomatic dispatch on the method of unloading ships at Guatemala's Pacific port of San José is typical of these observations:

The hoisting facilities of this monopoly are bad enough for freight, but are simply frightful for the human lives entrusted to them. They consist of a common donkey engine, and a hemp rope passing over a derrick, with an open cage attached to it. People are hoisted and lowered by this miserable apparatus daily; suspended in mid air over the sea, and liable to be drowned at any moment by the breaking of the rope, or some part of the cheap engine holding it. In our country, such a contrivance would not be permitted for 24 hours.[54]

The lack of modern tools, machines, and conveniences in everyday life as well as in farming, mining, and other economic enterprises was commonly regarded as a symptom of a deplorable degree of backwardness.[55] These conclusions are somewhat ironic because during the last two decades of the nineteenth century several Latin American countries experienced unusually high growth rates driven by demand from a rapidly industrializing Europe for foodstuffs, minerals, and other raw materials. This export-led growth produced major changes in many countries, most particularly in Argentina, Brazil, Chile, and

52. For an example of the symbolic importance of the railroad as a sure sign of progress, see the speech delivered at the inauguration of Peru's Arequipa railroad in 1871 by Henry Meiggs, as quoted in Stewart, *Henry Meiggs*, 142.

53. William H. Beezley, *Judas at the Jockey Club and Other Episodes of Porfirian Mexico* (Lincoln, Nebr., 1987), 71. On pages 67–79, Beezley provides a fascinating account of technological backwardness in rural Mexico during the rule of Porfirio Díaz.

54. Department of State, Diplomatic Dispatches, Central America, Vol. XVII, Cornelius A. Logan, U.S. Minister to Central America, Guatemala City, February 2, 1881, to Secretary of State William M. Evarts, Record Group 59.

55. John H. Coatsworth, "Obstacles to Economic Growth in Nineteenth Century Mexico," *American Historical Review*, LXXXIII (1978), 81–83. Coatsworth has shown that the perception of a growing gap between U.S. and Mexican standards of living was real; between 1800 and 1877 Mexican per capita income as a percentage of that of the U.S. fell from 44 to 14 percent.

Mexico. Most observers, however, focused on the large gap between the quickly maturing industrial economy of the U.S. and the traditional agricultural and extractive economies of Latin America.

In addition to race and climate, the other principal explanation for Latin American backwardness was the Black Legend. It received great stimulus from the Spanish-American War, but even before the war, popular school texts emphasized the cruelty of the Spanish conquest, and observers frequently referred to the colonial era as a period of "butchery and crime," as a "tyrannical choking" of the Indians, and as "four [sic] centuries of Spanish tyranny, duplicity and deception."[56] Perhaps the most-extraordinary condemnation of Spanish colonization is found in E. George Squier's 1877 travel book on Peru. Squier was a businessman and amateur archaeologist whose book created less of a stir than had his classic descriptions of Central America in the 1850s. It was, nevertheless, a work of high quality based on two years of travel and archaeological work. Squier speculated on what might have been the future of Peru had not the "untoward" Spanish conquest subverted the Inca empire: "I call it untoward because there was, under the Incas, a better government, better protection for life, and better facilities for the pursuit of happiness than have existed since the Conquest, or do exist today. The material prosperity of the country was far in advance of what it is now." Economist David A. Wells commented at length on the obstacles to Mexico's progress, and he concluded that the major factors included the traditions and practices inherited from Spain, that is, the "relics of European medievalism" that, though having disappeared in Europe, in Spanish America had become "embalmed" survivals. Among such relics he included a tax system that defied entrepreneurship, a pattern of land tenure that promoted stagnation, and a "long continued absolutism and tyranny in respect to both government and religion." Wells also saw the Spanish language, which he did not speak, as a barrier to advancement, arguing that it was "not well fitted for the uses and progress of a commercial nation" and that it was an obstacle to the adoption of the ideas and methods of Mexico's "great Anglo-Saxon neighbors."[57]

John Fiske, a noted historian and popular lecturer in his day, espoused the Black Legend in a multivolume history of the discovery

56. George Payn Quackenbos, *Elementary History of the United States* (1884 ed.; New York, c. 1860), 19; Elson, *Guardians of Tradition*, 75–76; Ira Nelson Morris, *With the Trade-Winds: A Jaunt in Venezuela and the West Indies* (New York, 1896), 155–56; Curtis, *Between the Andes*, 54. The Portuguese and Brazilians were criticized, though less intensely than the Spanish and Spanish Americans. See Joseph Smith, "Brazil and the Brazilians," *Harper's Weekly*, XXXVII (December 30, 1893), 1255–56.

57. Wells, *A Study of Mexico*, 174, 163, 181, 118, 113, 86, 94.

and conquest. In some regards Fiske's work was quite balanced, but his treatment of the Inquisition and its impact on Spanish-American history and character was pure Black Legend. He asserted that the Inquisition worked with "such fiendish efficiency" that it was nearly impossible for people of intelligence and moral courage to escape it. "They were strangled and burned by tens of thousands, and as the inevitable result, the average character of the Spanish people was lowered. The brightest and boldest were cut off in their early prime, while duller and weaker ones were spared to propagate the race. . . ." In his condemnation of the Inquisition, Fiske cited Henry Charles Lea, who had established a formidable reputation among historians for his scholarship on Spanish medieval and religious history and whose stature would be further enhanced in 1903 by election to the presidency of the American Historical Association. Lea did his part to fan the flames of hatred against Spain in an article entitled "Decadence of Spain" published in the *Atlantic Monthly* in the midst of the war. The article was not mere propaganda, for it reflected Lea's professional judgment about the Spanish colonial period, and it constituted a forthright expression of the Black Legend. Lea contended: "The discoveries of Columbus did not open up a new continent to be settled by industrious immigrants coming to found states and develop their resources in peaceful industry. The marvelous exploits of the Conquistadores were performed in the craziest thirst for gold, and those who succeeded them came in the hope of speedy enrichment and return, to accomplish which they exploited to the utmost the unhappy natives, and when these were no longer available replaced them with African slaves."[58]

The most-forceful indictment of the Spanish legacy to appear in the immediate aftermath of the Spanish-American War was *Harper's Pictorial History of the War with Spain*. This beautifully designed book of 508 pages in large format celebrates American achievement against a brutal, sadistic colonial regime at the end of its historic era. The central theme of the first section is Spanish cruelty—against the Indians, against the Dutch in their wars for independence, and against the French during the Napoleonic invasion. This section relies heavily on citations from Bartolomé de Las Casas—one of whose tracts, incidentally, was reissued at this time—and it contains many drawings illustrative of the cruelty theme. The following suggests the flavor of the book:

58. John Fiske, *The Discovery of America with Some Account of Ancient America and the Spanish Conquest* (Boston, 1899), II, 88, 401–402; Henry Charles Lea, "Decadence of Spain," *Atlantic Monthly*, LXXXII (July, 1898), 42, 46.

"Natives Penned Up and Burned, Shot, and Put to the Sword"
Harper's Pictorial History of the War with Spain (New York, 1899), p. 6.

The providence of God has doubtless had to do with the decline of Spain as a colonial power. . . . Morality sees in the sceptre of Spain a godless wand of necromancy that can be a cross or a sword at will or whim; philosophy finds beneath accumulated coatings of the why and wherefore of her doings an inner core of cruelty in Spanish character; and history traces this blood-red line of cruelty, entwined with a strand of golden greed, back through the black ages to the Gothic laws of a remote ancestry.[59]

Many Americans became convinced of the essential accuracy of the Black Legend through the reporting and the voluminous writing of one of the most respected Latin American thinkers of his generation, José Martí, Cuba's greatest hero and a symbol of liberty throughout the hemisphere. Best known as a leader in the cause of *Cuba libre,* Martí was a celebrated poet and essayist who came to know Latin America during several years spent in exile in the 1870s in Guatemala, Mexico, and Venezuela; he lived in New York from 1880 until his death in 1895 in a military skirmish on behalf of Cuban liberation. During his many years as a reporter and teacher in New York, he developed a strong following among his Latin American readership, the Cuban exile community, and U.S. citizens who supported his revolutionary cause. For Americans, one of the most-resonant notes in Martí's writing was the anti-Spanish theme that blamed Cuba's enslavement as well as Latin American backwardness on the mother country. In writing about Guatemala, Martí believed that the task was to overcome the result of three centuries of colonial "darkness" and "poison" left by Spain, and in reference to Cuba he held that the goal was not just to get Spain out of Cuba, "but to get it out of our habits."[60]

Latin America's Roman Catholic tradition was a central element of the Hispanic heritage, and, although essentially a part of the Black Legend, it was so frequently affirmed as an explanation for the region's backwardness that it can be viewed as a distinctive factor in this period. Anti-Catholic observations about Latin America were standard fare throughout the nineteenth century from the time of Thomas Jefferson's assertion about a "priest-ridden people" to the comments of travelers such as William Eleroy Curtis late in the century, by which time some observers were drawing a distinction between U.S. and Latin American Catholicism. The charges against the latter were that it engendered an authoritarian tradition inimical to democracy, hindered progress by keeping minds closed to free inquiry, and instilled negative character traits. In traveling through Mexico in 1878, a Protestant minister attributed the "degraded" condition of the

59. *Harper's Pictorial History of the War with Spain* (New York, 1899), 2.
60. Peter Turton, *José Martí: Architect of Cuba's Freedom* (London, 1986), 72, 52.

population to a flourishing Spanish heritage of "ignorance, bigotry, and intolerance." He vigorously condemned the church for having "fattened upon the land," and he asserted that the human sacrifices of the Aztecs "pale beside the subsequent atrocities, both of Church and State, committed against these heathen Indians under the name of Christianity!" A firm linkage between character and Catholicism is found in a dispatch of 1881 from the U.S. minister to Central America in which he noted that the Catholic church of Central America cannot be judged by the Catholic church of the United States, which produces "not only good, but intelligent people." The teachings of the former "have moulded the character of the people into a type almost *sui generis*. They are religious fanatics, and as is usually the case, without much true religion; they are avaricious and selfish; essentially narrow in view; intolerant in everything; with insincerity personified, untruthfulness cultivated as a fine art, deception a test of cleverness, and secret revenge installed as a household god."[61]

Even though the great bulk of commentary on Latin America in the late 1800s remained in the negative vein of the immediate post–Civil War period, some writers made an effort toward a more-evenhanded approach. During the Spanish-American War an editor of *Harper's* wrote: "I have read a good deal lately about Spain's ignorance of the United States, and I have witnessed the Mexican ignorance of our great country; I should say that it was only matched by our ignorance of Spain and Mexico." Traveling through Yucatan and southern Mexico, one observer noted that despite the conquerors' tyranny and greed, they "left the natives in possession of the coasts, fields, and forests. An Anglo-Saxon invasion would have swept them into the Pacific."[62] A rather extreme example of historical revision is *The Spanish Pioneers* by Charles F. Lummis, who sought to correct the distorted record of Spanish Indian policy presented in U.S. textbooks. He referred to the Spanish colonizing enterprise as "the largest and longest and most marvellous feat of manhood in all history," a feat marked from first to last by a "humane and progressive spirit" that, when placed alongside the American record, "puts us to the blush."[63]

61. Gray, *Mexico As It Is*, 63, 129, 45–46; Department of State, Diplomatic Dispatches, Central America, Vol. XVII, Cornelius A. Logan, U.S. Minister to Central America, Guatemala City, June 15, 1881, to Secretary of State James G. Blaine, Record Group 59.

62. C. D. Warner, "Editor's Study: Life in Mexico," *Harper's New Monthly Magazine*, XCVII (July, 1898), 312; Ford, *Tropical America*, 292.

63. Charles F. Lummis, *The Spanish Pioneers* (Chicago, 1893), 11–12, 23–24. This book was very popular and went through many editions between 1893 and 1936.

These occasional efforts at balanced treatment probably had slight impact on the educated public's judgment of Latin American civilization, particularly if one considers the negative stereotypes used by prominent journalists and writers of popular fiction to depict Latin Americans. In a study entitled *Myths and Mores in American Best Sellers, 1865–1965*, Ruth Miller Elson concluded that popular American writers assumed that the Spanish and Portuguese in Europe and America had a nature that embraced "laziness, violence, vengefulness, superstition, loyalty to a venal clergy, dishonesty and unreliability."[64] The most-prominent journalist to report on Latin America during the 1890s and the early years of the twentieth century was Richard Harding Davis, whose first exposure to the region came during a brief visit to Cuba in 1886. Although his journalistic reputation rested largely on his work as a war correspondent during the Cuban insurrection, the Spanish-American War, and the Boer War, his condescending attitude toward Latin America "influenced American opinion of Latin America for several decades," according to his biographers. That influence derived not only from his many articles on the region in large-circulation Philadelphia and New York City newspapers, in various magazines, and from his editorship of *Harper's Weekly* but also from the popularity of his many works of fiction. His reporting on Latin America was superficial, impressionistic, and shaped by his quest for spectacular scenes and romantic adventure.[65] *Three Gringos in Venezuela and Central America* (1896), a book based on several weeks of travel in Central America and a stopover in Caracas, Venezuela, was openly disdainful of the Central Americans. After riding across Honduras on muleback, Davis judged that life in the rural areas was "as near an approach to the condition of primitive man as one can find on this continent" and that poverty prevailed "not because the people are poor, but because they are indolent." Though he delighted in the beauty and potential wealth of Central America, he likened its people to "a gang of semi-barbarians in a beautifully furnished house, of which they can understand neither its possibilities of comfort nor its use." He described those small countries as "dis-

64. Ruth Miller Elson, *Myths and Mores in American Best Sellers, 1865–1965* (New York, 1985), 163–64. For studies of the characterization of Latin Americans and Mexican Americans in American fiction see: Cecil Robinson, *Mexico and the Hispanic Southwest in American Literature* (Tucson, Ariz., 1977); Pettit, *Images of the Mexican American*; Arnoldo De León, *They Called Them Greasers: Anglo Attitudes Toward Mexicans in Texas, 1821–1900* (Austin, Tex., 1983).

65. Scott Compton Osborn and Robert L. Phillips, Jr., *Richard Harding Davis* (Boston, 1978), 63, 67; Charles Belmont Davis, ed., *Adventures and Letters of Richard Harding Davis* (New York, 1917), 159.

organized military camps" in which progress and prosperity were impossible because of the turmoil caused by frequent revolutions. Davis darkly concluded that "the Central-American citizen is no more fit for a republican form of government than he is for an arctic expedition," and, consequently, "it would have been a very good thing . . . if [William] Walker, or any other man of force, had put his foot on the neck of every republic in Central America and turned it to some account."[66]

The work of Stephen Crane is illustrative of the negative stereotypes found in popular fiction. Crane, who achieved international fame during the last decade of his brief life, 1871–1900, as a novelist, poet, and master of the short story, spent several months in Mexico in 1895 and published within the next three years a series of short stories based on his experiences there. In three of those stories the central event used by Crane to explore human nature involved life-or-death confrontations between Americans and Mexicans. In "A Man and Some Others," several "greasers," one with "a smile that was gently, almost caressingly murderous," ambushed and killed, for no apparent reason, an innocent American sheepherder by approaching stealthily in the night "with the finesse of the escaping serpent." Crane described another confrontation in "The Five White Mice," in which one sober and two drunken Americans suddenly encountered three Mexicans late one night on a narrow Mexico City sidewalk. The boldest of the Mexicans expected a quick, easy fight, for his face was "a yellow mask smiling in eager cruelty, in satisfaction, and above all it was lit with sinister decision." All escaped injury when the sober American drew his revolver in self-defense. In this story the two Americans were happily, joyously drunk, whereas in "One Dash—Horses," excessive drink had an opposite effect on a Mexican described by Crane as "a fat, round-faced Mexican, whose little eyes were black as jet. He was insane with the wild rage of a man whose liquor is dully burning at his brain."[67] These sketches of Mexicans as sinister, treacherous, greaser bandidos by a major American author were muffled echoes of the portraits drawn by writers of lesser caliber in dime novels, weekly pulps, and historical romances.

Late-nineteenth-century observations on Latin American civilization reflected a general consensus on the causes of what was universally acknowledged to be a state of backwardness throughout the re-

66. Richard Harding Davis, *Three Gringos in Venezuela and Central America* (New York, 1896), 92–93, 146–47, 139.

67. Fredson Bowers, ed., *Tales of Adventure* (Charlottesville, Va., 1970), 54, 61, 47, 16, 18, Vol. V of Bowers, ed., *The Works of Stephen Crane.*

gion. There was substantial agreement on three fundamental causes: an inferior racial makeup, a tropical climate inimical to progress, and an inherited cultural pattern stamped with such retarding characteristics as corruption, indolence, and enslavement to a form of Catholicism that produced "cramped and narrow minds." To dramatize and give emphasis to the retrogressive influence of these factors, commentators often presented them in conjunction with a detailed description of the region's undeveloped abundance, which was certain to yield vast rewards given the proper application of energy and enterprise. Additional factors contributing to Latin American problems were discussed but with no frequency or regularity. For example, some writers examined Latin America's rugged terrain and severe transportation problems that impeded the marketing of raw materials; others mentioned the problems of inequitable systems of land tenure and taxation; and many wrote of the need for an influx of industrious immigrants. Surprisingly few observers emphasized the need for foreign capital, and, indeed, some remarked on the dangers it posed.[68] Some of the writing on Porfirian Mexico, however, assumed that because of Mexico's stability, development would occur behind the locomotive of U.S. capital and enterprise.[69]

The absence of close analysis of developmental problems in this period is to be expected, for the obstacles to development would not become subject to rigorous study until after World War II. As has been shown, there was an abundant commentary on the topic, but it was incidental and it lacked urgency. Evaluations of Latin America's prospects for development carried the underlying assumption that both nature and culture decreed the region would continue forever as a producer of raw materials for the industrial world and an importer of manufactured goods. This did not mean, however, that progress was ruled out. It meant that while Latin America could not expect to join the ranks of the advanced, industrializing nations, it could, nevertheless, make headway as a raw materials exporter. Some of the more widely traveled observers acknowledged that, within the region, Argentina and Chile were making progress because of temperate climates and the achievement of political stability, that Argentina was further

68. Curtis, *Between the Andes*, 203, 343, 394; Child, "Impressions of Peru," 274; Henry Ware Allen, "The Annexation of Mexico," *Arena*, LX (March, 1894), 479; "American Trade in Venezuela," *Scientific American*, LXXIV (February 8, 1896), 87; Ford, *Tropical America*, 208; Howard Conkling, *Mexico and the Mexicans or, Notes of Travel in the Winter and Spring of 1883* (New York, 1883), 297.

69. J. Hendrickson McCarty, *Two Thousand Miles Through the Heart of Mexico* (New York, 1886), 112.

advantaged by a large European-based population, and that Mexico, too, was showing signs of advancement because of its recently gained stability and its proximity to the U.S. In the final analysis, however, the many factors handicapping Latin America's progress appeared to condemn even the most favorably endowed nation of the region as a laggard to the rapid technological and material advance of the United States.

Knowledge of Latin America had advanced little between the end of the Civil War and the end of the century. Although the U.S. found itself with ownership of Puerto Rico, a protectorate over Cuba, a revitalized Monroe Doctrine, high ambition for an isthmian canal, and a growing commercial and financial stake in Latin America, it possessed little expertise on the region, its culture, or its history. The leading interpreter of Latin America was a Chicago journalist who had gained prominence through political appointment. Latin American history as a discipline did not yet exist, and its study at the university level was a rarity. Journalists, businessmen, and tourists provided the bulk of what Americans knew of Latin America. And Americans knew in 1900 that they could rightfully boast of great material strides and that the U.S. had become a developed world power, while Latin America appeared to languish in a state of turbulent backwardness. There seemed little concern over this great disparity, for it was often presented as though it were the natural order of things. In a sense, the attitude toward Latin America was rather detached, even though interest in the region had grown perceptibly during the 1880s and 1890s. But this attitude would change during the next generation, when Americans came to believe that their own national interests were imperiled by events in the region.

3

Perceptions of Backwardness in the Era of Intervention, 1901–1921

When Theodore Roosevelt succeeded to the presidency upon William McKinley's assassination in 1901, the involvement of the United States in Latin American affairs had never been greater. But the further escalation of that involvement during the next two decades would be truly startling. The acquisition of Puerto Rico and occupation of Cuba were merely the first steps toward a greater hemispheric intrusion that continued to be undergirded by the desire for more trade, investment, and contact. Fear that European intervention posed a threat to the nation's expanding interests in the Caribbean energized policy toward Latin America. This fear impelled the U.S. to reduce that threat by substituting a U.S. for a European presence, particularly after acquiring the Panama Canal site in 1903. Policy was also driven by the Progressive Era's moralistic impulse toward reform, which contributed to an attitude that saw in the smaller Latin American nations vast opportunities for the uplift of mankind. In addition, the chaos of revolution that engulfed Mexico during the second decade of the century inevitably drew the attention of a fascinated and appalled American public and led to lasting complications in relations with Mexico. Although those relations became embittered during the administration of Woodrow Wilson, 1913–1921, the outbreak of World War I in 1914 opened wide the door to the rest of Latin America for the expansion of U.S. commercial and financial interests by destroying existing patterns of European–Latin American trade and investment. By 1921 the U.S. had become deeply entangled in Latin American affairs. It exercised sovereignty over Puerto Rico and control over the Panama Canal; Cuba and Nicaragua were virtual protectorates; the U.S. was the major trading partner and foreign investor in several Latin American countries, and in some of the Caribbean nations it had established customs receiverships, stationed marines, and unseated presidents.

It was altogether fitting that the ebullient, energetic, forty-two-year-old Roosevelt should assume leadership, in the opening years of the century, in expanding the U.S. role in Latin American affairs. He had been an articulate spokesman for a more-dynamic foreign policy in the 1890s, and he was a "confident imperialist," convinced that great nations such as the U.S. had a duty to spread civilization, uphold law and order, and elevate mankind. Roosevelt's policies in Latin America were based on his and his generation's conviction of the superiority of the white race, especially of the Anglo-Americans, and of the nation's civilizing mission. In the several instances of major involvement in Latin America during Roosevelt's presidency, 1901–1909, U.S. policy was most strongly shaped by his use of a reinterpreted and reinvigorated Monroe Doctrine to forestall European intervention. Protection of American lives and property and promotion of the nation's economic interests also influenced the evolution of Roosevelt's Latin American policy toward greater activism.[1]

Military occupation of Cuba ended in 1902, but the island remained a U.S. protectorate as defined by the Platt Amendment, which the Cubans were compelled to incorporate into their constitution. In 1903 the two nations agreed on terms for the long-term lease of a base at Guantánamo Bay, and they ratified a reciprocity treaty strengthening their already close economic ties. Disorders that accompanied Cuba's 1905 elections led Roosevelt to dispatch marines to the island the following year, and they remained until 1909.[2] Another legacy of the Spanish-American War was a strengthened determination to obtain an isthmian canal. Little time was wasted in removing the major impediment to the canal project—the 1850 Clayton-Bulwer Treaty with Great Britain. That treaty was abrogated by terms of the 1901 Hay-Pauncefote Treaty, which granted to the U.S. sole rights of canal construction. From the time of the Venezuelan boundary controversy in 1895 to the signing of the Hay-Pauncefote Treaty, Great Britain had substantially acquiesced to U.S. hegemony in the Caribbean, and in the next few years the British further acknowledged U.S. ascendency by reducing their Caribbean fleet.

The Panama Canal opened for business in 1914, but the events that gave birth to the canal and to the Republic of Panama still haunt U.S.–Latin American relations. The Isthmian Canal Commission formed by Congress in 1899 to investigate future sites centered its attention on Nicaragua and Panama but ultimately recommended Panama, a department of Colombia. Negotiations in 1902 between Colombia and the U.S. produced a treaty that the Colombian National Assem-

1. David Henry Burton, *Theodore Roosevelt: Confident Imperialist* (Philadelphia, 1968), vii, 61, 69, 102, 114, 118–19.

2. Dana G. Munro, *Intervention and Dollar Diplomacy in the Caribbean, 1900–1921* (Princeton, 1964), 24–37, 125–40; Federico G. Gil, *Latin American–United States Relations* (New York, 1971), 91–93.

"Held Up the Wrong Man"
Cover of *Harper's Weekly* (November 21, 1903).

bly rejected in 1903. Events following the rejection are still clouded, but Roosevelt's impatience with this heretofore friendly republic and his conduct toward the Colombians, whom he later referred to as a "corrupt pithecoid community," were shabby. Agents of the New Panama Canal Company, which stood to gain from U.S. purchase of its rights in Colombia, accurately discerned Roosevelt's attitude and fomented a revolution for Panamanian independence. U.S. naval units prevented the landing of Colombian troops dispatched to suppress the rebellion, the Republic of Panama was proclaimed, and three days later the U.S. granted recognition. Shortly thereafter, the two nations drew up a treaty yielding to the U.S. all concessions it sought.[3]

European threats to intervene in the Dominican Republic as a result of indebtedness and civil disorders in 1903–1904 provided Roosevelt an opportunity to advance U.S. preeminence in the Caribbean by reinterpreting the Monroe Doctrine to make it an instrument to preclude such intervention. After the claims of a U.S. company against the Dominican Republic were settled by an arbitral commission, European creditors sought to have the U.S. collect Dominican debts owed them. To avoid European intervention, Roosevelt negotiated a treaty with the Dominican Republic to establish a customs receivership, whereby an American official would collect Dominican customs and apportion a percentage of them to the republic's European creditors. Establishment of the Dominican customs receivership in early 1905 was the first implementation of Roosevelt's corollary to the Monroe Doctrine announced in his December, 1904, State of the Union address, which proclaimed the duty of the U.S. to intervene in Latin America and exercise an "international police power" in cases of "chronic wrong-doing."[4]

Disorders in Central America that had gone largely unnoticed before acquisition of the Panama Canal became matters of high concern

3. Munro, *Intervention and Dollar Diplomacy*, 37–60; Gil, *Latin American–U.S. Relations*, 122–28; Lester D. Langley, *The United States and the Caribbean in the Twentieth Century* (Rev. ed.; Athens, Ga., 1985), 30–38; Theodore Roosevelt to Rudyard Kipling, November 1, 1904, as cited in Thomas G. Dyer, *Theodore Roosevelt and the Idea of Race* (Baton Rouge, 1980), 140; Charles D. Ameringer, "Philippe Bunau-Varilla: New Light on the Panama Canal Treaty," *Hispanic American Historical Review*, XLVI (1966), 28–35, 52; Thomas D. Schoonover, *The United States in Central America, 1860–1911: Episodes of Social Imperialism and Imperial Rivalry in the World System* (Durham, N.C., 1991), 97–110.

4. Langley, *The U.S. and the Caribbean*, 22–29; Munro, *Intervention and Dollar Diplomacy*, 66–111; Theodore Roosevelt, "Fourth Annual Message," December 6, 1904, in *Messages and Papers*, comp. Richardson, X, 831; John Bassett Moore, "Santo Domingo and the United States," *American Monthly Review of Reviews*, XXXI (March, 1905), 293.

NEXT!

"Next!"
Washington *Post*, January 31, 1905.

thereafter. In mid-1906 the U.S. persuaded El Salvador, Guatemala, and Honduras to sign an armistice to resolve a conflict, and early the following year the U.S. again mediated a dispute in the region. To establish a more-lasting peace, the U.S. and Mexico jointly sponsored a Central American Conference in Washington, D.C. in 1907, but its results were disappointing, in part, because of the disruptive enmity of the region's two strongmen, Manuel Estrada Cabrera of Guatemala and José Santos Zelaya of Nicaragua.[5] The isolation or removal of Zelaya, who was a thorough-going nationalist but was intensely disliked in official U.S. circles, became a principal goal of U.S.–Central American policy.[6] Revolution against Zelaya began in 1909 under the leadership of Juan J. Estrada and with encouragement from the U.S. consul. During the struggle Zelaya's forces captured, tried, and executed two U.S. mercenaries employed by the revolutionaries. This led the administration of William Howard Taft, 1909–1913, to break diplomatic relations and support the revolution that ousted Zelaya. The U.S. presence in Nicaragua was prolonged—a 100-man contingent of marines remained as a legation guard until 1925—and extensive; it involved loans, a customs receivership, and control of the national railroad by U.S. bankers.[7]

The U.S. was also sensitive to developments in the rest of Central America, Haiti, and the Dominican Republic. For example, after civil war broke out in the Dominican Republic in 1911, the Taft administration dispatched two commissioners who forced the interim president to resign by withholding customs receipts, persuaded the archbishop to accept the presidency, and arranged an end to the fighting. The commissioners also facilitated negotiations for a new loan from U.S. bankers to meet war-related expenses. To bring a halt to the government's improvidence, funds from the new loan were disbursed only with the approval of the U.S. legation and the customs receiver, a U.S. citizen.[8]

By the end of the Taft administration the U.S. was well on its way toward establishing a secure hegemony in the Caribbean. The underlying rationale of the Roosevelt and Taft administrations' inter-

5. Langley, *The U.S. and the Caribbean,* 45–49; Munro, *Intervention and Dollar Diplomacy,* 151–58.

6. Munro, *Intervention and Dollar Diplomacy,* 176, 167–70; Charles L. Stansifer, "José Santos Zelaya: A New Look at Nicaragua's 'Liberal' Dictator," *Revista/Review Interamericana,* VII (1977), 476–79, 483.

7. Munro, *Intervention and Dollar Diplomacy,* 171–77, 184–91, 199–202, 205–11; Langley, *The U.S. and the Caribbean,* 50–58.

8. Langley, *The U.S. and the Caribbean,* 59–62; Munro, *Intervention and Dollar Diplomacy,* 217–55, 259–68; Langley, *The U.S. and the Caribbean,* 69–71.

ventionism was securing the region from the danger posed to U.S. economic and strategic interests by European powers and protecting U.S. and foreign lives and property. Both administrations argued that to achieve those goals it was essential to establish financially sound and politically stable regimes by transferring indebtedness from European to U.S. creditors, negotiating customs receiverships to secure the loans, and using military force if necessary. Alongside the interventionism, Roosevelt and Taft promoted continuation of the Pan American movement, which the U.S. had initiated at the 1889 Washington Conference and which remained a product made in the U.S. Three conferences were held in the early twentieth century—Mexico City in 1901, Rio de Janeiro in 1906, and Buenos Aires in 1910—but the results were meager. By controlling the agenda, the U.S. kept discussion of political issues that interested the Latin Americans to a minimum and focused attention on commercial matters. Despite its limited accomplishments, Pan Americanism elevated U.S. interest in Latin America through the publicity spawned by the periodic meetings.[9]

Given such notable activism in U.S.–Latin American policy, one would expect a commensurate burgeoning of information on Latin America and a marked improvement in its quality. But a review of the information available to the public shows that the nineteenth century's deficiencies in knowledge and understanding persisted. Editorialists, essayists, reviewers, and journalists continued to complain of disinterest in Latin America, lack of contact, and distorted reporting. As an example, the reviewer of a text on South American history exclaimed how surprising it was, considering the size and growing importance of some of the South American states, "that so little has been written about them." A 1906 article in *Harper's Weekly* noted, "In leading North American newspapers there is now an almost total disregard of important Latin-American news, political movements, and national developments." Other writers complained that editorial comment often showed "total ignorance of real conditions" in Latin America and that daily periodicals "either rabidly attack" Latin Americans "or openly sneer at their attempts to follow modern methods."[10]

9. Walter V. Scholes and Marie V. Scholes, *The Foreign Policies of the Taft Administration* (Columbia, Mo., 1970), 12–13, 26, 36; Mecham, *The U.S. and Inter–American Security*, 58–68, 70–72.

10. Review of Charles Edmond Akers's *A History of South America, 1854–1904*, in *Nation*, LXXIX (December 29, 1904), 524; "Latin America," *Harper's Weekly*, L (October, 1906), 1414; "The United States and Latin America," *North American Review*, CLXXXIII (September, 1906), 479; "Panama and Central America To–Day," *Outlook*, LXXVIII (October 22, 1904), 475.

As a consequence of this inadequacy of information, many Americans found it impossible to comprehend Latin Americans or to invest any reality in their images of the region. The following letter to the author of a book on Mexico, who had resided there many years, expressed this incomprehensibility:

I notice that now and then you refer casually to "an American man" or "an English woman who lives here," and although I know there must be Americans and English living in Mexico as well as everywhere else, it always gives me a feeling of incredulity to hear that there are. I suppose I ought merely to consider the fact that you are there and then multiply you by a hundred or a thousand—or ten thousand perhaps; I have no idea, of course, how many. But to tell the truth I never altogether believe that *you* go to Mexico when you say you do. You go somewhere, but is it really Mexico? Why *should* anyone go to Mexico? It seems such a perverse—such a positively morbid thing to do.[11]

Similarly, the U.S. vice-consul-general at Rio de Janeiro complained that if an American "should decide to go down to Brazil to have a look-in and trade with the natives, he would not be quite sure whether to take a letter of credit or bright beads and red cloth."[12]

One of the striking features of the commentary on information about Latin America from 1901 to 1921 is that the first decade's widespread complaints of inadequacies were replaced by delight over its relative abundance and improved quality during the second decade. The reality, of course, was much less dramatic than the perception, but the gradual increase—under way since the 1880s—in contact with Latin America, trade, investment, travel, and the flow of information seemed rather suddenly to catch the public fancy late in the Taft administration. Curiously, no single, dramatic event signaled this change in perception, but it was stimulated by the publicity surrounding Roosevelt's extended trip to South America and his explorations in the Amazon Basin during the winter of 1913–1914, the nearing completion of the Panama Canal, and the beginning of revolution in Mexico.

An example of this change was a 1911 article entitled "The Promise of Latin America," which listed eleven recent books on Latin America—all published in London—and cited their appearance as evidence of a growing appetite for information. A year later a reviewer of four travel books on South America noted that "with the ever-increasing flood of Latin-Americana, there seems little need for a further essay in a field which for the last ten years has been covered to satiety."[13]

11. Charles Macomb Flandrau, *Viva Mexico!* (New York, 1908), 197.

12. George Agnew Chamberlain, "Our Neglect of South-American Markets," *North American Review*, CLXXXI (July, 1905), 120–21.

13. "The Promise of Latin America," *Living Age*, CCLXVIII (February 11, 1911),

Another observer commented on the increase in tourism and asserted that "the professional stereopticon lecturers have found that the Panama Canal and South America are the most popular subjects to present to the average well-informed audience." At the same time, guided summer tours of Latin America for teachers were getting under way, and the number of Latin American students attending U.S. institutions of higher learning was growing. Then too, the banana export trade from Central America and northern South America to U.S. ports grew rapidly in the early decades of the century, and the Great White Fleet formed by the United Fruit Company to transport the fruit efficiently also conveyed increasing numbers of tourists at low cost to Caribbean ports.[14]

Concurrent with the augmented popular interest in Latin America, academicians began laying the foundation for its formal study. Historians made noteworthy advances, but among the other disciplines only anthropology boasted significant contributions. At the turn of the century two universities offered courses in Latin American history—the University of California at Berkeley, where Bernard Moses taught the first such course in 1894–1895, and the University of Pennsylvania. By 1910 courses had been or were being offered by pioneers in the field—Edward Gaylord Bourne and Hiram Bingham at Yale, William S. Robertson at the University of Illinois, Leo S. Rowe at the University of Pennsylvania, and William R. Shepherd at Columbia University. One of the first academic conferences devoted to Latin America was held at Clark University in 1913 under the leadership of historian George H. Blakeslee. In 1914 the *Annals of the Academy of Political and Social Science* devoted the bulk of its July bimonthly issue to an examination of the Monroe Doctrine and the Mexican Revolution. Two events that signaled the end of the pioneering days in Latin American history were the publication in 1918 of the first issue of the *Hispanic American Historical Review*, the premier journal in its field, and the appearance a year later of the first college text on the subject, William W. Sweet's *A History of Latin America*.[15]

346; Julian Park, "Aspects of South America," *Dial*, LIII (December 1, 1912), 444–45.

14. George H. Blakeslee, "Introduction," in *Latin America: Clark University Addresses, November, 1913*, ed. George H. Blakeslee (New York, 1914), ix–x; George W. Nasmyth, "Universities and International Relations," in *ibid.*, 322; Stacy May and Galo Plaza, *The United Fruit Company in Latin America* (1958; rpr. New York, 1976), 18.

15. The small group of anthropologists conducting research in Latin America in this period included Carl Lumholtz, Frederick Starr, and Max Uhle. See Charles Wagley, "Introduction," in *Social Science Research on Latin America*, ed. Charles Wagley (New York, 1964), 7; Cline, "Latin American History: Development of Its Study and

In its practical consequences professionalization meant that eventually much of the misinformation that suffused commentary on Latin America would face stiff challenge, but this corrective process was a matter of decades, not years. The professionals themselves were not exempt from the long-standing and deeply engrained prejudices of the larger culture, and even when on the right track they often failed to address the nonacademic audience. Then, too, many of them were ineffective publicists. Hiram Bingham and Bernard Moses were notable exceptions to this generalization.[16] One can cite major studies in Latin American history published in this early period that were solid, balanced works but whose impact on public perceptions was much delayed. An example is Bourne's *Spain in America, 1450–1580* (1904), which "initiated a scholarly reaction" against the Black Legend, though the reaction must be measured in decades. The influence of Latin American historians was also limited by the uninspired, insipid quality of the available histories, which often conveyed a distorted, ahistorical impression of societies overcome by stagnation and lacking a destiny. A critic complained of the "dreary reading" abounding in one of the early studies used in the classroom, Charles Edmond Akers's *History of South America* (1904), which described a "shifting kaleidoscope of revolutions" but seemed to reveal "no real, progressive development of social and political life."[17]

The upward trend of U.S. investment and trade with Latin America in this period conformed to the general pattern of escalating involvement and interest. Until the 1890s, U.S. investments in the region were negligible and limited largely to mines and railroads in Mexico. After the Spanish-American War, U.S. capital began investing heavily in enterprises producing exports for the U.S. market, such

---

Teaching in the United States Since 1898," in *Latin American History*, ed. Cline, I, 7–11; Jorge Basadre, "Introduction" to *Latin American Courses in the United States*, by Pan American Union (Washington, D.C., 1949), as reprinted in *Latin American History*, ed. Cline, II, 419–20.

16. For an example of a well-balanced presentation of the historical origins of American misunderstanding of Latin America, see Bernard Moses, "The Relation of the United States to Latin America," *Annual Report of the American Historical Association*, I (1907), 139.

17. Benjamin Keen, "Introduction" to *Spain in America, 1450–1580, with New Introduction and Supplementary Bibliography*, by Edward Gaylord Bourne (1904; rpr. New York, 1962), vii–xi, as reprinted in *Latin American History*, ed. Cline, I, 58; Paul Samuel Reinsch, "Some Notes on the Study of South American History," in *Essays in American History Dedicated to Frederick Jackson Turner*, ed. Guy Stanton Ford (New York, 1910), 269–93, as reprinted in *Latin American History*, ed. Cline, I, 69.

as silver mining and petroleum extraction in Mexico, sugar production in Cuba, banana cultivation in the Caribbean nations, and copper mining in Chile. By 1914 U.S. investment in Latin America totaled approximately $1.7 billion or 20 percent of the total foreign investment in the region. U.S.–Latin American trade increased about 150 percent from 1900 to 1913, but about half of it was carried on with Mexico and the Caribbean island republics; the U.S. trade balance with Latin America was highly unfavorable, and Latin America's foreign trade remained under British and German domination.[18]

The erosion of European financial and commercial power resulting from the outbreak of World War I presented the U.S. with a unique opportunity. Because the war closed European money markets and ended European trade with the Latin American states, they turned to the U.S. for essential supplies and credits. The investment predominance that the U.S. would subsequently achieve in Latin America began in 1914. From that year to 1919, U.S. investments in the region increased about 50 percent while the level of European investment remained at former levels. The value of U.S.–Latin American trade from 1914 to 1920 showed an approximate fourfold increase, moving from 18 to 42 percent of Latin America's foreign trade.[19]

Woodrow Wilson's administration deserves major credit for its work in helping financial and commercial interests take advantage of the opportunity provided by war. Passage of the Underwood Tariff in 1913 brought lower tariffs, and the Federal Reserve Act of the same year allowed national banks for the first time to open branches in foreign countries and to accept drafts drawn on foreign trade, thereby providing the credit mechanisms necessary for direct trade arrangements with Latin America. In 1915 the U.S. hosted the Pan American Financial Conference, attended by delegates from nineteen countries. At that meeting, one held in 1916 in Buenos Aires, and a postwar conference in 1920, delegates took steps to extend banking and credit fa-

---

18. United Nations Department of Economic and Social Affairs, "The Growth of Foreign Investments in Latin America," in *Foreign Investment in Latin America: Cases and Attitudes*, ed. Marvin D. Bernstein (New York, 1966), 39–40; Paul V. Horn and Hubert E. Bice, *Latin-American Trade and Economics* (New York, 1949), 145; Burton I. Kaufman, "United States Trade and Latin America: The Wilson Years," *Journal of American History*, LVIII (1971), 343–45; Schoonover, *The U.S. in Central America*, 76, 173.

19. Joseph S. Tulchin, *The Aftermath of War: World War I and U.S. Policy Toward Latin America* (New York, 1971), 10, 23–24, 39–41; Marvin D. Bernstein, "Introduction," in *Foreign Investment in Latin America*, ed. Bernstein, 10; U.N. Dept. of Economic and Social Affairs, "The Growth of Foreign Investments in Latin America," in *Foreign Investment in Latin America*, ed. Bernstein, 42; Horn and Bice, *Latin-American Trade*, 363, 145.

cilities and improve transportation and communication among member nations. These achievements were facilitated by a growing spirit of cooperation among commercial interests, evidenced by formation of the U.S. Chamber of Commerce in 1912, by organized tours such as that by a delegation of the Boston Chamber of Commerce to South America in 1913, by the enthusiasm for hemispheric trade that accompanied the Panama Canal opening, and by the gradual shift in the composition of the nation's exports from foodstuffs to manufactured goods, a change that helped direct attention to underdeveloped regions such as Latin America.[20]

Wilson's righteous indignation over the political turmoil and economic disorder of the Caribbean nations also shaped his policies. His missionary zeal for American tutelage led him to expand the interventionist policies inherited from his Republican predecessors despite his lofty moral preachments and his denunciation of dollar diplomacy and foreign economic exploitation in Latin America. Wilson ordered the occupation of Haiti in 1915, following political violence of unusual savagery and the threat of European intervention. The occupation force became deeply involved in Haiti's internal affairs and remained until 1934. Less than a year after the Haitian landings, U.S. forces occupied the Dominican Republic because of recurring political instability and resistance to an expansion of U.S. control beyond that authorized by the existing treaty. During the eight-year occupation, the U.S. controlled the customhouses and treasury, established a *guardia nacional,* and promoted public works and education—but not without resistance from the Dominicans. The Wilson administration also landed marines in Cuba in 1917, under provisions of the Platt Amendment, to sustain a shaky regime, and it upheld the minority government in Nicaragua by continuing the marine presence.[21]

The greatest challenge to Wilson's Latin American policy came from Mexico, where revolution convulsed the country during much of the century's second decade. The tortuous course of the Mexican Revolution from the fall of long-term dictator Porfirio Díaz in 1911 through the brief, ineffective rule of Francisco Madero and his assassination, apparently under orders of his successor Victoriano Huerta in early

20. Kaufman, "U.S. Trade and Latin America," 342–43, 347–48; Robert Neal Seidel, "Progressive Pan Americanism: Development and United States Policy Toward South America, 1906–1931" (Ph.D. dissertation, Cornell University, 1973), 55.

21. Langley, *The U.S. and the Caribbean,* 68–88; Gil, *Latin American–U.S. Relations,* 92–107; Edward G. Lowry, "What the President Is Trying to Do for Mexico," *World's Work,* XXVII (January, 1914), 261–66.

1913, demanded decisions from newly inaugurated Wilson that he was unprepared to make. From indecision the appalled Wilson moved to a policy of nonrecognition and then to a stubborn insistence on Huerta's ouster. This he accomplished in mid-1914 by lifting the arms embargo to Huerta's enemies and by sending marines to occupy Veracruz under the pretexts of righting an insult to U.S. honor and preventing the landing of a European arms shipment. Anarchy became generalized during the ensuing struggle for power among forces led by Venustiano Carranza, Pancho Villa, and Emiliano Zapata. Carranza gained a dominant position, and after mediation between the U.S. and Mexico by six Latin American states, Wilson granted Carranza recognition in late 1915. Early the following year Villa brought the two nations close to war by murdering sixteen Americans in northern Mexico and raiding Columbus, New Mexico. Wilson then ordered American forces into Mexico in pursuit of Villa, a futile mission lasting a year and ending just before U.S. entry into World War I. Distrust of Mexico reached new heights early in 1917 upon publication of the Zimmerman note, a German proposal for an alliance with Mexico envisioning the restoration to Mexico of territory lost to the U.S. after the Mexican-American War. By the time U.S. attention became fully engaged in the European conflict, tensions with Mexico were easing, although promulgation of the 1917 constitution promised to embitter future relations because this revolutionary charter contained provisions designed to allow Mexico to regain control over its own natural resources, thereby threatening property rights of U.S. companies.[22]

The extraordinary expansion of the U.S. role in Latin American affairs during the first two decades of the century greatly stimulated the flow of information; the relative disinterest of the first decade gave way to an increasing appetite for information that World War I only temporarily eclipsed during the second decade. But the quality of that information was lacking. As the nation moved toward ever-larger involvement in the region's affairs, the perceptions of Latin America, its people, and its developmental problems conveyed by this growing reportage showed little change from the beginning to the end of the period.

One theme repeatedly stated by observers—a theme common to the nineteenth century—was the axiom that Latin America was a veritable treasure house of natural wealth. Descriptions of this potential abundance were applied to every country in the region. A brief survey

22. Gil, *Latin American–U.S. Relations,* 108–13; Howard F. Cline, *The United States and Mexico* (Rev. ed.; New York, 1971), 139–83; Robert Freeman Smith, *The United States and Revolutionary Nationalism in Mexico, 1916–1932* (Chicago, 1972), 31–189.

of these descriptions from travel books and articles, essays, editorials, and speeches illustrates the rampant hyperbole common to these sources, and it partially explains the impossible expectations resulting from assessments so far removed from reality.

Brazil's underpopulated vastness invited easy exaggeration of its "unimaginable resources." In a 1910 travel account, an author with wide experience in Latin America described Brazil's enormous acreage of unused fertile land and asserted that when all of Brazil's "latent possibilities are uncovered, it will be a towering giant." The author of a highly literate account of travels along the Andes and down the Amazon River reported that the iron ore deposits in Peru's eastern Andean slopes "amount to several hundred million tons—enough to supply the whole of South America with iron for centuries to come." An article on Colombia pictured it as "an untouched coffer of nature" possessing "incalculable wealth" in minerals. A traveler to Venezuela described as "yet untouched" its "pearl fisheries, the mountains of iron, the brooks with beds of gold."[23] Despite Mexico's propinquity, accounts of its resource base were also wildly inflated even during the years of revolution, when dispositions toward Mexico were most unneighborly. The author of *Benighted Mexico*, a harsh attack on its political system, wrote in 1916: "Mountains of copper, silver, gold, rare ores of almost metal purity and some of the richest deposits of petroleum in the world, yet in their virgin state, await development and world's markets. The agricultural possibilities of some of its rich valleys and highlands, in many instances thus far untouched by the hands of man, can hardly be exaggerated."[24] Even the most poverty-stricken and poorly endowed countries were depicted as wonderlands of abundance. A traveling clergyman familiar with Bolivia described it as the "Switzerland of South America" and asserted that it "has resources unequalled by any country of its size in the world." A Caribbean traveler portrayed Haiti as "potentially the richest island in the world with the possible exception of Java." In a study of lands surrounding the Caribbean published in the *National Geographic Magazine*, the author stated: "Nowhere else in the world has Nature been

23. Edwin A. Start, "The United States of Brazil," *Chautauquan*, XXXIV (March, 1902), 585; Nevin O. Winter, *Brazil and Her People of To-Day* (Boston, 1910), 353; Harry Weston Van Dyke, *Through South America* (New York, 1912), 137–38; John Augustine Zahm [H. J. Mozans], *Along the Andes and Down the Amazon* (New York, 1911), 117; Francis P. Savinien, "The New Era in Colombia," *American Monthly Review of Reviews*, XXXIII (May, 1906), 568–69; Eugene P. Lyle, Jr., "Venezuela and the Problems It Presents," *World's Work*, XI (December, 1905), 6953.

24. Randolph Wellford Smith, *Benighted Mexico* (London, 1916), 37.

more bountiful in her blessings of natural resources than in the Caribbean region."[25]

The following paragraph from a 1903 article on U.S.–Latin American relations nicely summarized the theme of Latin America's abundant natural endowments:

Rich in resources beyond the dreams of avarice, its tinted mountains filled with priceless gems and precious metals of untold worth, its vast prairies and mighty forests one unending panorama of nature's most stupendous effort, its shores indented by a thousand harbors wherein might ride secure the commerce of the world, a land of beauty comparable to no other in its myriad pictures formed by nature's whims, capable of containing the population of the earth and housing it all in luxury and splendor, this Queen of Continents is held in slavery and blood, in the blackness of intrigue and hate, at the mercy of brutal violence, perfidy and anarchy.[26]

This passage illustrates the common practice of painting surrealistic landscapes of idle bounty and using them to criticize the Latin Americans for their needless poverty and patent failures. Many writers conveyed their message of Latin America's willful backwardness by quoting Alexander von Humboldt's remark about Peru resembling a "beggar sitting on a pile of gold." One writer insisted that Venezuela's wealth was equal to that of the U.S., and yet Venezuela was "the poorest among the nations and an intolerable nuisance as well." An essayist wrote of South America: "When one considers its possibilities and its performance, one gets the impression of a vast continent almost literally going to waste." An editorialist noted that anyone with even a cursory knowledge of Latin America cannot fail "to feel profound disappointment at the almost tragic misuse that has been made of splendid opportunities." Woodrow Wilson also voiced the apparent anomaly of misery amidst abundance when, in accepting the presidential nomination in 1916, he characterized the Mexican people as "fifteen million oppressed men, overburdened women and pitiful children in virtual bondage in their own home of fertile lands and inexhaustible treasure!"[27]

25. Francis E. Clark, "The Switzerland of South America," *Independent*, LXIII (October 10, 1907), 866; Stephen Bonsal, *The American Mediterranean* (New York, 1912), 72; William Joseph Showalter, "The Countries of the Caribbean," *National Geographic Magazine*, XXIV (February, 1913), 227.

26. "Is the Monroe Doctrine a Bar to Civilization?" *North American Review*, CLXXVI (April, 1903), 528.

27. Lyle, Jr., "Venezuela and the Problems It Presents," 6952; W. M. Ivins, Jr., "South America and Our Responsibility," *World's Work*, VII (February, 1904), 4483–84; "The Promise of Latin America," *Living Age*, CCLXVIII (February 11, 1911), 347; Woodrow Wilson, "Speech in Long Branch, New Jersey, Accepting the Presidential Nomination,"

Although the great majority of observers expressed high enthusiasm about Latin America's natural endowments, a few writers added caveats to the usual encomiums about Nature's work south of the border. The most noteworthy example is a 1919 book carrying the prosaic title, *The Mineral Deposits of South America.* Its co-authors, Benjamin L. Miller and Joseph T. Singewald, Jr., professors of geology, compiled data obtained from field research into a scholarly, country-by-country survey. Though concluding that "the continent possesses both varied and rich mineral deposits," they noted that the bulk of its minerals had to undergo some elaboration prior to use and that the minerals were exported unrefined because of the lack of labor and fuel. They also concluded that the "topographic obstacles in the way of railroad construction" meant South America would not soon be in a position to develop a significant manufacturing industry and that its economy would necessarily continue to rely on the export of agricultural products and unrefined minerals. Another cautionary note is found in a delightful account of a four-year journey through South America, mainly on foot, in which the author expressed frustration over the abominable geographic obstacles encountered. At one point in the Peruvian Andes the traveler exclaimed: "We went down and ever down into an unconscionable gorge, to cross—such is the ghastly futility of Latin America—an insignificant stream; then quickly began to climb again."[28]

The paradox conjured up by frequent depiction of the Latin American as a "beggar sitting on a pile of gold" invited more substantive analysis than offered by this aphorism. Analysis of Latin America's lagging development was also encouraged by the striking contrasts observed by Americans between their own dynamic society and a seemingly stagnant Latin America. Most observers yielded to the urge to comment on the causes of this stagnation, and, as in the nineteenth century, their explanations centered on climate, race, and cultural legacy.

Climatic conditions attracted widespread attention as a fundamental factor in the process of development. Many sophisticated writers and experienced travelers assumed that the great majority of Latin

September 2, 1916, in *The Papers of Woodrow Wilson,* ed. Arthur S. Link (Princeton, 1966–1986), XXXVIII, 134.

28. Benjamin L. Miller and Joseph T. Singewald, Jr., *The Mineral Deposits of South America* (New York, 1919), 29–31; Harry A. Franck, *Vagabonding Down the Andes: Being the Narrative of a Journey, Chiefly Afoot, from Panama to Buenos Aires* (Garden City, N.Y., 1917), 313.

Americans lived in the tropics, and tropical conditions were widely presumed antithetical to progress. Even travelers who visited high-altitude cities such as Bogotá or Quito and sojourned through the temperate highlands of the Andean republics, where the bulk of their populations resided, failed to temper their complaints that tropical lethargy rendered those nations perpetual laggards. The author of an article published in a scholarly journal asserted that "the great mass of South America falls in a climate which discourages" effort, and for emphasis he specified that "fully seven-eighths of South America is essentially tropical."[29]

Many writers who blamed Latin America's apparent stagnation on the tropical climate argued that life in such regions was so easy that it instilled slothful habits, which were sufficient to survive in a benign, tropical setting. A U.S. naval officer familiar with Cuba wrote: "Nutritious fruits grew in rich abundance, almost without cultivation; comfort demanded but a poor house, little clothing and less fire; it was hardly necessary to work." Similar thinking led a visitor to Brazil to observe that nature was perhaps "too bountiful, and man depends upon that bounty rather than his own exertions." Another writer asserted that the Latin American masses "can live practically without labor. . . . Most of their food grows without cultivation. . . . They have no ambition, no desires, that cannot be satisfied."[30]

While portraying life in the tropics as free of care and stress, some commentators also alleged that it produced highly deleterious effects. In a study entitled "Self-Government in the Tropics" prepared for the Sixty-fourth Congress, the author asserted that tropical conditions have rendered Latin Americans incapable of self-government. "The enervating character of the climate, combined with the bounty of nature, which, in return for little labor, supplies the limited wants of the natives, has from time immemorial with these zones produced a population essentially inefficient as compared with that of the Temperate Zone." Some observers also argued that the tropics triggered a tendency toward moral degeneracy. A traveler in the West Indies speculated that it was perhaps natural "that the heat of the tropics should breed hatred for work and cause men to become tricky instead." Edward Alsworth Ross, a founder of American sociology, claimed that "sex is an overmastering concern in males from puberty on" because of the

29. Talcott Williams, "Ethnic Factors in South America," *Annals of the American Academy of Political and Social Science*, XXII (1903), 25–26.

30. R. L. Bullard, "The Cuban Negro," *North American Review*, CLXXXIV (March 15, 1907), 624; Winter, *Brazil*, 93; C. Mayer, "Latin America and the United States," *Outlook*, LXXIV (August 15, 1903), 950–51.

tropical climate. "There is, indeed, very unequivocal evidence that, irrespective of altitude, the human organism in the tropics is affected in ways adverse to the moral standards wrought out in the lands of the slanting sun."[31]

The pernicious effects of the tropics were alleged to apply with particular severity to Caucasians. A traveler with wide experience throughout the continent refuted claims that scientific sanitation was making it possible for Caucasians to thrive in the tropics: "[H]owever well they keep in hot countries the blood gets thinner all the time; the face paler and walk slower every month." The same sentiment was expressed in the glib remark attributed to the anti-imperialist Republican senator from South Dakota, Richard Pettigrew: "You can't make a white man and a banana grow on the same quarter section of land." A visitor to Mexico vividly portrayed the inevitable degeneration visited upon the white resident in the tropics:

In this torrid zone the white man fights the good fight with rum and nature—and loses. Scorpions and pinolias assail him; infinite gnats, countless flies, unspeakable bugs lie in wait. The heat melts his backbone; the ceaseless rain depresses. Slowly and surely the insatiate jungle closes in, claiming her own.

If the white man labours, he also drinks deep.

"A man must drink more in this climate," he meditates.

Presently he takes to himself a yellow woman. His liver swells and his nose turns red. He goes without a collar; his shoes are unbrushed—for what does a yellow woman know of these things? . . . Well if the adventurer escapes before it is too late—flees from the jungle, the yellow woman, and the bottle. Else he gets tropical paresis, and his usefulness is over.[32]

Ellsworth Huntington, the noted Yale geographer, published in 1915 *Civilization and Climate,* which had a profound and long-lasting impact on the question of the relationship between climate and level of civilization. His prominence as a research-oriented geographer and his prolific writing enabled him to exert a powerful influence throughout his career to the 1940s. His 1915 study was based on correlations between average daily temperatures and daily marks of students at West Point and Annapolis and work records of thousands of factory work-

31. Samuel L. Parrish, "Self-Government in the Tropics," *Senate Documents,* 64th Cong., 1st Sess., No. 364, p. 3; Harry A. Franck, *Roaming Through the West Indies* (New York, 1920), 102; Edward Alsworth Ross, *South of Panama* (New York, 1914–1915), 184, 223.

32. H. C. Stuntz, "South America: Land of Promise," *World Outlook,* II (February, 1916), 21; Arthur Wallace Dunn, *From Harrison to Harding: A Personal Narrative, Covering a Third of a Century, 1888–1921* (New York, 1922), I, 292; Stanton Davis Kirkham, *Mexican Trails* (New York, 1909), 207–208.

ers from Connecticut to Havana. Huntington concluded that the most-important climatic factors influencing productivity were mean temperature, temperature change from day to day, and relative humidity, but that uniformity of climate was more enervating than heat. He maintained that climate was not the only factor nor the main one in determining the conditions of a civilization, but that it was as essential as any other. Among his assumptions were that the white race was superior to others and that "native races within the tropics are dull in thought and slow in action." He also asserted that when whites moved to the tropics, the result was a weakness of will that manifested itself in several ways such as "lack of industry, an irascible temper, drunkenness, and sexual indulgence." Huntington contended that "white men who spur themselves to work within the tropics as hard as at home are in great danger of breaking down in health" and that deterioration takes place even at high elevation in the tropics, although at a slower rate.[33]

It was generally conceded that the highlands within tropical countries offered a salubrious climate, but several commentators, such as Huntington, claimed that, although the tropical problems of disease and stifling heat were absent, the high altitude presented other, equally grave problems. A traveler and U.S. diplomatic agent familiar with Bogotá, situated at an 8,500-foot elevation, reported that work beyond four hours a day will yield "alarming symptoms" such as "loss of appetite, insomnia, restlessness, and nervous exhaustion; and unless these premonitions are heeded, nervous prostration, paralysis and sometimes partial insanity are likely to follow." In a fascinating review of a sociological study of crime in Mexico, the reviewer strongly endorsed the author's conclusions:

The chief factor in moulding the character of the inhabitants of the City and Valley of Mexico is stated to be the high altitude. The very great elevation of this plateau, combined with its tropical situation, causes an extreme rarification of the atmosphere and a great diminution in the amount of oxygen contained in a given volume of air. This had led to an organic laziness upon the part of the inhabitants, to a confirmed quietism and a consequent distaste and contempt for work. To the same cause [the author] assigns the lack of civil valor, the political quiescence in the face of governmental or private oppression. . . . [I]n the dry season, the nervous tension becomes so great that no action is felt to be extravagant or extraordinary.[34]

33. Ellsworth Huntington, *Civilization and Climate* (New Haven, 1915), 35, 41–42, 136–37, 218.
34. William L. Scruggs, *The Colombian and Venezuelan Republics, with Notes on Other Parts of Central and South America* (Boston, 1900), 79–80; Walter E. Weyl, Re-

Views contrary to the prevailing perception that Latin America's tropical setting condemned it to stagnation were voiced on occasion. Some writers pointed to the southern cone as a region whose temperate climate assured it a bright future. Others asserted that Caucasians would prevail in the tropics as they had in temperate regions and that advances would therefore come to the tropics. Some observers argued that progress in tropical medicine rendered formerly pestilential areas habitable and productive.[35]

Recognition of the role of tropical disease as an impediment to development was somewhat heightened in the early twentieth century, though it did not gain its deserved prominence. The added importance attached to disease derived from the U.S. experience in Cuba and from a decade of work on the Panama Canal. In both countries American soldiers and workers suffered heavy losses from disease, and those losses were widely reported throughout the nation. For example, in the Fifth Army Corps, which laid siege to Santiago de Cuba in mid-1898, the death toll from disease was three times as great as from combat. There was also extensive reporting of the breakthroughs achieved against malaria and yellow fever in Cuba by Walter Reed and William Gorgas. Though the knowledge acquired in Cuba was not immediately applied in Panama, the persistent efforts of Gorgas toward improved sanitation on the isthmus brought a dramatic reduction in the death toll from tropical disease and demonstrated the procedures necessary to create healthy work conditions in the tropics.[36] Publicity related to the fledgling banana industry's rapid growth, which was based on those medical breakthroughs, contributed to expressions of confidence that tropical Latin America would soon embark upon an era

---

view of Julio Guerrero's *La Génesis del Crimen en México: Estudio de Psiquiatría Social,* in *Annals of the American Academy of Political and Social Science,* XVIII (1901), 331.

35. A recent study by J. Valerie Fifer, *United States Perceptions of Latin America, 1850–1930: A 'New West' South of Capricorn?* (Manchester, Engl., 1991), examines the optimism of outside observers about the southern cone's rapid development through railroad construction, following the American West model, and the decline of that optimism in the early twentieth century. John Barrett, "Latin America: A Great Commercial Opportunity," *World Today,* XIV (April, 1908), 416; Thomas C. Dawson, "The Caucasian in Brazil," *Popular Science Monthly,* LXIV (April, 1904), 550–51, 556; William Seymour Edwards, *On the Mexican Highlands with a Passing Glimpse of Cuba* (Cincinnati, 1906), 277; Frederick Upham Adams, *Conquest of the Tropics* (1914; rpr. New York, 1976), 50, 163.

36. Trask, *The War with Spain,* 324–35; McCullough, *The Path Between the Seas,* 415, 451–54, 465; William Crawford Gorgas, *Sanitation in Panama* (New York, 1915), 148–240.

of rapid development. But that confidence was not widely affirmed, and the disease factor in the region's underdevelopment was not strongly emphasized. The common view was that tropical regions failed to progress not only because of disease but also because of the debilitating effect of the climate itself—the heat, the monotony of temperature, and the excessive exposure to sunlight. One writer summarized the secondary role of the disease factor in his assertion, "Escaping disease, as at Panama, is one thing, thriving in such a climate is another."[37]

More widely accepted than climate as an explanation for Latin America's manifest lag was the racial factor. Americans clearly understood that the Latin American racial pattern differed substantially from that in the U.S., but they were terribly muddled about the details. A writer who attempted to define the Mexican noted that many Americans were "under the misapprehension that the Mexican is some kind of negro—or, at least, that there is a strong infusion of African blood, as in Haiti." According to an essay of 1908, Americans pictured Latin Americans as "the miscegenated descendants of Spanish hidalgos, negroes and Indians, a motley aggregation of vindictive, cigaret-smoking half-breeds, dominated by a corrupt Church in a corrupt State, and perpetually engaged in revolutions over nothing in particular."[38]

This emphasis on race was a product of the acute racial consciousness that Americans brought into the twentieth century, which was intensified by an alarming growth in immigration, whose changing profile fueled a movement for restriction. Much of the commentary on Latin America and on U.S. policy toward the region mirrored these domestic concerns. When Roosevelt was struggling over the problems caused by disorder in the Dominican Republic, Senator Francis G. Newlands proposed establishment of a protectorate over that country and Haiti. Aside from insuring stability on that strategic island, his goal was "to adjust the race question in this country by providing for the gradual colonization of the blacks in the United States on these islands." When Wilson ordered the occupation of Veracruz in 1914, Senator Charles S. Thomas opposed the policy, fearing it would lead to intervention on a much-larger scale and declaring, "We can not assimilate its people." His desire for restraint derived from concern over

37. Adams, *Conquest of the Tropics*, 50–54; Hiram Bingham, "Certain Characteristics of the South Americans of To-Day," *Popular Science Monthly*, LXXVII (December, 1910), 587; F. E. Chadwick, "The Present Day Phase of the Monroe Doctrine" in *Latin America*, ed. Blakeslee, 113.

38. Alexander Craig, "The Mexican As He Is," *World Outlook*, II (February, 1916), 10; "Land of Tomorrow," *Independent*, LXIV (May 21, 1908), 1157.

racial problems already facing the nation. "The South is confronted with an age-old problem, . . . the advance guards of the hordes of a more populous race" are already on the Pacific coast, and "another tide of immigration" is entering from southeastern Europe. Ellsworth Huntington also voiced concern over the new immigrants' alleged inferiority and noted, "In these last decades we are taking into our midst many people scarcely better than the Mexicans."[39]

The most thoroughly negative commentary on Latin America's racial configuration was directed toward its mixed races. A Department of Agriculture specialist in tropical farming who had done research in Latin America asserted that among Anglo-Saxons, "There is a growing feeling that an individual with pure ancestry running back for a thousand years or more should have too much race pride to allow his family tree to terminate in a non-descript twig of the half-breed type." Harvard historian Archibald Cary Coolidge argued that Cuban misconduct strengthened the "rough contempt" Americans had for Latin Americans, and it raised the "question of the ability of the Latin-American population of mixed blood to rule themselves without disturbance."[40] Public opinion had indeed become sensitive, since the turn of the century, to the record of misgovernment in the Caribbean nations, and observers often attributed this record to the racial factor. In advocating prolonged U.S. tutelage of the Dominican Republic, one writer argued: "The bulk of the Dominican population are mulattoes, and the Spanish mulatto has proven in the main a weak and degenerate stock. . . ." A description of the Cuban lower class written at the time of the second U.S. occupation is particularly memorable: "But the riff-raff; Lord, the riff-raff; injin, nigger, beggar-man, thief,—both mongrel, puppy, whelp and hound, and cur of low degree."[41]

The chaos of the Mexican Revolution inevitably evoked highly critical remarks directed at mixed races. An article in *Collier's* explained the revolution on the basis of the mixed Mexican ancestry and noted,

39. Francis G. Newlands, "The San Domingo Question," *North American Review*, CLXXX (June, 1905), 897–98; remarks of Charles S. Thomas, *Congressional Record*, Senate, 63rd Cong., 2nd Sess., Vol. LI, Pt. 7, p. 6984; Huntington, *Civilization and Climate*, 215. For a discussion of the relationship between racist sentiment and the debate over imperialism, see Rubin Francis Weston, *Racism in U.S. Imperialism* (Columbia, S.C., 1972), 258–60.

40. Earley Vernon Wilcox, *Tropical Agriculture* (New York, 1916), 38; Archibald Cary Coolidge, *The United States as a World Power* (New York, 1908), 304, 286.

41. T. Lothrop Stoddard, "Santo Domingo: Our Unruly Ward," *American Review of Reviews*, XLIV (June, 1914), 731; Henry Watterson, "Again 'Cuba Libre,'" *Havana Post*, January 29, 1909, as cited in Charles E. Chapman, *A History of the Cuban Republic* (New York, 1927), 263–64.

"If you are a Mexican you are a descendant of Spanish adventurers and Indians, with the boldness of the one, the treachery of the other, and the cruelty of both." John Lind, Wilson's special agent in Mexico who, incidentally, gained a reputation while there of being "anti-Latin, anti-British, and anti-Catholic," reported that "the hope of Mexico is in her Indian blood rather than in the mongrel progeny of the early moorish Spaniards." Edith O'Shaughnessy, wife of a U.S. diplomat stationed in Mexico during the early years of the revolution, wrote three fascinating books covering her experiences, and she attributed many of Mexico's problems to the mestizo who "generally knows envy and brotherly hate in their perfected forms."[42]

In a provocative article arguing that the U.S. was retarding progress in Latin America by preventing European intervention and chastisement of misbehavior, the author blamed Latin American problems on the ruling class, which he characterized as a mixture of Spanish and Indian blood with a heavy sprinkling of Negro, resulting in "an atrocious composition." "Taken altogether, it is the most aggressive, pretentious, good-for-nothing, nondescript, villainous, treacherous set of semi-banditti which was ever organized on the face of the earth, held together by the cohesive power of public plunder, and by the ambition to tyrannize over others."[43]

Two books dealing with the racial theme are of particular note because both used Latin America to illustrate the evils of miscegenation, and their authors were men of distinction. Albert Galloway Keller of Yale published *Colonization: A Study of the Founding of New Societies* (1908), which examined European colonization and concluded that climate and race were the factors most responsible for the greater success of temperate over tropical colonies. He noted that in the latter, irregular relations with native women, "especially on the part of the Latin nations, have produced a multitude of half-breeds, whose general character is but rarely an improvement upon that of either of the uniting races...." The second book, *The Passing of the Great Race*, by Madison Grant, a founder and chairman of the New York Zoological Society and an activist in the eugenics movement, stirred considerable comment when it appeared in 1916 and became a factor in the successful struggle of the following year to enact over Wilson's

---

42. Porter Emerson Browne, "The Mexican Mess," *Collier's*, LVII (July 22, 1916), 12; John Lind to William Jennings Bryan, September 19, 1913, in *The Papers of Wilson*, ed. Link, XXVIII, 294; Edith O'Shaughnessy, *Intimate Pages of Mexican History* (New York, 1920), 123.

43. "Is the Monroe Doctrine a Bar to Civilization?" *North American Review*, CLXXVI (April, 1903), 523.

veto a law requiring aliens to pass a literacy test to gain admission into the country. Grant's thesis was that the original populating race in the U.S., the Anglo-Saxon, was losing its purity and was degenerating as a result of the diluting effect of large numbers of inferior immigrants. To illustrate the degeneration resulting from race mixing, he pointed to Latin America and specifically to Mexico, which, according to Grant, "is now engaged in demonstrating its incapacity for self-government." Grant was decidedly pessimistic even concerning those parts of Latin America into which large numbers of Europeans were immigrating, such as Argentina and southern Brazil, because the immigrants were "of the Mediterranean type."[44]

Although commentators directed their most-censorious attacks against the mixed races, all racial strains going into that mix were considered deficient in various degrees. On the positive side, most observers attributed the stability and relative progress of Argentina and Costa Rica to their overwhelmingly white populations, but at the same time, the Spanish and Portuguese were considered inferior to the Anglo-Saxon and "destitute of the energy which is characteristic of the Anglo-Saxon." Rear Admiral F. E. Chadwick, who wrote extensively on Latin American affairs, maintained that the Spanish were less Latin than African, which explained "why the Spanish race wherever found is ready for revolution or insurrection."[45] Comments concerning the blacks were unambiguously negative and were commonly voiced during the periodic outbursts of disorder in the Caribbean nations.[46] Though some observers professed to see in the Indian the possibilities for nation building, the great majority saw him as an insuperable obstacle to national progress.[47]

---

44. Albert Galloway Keller, *Colonization: A Study of the Founding of New Societies* (Boston, 1908), 7, 219; Madison Grant, *The Passing of the Great Race, or the Racial Basis of European History* (New York, 1916), 15–16, 69–70. A similar theme is found in T. Lothrop Stoddard, *The Rising Tide of Color Against White World-Supremacy* (New York, 1920), 108–14, 120, 128, 141.

45. Frank G. Carpenter, *South America* (New York, 1900), 298; F. E. Chadwick, "A Study of Iberic-America," *Annals of the American Academy of Political and Social Science*, LIV (1914), 6–7.

46. Charles Francis Adams, "Reflex Light from Africa," *Century Magazine*, LXXII (May, 1906), 105, 109; R. L. Bullard, "The Cuban Negro," 624; Sydney Brooks, "Cuba," *Living Age*, CCLXVII (December 10, 1910), 657; Walter Wigdil, "Addition Without Division = Revolution," *Independent*, LXXII (June 13, 1912), 1352, 1356; remarks of Townsend Scudder, *Congressional Record*, House, 56th Cong., 2nd Sess., Vol. XXXIV, Pt. 4, p. 3370.

47. Albert Bushnell Hart, "The Postulates of the Mexican Situation," *Annals of the American Academy of Political and Social Science*, LIV (1914), 137; Harry A. Franck, *Tramping Through Mexico, Guatemala and Honduras* (New York, 1916), 232; Hiram

Many commentators who concluded that the racial configuration was the major obstacle to development called for large-scale immigration from Europe. The highly regarded Progressive editor, Herbert Croly, though not noted for his expertise on Latin America, expressed the common view when he wrote: "South America cannot develop without the benefits of European capital, additional European labor, European products, and European experience and training." Professor Edward Alsworth Ross reported that "Natives and foreigners alike declare that a large white immigration is the only hope for Ecuador." He also noted that South American statesmen are counting on a "great immigration of Europeans . . . to relieve their countries from mestizo unprogressiveness and misgovernment." In an article examining political unrest in Central America, another author asserted that the U.S. had a duty to use its moral influence to make the Central Americans "behave themselves," but even under such influence he argued that the region had no future until "foreign immigrants and foreign investors" could be attracted.[48]

As suggested by these quotations, the need for foreign capital was also recognized as an essential ingredient for Latin American development. This view, however, was often muted because of entanglement with the domestic struggle for regulation of capital and with the effort to replace European with U.S. capital in Latin America. Furthermore, plenty of voices expressed the minority view that "financial scheming by foreign concessionaires" lay at the bottom of Latin America's difficulties. Those voices included President Wilson, Secretary of State William Jennings Bryan, Progressive members of Congress, and radical journalists such as John Reed and Lincoln Steffens. For example, Bryan wrote privately in 1913, "the whole trouble in Mexico is due to the active influence of foreign investors who are denying to the people there the right to run their own government."[49]

Bingham, *Across South America: An Account of a Journey from Buenos Aires to Lima by Way of Potosí, with Notes on Brazil, Argentina, Bolivia, Chile, and Peru* (Boston, 1911), 155; William Warren Sweet, *A History of Latin America* (New York, 1919), 222.

48. Herbert Croly, *The Promise of American Life* (Cambridge, Mass., 1909), 295; Ross, *South of Panama*, 30, 92; Edwin Emerson, "The Unrest in Central America," *Independent*, LXVII (December 9, 1909), 1291, 1286.

49. "Central America in General and Nicaragua in Particular," *Outlook*, CVI (January 3, 1914), 23; William Jennings Bryan to Walter Hines Page, October 29, 1913, in *The Papers of Wilson*, ed. Link, XXVIII, 471; remarks of Charles S. Thomas, *Congressional Record*, Senate, 64th Cong., 1st Sess., Vol. LIII, Pt. 1, p. 946; remarks of Charles A. Lindbergh, *Congressional Record*, House, 63rd Cong., 2nd Sess., Vol. LI, Pt. 7, p. 6952;

The third major factor, in addition to climate and race, offered to explain Latin America's purported backwardness was its Hispanic legacy of an authoritarian structure for state, church, and society; ruthless exploitation of natives; and cultural values engendering greed, ignorance, bigotry, and a contempt for labor. Espousal of the Black Legend had seldom been more forthright or more pervasive. Commentators typically contrasted the English and Hispanic colonizing experiences to the decided disadvantage of the latter. An article of 1904 noted, "The primary fact in South American history and culture is that the continent was never colonized as were the English and French possessions of North America, but was exploited by small and isolated bodies of armed treasure-hunters." An author of several Latin American travel accounts charged that Brazil's advance was "stunted by the lust for gold" of the early Portuguese colonists. "It was different from the motive that influenced either Puritan or Cavalier in our own land, for they sought liberty."[50]

The importance attached to the influence of the cultural heritage is suggested by the passion that accompanied discussion of it and the sweeping effects attributed to it. Professor Ross argued that South America was the victim of a bad start that began when the conquering race "simply climbed upon the backs of the natives and exploited them. Thus, pride, contempt for labor, caste, social parasitism, and authoritativeness in Church and State fastened upon South American society and characterize it still." A traveler to western Mexico observed on the eve of the Mexican Revolution: "During the three centuries of Spanish occupation, the mass of native inhabitants of Mexico, reduced to slavery and serfdom, bowed under the lash of the hidalgo and cowed by the sword of a cruel and inhuman soldiery, lost their initiative and self-reliance." He also quoted with approval a mestizo's comments about the Spanish: "They robbed us of our land and our homes, they debauched our women, they murdered our sons, they taught us to be lazy and proud; and all they left us as a heritage was the priest, the prostitute, and the bull ring." In a speech of 1916 concerning Spanish rule in Mexico, Senator William E. Borah declared: "I have read a good many pages of history . . . but I have never read any story of frightfulness anywhere equal to the dismal, monotonous, ruth-

Lincoln Steffens, *The Autobiography of Lincoln Steffens* (New York, 1931), 719; Donald Lewis Zelman, "American Intellectual Attitudes Toward Mexico, 1908–1940" (Ph.D. dissertation, Ohio State University, 1969), 51, 67–68.

50. W. M. Ivins, Jr., "South America and Our Responsibility," *World's Work,* VII (February, 1904), 4480; Winter, *Brazil,* 22.

less, unbroken, and unending story of oppression and injustice in Mexico. In duration and in demoniacal heartlessness, in unvarying fiendishness it has no parallel, so far as I know."[51]

The period's harshest indictment of the Spanish heritage appeared in a book entitled *Rotten Republics: A Tropical Tramp in Central America* by G. L. Morrill, a much-traveled Protestant minister. He lucidly conveyed the tone of the book in the foreword: "Hamlet found something 'rotten in the state of Denmark,' but it was sweet compared with what I discovered in Central America—the land of dirt, disease, destitution, darkness, dilapidation, despots, delay, debt, deviltry and degeneracy, where a conservative estimate makes 90 per cent of the women immoral, 95 per cent of the men thieves and 100 per cent of the population liars." Morrill then proceeded to fix the blame for this state of affairs on Spain. "The word 'Spanish' in Latin America spells S-slaughter P-persecution A-avarice N-nefariousness I-ignorance S-superstition H-hell." Even the Spanish language, which he could not speak, invited his scorn. It is, he declared, "smutty and seems to have been invented to convey licentious lines, songs, and stories with a meaning no other language can bear or tolerate. It is a splendid tongue for the hypocrite."[52]

Latin America's Catholic tradition was the focus of attack in a genre of books by Protestant evangelicals, such as Morrill, who looked upon the region as a prime mission field. A missionary with sixteen years of experience in Mexico succinctly summarized the evangelical attitude and, at the same time, the significance of the role of the church: "On a corrupt church rests, in large measure, the responsibility for the undeveloped state of all the Roman Catholic countries which lie south of the United States." An evangelical tract published by the Disciples of Christ compared the U.S. and Mexican colonial experiences as follows:

The Puritans came to establish a state where God might be worshiped in freedom of conscience and where equal rights for all might prevail. The Spaniards sought wealth and power, the means to gratify their self desires. Secondarily they came to establish a system of religious bondage under which Europe had groaned for centuries, whose logical outcome was the Inquisition, with all its bloody horrors and the even worse deadening of the moral and spiritual fac-

51. Ross, *South of Panama*, as cited in "Spiritual Differences Which Interfere with Pan-American Sentiment," *Current Opinion*, LIX (July, 1915), 41; Dillon Wallace, *Beyond the Mexican Sierras* (Chicago, 1910), x, xii, 58; William E. Borah, *Congressional Record*, Senate, 64th Cong., 1st Sess., Vol. LIII, Pt. 2, p. 1443.

52. G. L. Morrill, *Rotten Republics: A Tropical Tramp in Central America* (Chicago, 1916), 281–82.

ulties of the people that must ever come where a system of dead works and of meaningless penances takes the place of a heartfelt faith. . . .[53]

Lay observers made similar anti-Catholic assertions. One traveler to Mexico claimed that during the colonial period the Spanish forced the Indians "under the pain of death . . . to relinquish their old ideals of morality and religion, and accept instead bigotry, sensualism, and superstition."[54] The nineteenth century's anti-Catholic perspective thus continued into the twentieth century, and it was by no means limited to Protestant evangelicals.

Traits of character assigned to the Latin Americans were often attributed to the influence of climate, race, or cultural heritage, but they were sometimes discussed without reference to their origins. And those traits, in themselves, could adequately explain the region's lagging development. Latin Americans were typically portrayed as ignorant, incompetent, lazy, and childlike—as people fundamentally flawed in character. Senator Albert Beveridge, an avowed imperialist, in a speech urging the annexation of Cuba in 1906, complained that after the U.S. had "purified and cleansed" the island, everything had come undone in four short years. Disorder, panic, and confusion had come about "because the character of the Cuban people made them absolutely certain." At the same time, Senator Henry Cabot Lodge privately noted that the common feeling was that the Cubans "ought to be taken by the neck and shaken until they behave themselves." Professor William W. Sweet concluded that the backwardness of Latin America was partly the result of an aversion to manual labor, the lack of a middle class and an intelligent laboring class, and a weakness of character that he summed up in these words: "Mutual distrust, excessive pride, self-indulgence, indolence, and want of persistence."[55] In a letter of 1911, Roosevelt described "our Spanish-American friends" as people with many good points but who "often act as if they were children solemnly engaged in making believe to be something that they are not." A traveler to Honduras noted, "Everywhere one has the impression of watching peculiarly stupid children playing at being a republic." In a variation on this theme, an article on Colombia written shortly after the separation of Panama held that "unquestionably

53. Hubert W. Brown, *Latin America* (New York, 1901), 120; Jasper T. Moses, *Today in the Land of Tomorrow* (Indianapolis, 1909), 2.
54. Wallace, *Beyond the Mexican Sierras*, xii.
55. New York *Times*, September 30, 1906; Henry Cabot Lodge to Theodore Roosevelt, September 16, 1906, in *Selections from the Correspondence of Theodore Roosevelt and Henry Cabot Lodge*, ed. Henry Cabot Lodge (New York, 1925), II, 233; Sweet, *A History of Latin America*, 238, 245, 223.

the Colombian character is essentially feminine. It requires guidance, considerate treatment, and the deft hand."[56] The list of traits held up as major obstacles to progress seems endless. To the author of a travel account on Mexico the critical trait was "authoritative robbery on a colossal scale," and to a long-term resident of Cuba it was a population "diseased, physically and morally, and also mentally." In view of the utter absence of "virtue, intelligence, and industry" among Latin Americans, the author of an article reviewing U.S.–Latin American relations exclaimed in exasperation: "Geologists claim that the northern coast of South America is fast sinking—why not await developments?"[57]

Such harsh judgments were also advanced by prominent Latin Americans, whose conclusions U.S. commentators frequently cited in support of their own analyses. In fact, in the history of Latin American thought, the early decades of the twentieth century are distinguished by an extraordinarily self-critical and pessimistic literature. It was every bit as disparaging of the peoples and cultures of Latin America as any serious work on the subject to appear in the U.S. This self-denigration followed the earlier diagnoses of Simón Bolívar and Domingo F. Sarmiento, but it was additionally sparked by the easy defeat of Spain in 1898, with the result that the analyses focused on the negative features of Spain's legacy. This literature was also characterized by a racial and geographic determinism that flowed from the late-nineteenth century's very popular positivist philosophy. Examples of prominent and widely read Latin American thinkers who led this paroxysm of self-flagellation include Brazilian physician, psychologist, and political writer José de Manoel Bomfim, who in his 1903 work, *O parasitismo social e evolucao: A América Latina,* wrote harshly about the Brazilian and Spanish-American colonial heritage of "parasitism" and decadent political traditions. Argentine novelist and sociologist Carlos Octavio Bunge addressed Latin American character in his *Nuestra América* (1903), described each of the racial groups in highly negative terms, and concluded that the outcome of race mixing was a Hispanic American fundamentally marked by laziness, sadness, and arrogance. Alcides Arguedas, Bolivian novelist, diplomat, and historian, achieved fame through his 1909 diagnosis of the fail-

56. Theodore Roosevelt to Maurice Francis Egan, September 5, 1911, in *The Letters of Theodore Roosevelt,* ed. Elting E. Morison (Cambridge, Mass., 1951–1954), VII, 341; Franck, *Tramping Through Mexico,* 369; Marion Wilcox, "Colombia's Last Vision of Eldorado," *North American Review,* CLXVII (December, 1903), 932.

57. George Agnew Chamberlain, *Is Mexico Worth Saving?* (Indianapolis, 1920), 229; Irene A. Wright, *Cuba* (New York, 1910), 97; C. Mayer, "Latin America and the United States," 952.

ures and defects of the Bolivian people, *Pueblo enfermo*, in which he denounced their character and customs and at the same time faulted Bolivia's geography and racial makeup for its multiple problems. Equally unsparing in the analysis of his people and their failures was Salvador Mendieta, a Central American political activist born in Nicaragua and leader of the struggle for Central American unity, who published the first volume of his three-volume work, *La enfermedad de Centro-América* in 1910.[58] Though this "sickness" literature had passed its highwater mark by the 1920s and quickly faded thereafter, it would never disappear entirely.

The most influential Latin American-authored study of the region to circulate in the U.S. in this period was *Latin America: Its Rise and Progress* by Peruvian diplomat Francisco García Calderón, which appeared initially in French in 1911 and in English translation two years later. The book offered a country-by-country survey of the postindependence period and an extended concluding section that discussed foreign "perils" and political, social, and economic problems facing Latin America. García Calderón's overall tone was pessimistic, and his assertions paralleled the themes emphasized by Latin American intellectuals and U.S. commentators. He characterized the colonial period as a dark age of stagnation and degeneration, and he argued that "unexploited wealth abounds" and that Latin America suffered from a stark contrast between "the wealth of the soil and the poverty of the State." In discussing the Central American and Caribbean nations, he wrote that "the peoples of the Tropics seem incapable of order, laborious patience, and method" and that throughout Latin America the Spanish Creole has been "enervated by miscegenation and climate." Somewhat preoccupied with the racial theme, the Peruvian held that "the mixture of rival castes, Iberians, Indians, and negroes, has generally had disastrous consequences." This widely circulated perspective from a Latin American intellectual, though not original, offered satisfying confirmation of the established American view.[59]

One additional non-American perspective of considerable influence

58. Discussion of these writers and others who shared their ideas, their major works, and turn-of-the-century intellectual currents can be found in Harold Eugene Davis, *Latin American Social Thought: The History of Its Development Since Independence, with Selected Readings* (Washington, D.C., 1961), Pt. 3 *passim;* William Rex Crawford, *A Century of Latin-American Thought* (Rev. ed.; Cambridge, Mass., 1961), Chapters V, VII *passim;* Martin S. Stabb, *In Quest of Identity: Patterns in the Spanish American Essay of Ideas, 1890–1960* (Chapel Hill, N.C., 1967), 12–33.

59. Francisco García Calderón, *Latin America: Its Rise and Progress*, trans. Bernard Miall (London, 1913), 378, 51, 231, 29, 361.

came from James Bryce, a highly regarded British legal scholar, states-
man, former ambassador to the United States, and author of a classic
study of the U.S. constitutional system. Bryce devoted four months
to a tour of much of South America and recorded his lengthy and
thoughtful reflections in *South America: Observations and Impressions* (1914), which was distinguished by a plea for a more-tolerant attitude toward South Americans from Europeans and North Americans. While freely acknowledging the continent's geographical
disabilities, Bryce argued that nature had, at the same time, bestowed
bounteous treasures and that the failure to develop those offerings was
largely a consequence of the colonial background and the racial pattern. He characterized the Spanish colonial government as "the most
ill-conceived and ill-administered scheme of government that self-
ishness and stupidity ever combined to devise." That experience, in
his view, caused the Spanish-American countries to drop "two centuries behind the general march of civilized mankind." Bryce gave particular attention to the problems of race, asserting that the large numbers of unassimilated "backward" races in countries such as Peru and
Brazil could only evoke despair for the future. Fittingly, Bryce was optimistic about Chile's prospects, because "here are no loitering negroes, nor impassive Indians."[60]

A factually based story, "so typical its name is Legion," bears retelling
at this point because it is an allegorical presentation of themes familiar to the period. Reported in a 1919 issue of the *Forum*, and highlighted
in the journal, this story by Agnes C. Laut, a much-published author
of articles on Latin America, is of a pioneering Nebraska family that
emigrated to southern Mexico in the hope of restoring the father's
health through outdoor labor in a sunny climate. "The little family
sprang from a race of pioneers, that had moved in tented wagons
over the mountains of Tennessee to the great Middle West, which they
colonized and civilized, and with the same urge of Destiny in their
blood, which has made Democracy what it is in the United States,
they now uprooted family ties and moved to a great South Land, where
the government was calling for new blood, new colonists, new capital, to do for that land what the colonization spirit had done for the
United States." The family began to prosper in a potentially rich land
made bountiful through the "sweat of brawn and brain," and relations
with the peons were neighborly. The pillar of the family was the el-
dest daughter, Grace, a name chosen because her parents "wished her
to become the embodiment of all the grace and freedom and beauty

---

60. James Bryce, *South America: Observations and Impressions* (New York, 1914),
16, 116, 464, 35, 549, 218.

that outdoor life in a western land could impart to body and spirit.
. . . She was sixteen and stood six feet tall. She could ride. She could
shoot. She could peg a tent, or break camp, or saddle a broncho; and
she grew in self-reliance every year because her family leaned upon
her strength; and she faced life with dauntless radiant happiness."

But the turmoil of revolution engulfed the countryside and shattered this idyllic scene. One evening two-score men burst into the
peaceful home, brutally beat and bound Grace's parents while she hid.
"Then a lantern was raised by the long naked hairy arm and faces shiny
with the sweaty ooze of drunken frenzy filled the darkness; and the
voice of the man holding the lantern shouted 'Now, where is your
Niña? Where is the Señorita?'" To save her parents, Grace surrendered
her body to the brutes who, after satisfying their savage lust, carried
her away. Months later she was rescued but was "past all healing in
body and soul; and that girl is today dying in the dusky hells of the hot
country, where white men seldom go and never stay." In conclusion,
the author warned that "if a Redemptive Power is not found, and found
swiftly, it is not into the Swine the Devils will go, and so over the
precipice into the sea, but into the blood of white-man civilization the
poison will course, cancelling all the world has fought for, and, won,
in ten thousand years," thus leading us all into "a primordial cesspool
of beastliness."[61]

Pure fiction also played an important role in popularizing the negative imagery of the peoples and culture of Latin America. Pejorative stereotypes were powerfully drawn in the work of O. Henry, whose
literary career rose rapidly to its peak in the century's first decade when
he became the nation's "most widely read storyteller." His first book,
Cabbages and Kings (1904), is a collection of loosely connected stories set on the tropical north coast of Honduras, where he lived for two
years in the 1890s. The stories are peopled by sleazy politicians, op-
portunistic revolutionaries, lazy grafters, and by a variety of local characters: "Simple-hearted children of nature" easily incited to revolution; "rambling, care-free and indolent" natives; "ox-eyed women,"
and a mestizo who worked with the "dawdling minuteness of inherited sloth." In contrast to such local characters is an American who
served as private secretary to the president and whose secret graft was
that of being the only honest man in the republic. "I run a monopoly
of square dealing here," he bragged. "There's no competition." O.
Henry referred to this Central American country as a "ginger cake
commonwealth," a "grocery and fruit stand," and as a place "where
it always seems to be after dinner." The tropical scenes in this never-

61. Agnes C. Laut, "In the Hells of Tehuantepec," *Forum*, LXI (June, 1919), 641–51.

FORUM

In The Hells of Tehuantepec

By AGNES C. LAUT

"An American Girl's Fate in Darkest Mexico"
(Cover of *Forum*, June, 1919).

never land are vividly drawn, the situations are comical, and many of the characters are memorable. The overall impression of tropical futility created by O. Henry is lasting.[62]

In the minds of U.S. observers it was a very short step from analyzing Latin America's failures and enumerating the deficiencies of character to suggesting adoption of American customs and values as a remedy. Such suggestions appeared often during the first decade of the century when they were applied most commonly to Mexico. A 1905 article, "The Americanization of Mexico," expressed exuberant delight at the course being followed under the rule of Porfirio Díaz and affirmed that "modernization and Americanization are almost synonymous terms in Mexico." In addition to teaching Mexicans modern mining and farming techniques, the author claimed that Mexicans were even learning American manners. He confidently predicted that more change was coming, "just as the American house has come, just as Mexican women are learning how to dress, just as Mexican men are learning how to transact business upon a business and not a social basis." In a similar assessment another writer enthusiastically related how the gradual spread of American culture was guiding Mexico into the modern era: "The S.P.C.A. has arrived, and bargain sales, and baseball, and the Y.M.C.A., and night schools, and the three-ring circus." The author clinched his argument with this rhetorical question: "When a Spanish-American country agitates the abolishment of bull-fights and introduces prizefights, does that not show an awakened sensitiveness to civilization?" One traveler predicted that in a few years "Mexico will tend to become an English-speaking country," and he concluded that it would not be surprising if "an Americanized Mexico should some day—perhaps in twenty-five years, or so—become peacefully annexed to the United States."[63] In addition to advocating adoption of the material symbols, customs, and language of U.S. culture, many writers argued that the long-term hope for Latin America was to embrace U.S. ideals and institutions. A political scientist specializing in Latin American affairs expressed confidence that progress would gradually come when "individual initiative and enterprise" replace "the old Spanish tradition of paternalism." Others placed their

62. Harry Hansen, "Foreword," vii, in William Sidney Porter [O. Henry], *The Complete Works of O. Henry* (Garden City, N.Y., 1953). The quotations are from stories in Book 5, "Cabbages and Kings," *ibid.*, 590, 566, 555, 552, 592, 587, 622.

63. Edward M. Conley, "The Americanization of Mexico," *American Monthly Review of Reviews*, XXXII (December, 1905), 724–25; Eugene P. Lyle, Jr., "Mexico at High-Tide," *World's Work*, XIV (August, 1907), 9196; W. E. Carson, *Mexico: The Wonderland of the South* (New York, 1909), 149, 176.

hope in the rise of a middle class, a system of public education following the U. S. model, division of land into quarter-section farms, or introduction of "the spirit of American commercialism" to supplant "Latin sentimentality."[64]

This missionary zeal for transplanting U.S. culture to Latin American soil reached its peak and encountered its most severe check during the compass of the Wilson administration. The moral imperialism so characteristic of the Wilson years formed an easy compatibility with the Progressive agenda of domestic reform. Wilson's journalist friend, William Bayard Hale, sent by him to Mexico in 1913 on a fact-finding mission, expressed the Progressive's view of the U.S. purpose in Mexico in a report to the president. Hale regarded U.S. businessmen and entrepreneurs residing in Mexico as "outposts and pioneers . . . of our higher civilization. . . . We are, in spite of ourselves, the guardians of order and justice and decency on this Continent; we are, providentially, naturally and unescapably, charged with the maintenance of humanity's interest here." In a thoughtful interview on this theme, Secretary of the Interior Franklin K. Lane commented on the American's "perfect, self-complacent appreciation" of his ability to "develop the backward peoples of the earth." Lane further noted, "There is a good deal of the special policeman, of the sanitary engineer, of the social worker, and of the welfare dictator about the American people. We are quite conscious that in the development of this great country of ours, in our march across the continent, we have done a perfectly good job, and the pioneering spirit is very much alive."[65]

The expectation, commonly voiced through the early years of the Wilson administration, that Latin America would find its way into the modern era through Americanization—first of Mexico, then of the Caribbean nations, and eventually of South America—had become a tarnished hope by 1921. The Mexican Revolution was the principal factor in that spreading disillusionment. One indication of this marked change in attitude can be found in the writing of Nevin O. Winter, a prolific writer on Latin America and an experienced traveler throughout the region. In a 1909 article he reported with much approval the rapid progress of Americanization in Mexico. He had in mind not just the construction of railroads, sewage systems, and ice-plants, for he

64. L. S. Rowe, "Some Fundamental Misconceptions Concerning South America," *North American Review,* CLXXXVII (January, 1908), 85; Henry Litchfield West, "What Does the Future Hold for Mexico?" *Harper's Weekly,* LI (June 1, 1907), 815.

65. Franklin K. Lane, "Memoranda on Affairs in Mexico," July 9, 1913, in *The Papers of Wilson,* ed. Link, XXVIII, 33; New York *World,* July 16, 1916, as cited in *Congressional Record,* House, 64th Cong., 1st Sess., Vol. LIII, Pt. 15, Appendix, 1578.

noted, "It is said that wheat bread is even replacing the beloved tortillas . . . so that Mexico may eventually take to eating prepared breakfast foods. Add to this, the wearing of American shoes, and teach them to sleep on beds instead of mats, and their civilization will be complete." Note the remarkable shift in attitude reflected in his assessment of 1918: "Things cannot be changed to Anglo-Saxon standards in a year, or two years, or even a generation. To Americanize Mexico will be a difficult if not impossible undertaking, and there are no signs of such a transition."[66] A similar shift took place in New York *Times'* editorials on Mexico. The change in tone was from confidence and optimism about Mexico's future before the revolution to puzzlement, uncertainty, frustration, and finally impatience, anger, and disillusionment during the course of the struggle.[67]

The dawning awareness that Latin America would not readily be Americanized was a sign of maturing judgment, but at the same time a sense of disillusionment and resignation accompanied that conclusion. Mexico's ghastly ordeal was the immediate source of that despair, but it was more generally a manifestation of the spirit of the times—an ironic close to a period dominated by a confident drive for reforming interventionism. The period began with the can-do enthusiasm of the American pioneer, missionary, businessman, and reformer when the U.S. was quickly moving toward world-power status. When this twenty-year span concluded, the nation had met its hemispheric security needs, and it was on its way toward financial and commercial dominance in Latin America. During the same period, the U.S. moved from debtor to creditor status, and the world's financial center shifted from London to New York. But having gained such gratifying rank, a postwar disillusionment settled over the public's feeling for foreign affairs and sapped the reforming zeal for the uplift of mankind. Attitudes toward Latin America in the following decade would reflect this loss of idealism.

During the half century that had elapsed since debate on the annexation of the Dominican Republic, the negative, distorted perceptions of Latin America and its people had changed but little, even though interest, contact, and the flow of information had increased

66. Nevin O. Winter, "The Progressive Mexico of To-Day," *World Today,* XVI (May, 1909), 551; Nevin O. Winter, *Mexico and Her People of Today* (Rev. ed.; Boston, 1918), 20–21.

67. Editorials from the following issues of the New York *Times* illustrate the trend: October 18, 1910; December 21, 1912; February 12, 1913; November 21, 1913; December 3, 1913; April 18, 1914; January 20, 1915; February 5, 1915; March 29, 1915; January 19, 1919.

substantially, particularly after the Spanish-American War, which marked the beginning of deep U.S. entanglement in the region. A start had been made toward the ordered, scholarly study of Latin America, but the impact of that information and scholarship on public perceptions was not yet evident. There had not emerged by the end of this period a corps of regional specialists who were trained in the language, culture, and history of Latin America and who had acquired an empathy for its peoples from extended residence there. Consequently, everyone was a specialist—storyteller, naval officer, businessman, journalist, missionary, congressman, diplomat, textbook author, and tourist. These commentators had been generous in discussing the causes of Latin American developmental problems but short on solutions, other than suggestions to follow the U.S. model. Discussion of causation continued the late-nineteenth-century focus on climate, race, and cultural legacy. That assessment received ready confirmation from an impressive body of Latin American intellectuals, thus suggesting that these conclusions emerged from common currents in Western thought and not solely from American ethnocentrism. Conviction that Latin America's Roman Catholic faith was disabling also remained as strong as ever. The factors identified as major impediments to progress were seemingly immutable. Even the calls for massive European immigration flew in the face of the overpowering influence attributed to climate, and arguments favorable to large-scale foreign investment were countered at the highest level in the Wilson administration with the assertion that foreign capital contributed to Latin America's problems. Indeed, one of this period's striking characteristics is the absence of an emphasis on capital needs. The need was, of course, mentioned—usually in the context of a cataloguing of undeveloped wealth or of the argument for replacing European with U.S. credit sources—but it was not highlighted. Other factors receiving more mention than in the past included the handicaps of geography and tropical disease. The coming and going of the campaigns for Progressive reform and to make the world safe for democracy had left America's inherited, negative perceptions of Latin America largely intact, for those perceptions were deeply rooted in the nation's racism and its ethnocentric vision of the world. After all, only with such a vision could an Americanized Latin America be hypothesized.

4

Continuity and Discontinuity:
The Emerging Challenge to Traditional Views,
1921–1930

Though the decade of the 1920s is often treated in histories of United States–Latin American relations as part of the era of intervention, 1898–1933, the decade merits separate treatment here. During the previous half century an overwhelming majority of commentators on Latin America attributed the region's developmental problems to climate, race, and cultural legacy, and although those views remained clearly dominant during the 1920s, they met significant challenge for the first time from intellectuals, scientists, and radical journalists who rejected the prevailing racism and ethnocentrism that shaped perceptions of Latin Americans. More characteristic than the dissent was an expanding flow of information on the region that was of better quality, more evenhanded, and more reflective of the Latin American point of view. Also, policies toward Latin America were more thoroughly debated than in the past and they underwent some shift, although they too reflected more continuity than discontinuity from the years of the Wilson presidency through the period of "Republican ascendancy." The changes in perceptions and policy were moderate and hardly commensurate with the cultural maelstrom that shook the decade, but they are critical to understanding the deeper changes of subsequent decades.

The long-standing consensus of views on Latin America's developmental problems was largely intact when the decade began, and it is indeed ironic that, during a decade noted for its xenophobic nationalism and violent racism, that consensus—which rested heavily on racism—would begin to crumble. Items such as the Scopes trial, Ku Klux Klan activism, severely restrictive immigration laws, and Prohibition laws demonstrated the strong drive of the 1920s for conformity, homogeneity, and standardization of values, and at the same time they suggest a cultural ambience offering fertile ground for racism and ethnocentrism. Popular racial prejudices had received strong support from science during the first two decades of the century; scientists gave respectability to the notion that races differed in innate intelligence, character, and temperament, and the mainstream of the newly emerging social sciences promoted the scientific basis of racism.

In the 1920s, however, psychological testers began questioning the immutability of intelligence, and cultural anthropologists successfully advanced the concept that human diversity was the product of culture and not of race. The beginning of an Indian reform movement in the 1920s was one manifestation of the sweep and influence of this concept of cultural pluralism. Inevitably such intellectual currents would in time have an impact on attitudes toward foreign cultures.

Warren G. Harding's landslide victory in his 1920 presidential campaign to return the nation to "normalcy" registered a major shift in national mood. The zeal of the Progressive Era for domestic reform and foreign crusades yielded to postwar disillusionment and ultimately to the cynicism and hedonism that marked the decade. Such attitudes diminished enthusiasm for foreign entanglements and induced a more-cautious foreign policy. The genial Harding's predilection for compromise and conciliation set him quite apart from his stern Presbyterian predecessor, who preferred the path of moralistic coercion in dealing with Latin American problems. In the postwar years the nation's security needs could no longer be convincingly invoked to justify interventions in Latin America, because World War I had devastated the economies and spirit of those European powers once seen as a threat. Also, the penchant for economy in the Republican administrations of the 1920s strengthened the tendency to avoid costly interventions. In a decade in which Calvin Coolidge could proclaim, "The business of the United States is business," it was only natural that in dealings with Latin America the emphasis should be on trade and investment and that private loans to the region should be seen as economic rather than political issues. All of this is not to suggest that the nation's Latin American policy underwent fundamental change in the 1920s, for it did not, but rather that the attitudes that had sustained an interventionist policy since the turn of the century were indeed changing and would in time alter that policy.[1]

Symbolic of change were the visits to Latin America of the three Republicans who held the presidency during the 1920s: President-elect Harding traveled to Panama in November, 1920; Calvin Coolidge went to Havana for the 1928 Pan American Conference despite his want of knowledge and interest in the region's affairs, and President-elect Herbert Hoover toured Central and South America on a ten-week cruise after his 1928 election. Although there was no formal rejection of intervention during the decade, the marines were used with di-

---

1. Kenneth J. Grieb, *The Latin American Policy of Warren G. Harding* (Fort Worth, Tex., 1977), ix–xii, 1–8; L. Ethan Ellis, *Republican Foreign Policy, 1921–1933* (New Brunswick, N.J., 1968), 32–34, 37, 229–32; Langley, *The U.S. and the Caribbean,* 95–96.

minishing frequency as an instrument of policy, the Roosevelt Corollary was repudiated as a basis for intervention, and Hoover adopted a policy of nonintervention. Hegemony was still sought and control was still exercised but more often through diplomatic and economic pressure rather than overt, formal instruments of power. Governmental encouragement and support of private efforts to expand tourism, trade, and investment in Latin America successfully maintained the momentum toward economic expansion into the region, which World War I had so notably advanced. For example, in 1926 four troop carriers were sold and converted to form the first private American-flag service to South America's east coast since the 1860s. Following a sharp rise and then a decline in the value of U.S.–Latin American trade in the immediate postwar years, exports to the region grew steadily from 1921 to 1929, and the value of U.S. investment more than doubled. The collapse of trade occasioned by the onset of depression in 1929, together with increasingly sharp criticism of U.S. policy both from Latin Americans at the 1928 Pan American Conference and from within the country, contributed to initiatives taken at the end of the decade by the Hoover administration for further policy change.[2]

One sign of change in U.S.–Latin American policy evident even before Harding's inauguration was Wilson's decision to begin preparations for eventual U.S. departure from the Dominican Republic. Senate investigations in 1921–1922 of interventions in Haiti and the Dominican Republic drew generally unfavorable conclusions about U.S. governance of those republics and spurred the Harding administration to act. Plans for withdrawal from the Dominican Republic were negotiated in 1922, and formal departure came in 1924, although the customs receivership continued under U.S. control. Haiti remained a U.S. protectorate throughout the decade, and, despite administrative reforms implemented under Harding, governance remained largely racist and uninspired, a factor contributing to an outbreak of strikes and riots in 1929. These led to another investigation and the decision to prepare for departure, which finally came in 1934. In Cuba, economic hardship caused by collapse of the sugar market and disputed

2. Tulchin, *The Aftermath of War*, 234–35; Grieb, *The Latin American Policy of Harding*, 5; Sumner Welles, *The Time for Decision* (New York, 1944), 187–88; Langley, *The U.S. and the Caribbean*, 125–28; John G.B. Hutchins, "The American Shipping Industry Since 1914," *Business History Review*, XXVIII (1954), 113–14; Alexander DeConde, *Herbert Hoover's Latin-American Policy* (Stanford, 1951), 13–24, 49; Ellis, *Republican Foreign Policy*, 269–70; U.N. Dept. of Economic and Social Affairs, "The Growth of Foreign Investments in Latin America," in *Foreign Investment in Latin America*, ed. Bernstein, 42, 45–46.

"Winter Sports in the Sunny Caribbean"
Edmond Duffy in the Baltimore *Sun*, December 8, 1929. This cartoon used courtesy
of the Baltimore Sun Company © 1993, *The Baltimore Sun*.

elections in 1920 led Harding to dispatch General Enoch Crowder to the island. Crowder, who had earlier devised Cuba's electoral law, served as the power behind the president until mid-decade when the presidency was assumed by Gerardo Machado, whose rule from 1925–1933 was characterized by rampant corruption, a move toward dictatorship late in the decade, and the rapid growth of U.S. economic interests on the island. The 1920s also witnessed final settlement, through U.S. support, of the intransigent Tacna-Arica dispute between Chile and Peru and ratification of the long-dormant treaty with Colombia providing for payment of a $25 million indemnity for the loss of Panama.[3]

In Central America, Nicaragua remained the trouble spot for U.S. policymakers, particularly during the last half of the decade. Early in the 1920s the U.S. hosted a Central American conference that produced several treaties designed to enhance peace and stability, but revolution in Honduras in 1923–1924 led to a brief U.S. military intervention. The Coolidge administration attempted to terminate intervention in Nicaragua by withdrawing the legation guard in 1925, but a renewal of fighting led to the reluctant decision to reintroduce the marines in 1926. Under terms of an agreement negotiated by Henry L. Stimson, Coolidge's personal representative, the U.S. sustained the incumbent regime, supervised the 1928 elections, and trained the national guard. Forces commanded by a dissident military officer turned guerrilla leader, Augusto Sandino, refused to honor the agreement and resorted to terrorism; they stubbornly fought the U.S. presence, which by the late 1920s totaled more than five thousand troops. Sandino's actions elevated him to cult-hero status among many Latin Americans for his anti-Yankee daring and fueled the debate in the U.S. on policy toward the region. While Sandino was still at large, the Hoover administration decided to withdraw, and that decision was carried out in 1932. The prolonged involvement in Nicaragua created possibly more acrimony and debate within the U.S. during the 1920s than did relations with Mexico.[4]

Wilson had left to Harding the decision to grant or withhold recognition of the newly elected Mexican president, Alvaro Obregón, and Harding withheld it pending successful negotiation of several issues

3. Langley, The U.S. and the Caribbean, 97–105, 134–36, 110–14; Ellis, Republican Foreign Policy, 266–67, 270–75, 279–83; Grieb, The Latin American Policy of Harding, 29–31; John D. Hicks, Republican Ascendancy, 1921–1933 (New York, 1960), 28–30.

4. Langley, The U.S. and the Caribbean, 106–10, 116, 25; DeConde, Hoover's Latin-American Policy, 79–84; Donald R. McCoy, Calvin Coolidge: The Quiet President (1967; rpr. Lawrence, Kans., 1988), 351–54.

"In the Wilds of Nicaragua"
Fitzpatrick in the St. Louis *Post Dispatch*, January 14, 1927.

that had arisen from the revolution involving satisfaction of claims and the status of land and oil property rights of U.S. citizens and companies. In 1923 a gentleman's agreement resolved some of the issues, recognition was granted, and in 1924 the U.S. actively aided the Obregón regime in suppressing an armed revolt. Under terms of the gentleman's agreement the U.S. accepted payment in bonds for expropriated lands, and the Mexican government agreed to honor titles to petroleum holdings acquired before 1917 in cases in which a "positive act" toward exploiting the resource could be demonstrated. At middecade tensions revived under the regime of Plutarco Elías Calles as the Mexican government appeared to renege on terms of the gentleman's agreement, and calls for intervention were renewed in some U.S. quarters. In 1927 Coolidge appointed Dwight Morrow ambassador to Mexico, and his arrival marked a turning point in U.S.-Mexican relations. His genuine goodwill toward Mexico and Mexicans, his informal diplomacy, and his direct negotiations with Calles enabled him to resolve or defuse many of the troublesome issues by the end of the decade.[5]

Postwar changes in U.S. foreign policy signaled by Senate defeat of the Treaty of Versailles and rejection of membership in the League of Nations, together with the inconsistency between Wilson's espousal of self-determination and his interventions in Latin America, inevitably invited debate on policy toward the region, and that debate remained vigorous throughout the decade. It began during the presidential campaign of 1920, when Harding and the Republicans criticized Wilson's interventions in the Caribbean and his Mexican policy.[6] For example, a few weeks before the elections, the *Nation* published a series of articles by the black writer, James Weldon Johnson, blistering the Wilson administration for its military occupation and racist rule of Haiti. Johnson reminded his readers that "the ruthless slaughter" of three thousand Haitians took place when "our sons were laying down their lives overseas," quoting Wilson, " 'for democracy . . . and for the rights and liberties of small nations.' "[7] Such perfervid attacks on U.S. policy continued throughout the decade in journals such as the *Nation*, the *New Republic*, and *Current History*, and Sena-

5. Cline, *The U.S. and Mexico*, 203–13.

6. Langley, *The U.S. and the Caribbean*, 97; Grieb, *The Latin American Policy of Harding*, 1.

7. John W. Blassingame, "The Press and the American Intervention in Haiti and the Dominican Republic, 1904–1920," *Caribbean Studies*, IX (1969), 29, 37, 40; James Weldon Johnson, "Self-Determining Haiti," *Nation*, CXI (September 25, 1920; August 28, 1920), 347, 238.

tors Hiram Johnson, William H. King, George W. Norris, Thomas J. Walsh, and William E. Borah added biting criticisms to these attacks. Samuel Guy Inman, a leading advocate of better understanding and more-friendly dispositions toward Latin America and author of many articles on the region, wrote a short piece in 1924 entitled "Imperialistic America" that conveyed the central message of these critics, namely, that the U.S., through the use of military force and financial advisers, had assumed an imperialistic stance in the hemisphere. Late in the decade a traveler to Bolivia and Peru registered his astonishment at the many foreigners directing branches of government and running key enterprises; while acknowledging the lack of trained personnel in these countries, he deplored what he perceived to be exploitation by foreigners—primarily Americans, British, and Germans— who "are running away with the money of these countries" and causing them to be "so outrageously fleeced." At the same time, a Southern congressman, who conceded that Haitians may be "just a lot of monkeys, . . . a lot of savages, a lot of cannibals," nevertheless espoused the anti-imperialist stance and insisted that "God has not given us the right to rule over them because of their own incapacity."[8]

In keeping with the often-frivolous, often-cynical spirit of the decade, critics of U.S. policy occasionally rendered it indefensible with their caustic humor. Will Rogers remarked, "Nicaragua voted the other day not to have us supervise their elections, but that's not official, as we didn't supervise their vote." Reports of violence involving Al Capone's men in recent Chicago elections evoked the following editorial in a Montana newspaper concerning U.S.-Nicaraguan relations:

The suggestion . . . that the Government might profitably call in the Nicaraguan Army to supervise the [Chicago] election is a good one. It would be a graceful act of reciprocity and while our marines are handling the coming election for the Nicaraguans the troops of the little Republic could protect Chicago citizens against the Capone insurrectos. . . . There should be an understanding that Nicaragua is not to keep her army of occupation in Chicago after that city has reached a point to exercise independence. It is reasonable to expect that the city will be fit for self-government, say, in about 50 or 60 years. The percentage of literacy is higher here than in Nicaragua, and great numbers of

8. Ellis, *Republican Foreign Policy*, 233; Langley, *The U.S. and the Caribbean*, 97; Samuel Guy Inman, "Imperialistic America," *Atlantic Monthly*, CXXXIV (July, 1924), 107–16; Department of State, Records Relating to Internal Affairs of Peru, 1910–1929, "General Conditions," Laurence Duggan, La Paz, Bolivia, July 28, 1929, to Stephen P. Duggan, Director, Institute of International Education, as enclosure in Stephen P. Duggan, New York, October 10, 1929, to Secretary of State Henry L. Stimson; remarks of George Huddleston, *Congressional Record*, House, 71st Cong., 2nd Sess., Vol. LXXII, Pt. 1, p. 317.

Chicagoans can read and write. Probably by the time both Nicaragua and Chicago are ripe for self-government we could give the order to withdraw our marines from the little Republic at the same time an order comes from Nicaragua for her troops to come home. Both Governments would then be on an equal footing and the exchange of international courtesies would excite the admiration of the world.[9]

One favorable trend apparent in the debate on Latin American policy was that a few voices, often of prominent Americans, began to be raised on behalf of such notions as greater understanding of Latin American problems, the unfairness of comparisons between the U.S. and Latin America, and tolerance for diversity. For example, the author of a survey history of Central America asked: "How many of our instinctive American notions of the blessedness of work, of inalienable freehold rights in land, etc., are founded on 'absolute' facts and how much on the chance facts that the North American pioneers settled in a healthful, temperate climate, with unlimited amounts of easily accessible, level, and fertile land?" Similar views were expressed by George Creel, journalist, chairman of the Committee on Public Information during the war, and President Wilson's unofficial agent to Mexico in 1920. In the foreword to his book, *The People Next Door,* Creel wrote: "Americans, favored as no other race in history, have come to ascribe success to intrinsic merit and sheer natural ability. Confident to the point of cocksureness, we are prone to look upon less fortunate peoples with intolerance, attributing their failures to fundamental inferiorities."[10] Latin American economic problems were also, on occasion, treated with empathy as illustrated by an article in *Barron's* that provided a detailed look at Brazil's experience with coffee valorization. The account was sympathetic in that the author compared the Brazilian coffee program with the frustrating efforts of the Federal Farm Board to cope with similar problems of wheat overproduction in the U.S. Another sign of improved reporting on Latin America was the appearance in 1927 in the *Saturday Evening Post* of a series of six articles on Mexico that were lengthy, detailed, and of good quality.[11]

9. Washington *Post,* March 24, 1928, as cited in remarks of Gerald P. Nye, *Congressional Record,* Senate, 70th Cong., 1st Sess., Vol. LXIX, Pt. 7, p. 7621; "Call in the Nicaraguan Army," Helena (Mt.) *Daily Independent,* April 5, 1928, as cited in remarks of Burton K. Wheeler, *Congressional Record,* Senate, 70th Cong., 1st Sess., Vol. LXIX, Pt. 6, pp. 6175–76.

10. Arthur Ruhl, *The Central Americans* (New York, 1928), 45; George Creel, *The People Next Door* (New York, 1926), xi.

11. "Brazil Pays the Price," *Barron's,* August 18, 1930, pp. 22, 28; the first of the six articles on Mexico was Isaac F. Marcosson, "Calles," *Saturday Evening Post,* Febru-

Debate on relations with Mexico during the decade, though intense, was more balanced and offered a clearer exposition of the Mexican point of view than ever before. One editorialist attempted to evoke an open-minded attitude by reminding his readers that "the Mexico most familiar to us . . . is the border country of towns built to serve our own vices." In 1924 the *Nation* and the *Survey* each devoted an issue to sympathetic presentations by U.S. and Mexican authorities of the various components of Mexico's reformist agenda and of its impressive achievements in education and the arts. Elsewhere, Albert Shaw, editor of the *Review of Reviews* and respected interpreter of political events, urged Americans to show patience toward the Mexican people "in their endeavor to make political and social advancement," and educational philosopher John Dewey, after observing the efforts to bring education to the Indian masses, described those programs with compassion and understanding.[12] In addition to favorable assessments by these and other intellectuals and scholars such as Van Wyck Brooks, Waldo Frank, and Herbert Croly, the pro-Mexican perspective was also provided by radical journalists and members of the counterculture who despised the enforced propriety, boosterism, and crass materialism of the atomized modern American industrial society. Many of these disillusioned intellectuals, literati, and artists looked for salvation to the collectivist and natural life that they seemed to perceive among American Indians. Mexico was elevated in their esteem because of its "Indianness" and its resistance to the worst aspects of modern American business culture. This partially explains the sudden popularity in the 1920s of Mexican art, which was featured, along with Indian art, in a very successful exhibition that toured several U.S. cities in 1930. The work of Mexico's three great muralists—David Alfaro Siqueiros, Diego Rivera, and José Clemente Orozco—which graced the walls of several public buildings in Mexico City, received particular acclaim for its authenticity and power. Several American intellectuals, instead of following the crowd to Paris, took up residence in Mexico, where they developed deep attachments to the people and culture and a sympathetic view of the goals of the revolution, espe-

ary 26, 1927, pp. 3–5. It should be noted that within some circles in Mexico and the U.S. the articles by Marcosson were considered offensive to Mexico.

12. "Our Southern Neighbors," *Nation*, CXIX (August 27, 1924), 204; the issues of *Nation* and *Survey* are *ibid.* and LII (May 1, 1924), respectively. Albert Shaw, "The Human Element in American Relations," *Annals of the American Academy of Political and Social Science*, CXXXVIII (1928), 55; John Dewey, "Mexico's Educational Renaissance," *New Republic*, XLVIII (September 22, 1926), 116–18; John Dewey, "From a Mexican Notebook," *New Republic*, XLVIII (October 20, 1926), 239–41.

cially in the areas of land reform and public education. These exiles included three radical journalists—Carleton Beals, Ernest Gruening, and Frank Tannenbaum—who wrote dozens of articles for U.S. publications. These writers exhibited a good understanding of Mexico, its culture, and language, which they had acquired from long-term residence, extensive travel, and contact with all levels of society, and their writing was reasoned. The central themes expressed by their collective writing were that Mexico was beginning to make headway toward the goals of the revolution, those goals were just and humane, and Mexico should be allowed to proceed without threat of U.S. intervention.[13]

One of the best-known American writers to spend much of the decade in Mexico was Katherine Anne Porter, who came to regard Mexico less as an exotic land than as "familiar country." In the several essays she wrote about Mexico in the 1920s, she argued that the goals of the revolution were utterly fair and reasonable, and she strongly opposed pressure from the U.S. government and outside oil interests to abandon those goals. She was most eloquent in expressing her admiration of Mexican art and of what she called the "aesthetic magnificence" of the people. In concluding an essay on the Mexican *corrido*, a form of ballad, she wrote: "A race of singing people . . . used to sorrowful beginnings and tragic endings, in love with life, fiercely independent, a little desperate, but afraid of nothing. They see life as a flash of flame against a wall of darkness. Conscious players of vivid roles, they live and die well, and as they live and die, they sing."[14]

The dichotomy in sentiment toward Mexico that crystallized in this decade was summarized by Walter Lippmann in his popular book *Public Opinion* as follows: "When we use the word 'Mexico' what picture does it evoke in a resident of New York? Likely as not, it is some composite of sand, cactus, oil wells, greasers, rum-drinking Indians, testy old cavaliers flourishing whiskers and sovereignty, or perhaps an idyllic peasantry a la Jean Jacques, assailed by the prospect of smoky industrialism, and fighting for the Rights of Man." This

13. John A. Britton, "In Defense of Revolution: American Journalists in Mexico, 1920–1929," *Journalism History*, V (1978–1979), 124–30; Fredrick B. Pike, "Latin America and the Inversion of United States Stereotypes in the 1920s and 1930s," *The Americas*, XLII (1985), 138, 145–48; Zelman, "American Intellectual Attitudes Toward Mexico, 1908–1940," 131–46.

14. Katherine Anne Porter, *The Collected Essays and Occasional Writings of Katherine Anne Porter* (New York, 1970); the relevant essays and dates of publication are as follows: "Why I Write About Mexico," 1923; "The Fiesta of Guadalupe," 1923; "The Mexican Trinity," 1921; "Where Presidents Have No Friends," 1922; "La Conquistadora," 1926. The quotation is from "Corridos," *Survey*, LII (May 1, 1924), 159.

comment illustrates Professor Fredrick B. Pike's observation that it is impossible for the North American to approach the Latin American without either sentimentality or dislike. In the 1920s these feelings coexisted.[15]

Another notion new in the commentary was the warning against the tendency to universalize American ideals and institutions. Norman Hapgood, an influential editor and advocate of various reformist causes, asserted that he would like to see the world develop an appreciation for the traditions of such places as China, Palestine, and Latin America. "I can easily be reconciled," he observed, "if in tolerating such things we fail to carry to the whole world the civilization which may be finding its apex in Chicago and Pittsburgh." The author of a study of foreign investment in Bolivia argued that Americans should permit other nations to work out their own destinies, "rather than to try to transplant a ready-made civilization upon a soil and people neither ready nor anxious for it." In his usual pithy style H. L. Mencken lambasted Americans for failure to recognize the diversity among Latin Americans and for bracketing them all in the same negative category. "It is as embarrassing," wrote Mencken, "for an Argentino to be put in the same box with the Haitians as it is for a civilized San Franciscan to be grouped with the morons of Los Angeles."[16]

An examination of journals of opinion suggests that the growing appearance in the 1920s of the Latin American perspective as expressed by its people themselves also helped create a more-balanced and informed public opinion. To cite one example, the following is from a 1924 article in the *Survey* by Plutarco Elías Calles a few months before he was inaugurated president of Mexico: "It has been human, altogether too human, for the people of the United States to judge Mexican history by the standards of their own career as a nation. They have, for instance, likened our war of independence to their own revolution against England. This attitude is fundamentally erroneous and is responsible for much of the misunderstanding between the two nations." The more-frequent appearance in U.S. periodicals of articles translated and reprinted from the Latin American press also indicated the trend toward more-balanced reporting. Several articles by the highly

15. Walter Lippmann, *Public Opinion* (New York, 1922), 68; Pike, "Latin America and United States Stereotypes," 152–53. Pike credits D. H. Lawrence with the observation, paraphrased by Pike, that it was "impossible for the White people to approach the Indian without either sentimentality or dislike."

16. Norman Hapgood, "Public Opinion on Mexico," *Annals of the American Academy of Political and Social Science*, CXXXII (1927), 179; Margaret Alexander Marsh, *The Bankers in Bolivia: A Study in American Foreign Investment* (New York, 1928), 122; H. L. Mencken, "Editorial," *American Mercury*, XIII (April, 1928), 410–11.

regarded Mexican minister of education, José Vasconcelos, explained his nation's ambitious program of educational reform and pleaded for Mexico's right to pursue its reformist goals free from outside interference and pressure.[17] In addition, Latin Americans began to show increasing sophistication in their efforts to mold U.S. opinion by employing lobbyists and publicists. Senator Borah complained that "'publicity' for the competing politicans and military leaders in Latin America has come to be highly organized," and the practice had created a "swarm of parasites," meaning the lobbyists thus employed.[18]

The formal study of Latin American history and civilization and of the Spanish language, major factors in the ultimate shaping of attitudes toward the region, continued to advance at a gradual pace. A mid-decade survey showed that 135 colleges and universities regularly offered courses in Latin American history. The University of California at Berkeley offered nine or ten such courses and at the same time provided rigorous graduate training under the guidance of scholars such as Charles E. Chapman and Herbert E. Bolton, but other major institutions such as Princeton and the University of Chicago offered no courses on Latin America. By the end of the decade, however, almost every university of consequence provided such courses. Formal study of Spanish had advanced somewhat more rapidly. One survey noted that "by 1919 it had become routine in the programs of all of the better institutions of learning." Publication of the *Hispanic American Historical Review*, which had begun in 1918 with limited resources and a total of fifty subscribers, was suspended in 1922, but it resumed in 1926 and since then has continued regularly.[19] Of some

17. "A Hundred Years of Revolution," *Survey*, LII (May 1, 1924), 133; José Vasconcelos, "Latin America: An Interpretation and a Prophecy," *Living Age*, CCCXXIX (May 1, 1926), 233–38; José Vasconcelos, "Educational Aspirations," *Survey*, LII (May 1, 1924), 167–69; José Vasconcelos, "Freedom or Imperialism?" *Nation*, CXIX (August 27, 1924), 212–13.

18. Ramiro de Maeztu, "Why There Are Two Americas," *Living Age*, CCCXXXII (February 15, 1927), 312–18, as reprinted from *La Prensa* (Buenos Aires), December 23, 30, 1926; "Chronic Revolution in Brazil," *Literary Digest*, LXXXIII (December 13, 1924), 20, as reprinted from several Brazilian newspapers such as *Combate* (São Paulo); New York *Times*, December 29, 1926.

19. William Spence Robertson *et al.*, "Report of a Committee of the Pan American Union on the Teaching of Latin-American History in Colleges, Normal Schools, and Universities of the United States," *Hispanic American Historical Review*, VII (1927), 355–56; A. Curtis Wilgus, "New Interest in the Teaching and Study of Hispanic American History—Abstract," *Annual Proceedings, National Education Association*, LXVII (1929), 635; Basadre, "Introduction" to *Latin American Courses in the U.S.*, as reprinted in *Latin American History*, ed. Cline, II, 424; Williams, *The Spanish Background*, I, 195; William Spence Robertson, "Introduction" to Ruth Lapham Butler, comp., *Guide*

help to the growing number of instructors in the discipline, many of whom complained of the lack of atlases, syllabi, and quality readings, was the publication early in the decade of two new Latin American history texts for college undergraduates. Both suffered, however, from the same problem of dull, uninspired presentation as William W. Sweet's text already in use. The decade also witnessed publication of the first book of source material suitable for supplementary reading in college courses in Latin American history and the first high school text on the subject.[20]

Also in the 1920s distinguished scholars such as Charles E. Chapman, William L. Schurz, and Mary W. Williams contributed many articles on Latin American themes to the nonacademic press. Hubert Herring, a Congregationalist minister and future professor of Latin American history, advanced the cause of enlightenment by serving as executive director of the Committee on Cultural Relations with Latin America and by annually escorting groups of Americans to Mexico and introducing them to Mexican leaders; the cost, it should be noted, was to be denounced in Congress, along with other advocates of an evenhanded policy, for being a "hireling" of the Mexican government, a "piffling pacifist," and a "political eunuch" for defending Calles and "his cutthroats."[21]

Despite the growing balance and improved quality in the commentary about Latin America in the 1920s, observations about the region and about the possibilities and problems of its development reflected more continuity than discontinuity from the previous period. The dominant themes in American thought during the previous half century remained so in the 1920s. Although the emphasis here is on evidence of changing perspectives, it must be kept in mind that these changes represented the views of dissenters from the mainstream of commentary, offered within a context in which Latin America aroused

---

to the *Hispanic American Historical Review* (Durham, N.C., 1950), vii–xvi, as reprinted in *Latin American History*, ed. Cline, I, 121–22.

20. The major texts in use during the 1920s were: Sweet's *A History of Latin America*; William Spence Robertson, *History of the Latin American Nations* (New York, 1922); Herman G. James and Percy A. Martin, *The Republics of Latin America: Their History, Government and Economic Conditions* (New York, 1923). Basadre, "Introduction" to *Latin American Courses in the U.S.*, as reprinted in *Latin American History*, ed. Cline, II, 420.

21. Remarks of William C. Hammer, *Congressional Record*, House, 69th Cong., 2nd Sess., Vol. LXVIII, Pt. 5, p. 5834; remarks of James A. Gallivan, *ibid.*, Pt. 2, p. 2259. Some of these remarks were directed at activists other than Herring, who, like him, wrote favorably about Mexico in the popular press.

relatively minor interest in a public absorbed in more exciting and immediate developments.

Observers of Latin America in the 1920s continued to portray the region as a land of great potential wealth. Wallace Thompson's *Rainbow Countries of Central America*, cited in congressional debate, was a popular description of the five republics, written in a romantic, exuberant vein that lavishly described the region's wealth and expressed confidence that scientists and engineers would in the future uncover its hidden abundance. In an account of travels through Andean South America, another author wrote that "since the days of Pizarro South America has been the El Dorado of gold and silver and of emeralds and diamonds as well. It has now become the continent of tin, copper, and iron." He described Bolivia as "a mighty treasure vault" and portrayed Colombia as "an undeveloped empire" of mineral wealth that modern progress had recently roused, "like a sleeping princess, to arise and gather up her jewels."[22]

This vision of Latin America as a storehouse of latent wealth was a familiar image by the 1920s, but the decade did hear for the first time a significant number of demurrals clouding that happy vision. In the main, these voices of doubt qualified the exaggerated claims, pointed to the problems of terrain and location, and emphasized the great capital investment required to realize the potential. A popular book of 1929, *The Romance and Rise of the American Tropics*, expressed the prevailing view that U.S. business enterprise, capital investment, and technical skill had been key ingredients in fomenting economic progress in Central America and the northern South American republics since the turn of the century. But, argued the author, the wealth thus gained was not easily done so. "The myth of the easy wealth of the Indies has been a long time dying." He noted that in Colombia "the wealth potentialities are more than overcome by the troubles of transport," and in Central America the potential wealth was of a kind that responded "only to skilled and expensive engineering and agricultural development." In a series of lectures on Mexico, historian Herbert I. Priestley spoke of the country's difficult terrain and uneven rainfall, emphasizing that these obstacles had severely limited the achievements of both Aztecs and Spaniards.[23] Margaret

22. Wallace Thompson, *Rainbow Countries of Central America* (New York, 1926), 165; Frank G. Carpenter, *Lands of the Andes and the Desert* (Garden City, N.Y., 1924), 4, 197, 16, 24.

23. Samuel Crowther, *The Romance and Rise of the American Tropics* (Garden City, N.Y., 1929), 9–10, 50; Herbert I. Priestley, "Basic Features of the Mexican Problem," in *Some Mexican Problems (Lectures on the Harris Foundation 1926)*, eds. Moises Saenz and Herbert I. Priestley (Chicago, 1926), 96–97.

Alexander Marsh, author of an excellent study on the impact of foreign investment in Bolivia, offered the following assessment of the Bolivian mining enterprise that directly countered contemporary descriptions of the country's "mighty treasure vault" of wealth: "The high cost of fuel, heavy transportation charges, the necessity of importing practically all machinery, mining materials and provisions, the inaccessible character of the country, and other lesser causes combine to make mining in Bolivia a fairly costly process." In a college text on the economic geography of South America, Professor Clarence F. Jones summarized the general conclusions of these dissenters by contrasting the geographic and climatic conditions of North and South America as follows: "In practically every instance of major likeness or difference, the southern lands are less advantageously disposed than North America."[24]

Climate, race, and cultural legacy continued in the 1920s to be the principal factors offered in explaining Latin America's failure to live up to its potential and keep pace with the United States. A strong sense of American superiority, which reached full expression in this decade albeit in highly xenophobic form, underlay judgments about the backward condition of Latin America. As in the case of commentary on its potential wealth, dissent from prevailing explanations for underdevelopment was growing as well, particularly with regard to race and cultural legacy.

There is little evidence of change from previous decades in discussions of climate and tropical conditions or in assessments of the largely negative role of climate on the process of development in Latin America. Travel accounts, histories, geographies, and descriptive accounts reiterated the often-repeated message of earlier years: an abundant nature provided all of man's basic needs in the tropics, and the consequent ease of existence had, over centuries, produced a population essentially indolent, carefree, and improvident. Although there was less confusion in the 1920s about the location of the bulk of the population in relation to the tropics and less of a tendency to identify all of Latin America as tropical, the disadvantages attributed to tropical life were often generalized to nontropical Latin America.

In his book, *Mexico and Its Reconstruction*, Chester Lloyd Jones, a political scientist and a diplomat with Latin American experience, judged that tropical and semitropical conditions do not produce "that wholesome unrest which is the dynamic element in countries less fa-

24. Marsh, *The Bankers in Bolivia*, 43; Clarence F. Jones, *South America* (New York, 1930), 14.

vored by nature. Life is too easy. Poverty is always near but actual starvation is known hardly by report." The author of an article entitled "The Real Central America" also drew a contrast between the energetic, progressive peoples of the northern temperate regions and the lazy ways of the tropics. "Our race goes back to the hardy tribes of north Europe, where inhospitable climate and barren soil encouraged industry, thrift, self-denial, and group action. The Central American was born and reared in a land where food, clothing, and shelter might be had with little effort. . . ." In a 1927 Senate debate on policy toward Mexico, Senator George P. McLean expressed a fatalistic assessment, arguing that the troubles facing Mexicans and Central Americans "for the most part are anthropological and meteorological. . . . In other words, the weather is largely responsible for the variations in the color and the conduct of men and women the world over. . . ." Commentators also continued to stress the deleterious effect of tropical conditions on Caucasians. For example, Harry A. Franck, perhaps the decade's most-experienced and widely published traveler in South America—and, incidentally, a man who came to dislike South America rather intensely—concluded that the less said about a white man of long residence in the tropics, the better.[25]

One of the rare challenges to the thesis linking climate and level of civilization appeared in a popular textbook entitled *Contemporary Sociological Theories*. Authored by Russian-born Pitirim Sorokin, a highly regarded American sociologist, it offered a description and history of the major schools of sociological theory. Sorokin examined the thesis that climate determines the growth and decay of civilization, whose most-respected advocate was Elsworth Huntington, and concluded, "There may be some correlation between genius and civilization and climate but most of it remains to be discovered. Dr. Huntington's work, in spite of the talent and energy he displays, cannot be recognized as conclusive." This mild reproof somewhat understates the vigor of Sorokin's attack on Huntington's work.[26]

Some observers in the twenties still professed to see deleterious effects from residing in tropical highlands. The best statement of this is found in *The People of Mexico* by Wallace Thompson, who wrote: "There seems no doubt that on the plateau the rarefied air, with its

25. Chester Lloyd Jones, *Mexico and Its Reconstruction* (New York, 1922), 114; Thomas F. Lee, "The Real Central America," *Mentor*, XIII (February, 1925), 15; remarks of George P. McLean, *Congressional Record*, Senate, 69th Cong., 2nd Sess., Vol. LXVIII, Pt. 2, p. 2226; Harry A. Franck, *Working North from Patagonia: Being the Narrative of a Journey, Earned on the Way, Through Southern and Eastern South America* (New York, 1921), 477, 433–34.

26. Pitirim Sorokin, *Contemporary Sociological Theories* (New York, 1928), 192.

accompanying absence of oxygen, the strain of the long, dry period upon the nervous system, have a definite effect upon the inhabitants, tending to nervousness in the creoles and in foreign whites, and probably resulting in the early death of the nervous types of the lower classes, leaving the lethargic alone as the typical Mexican of the plateau as well as of the hot country."[27]

In setting forth the obstacles to development, the prevalence of disease remained a significant factor for many observers. Professor Priestley asserted that "the physical condition of the people is one of the most profound difficulties in the way of [Mexico's] well-being." A traveler in Mexico emphasized "an overwhelming death-rate," but declared, "In sapping the strength of the Mexican people, probably no single factor is greater than venereal disease." Following a tour of southern Brazil, the U.S. military attaché reported that three-fourths of Brazilians lived in rural areas, "90% of this rural population are suffering from hookworm, a curable disease," and also that large numbers were afflicted with malaria.[28]

Interpretation of Latin American underdevelopment based on racial factors continued to receive heavy emphasis in the 1920s, and that view was confirmed by a convergence of trends that led to a scientific consensus for racism. During the second half of the nineteenth century the polygenist view that racial differences arose from different primordial origins supplanted the Biblical chronology and the monogenist conception of humankind as a single species of common origin, whose differences evolved under the impact of different environmental conditions. At the same time, Darwinian biologists and social philosophers argued that societies followed natural and evolutionary laws of progress from savagery to barbarism to civilization and that the races could be ordered into hierarchies of progress. Much of the effort of comparative anatomy and physical anthropology had been directed toward the largely unsuccessful task of classifying and measuring racial differences that led to development of measurements such as the cephalic index. The underlying assumption of these efforts was that cultural differences were a function of differences in racial physical structure.[29]

27. Wallace Thompson, *The People of Mexico: Who They Are and How They Live* (New York, 1921), 103–104.

28. Priestley, "Basic Features of the Mexican Problem," 99; Thompson, *The People of Mexico*, 108, 105; Department of State, Records Relating to Internal Affairs of Brazil, 1910–1929, "Political Affairs," Major F. L. Whitley, U.S. Military Attaché, Rio de Janeiro, June 13, 1922, to War Department, as enclosure in Sheldon Crosby, Chargé d'affaires, Rio de Janeiro, July 18, 1922, to Secretary of State Charles E. Hughes.

29. Thomas F. Gossett, *Race: The History of an Idea in America* (Dallas, 1963),

Developments in psychological testing during the first two decades of the century also strengthened scientific racism. Henry H. Goddard's work in translating and publishing Alfred Binet's mental tests, beginning in 1908, stimulated rapid development of testing and the use of tests by teachers, administrators, and those working with the feebleminded. During World War I, by which time the IQ test was closely linked to hereditarian views, the intelligence test came of age when it was used as a group test given to army recruits. A basic assumption in a widely discussed report on the IQ test, published in 1921 by the National Academy of Sciences, was that it measured innate mental capacity. In the early 1920s, intelligence testing became firmly established in American education, and the tests were used to demonstrate innate differences among ethnic and racial groups.[30]

The founding and rapid growth of the eugenics movement during the second and third decades of the century also contributed to the acceptance of scientific racism. Inspired by the work of British scientist Francis Galton, biologist Charles B. Davenport founded the eugenics movement in the U.S. by establishing a well-funded research institute in 1910. Prominent Americans such as Alexander Graham Bell, Theodore Roosevelt, Margaret Sanger, Charles W. Eliot, and Luther Burbank were attracted to the movement by growing concern over immigration and fear of "race suicide." The American Eugenics Society, founded in 1923, quickly organized committees in twenty-eight states. The movement succeeded in spreading the concept that mental ability was strictly an inherited trait, and it obtained passage in several states of laws permitting sterilization of the "feebleminded." The eugenics movement was also one element of the diverse coalition that succeeded in enacting laws restricting immigration.[31]

Scientific racism strengthened the popular, vulgar racism of the 1920s, which manifested in race riots, the power of the Ku Klux Klan,

---

63–83, 164–75; George W. Stocking, Jr., *Race, Culture, and Evolution: Essays in the History of Anthropology* (Chicago, 1982), 52–56; Robert F. Berkhofer, Jr., *The White Man's Indian: Images of the American Indian from Columbus to the Present* (New York, 1978), 49–61.

30. Thomas P. Weinland, "A History of the I.Q. in America, 1890–1941" (Ph.D. dissertation, Columbia University, 1970), 73–79, 86–87, 96–99, 125–26, 157–65, 178–81; Daniel J. Kevles, *In the Name of Eugenics: Genetics and the Uses of Human Heredity* (New York, 1985), 80–82.

31. Kevles, *In the Name of Eugenics*, 59–64, 96–112; Weinland, "A History of the I.Q. in America," 98–104.

and immigration restriction. As a consequence, the role of racial factors during the previous half century in explaining Latin American underdevelopment remained prominent. Numerous sources can be cited to demonstrate that the dominant view during the 1920s was that the inferiority of the great bulk of Latin America's population—Indians, Negroes, and mixed races—was a major, lasting obstacle to progress. The half-breed attracted most of the negative comment—Indian and Negro inferiority was widely assumed—and the commonly used aphorism was that he had "the virtues of neither race and the vices of both" or, as stated by historian William L. Schurz, that Latin America was handicapped by "the indiscipline of the mixed breed."[32] In one of his books on Mexico, Wallace Thompson ridiculed the arguments of some Mexican leaders that they had created "a new race" from the Spanish-Indian mixture. "To us as we watch them," noted Thompson, "the only result of the mixture is the conflict, the weakness and the ineptitude of the half-breed type in every race." Harry A. Franck commented on the racial mixtures in Brazil, which many Brazilians believed were producing "a new type of humanity." He argued that "the results are not so promising; it looks less as if Brazil were solving the color question than as if color were dissolving Brazil." Traveling north into Venezuela, Franck observed that the population of Ciudad Bolívar resembled that of most Spanish-American cities: "few pure whites and fewer full Indians, but every possible mixture of the two, with a goodly dash of African blood thrown in to complete the catastrophe." A series of prominently displayed "Letters to the Editor" of the New York *Times* in 1926 also expressed this theme. The opening letter from Luis de Mendoza of Boston argued that climate was much less responsible for Latin America's problems than the racial hybrid who "is an active factor in all these countries, but a calamitous hindrance of their progress."[33]

Intelligence testing, whose explosive popularity in the 1920s is evidenced by an early 1930s, 251-page bibliographic listing of research on testing, was widely purported to provide proof of the inferiority of mixed races and of Mexicans, both subjects of extensive testing by schools in California and the Southwest. Two books published in 1930 summarized much of the work done through testing, and both concluded that the results of race mixing were generally unfavorable.

32. William L. Schurz, "One-Man Rule in Latin America," *Current History,* XXX (July, 1929), 604.

33. Wallace Thompson, *The Mexican Mind: A Study of National Psychology* (Boston, 1922), 44–45; Franck, *Working North from Patagonia,* 210, 611; New York *Times,* October 17, 1926, Sec. 8, p. 16.

Charles B. Davenport, in *Human Biology and Racial Welfare,* cited studies to show that mental traits as well as physical traits were inherited in race crosses. From his summary of the studies on race crossing he concluded: "In the absence of any uniform rule as to the consequences of race crossing and in view of the disharmony shown by many hybrids it is well to discourage hybridization between extreme types. . . ." In *The Biological Basis of Human Nature,* Herbert S. Jennings, a member of the eugenics priesthood and a colleague of Davenport at Johns Hopkins University, concluded with scholarly restraint that "a nation composed of races in process of mixture will not be among those happy peoples whose annals are vacant." The relevance of intelligence testing to the evaluation of Latin American societies was established most clearly by Edward Alsworth Ross, a respected sociologist, prolific writer, and adherent of the eugenics movement, who noted that if intelligence tests measure native ability, "we must not expect as much of the Mexican people, even after they have had a fair chance, as we may expect of (say) the Scotch or the Czecho-Slovaks." Ross then cited the results of IQ tests administered in California public schools showing the relatively low ranking of Mexican children. From this information he concluded: "If the red or Indian race is not the intellectual peer of the yellow race or the white race, and if from 75 to 85 per cent of the human germ plasm in Mexico is charged with determiners of the traits of the Indian race, then no amount of education and no release of stimulating ozone into the social atmosphere will avail to close quite the gap between Mexico and the onward countries."[34]

During the last half of the decade, debate—much enlivened by reports of IQ test results—surrounding Mexican immigration offered further testimony of the significance attached to race as a factor in Latin American development. Following passage of the National Origins Act in 1924, which excluded East Asians and sharply reduced southern and eastern European immigration through a national quota system, there were serious attempts to impose quotas on immigration from Mexico and other Latin American nations. Those who favored such quotas grounded their arguments on the alleged racial inferiority of Mexicans and fear of mongrelization of the American racial stock. Even the scholarly Frank Tannenbaum pandered to racist

---

34. Kenji Hakuta, *Mirror of a Language: The Debate on Bilingualism* (New York, 1986), 20; Charles B. Davenport, "The Mingling of Races," in *Human Biology and Racial Welfare,* ed. Edmund V. Cowdry (New York, 1930), 565; Herbert S. Jennings, *The Biological Basis of Human Nature* (New York, 1930), 288; Edward Alsworth Ross, *The Social Revolution in Mexico* (New York, 1923), 10, 13.

sentiment when he urged the government to cease working to undermine the Calles regime in Mexico, arguing that if revolution broke out again, the U.S. would intervene and intervention would mean annexation. "Annexation, in its turn," he cautioned, "would mean adding twelve million Indians to some twelve million negroes." An article in *Current History* pointed out the "anomaly of leaving our southern border wide open while we are trying to preserve our 'American stock' by the national origins plan." The author warned that the large numbers of Mexicans pouring into the Southwest were a detriment to the "schools, churches, community life and political and racial characteristics of the native American people of those regions." Articles in the popular press conjured up an alarming spectacle of Mexicans flooding across the border who were characterized as "the riffraff of the Mexican race" and as "chronic beggars . . . sizzling with disease."[35]

In 1928 Representative John C. Box of Texas, ranking Democrat on the House Committee on Immigration and Naturalization, who had been won over earlier in the decade to the eugenic point of view, introduced a bill to restrict Mexican immigration through quotas. The Harris bill, its counterpart in the Senate, passed, but the Box bill, though debated on and off for three years, failed. In advocacy of his bill, Box spoke as follows before a national immigration conference:

Another purpose of the immigration laws is the protection of American racial stock from further degradation or change through mongrelization. The Mexican peon is a mixture of Mediterranean-blooded Spanish peasant with low-grade Indians who did not fight to extinction but submitted and multiplied as serfs. Into that was fused much negro slave blood. This blend of low-grade Spaniard, peonized Indian, and negro slave mixed with negroes, mulattoes, and other mongrels, and some sorry whites, already here. The prevention of such mongrelization and the degradation it causes is one of the purposes of our laws which the admission of these people will tend to defeat.[36]

Several factors contributed to the defeat of the Box bill, including the reduced influx from Mexico in 1930 as a result of the onset of depression, the expectation that more-settled conditions in Mexico would further reduce the influx, and the perception that Southern support-

35. Frank Tannenbaum, "Mexico's Internal Politics and American Diplomacy," *Annals of the American Academy of Political and Social Science*, XXXII (1927), 175; Remsen Crawford, "The Menace of Mexican Immigration," *Current History*, XXXI (February, 1930), 902, 904; Kenneth L. Roberts, "Wet and Other Mexicans," *Saturday Evening Post*, February 4, 1928, p. 11.

36. Kevles, *In the Name of Eugenics*, 103; John C. Box, "Speech at Memorial Continental Hall," Washington, D.C., January 19, 1928, reprinted in *Congressional Record*, House, 70th Cong., 1st Sess., Vol. LXIX, Pt. 3, pp. 2817–18.

ers of the bill were selfishly motivated by desire to reduce the Southwest's ability to compete in cotton production.

One view of the relation between race and Latin American development, which had received little attention before the 1920s, was that the question was not so much one of inferior versus superior types but rather that progress in racially mixed societies was inhibited by the absence of racial, cultural, and national unity. For example, Senator Guy D. Goff, in a speech assessing Latin American problems, touched upon this concept when he noted that racially mixed groups, which he described as inferior in character and ability, were "a racial anomaly within the nation, but not of it." One of the major conclusions of the popular book *Mexico and Its Heritage* by Ernest Gruening was that "the blundering clash between racial cultures, and their lack of mutual adjustment, rather than the character of either have spelled failure."[37]

In a period as race-conscious as the 1920s, the popularity of the racial interpretation of Latin American problems is to be expected, but the growing resistance to that view is somewhat surprising. Commentators who argued that the Latin American racial profile was not a decisive factor in the region's halting progress represented a minority view that would, however, gain greater acceptance in the subsequent period. The countercurrent against scientific racism was led by the Franz Boas school of cultural anthropologists, by psychological testers unconvinced of the immutability of intelligence as measured by IQ tests, and by assorted laymen and scholars such as Walter Lippmann and John Dewey. The concept most efficacious in undermining scientific racism was cultural pluralism, whose elaboration was primarily the responsibility of Franz Boas, founder of cultural anthropology in the U.S. Boas and his students came to dominate American anthropology during the 1920s, and along with that dominance came the anthropological concept of culture and the explanation of human diversity on the basis of culture instead of race. Commentators on Latin America lagged in analyzing the region from the perspective of cultural pluralism, but now and then such an analysis was offered. For example, Professor Priestley argued that the racial hypothesis "neglects the factors of social environment which are as potent as heredity. Modern scientific thought rejects the theory of inherent inferiority of mixed races." Psychologists, though influenced by the cultural perspective, focused their attention during the 1920s

37. Remarks of Guy D. Goff, *Congressional Record*, Senate, 69th Cong., 1st Sess., Vol. LXVII, Pt. 1, p. 629; Ernest Gruening, *Mexico and Its Heritage* (New York, 1928), 86.

on a critique of the methodology and assumptions of intelligence testing, thus weakening the single most important buttress for scientific racism in the period. By the end of the decade the challenge to scientific racism by the academic social science community was strong,
although public opinion was little moved.[38]

In discussions of Latin American problems and proposed solutions,
a striking difference between the 1920s and preceding decades was
that few writers in the twenties proposed the earlier, favored remedy
of large-scale European immigration. Among the handful of writers to
propose it, few made it the centerpiece of discussion, and several mentioned it by way of quoting Latin Americans who favored it.[39] It was
not infrequently pointed out, however, that Argentina's relative progress
owed much to the past half century's heavy influx of European immigrants. It is not clear why the earlier enthusiasm for European immigration faded in the 1920s, but it is possible that the powerful anti-
alien sentiment of the decade, fueled, in part, by increased radical
tendencies among the immigrants, was simply generalized or that the
sorry spectacle of postwar European civilization in disarray diminished support for it.

The third factor widely noted as a cause of Latin American underdevelopment during the preceding half century was inheritance from
the colonial period of numerous fundamental flaws that characterized
the political, social, economic, and cultural makeup of the independent republics. Commentary on this allegedly defective heritage by
scholars, travelers, editorialists, and congressmen continued to per-
meate discussion of Latin America in the 1920s. Acceptance of the
principal tenets of the Black Legend appears not to have diminished
despite a greater depth of knowledge of the region and a higher degree
of participation by scholars and Latin Americans in the discussion.

A measure of the persisting strength of this interpretation is its appearance throughout the pages of Charles E. Chapman's *A History of
the Cuban Republic.* Chapman, professor of history at the University
of California, argued in the preface, "There is a handicap of evil political traditions that the Cuban, like other Hispanic Americans is
obliged to overcome," and Chapman liberally sprinkled the words

38. Gossett, *Race,* 409–27; Stocking, *Race, Culture, and Evolution,* 294–307; Herbert I. Priestley, *The Mexican Nation: A History* (New York, 1923), 118; Weinland, "A
History of the I.Q. in America," 184–211, 224; Berkhofer, *The White Man's Indian,*
62–64.

39. Ross, *The Social Revolution in Mexico,* 13; Victor Oscar Freeburg, "'El Dorado'
Rediscovered," *Forum,* LXXIII (April, 1925), 477; Thomas F. Lee, "Venezuela: Impressions of the Country and Its People, Gathered During Recent Months of Travel and Observations," *Mentor,* XIII (November, 1925), 18.

"evil political traditions" throughout the text. Among the unfortunate traditions passed on to Cuba and to all of Spanish America, according to Chapman, were the use of public office for private benefit, political graft and corruption, nepotism, and self-indulgence. Numerous writers emphasized these unsavory political traditions, reflecting, perhaps, America's frustrating experience in attempting to instill stable, democratic practices through its Caribbean and Central American interventions. A State Department official with some responsibility for U.S. policy in the Caribbean complained, "The evil traditions of corruption and favoritism inherited from the colonial regime made it difficult to inculcate respect for law or honesty in administration." Professor Isaac Joslin Cox of Northwestern University urged the U.S. to follow a policy of conciliation toward Mexico, because its heritage "rendered both Creole and Indian more or less irresponsible and seemingly incapable of self-directed progress." Such judgments seemed confirmed when Mexican Minister of Education José Vasconcelos complained in a speech translated and published in an American journal that the Spanish monarchs tried to make the colonies "a benefice for fortune-seeking place-hunters" and that "we still suffer from the blight of three centuries of blind obedience."[40]

Another frequently mentioned facet of this legacy was the alleged blight of Spanish exploitation. As an example, the author of an article on Mexican character wrote, "The rapacious gold-seekers, swashbuckling adventurers who wrenched the land from Montezuma, were not shopkeepers with thrifty slogans of 'a penny saved is a penny earned.' They were sons of Spain's great feudal families who saw life in terms of danger mastered, in riches accumulated without work." A rather different view of the Spanish conquering class, though just as negative, is found in a travel book on Ecuador in which the author asserted that the Indians "were dealing with the very scum of the cruel and ignorant Spain of the sixteenth century." An article by Wallace Thompson described colonial Spanish America as a "world of blood and oppression, of a ruthless search for gold, of exploitation and slavery in mines and plantations. . . . Misery and death stalked the length of all the Americas, and half a million negro slaves were imported from Africa to feed the greed of the oppressors."[41] The same

40. Chapman, *A History of the Cuban Republic*, 29–30, 525, 565, 590; Dana G. Munro, "The Basis of American Intervention in the Caribbean," *Current History*, XXVI (September, 1927), 857; Isaac Joslin Cox, "The Mexican Problem: Self-Help or Intervention?" *Political Science Quarterly*, XXXVI (1921), 227; José Vasconcelos, "Latin America: An Interpretation and a Prophecy," 233.

41. Remarks of Ralph F. Lozier, *Congressional Record*, House, 69th Cong., 2nd Sess.,

theme continued to appear in some U.S. history texts of the period. Perhaps most extreme was the lavishly illustrated history, *America*, by Dutch-born Hendrik Van Loon, who in due course would become a well-known journalist, historian, and illustrator. Van Loon wrote of the "profound and blood-thirsty devotion" and the "ruthless greed for gold" of the conquistadores and asserted that in their treatment of the Indians they "shot and hacked and hung and burned and robbed and lied and cheated and reduced half a dozen interesting experiments in statecraft to agglomerations of mud-hovels and cemeteries." On the other hand, in such popular texts as those by David Saville Muzzey and Charles A. and Mary R. Beard, the Spanish colonizing experience was either entirely omitted or only briefly presented.[42] It can be assumed that standard history texts such as these exercised a powerful influence in confining American public opinion, decade after decade, to its ethnocentric, anti-Hispanic limitations.

One of the most-influential promoters of the Black Legend in the 1920s was the liberal journalist Ernest Gruening, who interpreted Mexico, the Mexican Revolution, and the revolutionary goals of land reform and uplift of the Indian masses with much sympathy in his many articles and his widely read book, *Mexico and Its Heritage* (1928). In it Gruening touched every base in his assault on the Spanish heritage. After cataloguing in detail the evils acquired from Spain, the "corruption, ignorance, fanaticism, intercaste hatred," and many more, he contemplated Mexico's prospects for the future: "The largest 'if' which includes all others is the likelihood of Mexico's freeing itself from its heritage: To what degree can Mexico get rid of the legacies of political and social ill health?"[43]

Gruening was one of several observers in the 1920s who upheld the traditional emphasis on the nearly insuperable handicaps of the Catholic heritage—a three-hundred-year period of "absentee absolutism resting on military and religious domination." Laurence Duggan, who would enter the State Department as a career officer in 1930 and rapidly advance to become chief of the Latin American Division by mid-decade, wrote of his dismay, after visiting Peru, over the plight of the Indians,

Vol. LXVIII, Pt. 3, p. 2972; Eva A. Frank, "The Mexican 'Just Won't Work,'" *Nation*, CXXV (August 17, 1927), 156; Blair Niles, *Casual Wanderings in Ecuador* (New York, 1923), 56; Wallace Thompson, "The Rediscovery of Latin America," *Advertising and Selling*, XIII (October 2, 1929), 36.

42. Hendrik Van Loon, *America* (New York, 1927), 46, 51; David Saville Muzzey, *The American Adventure* (New York, 1922); Charles A. Beard and Mary R. Beard, *The Rise of American Civilization* (New York, 1927).

43. Gruening, *Mexico and Its Heritage*, 27, 657.

blaming their condition on the state and the church. "The Church came out with the Spaniards," he noted, "and like them, gouged the Indians to the last penny." Professor Ross, in a study of the impact of the revolution on Mexican society, wrote in sorrow: "Ever and anon as you go about, you reflect what a paradise this Mexico might be if it possessed the moral character and the social institutions of the descendants of the Puritans."[44] Though anti-Catholic observations were not uncommon during the decade, they were no longer standard fare, and they lacked the animus of earlier commentary.

Often intermingled with these accounts of Latin America's crippling heritage were vivid descriptions of its people as woefully defective in character. As in earlier periods, much of the commentary in the 1920s was merely descriptive, highly generalized, and lacking subtlety, and it often failed to distinguish among nations, racial groups, or classes. Informed scholars as well as those unfamiliar with Latin America freely extended the list of character defects. Americans persisted in regarding Latin Americans as childish, indolent, fatalistic, and "too proud to learn from others." Such attitudes were characteristic even of those observers who otherwise understood Latin American problems, such as Felix Frankfurter, who regarded Latin Americans as "non-adult peoples"; an editorialist for the *Northwestern Christian Advocate*, who described Mexico as "a temperamental child in the family of nations"; or scholar and diplomat Chester Lloyd Jones, who wrote that the Mexican native shows "in the work that he undertakes, an immaturity of character comparable to that of a child." A traveler familiar with South America noted that Brazilian character consisted of "Latin sensibility tinged with the African traits of superstition, fatalism, slovenliness, indiscipline, a certain happy-go-lucky cheerfulness, and an almost total lack of initiative; and to these the country owes most of its social and economic afflictions."[45] The latter statement cogently summarizes the significance of this persistent, negative depiction of the Latin American: progress seemed

44. *Ibid.*, 27; Department of State, Records Relating to Internal Affairs of Peru, 1910–1929, "General Conditions," Laurence Duggan, La Paz, Bolivia, July 28, 1929, to Stephen P. Duggan, Director, Institute of International Education, as enclosure in Stephen P. Duggan, New York, October 10, 1929, to Secretary of State Henry L. Stimson; Ross, *The Social Revolution in Mexico*, 7.

45. Remarks of George P. McLean, *Congressional Record*, Senate, 69th Cong., 2nd Sess., Vol. LXVIII, Pt. 2, p. 2227; Felix Frankfurter, "Haiti and Intervention," *New Republic*, XXV (December 15, 1920), 72; *Northwestern Christian Advocate* (Chicago), January 20, 1927, as cited in remarks of Lynn J. Frazier, *Congressional Record*, Senate, 69th Cong., 2nd Sess., Vol. LXVIII, Pt. 5, p. 5528; Jones, *Mexico and Its Reconstruction*, 108–109; Franck, *Working North from Patagonia*, 215.

beyond hope in societies whose citizens were so lacking in virtue.

Discussion of Latin America's perceived shortcomings generally remained descriptive, but to the extent that solutions were proffered they were of a technical nature focusing on such things as sanitation, scientific farming, road building, balanced budgets, and better-drawn laws and constitutions. A reporter who accompanied President-elect Hoover on his South American tour saw the solution to South America's "delayed development" as "an engineering job." Confidence was high in the ability of American technology to work wondrous material transformations, particularly in tropical areas. Proclaimed one writer, "It has been proved that drainage—and practically drainage alone—is all that is required for making the Tropics really healthy and habitable," and he proceeded to discuss prospects for draining the Amazon Basin![46] Efforts begun in 1913 by the Rockefeller Foundation to improve sanitation and health conditions in Latin America and to reduce the incidence of hookworm disease and yellow fever continued into the 1920s, when they were supplemented with campaigns against malaria and in favor of improved medical education. Increasing numbers of foreign technical experts had arrived in Latin America from the 1890s through the 1920s, by which time all but two countries, Argentina and Brazil, had hosted U.S. financial consultants. The most noted of the many U.S. technical advisers to provide his expertise in the 1920s was Princeton University economist Edwin Walter Kemmerer. Between 1923 and the early 1930s Kemmerer accepted invitations from the five Andean republics to head economic missions to each of them. The missions were instrumental in moving those nations toward central banking systems, adherence to the gold standard, more-"scientific" tax systems, and more-realistic budget procedures. In keeping with the laissez-faire atmosphere of the period, these agents of technological diffusion were private individuals whose activities were encouraged but not controlled by the U.S. government.[47]

The Kemmerer missions were quite successful in meeting their modernizing goals because in most cases the host governments were committed to reform, a general consensus on solutions already existed, and Kemmerer arrived with the renown of a foreign expert who was held to be a politically neutral, "scientific" economist. He

46. Will Irwin, "South America Awakes," *Nation's Business*, XVII (May, 1929), 27; Don Augustin Edwards, "Spanish America's Future," *Living Age*, CCCV (June 19, 1920), 705.

47. Raymond B. Fosdick, *The Story of the Rockefeller Foundation* (1952; rpr. New Brunswick, N.J., 1989), 33, 48, 59–61, 114; Paul W. Drake, *The Money Doctor in the Andes: The Kemmerer Missions, 1923–1933* (Durham, N.C., 1989), 19, 25.

was warmly welcomed as a messiah bringing a level of technical competence and integrity considered by his hosts to be available only from abroad.[48] The self-denigration so common at the turn of the century was also expressed in editorials and speeches welcoming Kemmerer. A Chilean economist noted in 1925 that the causes of Chile's defective monetary system were known but a solution could not be reached without the services of Kemmerer because of "parliamentary chaos." An editorial from a 1930 Colombian newspaper urging the return of Kemmerer noted, "We are incapable of increasing the value of our riches and of completing the most important public works. We do not understand finances, nor can we reach agreement on anything, nor can we succeed in economizing or putting order in our businesses."[49] The disparaging attitudes held by large numbers of Americans toward Latin Americans found frequent endorsement south of the border through the 1920s.

As noted in the previous chapter, the passion of the Progressive Era to Americanize Latin America, that is, to promote the wholesale transfer of U.S. institutions, ideals, and values, notably flagged in the postwar years, and that absence of zeal for Americanization persisted throughout the 1920s. There was, for example, virtually no mention of the possibility that Mexico would become an English-speaking nation in the foreseeable future. Some enthusiasm still attached to educational solutions for Latin America's problems, but even here skepticism predominated. A member of a U.S. educational mission sent to Peru in 1920 to establish a public school system following the U.S. model was extremely disheartened three years later by the disappointing results and complained, "It will be many years before Peru will have any real conception of the value of an efficient public school system along American lines."[50] In their examination of Latin America's agrarian question, however, some observers advocated a land tenure system based on the idealized American family-farm model. Commentary on the agrarian question, which had aroused only slight interest before the 1920s, was stimulated by Mexico's postrevolutionary effort to implement a land reform program. Some of the best

48. Drake, *The Money Doctor*, 90–91, 139, 251.

49. *Ibid.*, 87; *El Tiempo* (Bogotá), September 29, 1930, as cited *ibid.*, 68. Expressions of Colombia's racial inferiority and "spiritual infirmity" by major figures in the Liberal and Conservative parties were not uncommon in the 1920s. See James D. Henderson, *Conservative Thought in Twentieth Century Latin America: The Ideas of Laureano Gómez* (Athens, Ohio, 1988), 66–67; note 23, pp. 178–79.

50. "Reorganizing Peru's Schools," *School and Society*, XVII (February 3, 1923), 118; see also Guillermo A. Sherwell, "The Soul of Mexico," *Bulletin of the Pan American Union*, LIII (September, 1921), 239.

historical studies on Latin America published during the decade focused on land reform, and Mexico received most of the attention. These studies emphasized the deadening impact of latifundia, and they placed great hope in an agrarian reform program that held out the prospect of transforming Mexico "from a nation of serfs to one of small independent landholders."[51]

During the century's first two decades an unemphasized assumption existed that foreign capital had an important role to play in solving Latin America's problems. That assumption gained strength in the 1920s as many Latin American leaders lobbied for loans, investments, and business participation from the United States. Economists, businessmen, and nonspecialists agreed that the region required foreign capital for the kinds of projects essential for economic progress, such as railroad construction and mining development. Important voices in government—especially in the Department of Commerce—in trade associations, and the investment community also urged a favorable response to Latin America's requests for capital. The importance assigned to foreign capital's role in the region's development increased significantly as fear of European economic domination faded and U.S. capital moved toward ascendancy. Implicit in much of the commentary centering on this issue was the understanding that economic development in the region meant production of primary goods from mine, field, and forest; a few observers forthrightly stated the impossibility of development based upon manufacturing.[52]

As previously noted, some commentators during the Progressive Era dissented from this very positive view of the role of foreign capital in Latin American development, and the dissenters included figures prominent in the Progressive movement who attacked the evils of capitalist exploitation both within the U.S. and abroad. Dissent became more pronounced as foreign investment increased. Some of the accounts favorable to the objectives of the Mexican Revolution published in the 1920s included highly critical analyses of the role of foreign capital during the prerevolutionary period, and these analyses were more soundly based and objectively presented than were the

51. Gruening, *Mexico and Its Heritage*, 663; see also George McCutchen McBride, *The Land System of Mexico* (New York, 1923), 174; Frank Tannenbaum, *The Mexican Agrarian Revolution* (New York, 1929), 86–87, 130.

52. Seidel, "Progressive Pan Americanism," 649–50; Jones, *South America*, 719; Jacob Warshaw, *The New Latin America* (New York, 1922), 71; Francis R. Hard, "Changes in Our Relations with Spanish-America During the Last Quarter Century," *Harvard Business Review*, VI (1928), 389; Samuel Crowther, "Central America," *Saturday Evening Post*, November 5, 1927, pp. 22–23; New York *Times*, April 24, 1922, p. 14.

diatribes of the muckrakers in the previous period. For example, Professor Priestley asserted, "The foreigner built railroads, opened mines and farms, but he took his money away, and only a small residue went to benefit the Mexican nation in taxes and higher wages." In her study of foreign investment in Bolivia's tin mining industry, Margaret Alexander Marsh argued convincingly that the industry, owned and operated largely by foreigners, had brought Bolivia little benefit when compared to the riches taken out of the country. In addition to ultimately depleting the mineral deposits and leaving the dependent communities as "empty shells," the industry provided no lasting benefit because "no manufacturing or other industries grow up alongside the mining industry." Melvin M. Knight's *The Americans in Santo Domingo,* a book in the same series as Marsh's—*Studies in American Imperialism*—was more dogmatic and less persuasive than the Marsh study. Knight railed against the "Yankee peril," by which he meant the growth and spread of large-scale commercial agriculture in the West Indies for the production of such crops as sugar for the U.S. market. Americanization of West Indian agriculture has often been "a disaster for the natives," Knight claimed. "It leads to a few commercial crops, large holdings, a general landlessness of the native population, and economic vassalage."[53] This radical critique, which fixed prime responsibility for developmental problems on foreign capitalist exploitation, followed the tradition of earlier, leftist commentary on the Mexican Revolution, and it offered an approach to the analysis of economic development that would claim many disciples in future years.

Detailed consideration in the 1920s of such topics as land reform and foreign investment suggests that the highly generalized views of the past were yielding to specialization and to more-complex analysis. Attitudes toward the region exhibited a greater diversity than had ever previously existed. Besides the more-serious efforts made to understand Latin American problems, there was evidence of growing toleration of cultural diversity and recognition that traditional views were terribly condescending. Occasionally, countries such as Argentina and Costa Rica were distinguished from a categorically backward Latin America. These somewhat more sophisticated perspectives were the result of growing contact, more-frequent presentation of the Latin American viewpoint, and advances at the academic level. By 1930 a small but growing corps of regional specialists had emerged, and many of these experts actively worked to inform public opinion. Sympathetic analyses of the goals of the Mexican Revolution, empathy for

53. Priestley, *The Mexican Nation,* xv; Marsh, *The Bankers in Bolivia,* 54, 64–65, 135; Melvin M. Knight, *The Americans in Santo Domingo* (New York, 1928), 173.

Mexico's Indianness by members of the counterculture, and a radical critique of foreign investment and U.S. intervention in Latin America offer further evidence of discontinuity from earlier perspectives. In this context, the desire during the previous period to solve the problems of Latin America through a process of Americanization seemed quite out of place, not only because these specialized studies revealed complex societies with unique historical traditions, but also because many commentators 1) had come to accept the concept of cultural pluralism, 2) lacked the reformist, crusading urge of the Progressive Era, and 3) doubted that American society in the 1920s represented the acme of human achievement.

U.S. policy toward Latin America in the 1920s, which was in no sense isolationist, was better informed than at any time in the past, and it gradually evolved to form a basis for the Good Neighbor policy of the 1930s. Change came in response to the shifting perception of Latin America, vigorous public debate, diminished justification for intervention, and insistent reports of Latin American "Yankeephobia."[54] It would not be unfair to conclude, however, that by 1930 the American public remained largely ignorant of Latin America and uninterested in the region despite the noted improvements in the quality and flow of information. Confidence was high in the ability of American science, technology, and capital to transform Latin America's still greatly exaggerated potential wealth into real wealth. That transformation was generally welcomed by Latin American elites, many of whom justified their requests for technical assistance with a genuine self-disparagement that tended to strengthen traditional American perceptions. Despite a growing appreciation of the role of disease and the region's severe geographic handicaps in limiting development, and despite mounting challenges to the interpretation of Latin American underdevelopment based on climate, race, and cultural legacy, those three factors remained dominant.

---

54. J. Fred Rippy, "Literary Yankeephobia in Latin America," *Journal of International Relations*, XII (1922), 350–71, 524–38; W. E. Dunn, "The Postwar Attitude of Hispanic America Toward the United States," *Hispanic American Historical Review*, III (1920), 177–83; New York *Times*, May 13, 1921.

5

Semblance of a Changing Perspective, 1930–1945

Two events helped define United States relations with Latin America in the 1930–1945 period and contributed to major changes in U.S. policy—the Great Depression and the Second World War. The obvious economic failings associated with depression in the U.S. tended to soften the previously strident criticism of Latin America. In reaction to the economic devastation the country experienced during the 1930s, many writers searched for a collectivist societal model to replace a failed individualism; some claimed to find it in the Soviet Union and others in the idealized Mexican village. In addition, a craze for things Latin American swept the country midway through the period, and the wartime mandate for official friendship further restrained the customary faultfinding. Such favorable developments facilitated the emergence of a new official policy toward the region, the Good Neighbor policy, which brought unprecedented attention to Latin America and helped fashion a more cooperative hemispheric relationship. Depression also added a new dimension, economic analysis, to the discussion of developmental problems. For a brief time the period also witnessed elevation of the Latin American development issue to the level of official concern. These years were additionally distinguished by the opening of debate over whether Latin America should embark on a program of industrialization. But beneath the patina of the official Good Neighbor policy and the period's apparently enlightened outlook, climate, race, and culture continued as the prime explanations for the region's underdevelopment even while commentators showed growing appreciation of the complexity of the issue, raised new questions about Latin America's resource base, and challenged the validity of those traditional explanations.

During the first half of this period, depression undermined the established pattern of commercial and financial relations between the U.S. and Latin America, sharply altering the political landscape in the region and causing the traditional interpretation of its developmental problems to be amended. Since the late-nineteenth century, the stimulus of expanding markets in the U.S. and the industrializing countries of Europe had steadily moved Latin America toward an economic system based on producing for export raw materials such as bananas, coffee, sugar, and minerals in exchange for imported manufactured goods. As this trade pattern developed, U.S.–Latin American economic ties became close, particularly during World War I and in the following decade. By 1929, 20 percent of Latin American exports went to the U.S., and a third of all U.S. exports went to Latin America, where the U.S. also placed one-third of its foreign investment. The worldwide economic collapse of the early 1930s eliminated those overseas markets for Latin American goods and devastated the countries' economies. The total value of the region's exports for 1930–1934 fell by nearly half of what it had been for the previous five-year period, and domestic economic development, whether based on foreign exchange earned from exports or on foreign investment, practically ceased. During the early months of depression the Latin American nations, with few exceptions, defaulted or declared moratoriums on their debts.[1]

This economic devastation inevitably brought political turmoil in its wake. From 1930 to 1933 half of the Latin American republics suffered violent changes in government. Some countries endured an extended period of anarchy, as in the cases of Ecuador, Chile, and Cuba, while others witnessed sudden coups, as in Peru and El Salvador. Mexico weathered a constitutional crisis, and other regimes warded off armed challenges only through vigorous countermeasures. One frequent result of this turmoil was the appearance of more-authoritarian regimes. The transition of the early 1930s saw the emergence of strongmen such as Getúlio Vargas in Brazil, Rafael Trujillo in the Dominican Republic, and Jorge Ubico in Guatemala. Latin America in the 1930s was not only more authoritarian but also more nationalistic. This impulse toward nationalism resulted partly from vulnerability to external economic forces, which was exposed by the depression and detailed by debate on problems related to bond defaults, tariffs, and taxes.[2]

The task of adjusting U.S. policy to the disruptive effects of economic crisis and political turmoil fell to Herbert Hoover who, during his goodwill tour of Latin America as president-elect and in several speeches, had shown a predisposition to move in new directions.

1. Thomas E. Skidmore and Peter H. Smith, *Modern Latin America* (New York, 1984), 56, 331; Irwin F. Gellman, *Good Neighbor Diplomacy: United States Policies in Latin America, 1933–1945* (Baltimore, 1979), 7; DeConde, *Hoover's Latin-American Policy*, 66.

2. David Green, *The Containment of Latin America: A History of the Myths and Realities of the Good Neighbor Policy* (Chicago, 1971), 10–12; Skidmore and Smith, *Modern Latin America*, 56–57, 331.

"Unemployment" in Latin America

" 'Unemployment' in Latin America"
San Francisco *Chronicle*, September 13, 1930. © San Francisco *Chronicle*.
Reprinted by permission.

His inclination toward a less openly domineering role for the U.S. was strengthened by Latin America's growing stability during the 1920s, a much-reduced fear of European intervention, and the realization that U.S. intervention was expensive, troublesome, and unlikely to promote democracy. Although Hoover's Latin American policy was overshadowed by the depression and by dramatic events in Europe and Asia during the last half of his single-term presidency, he gave careful attention to the region and moved toward a policy of nonintervention. This substantive change led to abrogation of the Roosevelt Corollary and laid the groundwork for the Good Neighbor policy. The Hoover administration limited the "right" of intervention that the U.S. had upheld at the 1928 Pan American Conference, and, with the exception of Central America, his administration ceased withholding recognition from governments that came to power by unconstitutional means. The nonrecognition policy had its origins in the Central American Conference of 1907, and, though fitfully applied, it was often used as an interventionist tool. In addition, the Hoover administration refrained from interventions in situations that in the past would have been seen as offering ample justification for such action, as for example during revolutionary disturbances in Panama in 1931 and Cuba in 1931–1932, where treaty rights for intervention existed. Most noteworthy of a shift in policy was Hoover's completing the withdrawal of marines from Nicaragua in early 1933 and beginning the withdrawal process in Haiti.[3]

This record of positive achievement was partly nullified by a feverish effort at the beginning of the depression to find economic security in traditional Republican high tariff policy. The climax of the 1920s' protectionist trend came in 1930 when Hoover signed into law the high tariff schedules of the Hawley-Smoot Tariff Act, whose enactment evoked tariff retaliation from Latin America, thus further restricting trade and crippling the means to service debt. The Revenue Act of 1932 elevated additional barriers against Latin American products such as copper, petroleum, and sugar. Expansion of trade and access to Latin American markets, key policy objectives since the late-nineteenth century, were thus sacrificed to economic nationalism.[4]

Franklin D. Roosevelt has received generous credit for fundamen-

3. Bryce Wood, *The Making of the Good Neighbor Policy* (New York, 1961), 6–7; DeConde, *Hoover's Latin-American Policy,* 46–50, 53, 60–70, 83–89, 105–107; Gellman, *Good Neighbor Diplomacy,* 5–9; Martin L. Fausold, *The Presidency of Herbert C. Hoover* (Lawrence, Kans., 1985), 183–86; Charles L. Stansifer, "Application of the Tobar Doctrine to Central America," *The Americas,* XXIII (1967), 252–69.

4. Gellman, *Good Neighbor Diplomacy,* 7–8; DeConde, *Hoover's Latin-American Policy,* 75–77; Gil, *Latin American–U.S. Relations,* 155 and note 38 on pp. 305–306.

tally altering U.S. policy toward Latin America as architect of the Good Neighbor policy during his presidency, 1933–1945. Under the Good Neighbor, a policy built on Hoover's initiatives but with greater sweep, coherence, and public appeal, U.S. consciousness of Latin America—not just of one or two "problem" countries—and interest in things Latin American easily surpassed previous levels. The new policy and interest were a result not only of Roosevelt's predilections, his sense of timing, and the primacy of skilled, knowledgeable advisors, but also of superb public relations. At a time when Europe and Asia were largely excluded from the sphere of active U.S. diplomacy, Roosevelt recognized in Latin America an area offering opportunities for an international role for his country. And the benign actions implied by good neighborliness seemed not to violate the isolationist spirit of the times.[5]

Roosevelt early indicated support for nonintervention, and his administration gave formal expression to that position at the 1933 Pan American Conference in Montevideo. That commitment was enlarged at the succeeding conference of 1936 at Buenos Aires, which Roosevelt attended. Nonintervention was sorely tested by prolonged disorder in Cuba in 1933, during which the U.S. intervened in every sense but the military. Shortly after a stable regime gained power in 1934, the U.S. signed a treaty abrogating the Platt Amendment, which had provided the legal umbrella for intervention since 1902. In Haiti Roosevelt honored arrangements made by his predecessor for "Haitianization" of the administration and completed the withdrawal of marines in 1934, although control of customs was retained until 1941. With Panama the U.S. in 1936 negotiated a new treaty to replace the 1903 treaty and therein renounced the right of intervention. The U.S. retained rights of customs receivership in the Dominican Republic and Nicaragua throughout the decade but relinquished them in the 1940s. Early in its first term the Roosevelt administration extended to Central America traditional recognition practices already implemented by Hoover for the rest of Latin America. By the time of his second inauguration, Roosevelt had removed the most prickly irritants in relations with Latin America.[6]

Protectionism in the U.S. was more than an irritant in hemispheric relations, consequently commercial expansion became an early Good Neighbor goal. Roosevelt had committed the Democratic party to tar-

---

5. Wood, *Making of the Good Neighbor Policy*, 118–35; Green, *Containment of Latin America*, 13; Gellman, *Good Neighbor Diplomacy*, 9, 17.

6. Gil, *Latin American–U.S. Relations*, 155–64; Wood, *Making of the Good Neighbor Policy*, 6–7.

iff reduction during his 1932 campaign—though he later equivocated—and Secretary of State Cordell Hull was an ardent champion of free trade. But conflicting economic pressures led Roosevelt's enthusiasm to wane, and instead of pursuing unilateral tariff reductions or multilateral trade negotiations he chose a bilateral approach that was authorized in the 1934 Reciprocal Trade Agreements Act, whose most-favored-nation provisions would have great impact on U.S.–Latin American trade after World War II. Throughout his tenure as secretary of state, 1933–1944, Hull enthusiastically pursued bilateral trade agreements, and by 1940 he had negotiated agreements with eleven Latin American nations. But the obstacles in the way of worldwide trade expansion were formidable. The British system of commonwealth preference, German barter arrangements, and the Japanese economic sphere of influence in the Far East all limited trade expansion. Also, the competitive nature of some U.S. and Latin American exports such as beef and grain made trade expansion with such countries as Argentina and Uruguay quite impractical. All in all, U.S.–Latin American trade showed only modest gains during the 1930s, although the approach and outbreak of war in Europe caused Latin America to shift from European to U.S. markets at the end of the decade.[7]

The most-severe test of the Good Neighbor during the 1930s centered on an oil controversy with Mexico.[8] U.S.-Mexican relations had frequently been put to the test since the beginning of the Mexican Revolution, and during the 1930s the U.S. struggled to maintain restraint in the face of pressure from U.S. Catholics for action on behalf of oppressed coreligionists in Mexico and U.S. property owners whose lands were being expropriated as part of an agrarian reform program. The U.S. was ill-prepared, however, for the sudden expropriation and nationalization of foreign oil holdings in 1938. Faced with conflicting counsel, Roosevelt acknowledged the legality of the action if accompanied by appropriate compensation, and he urged a negotiated settlement. The dispute dragged on, but a rupture in the previously unified position of the oil companies and the Roosevelt administration, together with the imminence of Western Hemispheric involvement in the world conflict, led Mexico and the U.S. to an agreement late in 1941, which settled terms for compensation but left the parties far apart on the nationalization issue.[9]

7. Gellman, *Good Neighbor Diplomacy*, 24, 28, 40, 47–49, 57–58, 73; William E. Leuchtenburg, *Franklin D. Roosevelt and the New Deal, 1932–1940* (New York, 1963), 10.
8. There was also a serious oil controversy with Bolivia that began in 1937. See Gellman, *Good Neighbor Diplomacy*, 49–55; Gil, *Latin American–U.S. Relations*, 164–65.
9. Cline, *The United States and Mexico*, 229–50; Clayton R. Koppes, "The Good

Successful resolution of these controversies occurred within the context of rapid progress toward creation of a highly active, multi-leveled Pan American structure. The series of Pan American meetings held between the 1933 session in Montevideo and the foreign ministers' meeting in Rio de Janeiro shortly after the Japanese attack on Pearl Harbor steadily moved the Pan American nations toward an unprecedented level of cooperation. The understandings achieved through the varied avenues of consultation established at the Buenos Aires Conference of 1936 and thereafter, proved essential in working out such complex problems as military security, production and shipment of strategic goods, and control of enemy propaganda.[10]

In addition to strengthening U.S.–Latin American relations, the Second World War also altered the course of Latin American development. Early in Roosevelt's second term the U.S. began to respond to the region's desire, quickened by depression, for diversified economic development. Interest within the U.S. in a direct role in shaping the developmental process derived from fear of the spread of radical philosophies to the hemisphere, whether socialist or fascist, and from experience with threats to private investment from revolutionary nationalism, such as in Cuba in 1933 and Mexico in 1938. The agencies chosen to advance the developmental process included the Export-Import Bank, the Inter-American Development Commission, and a proposed inter-American bank. But several factors hindered progress toward assisting Latin America's industrial development. The administration was divided over the U.S. role, particularly over the issue of public versus private financing of projects in countries with default records and over the question of encouraging foreign industrialization, especially as the New Deal domestic programs were winding down. The Export-Import Bank began issuing small development loans as early as 1938, but concern for the interests of U.S. bankers limited the scope of its activities. The Inter-American Development Commission was not allowed to promote projects that competed with U.S. lines of production, and authorization for an inter-American bank stalled in Congress until the postwar period. By mid-1941 U.S. aid for diversified Latin American development had been put on hold, and entry into the war killed it.

The most conspicuous U.S.-supported development project be-

Neighbor Policy and the Nationalization of Mexican Oil: A Reinterpretation," *Journal of American History*, LXIX (1982), 81.

10. Gil, *Latin American–U.S. Relations*, 168–84; Wood, *Making of the Good Neighbor Policy*, 122–23.

fore funds were curtailed was Brazil's construction of a steel mill at Volta Redonda, ninety miles from Rio de Janeiro. The decision by the Roosevelt administration in 1940 to provide a $20 million loan for the project through the Export-Import Bank came after Brazil's failure to obtain participation from the United States Steel Corporation and in the context of an offer from Germany's Krupp interests to build the mill. Construction lasting from 1941 to 1946 was a joint U.S.-Brazilian endeavor, and Volta Redonda became an important symbol of both hemispheric solidarity during wartime and the launching of Brazilian industrialization.[11]

At the same time the administration was wrestling with the development issue, it began stockpiling strategic goods from the region as a contingency in case of entry into the war and also to deprive the Axis powers access to such goods. During the war the U.S. further increased its purchases of Latin American goods to help fill the gap in international demand left by the closure of European markets. By 1945 the U.S. had gained enormous power over the Latin American economies. By directing them toward the production of critical raw materials, the war returned Latin America to its traditional export-import pattern of dependence. Despite some progress toward export diversification and consumer-goods production, which depression and war had prompted, the principal results of the war economy on Latin America were to inflate its economy, increase dependence on the U.S., and sidetrack industrialization.[12]

War aborted the modest U.S. effort on behalf of Latin American development and confirmed its dependence, but it also evoked a felicitous level of hemispheric cooperation. Solidarity within the hemisphere, with the exception of Argentina, reached an unprecedented scale. But after Pearl Harbor, American attention was fixed on the theaters of war, and Latin America aroused slight public interest despite the comings and goings of U.S. military and civilian personnel involved in speeding up the flow of strategic goods, assuring access to military bases, and countering the activities of Axis agents. The change during the 1930s in official attitude toward Latin America laid the basis for this solidarity, but hemispheric economic ties had advanced to such an extent by the end of 1941 that any war that threatened the U.S. was indeed a common threat.

11. Green, *Containment of Latin America*, 35–37, 44–47, 59–60, 66–67, 73–76, 80–92, 101–107, 111; Gellman, *Good Neighbor Diplomacy*, 156, 162–67; Frank D. McCann, Jr., *The Brazilian-American Alliance, 1937–1945* (Princeton, 1973), 193–99.

12. Dick Steward, *Trade and Hemisphere: The Good Neighbor Policy and Reciprocal Trade* (Columbia, Mo., 1975), 275.

One factor provides striking unity to the 1930–1945 period and distinguishes it from earlier times: the remarkably tolerant, even benevolent, tone in the commentary about Latin America. The heretofore supercilious attitude that had distinguished such commentary was at no time dominant. The change became evident shortly after the onset of depression, and the new tone continued through the end of the war. Change came initially from the humbling experience of depression and from the sense of shared tragedy and failure that accompanied the economic debacle. A 1931 editorial expressed this feeling of humility born of suffering when it noted that after two years of depression Americans "no longer feel their overweening pride of excellence above all other nations." The same sentiment was attributed to Will Rogers who, after jokingly expressing a desire to become ambassador to Mexico, said: "I could attend the dinners and bullfights and make speeches at both, and listen without laughing (much) to the Americans saying 'We got to take this country over and civilize it like ours! Like ours! Ha! Ha!'" The very fact that a humorist would deliver such a line suggests that large numbers of people considered the notion of America's civilizing mission as utterly laughable in the early depression. On the harmony-through-mutual-suffering theme, a contributor to a missionary journal was persuaded that "being united in one great fellowship of pain predisposes the nations forming the Pan-American Union to regard one another in a much friendlier way than they have done for decades past."[13] Writers critical of the American individualistic, capitalist mainstream were most eloquent in proclaiming the demise of Western civilization, and in light of its announced failure they advocated a reassessment of Latin American culture. A study praising Mexico's accomplishments under the regime of Lázaro Cárdenas, 1934–1940, asserted that "the dominant trend of the present era is the destruction of competitive capitalism," and concluded: "Until we are certain that we ourselves have found the right road, it would appear presumptuous to attempt to shape the 'good neighbors' according to our own image." The tolerance toward Latin American revolutions exhibited by the following lines from a 1932 article in *Business Week* would have been most uncommon before 1930: "Yankees have come to see [Latin American revolutions] in their true light in recent years—as the Latin way of changing governments when it seems to the electorate that a change of government is a good thing.

13. New York *Times*, April 26, 1931; Will Rogers as quoted in Henry Grattan Doyle, "Chilean Dictatorship Overthrown," *Current History*, XXXIV (September, 1931), 918; John A. Mackay, "The South American Crisis," *Missionary Review of the World*, LVII (February, 1934), 77.

"This Cock-Eyed World!!"
Washington (N.C.) *Daily News*, November 28, 1936.

In most cases there is comparatively little rough stuff, sometimes less than in a normal election in the non-Latin republics of the world."[14]

The sympathetic attitude toward Latin America that introduced this period evolved during the decade into a fascination for all things Latin American. Tolerance and understanding were induced by the depression, but genuine interest arose from the popular appeal of the Good Neighbor policy and, as war approached, from an awakening sense of the region's strategic importance. A substantial growth in German–Latin American trade during the 1930s, together with energetic espionage and propaganda efforts by the Third Reich, convinced nearly 80 percent of the American public, according to public opinion polls in the late 1930s, that Germany was preparing to establish a foothold in the Western Hemisphere.[15] Article titles such as the following, which appeared frequently during the last half of the 1930s, conveyed a sense of alarm over the inroads into Latin America of radical ideologies and inevitably focused attention on the region: "Next Door to Communism," "Are the Americas Safe?" "Totalitarian Inroads in Latin America," and "The Coming Struggle for Latin America." Lewis Hanke, a rising Latin American historian, caustically observed in *Harper's Magazine* in 1940: "In the face of this [Nazi] menace our people are not idle. Groups of clubwomen tour the southern republics, two symphony orchestras play in the more sophisticated capitals, and a caravan of business men proposes to motor around Central and South America this fall. These and many other moves are designed, one learns, to improve our relations with Latin America and somehow or other help defeat the Nazis there."[16] As Hanke's comments suggest, a growing interest in Latin America produced a notable increase in the number and variety of contacts with the region.

The rapid evolution in attitude from sympathy in the early 1930s to enthusiasm at the end of the decade was evidenced by a popular fancy for Latin American music and dances, fashion designs and decorative motifs, as well as movies with Latin American themes; by a growth in course offerings, cultural exchanges, and tourism; and by an explosion of information. The craze for Latin dance rhythms, for the voice and lusty movements of "the Brazilian bombshell" Carmen Miranda, and for the use of angular Indian design in fashion in

14. Nathaniel and Sylvia Weyl, *The Reconquest of Mexico: The Years of Lázaro Cárdenas* (London, 1939), 380, 384; "Chile's Socialist Shift Is More Than Just Another Revolution," *Business Week*, June 15, 1932, p. 20.

15. Gellman, *Good Neighbor Diplomacy*, 111.

16. Lewis Hanke, "Plain Speaking About Latin America," *Harper's Magazine*, CLXXXI (November, 1940), 588.

the late 1930s and early 1940s suggests the sweep of the fad. Beginning suddenly in 1939 and lasting through the end of the war, Hollywood films used Latin American themes, stars, and locales. In Walt Disney films, the comical antics of Donald Duck and his feathered traveling companion Joe Carioca south of the border delighted children and parents alike. Many Hollywood films showed an unprecedented awareness of the differences among the Latin American nations and displayed an almost reverential attitude toward things Latin American. One student of this phenomenon concluded that Hollywood reversed its "Latin stereotype of the violent, dirty, and lazy South American, and presented a continent with educated classes and indigenous tribes with a valid culture." This striking change was the product of governmental pressure, the desire to capitalize on the popularity of Latin American music, and an attempt to expand sales in the Latin American market to compensate for losses in other foreign markets.

Course offerings on Latin America continued to grow during the 1930s, though not at the fast pace of the previous fifteen years. In 1931 three college textbooks on Latin American history were in wide use, and by the early 1940s eleven texts were available. When Latin American and borderlands specialist Herbert E. Bolton became president of the American Historical Association in 1932, he was able through his formal address entitled "The Epic of Greater America" to publicize his enthusiasm for Latin America's future and his interpretation of the Americas' common history. During Bolton's tenure at the University of California, Berkeley, spanning the 1920s and 1930s, he published a shelf of studies and trained hundreds of graduate students in Latin American history. These all had lasting and widespread influence among Latin American historians, not only on perceptions of the Spanish borderlands but also in acceptance of his thesis that the Americas share a common historical experience. In addition to the field of history, outstanding Latin Americanists made important contributions in geography and anthropology. Parallel with the gradual formation of a corps of Latin American specialists in the academic world, a similar development was occurring in the diplomatic service. Throughout the nineteenth century and into the 1920s, the nation had suffered a spoils-ridden diplomatic corps whose representatives in Latin America were, by and large, inept amateurs. Reorganization of the foreign service in 1924 and subsequent salary improvements led to professionalization and a consequent improvement in reporting from the region. This trend, together with the placement of personnel sympathetic to Latin America in key policy-making positions within the

State Department, had a favorable though indirect impact on shaping public opinion about Latin America.[17]

Throughout this period dozens of cultural exchange programs were sponsored by the Rockefeller and Carnegie foundations and the Pan American Union, and the U.S. government undertook a modest exchange program with Latin America beginning in 1936. Two years later the Department of State formed a Division of Cultural Relations that concentrated on Latin America, and in 1940 the Office of the Coordinator of Inter-American Affairs was established under the directorship of Nelson A. Rockefeller. To his role as advocate and coordinator of cultural diplomacy, Rockefeller brought youthful energy and prior experience in Latin America; aided by his direct ties to the White House and generous funding from Congress, he proved effective in combating Nazi penetration of the hemisphere and in promoting Pan American solidarity by improving dissemination of information through the mass media networks in the Americas. These and other official agencies also stimulated Latin American studies and financed field investigations by U.S. scholars.

Tourism to Latin America grew substantially in the 1930s as travel facilities by air, sea, and land expanded; this decade's growth of tourism followed more salutary channels than it had during Prohibition when Americans trooped to the drinking, gambling, fleshpot meccas of Havana and Tijuana. Pan American Airways initiated service to Latin America in 1928 and gradually extended it to both coasts of South America. By 1937 three flights a week departed Miami for Latin America, and Buenos Aires could be reached in five days. Ocean cruises to southern waters briefly spurted upwards in 1936 as a replacement for cruises to the Mediterranean, which were cancelled because of the "Mussolini problem." Extensive propaganda in "sound-color" film and elegant travel books about the largely fanciful Pan American Highway attracted overland visitors. But even before the outbreak of war

17. Bemis, *Latin American Policy of the U.S.*, 319–29; Allen L. Woll, "Hollywood's Good Neighbor Policy: The Latin Image in American Film, 1939–1945," *Journal of Popular Film*, III (1974), 278–85, 291; Herbert E. Bolton, "The Epic of Greater America," *American Historical Review*, XXXVIII (1933), 448–74; Cline, "Latin American History: Development of Its Study and Teaching in the United States Since 1898," in *Latin American History*, ed. Cline, I, 9–10; New York *Times*, January 1, 1933; James A. Robertson, "Cure Our Ignorance of Hispanic America," *American Scholar*, VI (1937), 498; "Courses on Latin America in American Colleges," *School and Society*, XXXIII (February 14, 1931), 233–34; Lewis Hanke, "Introduction," in *Do the Americas Have a Common History? A Critique of the Bolton Theory*, ed. Lewis Hanke (New York, 1964), 14–15; Thomas S. Estes and E. Allan Lightner, Jr., *The Department of State* (New York, 1976), 32–37.

ended tourism, the high cost of travel to much of Latin America kept it noncompetitive with sojourns in Europe.[18]

In the late 1930s and early 1940s an explosion of information about Latin America burst forth in academic monographs, travel books, newspaper editorials, articles in popular magazines, and children's books. The high school weekly *Scholastic* increased its Latin American coverage, the monthly *Rotarian* initiated a "Little Lessons on Latin America" section, and a new journal, the *Inter-American*—a high-quality monthly containing samples of Latin American press opinion and a synopsis of hemispheric news stories—appeared from 1942 to 1946. *Fortune* magazine published a series of lengthy, detailed, and well-written articles on South America in 1937 and 1938 to alert the public to the Fascist threat there. The entire March, 1940, issue of *House Beautiful* was devoted to Latin America. An article entitled "South Americana" in a 1937 issue of *Reader's Digest* consisted of eleven delightful vignettes offering sketches of the social life and customs of South American countries taken from popular works.[19] Frank Knox, publisher and Republican vice-presidential candidate in 1936, summarized the explosive growth of information on Latin America as follows: "There have been more than a 'five-foot shelf' of books on South America published in the past twelve months; popular picture magazines have made South American scenes familiar; the lecture platform has been crowded with returned travelers; news agencies have sharply increased the volume of 'spot news' from down under the equator, and newspapers have been finding space for such news in the forward pages—sometimes on page 1."[20]

The pre-1930 distortions of inattention and ignorance, however, too easily became the distortions of dilettantism and romanticism. A book reviewer claimed that "it seems that everybody who has been

18. Wagley, "Introduction," in *Social Science Research on Latin America*, ed. Wagley, 8–9; Gellman, *Good Neighbor Diplomacy*, 148–53; James Truslow Adams, "The Two Americas in Each Others Eyes," *New York Times Magazine*, September 13, 1931, p. 4; "South America I: The Continent," *Fortune*, XVI (December, 1937), 101; "Brass Tacks on Latin America," *Business Week*, February 4, 1939, p. 45; "To South America and Back," *Fortune*, XVI (December, 1937), 96; Harry A. Franck and Herbert C. Lanks, "Our Neighbors Down the Road," *Christian Science Monitor Magazine*, December 6, 1941, pp. 8–9; A. A. Berle, Jr., "After Lima," *Yale Review*, XXVIII (March, 1939), 470–71.

19. Maria Cimino, "South America in Children's Books," *Publishers Weekly*, CXXXVIII (August 31, 1940), 671–76; *Reader's Digest*, XXXI (December, 1937), 27–29. The articles in *Fortune* appeared anonymously, but at least two of them were authored by Archibald MacLeish.

20. Frank Knox, "Our Southern Arteries," *Atlantic Monthly*, CLXIV (July, 1939), 75.

to, over, around, by or inside our southern neighbors feels an unfortunate compulsion to tell about them." A somewhat exasperated Latin American specialist offered the following summary of the craze for Latin Americana at its peak in 1941:

Affection for Latin Americans has broken out like a speckled rash on the skin of the North American body politic. Clubwomen read papers on the Humboldt Current, dress up as Aymarás, listen to guitarists strum tunes reputed to come from the Amazon. College presidents substitute courses on the Incas for those on the Age of Pericles. Chambers of Commerce give dinners to visiting Argentine bankers, and keep a set of twenty-one flags among their props. Schoolgirls cut paper dolls which represent the dwellers by Atitlán. Official Washington takes a half-holiday to welcome itinerant Caribbean dictators. The army entertains Latin-American chiefs of staff, there is no ceiling on expense accounts.[21]

The problem with this vast outpouring of information was that it largely consisted of "flapdoodle," to use Lewis Hanke's term. It abounded with factual error such as the description of Colombia's inland city of Cali as a seaport that might be seized by the Japanese and used for landing fields and submarine bases. Also, many of the descriptive accounts were filled with "romantic nonsense." The author of a travel article touted Brazil as "Uncle Sam's best girlfriend among the South American states" and described its interior as "a vast unexplored wilderness, populated by strange tribes, queer animals, and all sorts of weird mysteries." A U.S. professor visiting at a Colombian university complained that an editor from *Reader's Digest* arrived "to write the biography of a famous Colombian in four days." And the publishers of a book about Bogotá explained on the jacket that the author "took with her a friendly spirit, a sense of humor, and an abysmal ignorance of everything South American." The great flood of dilettantes and novices into the field accounted for many of the inaccuracies and distortions. One academician lamented, "The fadists, having just heard about Latin America, are giving lectures, forming committees, excogitating 'projects' and so on, though some of them know neither enough Portuguese nor enough Spanish to buy a hat." During the last two years of this period, the frenetic publication of Latin Americana sharply dropped off and returned to the normal pace of the mid-1930s. In late 1943 one observer noted that during the year "there was hardly a notable volume" published on Latin America; "the heat is off and our interest wanes."[22]

21. Baily W. Diffie, Review of Lawrence Griswold's *The Other America*, in *Hispanic American Historical Review*, XXIII (1943), 313; Hubert Herring, *Good Neighbors: Argentina, Brazil, Chile, and Seventeen Other Countries* (New Haven, 1941), 327.

22. Lewis Hanke, Review of Waldo Frank's *South American Journey*, in *Hispanic*

Despite the flurry of good-neighbor activity and the promotion of Latin America, specialists complained during and after the craze that the public remained pitifully ignorant of the region. The craze had left little of enduring value because it promoted the superficial, highlighted the romantic, and distorted the real. Observed one historian in 1943, "We are all so officially fond of each other these days that realism is indecent."[23]

One important and concrete by-product of the interest in Latin America, however, was the appearance in 1944 of a landmark study, *Latin America in School and College Teaching Materials*, published by the American Council on Education. A committee of scholars under the chairmanship of Professor Arthur P. Whitaker organized teams of specialists who examined a wide variety of teaching materials used in the primary and secondary grades and in college. The study's goal was to evaluate and improve the treatment of Latin America in various fields such as history, geography, current events, and literature. Among its major findings, the study reported that the material available was better than it had ever been, and there was "no evidence of conscious and perverted antagonism toward Latin America." It also found, however, that the material examined tended to perpetuate the Black Legend, showed evidence of racial prejudice and condescension toward Latin Americans, slighted the region's literature, and treated Latin America with undue sentimentalism and excessive emphasis on the quaint and colorful. The scholars also noted that the field had produced its share of "overzealous cultists and superficial amateurs." This survey can be taken as a sign of the maturation of the first generation of truly professional Latin American scholars in the U.S. because it was a serious effort at self-criticism, conducted

---

American Historical Review, XXIII (1943), 715; Erna Fergusson, *Chile* (New York, 1943), 6; Roland Hall Sharp, *South America Uncensored* (New York, 1945), 235; "South Lies Hispanic America," *Review of Reviews*, XCII (December, 1935), 56–57; Frederick Sparks Stimson, "You, Too, Can Write a Book About South America!" *Saturday Review of Literature*, March 11, 1944, pp. 7–8; Edwin Ryan, "Latin America Is Dynamite," *Commonweal*, XXXIII (February 7, 1941), 396–98; "A Portent from Latin America," *Commonweal*, XXXIX (December 10, 1943), 195.

23. Henry Grattan Doyle, "Cultural Elements in Inter-American Understanding," *Modern Language Journal*, XXII (1938), 642–43; "To South America and Back," *Fortune*, XVI (December, 1937), 96; John W. Whitaker, *Americas to the South* (New York, 1939), 292; William Franklin Sands, *Our Jungle Diplomacy* (Chapel Hill, N.C., 1944), 119–20; Hubert Herring, Review of *Mexico and Central America: The New World Guides to Latin-American Republics*, Vol. I, ed. Earl Parker Hanson, in *Hispanic American Historical Review*, XXIII (1943), 532.

with thoroughness, judiciousness, and the support of prominent scholars in the field. In addition, it was widely and favorably reviewed.[24]

As already noted, the depression played an important role in initiating the greater tolerance that characterized this period, and it also inspired an economic emphasis in analyzing Latin American problems. This new emphasis grew out of attempts to understand the rash of defaults and revolutions of the early 1930s, but it persisted throughout the period and expanded to become the basis for a broad interpretation of the region's underdevelopment. In fact, examination of this problem from an economic perspective marked the first significant addition to traditional analyses, which heretofore had been made from the perspective of climate, race, and culture.

Principal themes of economic analysis were that the Latin American nations were helpless victims of international forces and that the export-import orientation of their economies made them highly vulnerable to the operation of those forces. It was further argued that dependence on only one or two export commodities exaggerated that vulnerability. To convey the sense that Latin America was struggling against the full weight of a long-standing tradition of exploitation and dependency, it became common during this period to refer to the region's economies as "colonial economies."[25] Many of the studies of Latin America published from 1930 to 1945 had a heavy economic emphasis, and they made the same points with little variation, e.g., a major handicap of "the Caribbean area has been its economic dependence upon a restricted list of export products"; Chile's "dependence upon unstable foreign markets [has] been largely responsible for her troubles"; and "our neighbors to the south are the victims of international forces."[26] This economic perspective was convincingly summarized in an article reprinted in the *Congressional Record* during debate in 1940 on a loan to Latin America: "These are commodity countries. Many of them are in the kind of trouble Kansas would have been in if it were an independent nation and dependent wholly on its wheat crop. The economic stability of the South American nations is at the mercy of the fate of single commodities."[27]

24. American Council on Education, *Latin America in School and College Teaching Materials* (Washington, D.C., 1944), 16, 21, 25–35, 43.

25. "Americas More Self-Sufficient," *Commonweal*, XXXVI (July 10, 1942), 267; George Soule, David Efron, and Norman T. Ness, *Latin America in the Future World* (New York, 1945), 302; Whitaker, *Americas to the South*, 15.

26. Chester Lloyd Jones, *Caribbean Backgrounds and Prospects* (New York, 1931), 174; P. T. Ellsworth, *Chile: An Economy in Transition* (New York, 1945), 49; Seymour E. Harris, ed., *Economic Problems of Latin America* (New York, 1944), 3.

27. John T. Flynn, "Plain Economics," as cited in remarks of Robert R. Reynolds,

The most-articulate and widely published exponent of this theme was Carleton Beals, whose career as a radical journalist specializing in Latin America spanned a half century from the early 1920s through the 1960s. Author of thirty-four books and more than two-hundred articles, the large majority on Latin American themes, Beals was near the peak of his career when he published in 1937 *America South*, which contained a fascinating chapter, "Why Latin-American Backwardness?" The views expressed here differed little from those contained in a lifetime of writings, namely, that the principal causes of Latin American developmental problems were a medieval heritage, geographical handicaps, and exploitation by the industrialized nations. Beals became marked as a radical journalist by his lifelong emphasis on the exploitation theme and by his journalistic assaults against U.S. intervention, whether in the form of overt military action as in Nicaragua in the 1920s, diplomatic pressure on Cuba in the early 1930s, or the more widespread economic interventions. Though a stubborn individualist, Beals nevertheless followed the tradition of Progressive critics of U.S. policy such as Lincoln Steffens, the anti-imperialist school of the 1920s represented by Margaret Alexander Marsh, and the sympathetic presentation in the 1930s of the peasant perspective by Robert Redfield. But in Beals's analysis the critical factor that worked as a catalyst in promoting various antidevelopmental tendencies was assigning to Latin America the role of producer of unfinished raw materials for the industrialized nations, thus throwing the region back "into a semi-colonial status." Beals concluded that "the extraction of vast quantities of raw materials has tended to accentuate feudal evils, to accentuate militarism, to forestall democracy and to prevent the amalgamation of the social groups, the classes, the races and the cultures."[28]

Foreign capital's role in Latin American development attracted more and more attention as the period unfolded. The question evoked controversy, and majority sentiment appeared to emphasize its negative results. Articles in *Barron's* and the *New Republic* early in the period blamed U.S. bankers for making loans and undertaking bond issues without sufficient caution, but more weighty indictments of foreign capital appeared later in the period. In his 1934 study, *Whither*

Congressional Record, Senate, 76th Cong., 3rd Sess., Vol. LXXXVI, Pt. 17, Appendix, p. 5306.

28. John A. Britton, *Carleton Beals: A Radical Journalist in Latin America* (Albuquerque, N.M., 1987), 85–86, 113, 115, 123, 144–45, 153, 164, 229; Carleton Beals, *America South* (New York, 1937), 354–55.

Latin America, Frank Tannenbaum argued that the region's development had been handicapped by foreign exploitation, and, as an example, he detailed foreign control in Peru during the 1920s of railroads, mines, large agricultural enterprises, and nearly a dozen other industries.[29] An article in *Harper's Magazine* that offered a coldly frank appraisal of conditions in Central America at the height of the Latin American fad asserted that U.S. dominance had been a major "handicap" to Central America's progress. "This dominance," claimed the author, "has lain like a weight on Central-American initiative." A thoughtful summary of the impediments to Latin American development appeared at the end of the period under the title *Latin America in the Future World*. Written in consultation with regional specialists, its authors concluded that "Latin America appears to be almost uniquely vulnerable to the hazards inherent in international economic intercourse." They acknowledged that foreign capital had opened many regions in the world, "but in few have so little of the consequent benefits remained in the country of development."[30]

There were, of course, positive assessments of foreign capital's role in development, but few of them ignored its drawbacks. In his 1931 study, *Caribbean Backgrounds and Prospects*, Professor Chester Lloyd Jones made a strong case for the contribution of foreign capital in developing the Caribbean countries, and he drew a parallel between their development and that which had taken place in the U.S., Canada, and South Africa in the late-nineteenth century. Four years later, however, he showed more caution when he observed that it was too soon to say whether foreign capital would serve "as a bridge from economic dependence to independence" in the tropical areas.[31] Likewise J. Fred Rippy, in his well-received study, *The Capitalists and Colombia* (1931), lauded the role of Yankee capital in developing Colombia, but he concluded, "There is the possibility that those who dominate and direct the process will be absentee capitalists without the incentive of patriotism to stir them to benevolence toward the Colombian public." A balanced assessment published near the end of the period noted that Latin America's economic development before the 1930s had come

29. "South America Faces Serious Problems," *Barron's*, July 6, 1931, p. 13; "Wrecking a Continent," *New Republic*, LXXI (July 27, 1932), 276–77; Frank Tannenbaum, *Whither Latin America: An Introduction to Its Economic and Social Problems* (New York, 1934), 32.

30. Lawrence and Sylvia Martin, "Four Strong Men and a President," *Harper's Magazine*, CLXXXV (September, 1942), 427; Soule, Efron, and Ness, *Latin America in the Future World*, 110, 134.

31. Jones, *Caribbean Backgrounds*, 157, 308; Chester Lloyd Jones, *Costa Rica and Civilization in the Caribbean* (New York, 1935), 155.

largely through foreign investment, but its "increasingly vulnerable international position . . . is the price of that development."[32] Reference to Latin America's economic vulnerability had become a commonplace observation by 1945, and it testified to a substantial shift in the focus of analysis caused by the depression experience. During the Progressive Era and in the 1920s, emphasis on foreign capital's role in the region's underdevelopment had been a theme espoused primarily by a leftist minority, but in the 1930s that view gained general respectability.

Depression also caused analysis to shift from political and legalistic factors to social and economic. During approximately the first half of this period, when concern over depression attracted attention to the socioeconomic factors in Latin America's development, commentators prognosticated an essentially agricultural, nonindustrial future for the region. This vision was most frequently applied to Mexico, and it was often based on a happy image of Mexican village life as communal, cooperative, and spiritually fulfilling as opposed to the neurosis-laden, atomistic, machine-governed life in the U.S., where people in the 1930s suffered relentless unemployment, despair, and unsettling evidence of sharp class divisions. This contrast between a salutary Mexican collectivism and a disordered U.S. individualism was evoked by observers from varied backgrounds, including Secretary of Agriculture Henry A. Wallace, Commissioner of Indian Affairs John Collier, writer Waldo Frank, anthropologist Robert Redfield, and economist Stuart Chase. These advocates of a more-integrated, harmonious social order were inspired—just as elements of the counterculture had been in the 1920s—by Latin America's *indigenistas,* prominent intellectuals such as Victor Raúl Haya de la Torre of Peru and Manuel Gamio of Mexico.[33]

Some analyses of Latin America's future were rooted in dark despair over the collapse of industrial capitalism, though counterculturalists could hardly conceal their glee. An example of the latter is a 1931 study of Mexico by Stuart Chase, who combined his rage at U.S. capitalism with an idealized view of the Mexican Indian. He doubted that Mexico would ever be able to industrialize—"the future for industri-

---

32. J. Fred Rippy, *The Capitalists and Colombia* (New York, 1931), 37, 41, 192–93; Paul R. Olson and C. Addison Hickman, *Pan American Economics* (New York, 1943), 196.

33. Waldo Frank, *America Hispana: A Portrait and a Prospect* (New York, 1931); Robert Redfield, *Tepoztlán, A Mexican Village* (Chicago, 1930); Stuart Chase and Marian Tyler, *Mexico: A Study of Two Americas* (New York, 1931); Zelman, "American Intellectual Attitudes Toward Mexico, 1908–1940," 174–75, 184, 190–212; Pike, "Latin America and the Inversion of U.S. Stereotypes in the 1920s and 1930s," 139, 155–56.

alism in the sense of mass production is not rosy, for which we may thank whatever gods there be"—because of limited natural resources, transportation problems, and a cultural disinclination on the part of the Mexican to become a machinist. This anti-industrial perspective was akin to the views of a vocal minority of European writers in the interwar period who concluded from the suicidal slaughter and devastation of trench warfare in World War I that European civilization was in a state of profound crisis deriving from the very nature of modern industrial civilization. The essays of anthropologist Bronislaw Malinowski and the stories and novels of D. H. Lawrence exemplify the desire to find alternatives to the dehumanizing industrial order in the simple but wholesome life-styles found in exotic lands.[34]

Two major studies of 1934 strongly affirmed the notion that Latin America's future was nonindustrial. H. Foster Bain and Thomas Thornton Read's *Ores and Industry in South America*, published for the Council on Foreign Relations, consisted of a country-by-country mineral survey of South America, which led the authors—distinguished scientists with impressive governmental and academic experience in the field of mineralogy—to conclude that "South America is destined for some time in the future to remain in its past role of exporter of minerals either in the raw or but simply processed state." They so concluded because of the lack of cheap fuel and because "both the natural resources of the continent and the habit of thought of its people favor making agriculture the dominant industry."[35] In the same year, Frank Tannenbaum's influential book-length essay, *Whither Latin America*, posed numerous research questions about Latin America and emphasized the paucity of knowledge about the region. He came to essentially the same conclusion as Bain and Read, arguing that Latin America was destined to remain an agricultural economy. Tannenbaum was particularly influenced by the limited prospects for export growth, which in his view derived from depression and Europe's small population increase. "Clearly enough," he argued, "Latin America in a greater degree in the future than even in the past . . . must learn to live within its own resources. The way of its life will be determined by the use it makes of its soil, not only for export but for local consumption."[36]

34. Chase and Tyler, *Mexico: A Study of Two Americas*, 219, 223, 240, 246, 314; Michael Adas, *Machines as the Measure of Men: Science, Technology, and Ideologies of Western Dominance* (Ithaca, 1989), 380–92.

35. H. Foster Bain and Thomas Thornton Read, *Ores and Industry in South America* (New York, 1934), 369.

36. Tannenbaum, *Whither Latin America*, 141, 170.

At the same time that many U.S. observers were projecting a non-industrial future for Latin America, Latin Americans themselves were of necessity beginning to embrace industrialization. Sharp declines in the price and demand for primary goods exports in the early 1930s meant that Latin Americans were unable either to pay their foreign debts or continue importing manufactured goods. When the world was rushing toward national economic self-sufficiency, the arguments of Latin America's economic nationalists for a policy of state-induced industrialization to preserve limited foreign exchange, attain economic diversification, and create badly needed jobs seemed compelling. In many Latin American nations industrialization had its real beginnings in the 1930s through the stimulus of state promotion, by means of such policies as protective tariffs, subsidies, government purchases, tax privileges, and direct government participation in key industries. As an example, in Brazil between 1929 and 1937, industrial production increased nearly 50 percent.[37]

A major work that marked a shift in U.S. perspectives on Latin American development toward the end of depression was Eyler N. Simpson's monumental study of 1937, *The Ejido: Mexico's Way Out.* Simpson focused on the agricultural sector and land reform, but he concluded that "internal pressure of necessity will inevitably force Mexico to embrace the basic procedures and attitudes of industrialism." He concluded, however, that heavy industry based on steel production offered no hope for Mexican development. Reflecting the experience of depression, he argued that Mexico had a chance to avoid industrialized societies' errors that had led to massive unemployment and vast urban problems. His central thesis was that Mexico's hope for development was through an agrarian-based development of small factories, specializing in food processing and the production of clothes and furniture, and "the application of science, power, and machinery to agriculture." Two years later in *The Reconquest of Mexico: The Years of Lázaro Cárdenas,* Nathaniel and Sylvia Weyl advocated full-scale industrialization, and they too warned that it must not follow the path of modern "competitive capitalism." They held that only through industrialization "can the masses drag themselves out of the dark caves of poverty and ignorance into the sunlight of a civilization of abundance," but they advocated industrialization under firm government control—control of the process, of foreign earnings, and of the export of capital.[38]

37. E. Bradford Burns, *Latin America: A Concise Interpretive History* (Rev. ed.; Englewood Cliffs, N.J., 1977), 202–203; John D. Wirth, *The Politics of Brazilian Development, 1930–1954* (Stanford, 1970), 12.

38. Eyler N. Simpson, *The Ejido: Mexico's Way Out* (Chapel Hill, N.C., 1937), 557; Nathaniel and Sylvia Weyl, *The Reconquest of Mexico*, 380, 371–72.

Both the Simpson and Weyl studies pointed to the rather dramatic change in the reading of Latin America's future that occurred between the anti-industrial perspective of the depression years and the wartime advocacy of industrialization. By the late 1930s there was growing recognition that Latin America desired to industrialize; the U.S. was increasingly willing to assist the process, and an effort was made to assure Americans that such a course would not damage U.S. economic interests. As the war-born competition for strategic raw materials intensified in the late 1930s, well-connected writers such as economics editor Eliot Janeway and New Dealer Raymond Moley argued that in order to guarantee access to such materials, the U.S. should respond to the Latin American desire to develop its own resources and should grant developmental loans and sell machinery and processing equipment. Some writers were convinced that the devastation wrought by depression and war on Latin America's highly dependent economies offered the most-compelling reason to industrialize.[39] During the war years, advocacy of Latin American industrialization grew, and it was more and more treated as a necessity rather than an option. At the same time, several commentators attempted to calm the often-expressed fear that it would pose harmful competition to U.S. industry. Geographer Preston E. James wrote that industrialization in Latin America would immediately create an expanding market for U.S. machinery and factory equipment, and in the long run "it will mean higher standards of living in Latin America, and only by raising standards in the rest of the world can the older industrial centers maintain the levels they have reached." This same line of reasoning was often advanced late in the war, when it was asserted that Latin American industrialization would help ease the transition in the U.S. from a wartime to a peacetime economy.[40]

A theme much discussed in previous periods that now intruded into the consideration of Latin America's future was the question of the region's potential wealth. Throughout the years of depression and war, the challenge made in the 1920s to the traditional view that Latin

39. Eliot Janeway, "America in the Post-Munich World: III—Alternative to War," *Nation*, CXLVIII (March 4, 1939), 261–62; Raymond Moley, "Defending Latin America," *Newsweek*, December 26, 1938, p. 40; William Lytle Schurz, *Latin America: A Descriptive Survey* (New York, 1941), 154; Olson and Hickman, *Pan American Economics*, 394.

40. Preston E. James, *Latin America* (New York, 1942), 838; New York *Times*, February 12, 1943; William P. Witherow, "Development by Latin-American Countries of Industrialization Urged by Witherow," *Commercial and Financial Chronicle*, May 18, 1944, p. 2062; Lawrence Duggan, "Introduction," vii, in George Wythe, *Industry in Latin America* (New York, 1945).

America possessed vast, untapped wealth gained impressive momentum under the guidance of a growing body of specialists whose conclusions were based on solid field work. But at the same time, the traditional view persisted, and it appears to have been temporarily strengthened during the 1930s by the depression. Many writers, for example, invoked visions of vast frontiers of opportunity beckoning in Latin America to those who despaired the lack of jobs, opportunities, and frontiers in the U.S. A sampling of opinion suggests the tenacious appeal of the traditional view. In his 1931 study of U.S. investment in Colombia, J. Fred Rippy wrote: "Mexico has been compared to a beggar sitting upon a bag of gold. The figure might be applied with almost equal appropriateness to Colombia." A high school social studies weekly proclaimed that Mexico was appropriately shaped like a cornucopia and that it was "a treasure house wherein is stored probably the greatest wealth ever bestowed by nature upon a single people." An author of popular travel accounts described the Venezuelan territory of Amazonas as "wealthy beyond the dreams of the wildest Venezuelan enthusiast," and the author of a journalistic survey of South America wrote: "Peru has mountain fastnesses fabulous with copper, gold, and silver . . . and deep jungles rich with oil and unexplored possibilities in coffee."[41] This colorful imagery included visions of Latin America as a frontier of opportunity for those with energy and ambition. An example is an article in the *Reader's Digest,* which began as follows: "While American economists ring a knell over the passing of the frontier and, presumably, the downfall of western civilization, a new and richer frontier, between the equator and the Caribbean, awaits Yankee pluck and ingenuity." The author then reported a conversation with an adventurer who had gone into the interior of British Guiana near the Venezuelan border to prospect for gold and who declared: "But before long I was throwing gold away. . . . Couldn't take the time to pan it out. Diamonds settle to the bottom of a pan quicker, and I found plenty of them."[42]

Despite abundant evidence that the traditional view of Latin America's potential wealth persisted at least into the 1940s, change was under way, and it was advanced primarily by the work of a handful of spe-

41. Rippy, *The Capitalists and Colombia,* 30; "A New Link Between the Americas," *Scholastic,* May 9, 1936, p. 19; Earl Parker Hanson, *Journey to Manaos* (New York, 1938), 132; Whitaker, *Americas to the South,* 14.

42. "A New Frontier for American Pioneers," *Reader's Digest,* XXXI (July, 1937), 59. Promoters of Latin America as a frontier of opportunity ignored the well-publicized failure of an American colony established in Bolivia in the 1920s by a colorful Oklahoma agrarian politician, William H. "Alfalfa Bill" Murray. For an account of his colonizing effort, see Keith L. Bryant, Jr., *Alfalfa Bill Murray* (Norman, Okla., 1968), 151–72.

cialists. Two previously mentioned studies were of special importance in undermining the traditional view. One, the survey of mineral resources by Bain and Read, concluded that "a belief that South America is a vast reservoir of untouched mineral wealth is wholly illusory and that the cost of producing such as exists has so far left but moderate returns. . . ." The other study, Tannenbaum's *Whither Latin America*, confirmed the conclusions of Bain and Read that Latin America lacked mineral resources, that those it possessed were poorly located, and that the cost of constructing a transportation system necessary to exploit those resources was prohibitive. One additional study advancing the same themes was the 1942 survey *Latin America* by Preston E. James, a preeminent student of Latin American geography. "We must learn," he admonished, "before it is too late, that Latin America is not a rich territory waiting to be exploited by North American business genius; we must learn that Latin America is not just a backward pioneer land, following the same course charted in so spectacular fashion by the frontiersmen of the United States." He acknowledged that much of Latin America could be described in superlatives, "but superlatives which are poorly combined in terms of the needs of modern industrial society."[43]

These specialists not only rejected the notion of Latin America's vast potential wealth, but they also broadly critiqued the region's natural conditions and concluded that it suffered many liabilities. James noted that the people lived in widely scattered clusters separated by scantily occupied territory; that South America was poorly provided with harbors and with navigable rivers usefully placed, and that it was remote from the patterns of international trade—it was "literally one of the ends of the habitable earth." Many writers commented on the poor distribution of rainfall and the lack of arable land. John Gunther, for example, noted that "Mexico, because of its precipitous geography and its pressing lack of water, produces very little soil—a commodity that can be as valuable as gold." Other writers commented on the paradox of lush vegetation in tropical soil that, because of the leaching process caused by frequent downpours, is mineral-deficient and humus-poor. "As a whole," noted an article on the tropics, "tropical soils are so poor that the price of their cultivation is poverty." A journalist with many years' experience in South America wrote a survey of the continent at the end of the period that expressed many of these points, thus indicating that the educated layman was beginning to get

43. Bain and Read, *Ores and Industry*, 7, 19; Tannenbaum, *Whither Latin America*, 23, 84; James, *Latin America*, viii, 19.

the point. He concluded that "it would be difficult to design a continent with more massive natural handicaps."[44]

These "natural handicaps" nicely supplemented the climatic factor that remained a nearly unchallenged explanation of Latin America's underdevelopment. Professor A. Curtis Wilgus, in his 1941 college text, *The Development of Hispanic America*, expressed the prevailing view as follows: "About three-fourths of Hispanic America lies within the tropics, which zone, even where the climate is modified by altitude, has invariably been a handicap to political, economic, and social progress." In *The Latin American Policy of the United States*, the standard work on the subject, Yale professor Samuel Flagg Bemis, the leading historian of U.S. diplomacy at the time, confirmed this thesis and, relying substantially on the work of Ellsworth Huntington, wrote: "In South America the cultural fruitage of human energy has been limited to the tapering temperate region, to the tropical highlands and to the cooler fringes of the sea." Specialist and nonspecialist adhered to the view that, in the words of Chester Lloyd Jones, "Life in the full tropics for a succession of generations is for the white race not practicable." According to the author of numerous travel books on Latin America, "The white man visibly deteriorates; wakes up with good resolutions, only to see them wither as the tropical heat and especially the humidity saps all energy, will-power and desire to do."[45] As was true in earlier periods, a few observers drew attention to the harmful effects of permanent residence in the tropical highlands, which reportedly produced "frequent nervous disorders." After his fleeting sojourn in Bolivia, John Gunther remarked, "Most Bolivians vary in character-pattern from extreme apathy, apathy almost to the point of physical numbness, to an intense nervous irritability that may burst out very suddenly, on account of the altitude."[46]

In the minds of most travelers to tropical America, the underlying cause of stagnation was the enervating heat and humidity, but, as in previous periods, many also blamed the ease of existence they professed to witness. Chester Lloyd Jones wrote that in the tropics, "'the blessings of adversity' have been denied to the local populations. They

44. James, *Latin America*, 4–6, 8, 23; John Gunther, *Inside Latin America* (New York, 1941), 57; Carl F. Westerberg, "Revolt in the Tropics," *North American Review*, CCXXXI (March, 1931), 257, 263; Sharp, *South America Uncensored*, x.

45. A. Curtis Wilgus, *The Development of Hispanic America* (New York, 1941), 633; Bemis, *Latin American Policy of the U.S.*, 7–8; Jones, *Costa Rica*, 152; Harry A. Franck, *Rediscovering South America* (Philadelphia, 1943), 386.

46. Charles A. Mills, *Climate Makes the Man* (New York, 1942), 252; Gunther, *Inside Latin America*, 219.

have been handicapped by the abundant yields of the tropics. . . ." Another writer explained underdevelopment by noting that the wants of the people "are few and easily supplied. . . . Where labor is content with mere subsistence, there cannot be the accumulation of capital needed for the development of a modern civilization."[47]

It must be noted that the predominant view, that of the climatic determinists, was on occasion rejected, perhaps most forthrightly by Preston E. James, who argued that factors such as diet and disease must be evaluated before accepting the notion that the backward conditions of the tropics were the result of climate. "There is no evidence," claimed the geographer, "which permits us to subscribe hopelessly to the idea that the low latitudes are forever condemned to backwardness and poverty." One of the few writers to emphasize the disease factor was Charles Morrow Wilson; in his book *Ambassadors in White* (1942), which told the story of modern achievements in tropical medicine, and in an article entitled "How Latin Americans Die," he characterized Latin America as a "sick man's society" in which at least fifty million out of a total population of roughly 120 million were sick. "Only gradually and partially," he noted, "has it begun to dawn on the experts in the field of public health that sickness in Latin America is as much a condition of life as weather or food."[48]

Race also remained a common explanation for Latin American underdevelopment, and during a period when racial segregation was the norm, when the Senate killed an antilynching bill with an angry filibuster, and when a senator could proclaim on the Senate floor, "I stand for white supremacy at all times," the persistence of the racial explanation is hardly surprising. Its prime target continued to be racially mixed groups, but Indians, blacks, and, on occasion, Spanish and Portuguese were included in the indictments against Latin America's peoples. These views had been challenged in the 1920s, and the challenge made headway in the following period as scientific racism weakened, IQ tests were used more judiciously, and the cooperative spirit of wartime softened the harshness of racist commentary.[49]

47. Jones, *Caribbean Backgrounds*, 316–17; Stephen Duggan, *The Two Americas: An Interpretation* (New York, 1934), 10–11.

48. James, *Latin America*, 391–92, 835; "How Latin Americans Die," *Harper's Magazine*, CLXXXIV (July, 1942), 141; Charles Morrow Wilson, *Ambassadors in White* (New York, 1942).

49. Remarks of Allen J. Ellender, *Congressional Record*, Senate, 75th Cong., 3rd Sess., Vol. LXXXIII, Pt. 1, p. 813. For evidence of greater sophistication in the use of IQ tests on minority children, see E. Lee Davenport, "The Intelligence Quotients of Mexican and Non-Mexican Siblings," *School and Society* XXXVI (September 3, 1932), 304–306.

The most avowedly racist views of the period were directed against racially mixed groups and were expressed by Senator Allen J. Ellender of Louisiana and by T. Lothrop Stoddard, a writer who had been promoting such views for two decades before he wrote *Clashing Tides of Colour* in 1935. Ellender, speaking on the Senate floor against the antilynching bill, argued that wherever progressive civilization exists in South America, it is in the hands of whites, and "wherever the mongrel prevails, wherever the mixed breed prevails . . . there is a decay of civilization." Like the senator, Stoddard claimed to see unmitigated disaster as the inevitable consequence of race crossing. "We see melancholy examples of it in peoples to the south of us, especially in the Caribbean area, where mixtures of whites, Negroes, and Indians are most common. The disastrous consequences on the national life of those peoples are only too clear."[50] Representatives John C. Box and Thomas A. Jenkins continued the crusade they had begun late in the 1920s to restrict Mexican immigration, and in support of that project they authored a study of the Mexican immigrant, whom they found to be racially inferior. Jenkins held that the Mexican possessed "an ancestry which promises little—a mixture of native Indian with West Indian negro and Spaniard," and Box asserted that admission of such people would accelerate the "distressing process of mongrelization." A 1936 article in the *Review of Reviews* that briefly surveyed contemporary Latin America portrayed its leadership in negative racial terms. The caption under a photograph of the Brazilian leader read: "Brazilian Strongboy: Getúlio Vargas." Rafael Trujillo was referred to as "this big negrocrat," the wealthy tin magnate Simon Patiño as a "Bolivian half-caste," and Fulgencio Batista as "mostly Indian."[51]

Indians and blacks were generally portrayed as a brutish people who could offer no basis for progress. The authors of an article on Mexico foresaw for the country nothing better "than a rickety continuance of the present rickety existence"—an outlook based on the inherent incapacity of the Indian. "We find that the indio is, when not definitely feeble-minded, generally addlepated; he is, moreover, psychopathically dirty, suicidally lazy, not preeminently honest, and, worst of all, of a black, brooding, sullen, revengeful and sanguinary character."[52]

50. Remarks of Ellender, *Congressional Record*, Senate, 75th Cong., 3rd Sess., Vol. LXXXIII, Pt. 2, p. 1687; *ibid.*, Pt. 1, p. 814; T. Lothrop Stoddard, *Clashing Tides of Colour* (New York, 1935), 21–22.

51. Remarks of Jenkins, *Congressional Record*, House, 71st Cong., 3rd Sess., Vol. LXXIV, Pt. 4, p. 3556; remarks of Box, *ibid.*, p. 3552; "Latin America Today: Peoples and Government," *Review of Reviews*, XCIV (December, 1936), 65–66.

52. Sean Niall and Katharine Mangan, "Mexico-Tierra Triste," *North American Review*, CCXLIII (March, 1937), 78–79, 67–70.

Among the most-arresting examples of similar treatment of the Latin American black were Senator Ellender's discussion of the history of Haiti and a chapter entitled "The Negro Problem" in a study of white settlement in the tropics, in which the author examined the encroachment of blacks onto the Costa Rican central plateau, a process he referred to as "negrodation." A survey of Mexico also indicted its Spanish heritage, which the author characterized as follows: "All that Western civilization had brought them in three hundred and ninety-one years was the horse, the gun, the ox-drawn plow, a number of new diseases and a new strain of blood that introduced an element of temperamental instability into the psychology of all who had it."[53]

One distinguishing feature of the commentary on race in this period was the renewal of proposals for large-scale immigration into Latin America. Even while urging this solution to the "population problem," many observers acknowledged that it was somewhat unrealistic because of the reduced European birth rate. Immigration was proposed as a way to improve the Latin American population and also as a solution to limitations caused by a too-scanty population. The former rationale was advanced by Kathleen Romoli in her highly regarded book on Colombia: "There has been almost no immigration to Colombia in the last century, very little infusion of vigorous new blood, and the people, taking them all in all, have had to get along on fare that is hardly just what the eugenist would order."[54]

The challenge of the 1920s to the racist interpretation made further headway in this period thanks to the work of a handful of young scholars. But as can be judged from the above citations, their views must still be seen as a minority's arguments against prevailing sentiment. The general position of these scholars was that evidence for a racist interpretation was lacking, and they noted that other factors such as absence of racial and cultural unity within a nation were often mistakenly interpreted as solely racial factors. Harvard historian C. H. Haring asserted in a series of lectures in 1933 that the question of inherited results of race mixing had yet to be studied in a scientific manner. "There is nothing in South American history to prove the essential inferiority of the mestizo. Whatever inconstancy of character or temperament he may display can easily be explained by circumstances of social inheritance and environment." Preston E. James ar-

53. Remarks of Ellender, *Congressional Record*, Senate, 75th Cong., 3rd Sess., Vol. LXXXIII, Pt. 1, p. 765; A. Grenfell Price, *White Settlers in the Tropics* (New York, 1939), 129; Virginia Prewett, *Reportage on Mexico* (New York, 1941), 46.

54. Kathleen Romoli, *Colombia, Gateway to South America* (Garden City, N.Y., 1941), 9.

gued that many factors explained Latin America's lack of development, but the readily observed "lack of energy, lack of ambition to achieve better standards of living through more efficient work, the general prevalence of ignorance, superstition, and apathy . . . are not the result of tropical climate, or inherited racial inferiority."[55] Robert Redfield insisted that more important than race in understanding Mexico were the isolation of peasant villages and the divisions between upper and lower classes and rural and urban residents. In a 1932 article Eyler N. Simpson expressed the same theme of social isolation: "It is the essential discontinuity of Mexican culture," he concluded, "produced and enforced through the centuries by the physical barriers of mountainous terrain, which lies at the base of Mexico's problem of creating a modern and integrated nation."[56]

The Black Legend, the third factor routinely offered to explain Latin American underdevelopment, had fewer advocates in this period than in earlier times, but advocacy of this constellation of anti-Hispanic beliefs seems not to have diminished in vigor. The horrors of the Spanish Civil War together with the authoritarian rule of Francisco Franco and his Falange played no small part in energizing those beliefs. Early in the period an editorial noted that the turmoil in the modern history of Spain and Portugal should remind us that when we contemplate "Latin America's chronic restlessness" we should give due credit to the "Latin element." Commentators who promoted the Black Legend continued to argue that the Spanish and Portuguese colonizers plundered the New World of its wealth, terrorized the native inhabitants with wanton cruelty, and introduced traditions of corruption, bigotry, and laziness, which together largely explained developmental problems. Some writers romanticized the pre-Columbian civilizations, to which the Spanish introduced the "untold horror of European exploitation through sword-and-cross." In reference to the Incas one author proclaimed that Latin America would be "a much happier and more stable area" if the Spanish had never arrived. "The marvelous Inca civilization of Peru, humane and communistic in the best sense of the word, was spreading slowly over South America, based on justice, social security, and all kinds of peace." A visitor to Mexico com-

55. C. H. Haring, *South American Progress* (Cambridge, Mass., 1934), 21; James, *Latin America,* 835.

56. Robert Redfield, "Folkways and City Ways," in *Renascent Mexico,* eds. Hubert Herring and Herbert Weinstock (New York, 1935), 34–35; Eyler N. Simpson, "Motor to Mexico Mañana," *Survey,* LXVIII (July 1, 1932), 299. Mexico's political, social, and cultural disunity was a central thesis of the very popular text, *Many Mexicos* (Berkeley, 1941), by Lesley Byrd Simpson.

plained of how "infinitely mournful" it was to contemplate "four centuries and more of cringing abjection in a land where once civilized men walked free, fearless and masters of their destiny," and to recall that when the Spanish came, it was a land "where the trees gave forth each its own sweet odour, the roses bloomed, and the birds sang." Respected specialists added their condemnation of the colonial heritage. Among the reasons listed by J. Fred Rippy for the "general backwardness in Colombia" was the "Spanish heritage of intolerance, intellectual repression, political corruption, and administrative inexperience."[57]

The author of a 1944 article in the *Christian Century* was so struck by the insight of a French essayist who had visited South America that he quoted at length from his speculation about North America had it been settled by Spain:

North America would be an uncultivated continent covered by immense woods, a silent continent divided into 198 republics. With very little precious metal to tempt the Latins the country would be largely an undeveloped pampa. In Canada half-breeds would dabble in politics, Negroes would vote in Alabama and Florida would be an independent Negro state. In Detroit, instead of the Ford factory there would be a grotto to some miraculous virgin and French prostitutes would be living in cozy apartments in San Francisco. . . . The Hawaiian Islands would be a government fortress large enough to accommodate all deposed presidents. Monasteries would cover the slopes of the Rockies and, in the evening, their bells would ring the Angelus in Hollywood![58]

Latin American character, which was still in this period presented in overwhelmingly negative terms, was judged a product of this unfortunate racial and/or cultural heritage, and Latin Americans were often portrayed as childish, ignorant, lazy, corrupt, and extremely individualistic. Roosevelt, frustrated over the pro-Fascist attitude of the Argentine government, in 1944 advised Secretary of State Edward Stettinius, "Ed, you make a face to the Argentineans once a week. You have to treat them like children." A journalist who claimed to have lived on the Mexican border or in Mexico for most of his life portrayed Mexicans as so densely ignorant that "to about eighty per cent of the country's population a crow bar is as complicated a piece of machinery as can be understood." In a discussion of conditions in Mexico, a Massachusetts congressman concluded that "Mexican graft is one of

---

57. New York *Times*, May 2, 1931; "America Hispana," *Review of Reviews*, XCIII (March, 1936), 51; Chase and Tyler, *Mexico*, 79; Rippy, *The Capitalists and Colombia*, 35–36.

58. George P. Howard, "What Ails Argentina?" *Christian Century*, LXI (January 26, 1944), 106, translated from Paul Morand, *Air Indien* (Paris, 1932).

the seven marvels of the world."[59] A traveler to Brazil in 1943 claimed that the majority of Brazilians were "interested only in food, shade and sexual satisfaction." A trait often observed and usually deplored was the Latin American's extreme individualism. In a sketch of the Colombian, Kathleen Romoli wrote: "Team work, personal responsibility in a common labor, the pride of being a consciously efficient cog in a comprehensive wheel are not yet part of his philosophy. . . . One does not know whether to pity, blame or envy this bone-deep individualism."[60]

In the expanding flow of information about Latin America and the evidence therein of greater awareness of each nation's distinctiveness, a few countries were applauded for their progressiveness and their better prospects for development, most especially Argentina, Chile, and Costa Rica.[61] All three were recognized for their political stability, democratic leanings, and growing middle classes. Export growth had enabled them to share in the worldwide prosperity of the 1920s, and following the depression of the early 1930s, the economies of Argentina and Chile made impressive comebacks based on rapid recovery of exports. Observers often attributed the relative progress of these countries to the lesser influence within them of factors traditionally invoked to explain Latin American backwardness. John Gunther noted that "the very climate of Costa Rica, with mild summer days and brisk cool nights the year round, stimulates orderly living. Its citizens are neither exhausted by altitude nor debilitated by moist tropical heat." Professor William L. Schurz, in his survey history of Latin America, argued that Argentina's predominant white population was a principal factor favoring the development of political democracy and stability. "It is free from the dead weight of a heavy Indian population, the too mercurial influence of the Negro, and the disturbing leaven of mixed peoples. . . ." These "onward" countries were also considered beneficiaries of the slight attention given them by the mother country during the colonial period. Professor Herring observed that "Spain's contempt for unprofitable Chile resulted in a wholesome neglect by colonial administrators. Chileans learned to fend for themselves."[62] Identification of the more-progressive states as those ben-

---

59. John Morton Blum, *Years of War, 1941–1945* (Boston, 1967), 206, Vol. III of Blum, *From the Morgenthau Diaries*; Owen P. White, "Next Door to Communism," *Collier's*, October 3, 1936, p. 12; remarks of John P. Higgins, *Congressional Record*, House, 75th Cong., 1st Sess., Vol. LXXXI, Pt. 10, Appendix, p. 2086.

60. Franck, *Rediscovering South America*, 345; Romoli, *Colombia*, 35.

61. Also included in this category, but mentioned less frequently, were Uruguay, southern Brazil, and Colombia's Department of Antioquia.

62. Gunther, *Inside Latin America*, 133; Schurz, *Latin America*, 140; Herring, *Good Neighbors*, 179.

efiting from the relatively slight influence of tropical climate, mixed races, and Hispanic legacy indicates the continuing importance of these factors in interpreting the region's underdevelopment.

Although these traditional explanations of underdevelopment retained their primacy in this period, they were supplemented with a growing variety of additional explanations. As previously noted, this period witnessed particular attention to the region's natural handicaps and the associated problems of transportation, communication, and national unity and to economic factors related to the dependency issue; the heavy burden caused by disease and malnutrition was also recognized. Past observers had mentioned other factors, but in this period these secondary factors were more numerous and presented somewhat more frequently. One writer noted that South America had never developed a "capitalistic spirit" sufficient to spur industrialization, and another declared that the Colombian lower class lacked an "acquisitiveness and a yearning to keep up with the Joneses." The same observation was often made about the Indians of Mexico, Peru, and Bolivia. The head of a U.S. technical mission sent to Brazil during wartime concluded that Brazil's delayed industrial development derived from the lack of a "technological inheritance, the inductive analytical habit, the zest for invention."[63] Other writers emphasized what Eyler N. Simpson, in his discussion of Mexican character, referred to as "a curious feeling of inferiority" and what a Brazilian-born, European-educated writer saw as a deep despair or pessimism born of a sense that "the poverty in South America is not an occasional crisis. It is a fact of centuries." An additional barrier to progress was seen in an entrenched upper class resistant to change, characterized by a conquistador mentality, and unwilling to place the public good above private gain.[64] Much of the commentary on these secondary factors contained the ethnocentric assumption that what ailed Latin America was the absence of qualities seen as essential to American achievement, such as a capitalistic spirit, technological inventiveness, a can-do optimism, and a dominant middle class.

An incident related by Professor Herring near the end of this period captures the essence of U.S. feeling toward the Latin American. Herring described a brief, casual conversation during a dinner party held

63. J. F. Normano, *The Struggle for South America: Economy and Ideology* (Boston, 1931), 225; Romoli, *Colombia*, 35; Morris Llewellyn Cooke, *Brazil on the March: A Study in International Cooperation. Reflections on the Report of the American Technical Mission to Brazil* (New York, 1944), 72.

64. Simpson, *The Ejido*, 580, 578; Normano, *The Struggle for South America*, 142; Soule, Efron, and Ness, *Latin America in the Future World*, 60.

in connection with a conference on hemispheric solidarity: "The charming faculty wife with whom I sat suddenly turned on me. 'Why is it,' she asked, 'that we all feel quite superior to the Latin Americans? We do, you know.' To which I could but return a feeble 'do we?' I have thought often of that lady, although her name is forgotten. I am inclined to agree with her. We *do* feel superior to the Latin Americans— at any rate, many of us do. . . . The prevailing opinion seems to be that Latin Americans are pleasant, impractical, shiftless people who cannot command serious attention."[65]

Changes in the perception of Latin America and its people were indeed slow in coming. Though the crises of depression and war softened criticism and brought greater mutual understanding, centuries-old stereotypes held sway. And even though the public became engrossed in the eccentricities of a Latin American craze, it left but a fleeting legacy. The period witnessed solid professional growth in Latin American studies and in the diplomatic corps accredited to the region, but the explosion of information on Latin America was still error-ridden, superficial, and filled with "flapdoodle." By the end of this period a corps of regional specialists had emerged who had formally studied Latin America, resided there for years, and become acquainted with Latin Americans from all levels of society. Acceptance of *indigenismo* by some of these specialists indicates that the American perspective was being influenced by Latin Americans and not just reinforced by the traditional elites, as in the past. It was also becoming clear that, as specialization advanced, it would be increasingly inaccurate to speak of an American public opinion on Latin American underdevelopment. The traditional emphasis on climate, race, and culture to explain underdevelopment continued to dominate commentary in the mid-1940s, but an emerging group of young scholars— including Robert Redfield, Preston E. James, Frank Tannenbaum, and C. H. Haring—who would assume academic leadership of Latin American studies in the postwar period, challenged traditional interpretations, particularly those based on race and culture. At the same time, more and more observers rejected the El Dorado myth and pointed out that Latin America's natural handicaps and resource limitations posed severe obstacles to development. The greater empathy for Latin America's problems, the slowly improving quality of information, and the growing challenge to traditional interpretations all contributed to the appearance of a somewhat more complex analysis of the forces impeding the region's development.

65. Hubert Herring, "Getting Along with the Neighbors," *Inter-American,* III (February, 1944), 13.

The most-important change in the discussion of Latin American underdevelopment was recognition of the critical importance of economic factors. Intrusion of economic analysis into the discussion arose naturally from the depression context, but it was largely sustained by Latin America's growing determination to move toward industrialization, by fear of introduction of foreign, radical ideologies, and by evidence of revolutionary nationalism. Tentative moves by the U.S. government to assist Latin American industrialization before World War II also promoted discussion of the economic forces impinging on industrialization. Before the depression the role of international economic forces had received consideration primarily from muckrakers, radical journalists, and leftist writers, but examination of the impact of those forces would become the basis for a sweeping theory of dependency in the 1960s. Although war confirmed Latin America's dependency and postponed policy decisions on the future course of the region's development, the debate on Latin America's future had already begun and, following transition to peacetime conditions in a Cold War setting, that debate would gradually resume and ultimately acquire urgency.

6

Latin America and the Discovery of Underdevelopment, 1945–1960

The level of interest in Latin America plunged dramatically a few years after the craze of the late 1930s and early 1940s, and the disinterest persisted for a decade and a half until a sudden recovery of concern late in the postwar period. That renewed interest spurred significant policy changes in the 1960s. As the United States abandoned isolationism and assumed the burdens of the world's dominant power in the late 1940s, Latin America became insignificant in U.S. policy formation and in public interest. Problems of inadequate and inaccurate reporting persisted, and the public's ignorance remained high even as scholarship in Latin American studies matured. Evidence of Latin America's growing economic nationalism and fear of communist advances, however, drew some attention to the region. Toward the end of the period, East-West competition—particularly in relation to alarming trends in Cuba—together with the inadequate performance of the Latin American economies, caused U.S. interest to rise. Concern over the quality of Latin America's political leadership, expressed in debate over aid to dictatorial regimes, was also voiced with a greater sense of urgency than in the past. In addition, the concept of "underdevelopment" emerged, and because Latin America was categorized as underdeveloped, the developed-underdeveloped conceptual framework directly influenced discussion of the region's problems. Consequently, commentary on those problems was more direct and clearly focused than ever before. The traditional explanations for Latin American underdevelopment still survived—except for the climatic factor, which largely disappeared—but they were supplemented by the new "modernization theory," which attempted to order and formalize increasingly complex explanations for underdevelopment and to propose remedies consonant with U.S. historical experience.

World War II and its aftermath had noteworthy political and economic consequences for Latin America. Even though only Mexico and Brazil had directly supported the Allied cause with combat units, all the Latin American states had severed ties with the Axis powers by the war's end, and most Latin Americans had experienced economic sacrifice in the form of severe shortages, inflation, and economic dislocation. Allied triumph over the fascist dictatorships sparked determination among many Latin Americans to claim their own democratic rights, which during the last two years of the war helped remove some long-standing dictators, including Jorge Ubico in Guatemala and Getúlio Vargas in Brazil. In the immediate postwar period until about 1948, the region enjoyed a wave of freer expression, an outpouring of rhetoric extolling democratic ideals, and the emergence of more-representative political parties that gained or shared power, such as Acción Democrática in Venezuela. Suffrage also expanded, and by the mid-1950s most Latin American states had granted women the right to vote. By the end of that decade only four states remained under military rule. It is too easy, however, to read a steady democratic trend in this postwar period. In fact, the trend was highly erratic, political turbulence still remained the norm, and subsequent events showed that the antidictatorial surge that marked the close of this period brought democracy to a very short-lived apogee.[1]

The war, like the depression before it, imposed serious strains on the Latin American economies, led to growing differences with the U.S. over the best path toward development, and stimulated economic nationalism. A student of U.S.–Latin American relations concluded that "Latin America emerged from the war years disorganized, dislocated, undersupplied, undernourished, and underprotected in the face of the vastly strengthened United States economic system." The loss of continental European markets during the war emphasized Latin America's dependence on the U.S. both as a market for exports and as a source of manufactured goods. In 1938 Europe bought about 55 percent of Latin America's exports and supplied about 44 percent of its imports; by 1944 those figures had fallen to 20 percent and 7 percent respectively. The U.S. took up much of that slack and encouraged production of critical raw materials, but joint Anglo-American purchasing commissions held prices down. In addition, the U.S. abruptly ended large-scale purchases of those goods after the war and in some cases restored former tariffs on them. The war also created shortages of food, consumer items, and capital goods, and the shortages spurred the growth of local consumer industries. Latin Americans sought to ensure the survival of those industries through tariffs, import controls, multiple exchange rates, and subsidies, while at the same time the U.S. argued for freer trade. A major economic theme throughout much

1. Burns, *Latin America*, 215–26; Cline, *The United States and Mexico*, 283–91; Leslie Bethall and Ian Roxborough, "Latin America Between the Second World War and the Cold War: Some Reflections on the 1945–8 Conjuncture," *Journal of Latin American Studies*, XX (1988), 168–72.

of Latin America in the postwar period was development through industrialization, a quest stimulated by depression, war, and the example of Mexico's shift in emphasis during the 1940s from land reform to industrialization.[2] The U.S. had, in fact, pledged its support for industrial development at the Third Meeting of Foreign Ministers in Rio de Janeiro a few weeks after Pearl Harbor and, under growing pressure from the Latin American states, had agreed at the February, 1945, Chapultepec Conference to a postwar hemispheric conference devoted to economic issues. Substantial differences with Latin America over the best path to economic development, however, led the U.S. to renege on its agreement to an economic conference.[3]

During the early postwar years Latin America enjoyed a healthy rate of development fueled by a high level of exports, favorable trade terms, and an expansion of imports made possible by the wartime accumulation of reserves. Observers complained, however, that vast amounts of those reserves were dissipated in luxury imports; for example, one writer noted that Mexico "bought herself silk sheets out of her war profits, while her people still need the basic elements of life."[4] By midcentury the development rate declined, and the decline became general throughout the region by 1955; it gave way to stagnation in many of the countries by 1960. Factors adversely influencing economic performance in the 1950s included the exhaustion of reserves, recovered production of primary goods in regions competitive with Latin America, the end of the Korean War and its accompanying export boom, and the onset of recession in the U.S. by late in the decade. The decline in rate of development is magnified when examined on a per capita basis because population grew so rapidly that the per capita product rose only 1.4 percent at the end of the period compared to 3.4 percent at the beginning. Because the region's economies remained so export-dependent, the performance of the export sector was critical to overall economic performance; the value of exports during the

2. Green, *Containment of Latin America*, 287; Samuel L. Baily, *The United States and the Development of South America, 1945–1975* (New York, 1976), 39, 55; David Green, "The Cold War Comes to Latin America," in *Politics and Policies of the Truman Administration*, ed. Barton J. Bernstein (Chicago, 1970), 151; Dean Acheson, *Present at the Creation: My Years in the State Department* (New York, 1969), 496–97; R. Harrison Wagner, *United States Policy Toward Latin America: A Study in Domestic and International Politics* (Stanford, 1970), 46–47; Sanford A. Mosk, *Industrial Revolution in Mexico* (Berkeley, 1950), 3–17.

3. Stephen G. Rabe, "The Elusive Conference. U.S. Economic Relations with Latin America, 1945–1952," *Diplomatic History*, II (1978), 279–86.

4. Alexander H. Uhl, "The 19th Century Comes to Mexico," *New Republic*, CXVI (May 5, 1947), 18.

1950s—excluding Venezuela because of the distortion caused by its petroleum exports—peaked in 1951 and did not regain that level until the following decade. Furthermore, Latin America's share of total world trade declined from 11.9 percent in 1950 to 6.8 percent in 1960. The region suffered a particularly unfavorable trend in the terms of trade from 1955 to 1960 because export prices declined relative to the stable prices of imports and because exports did not expand and diversify. In 1960 exports still consisted of traditional primary products. As a result of deterioration in the terms of trade, an acute balance of payments problem arose late in the period. Despite the strong desire for industrialization, the annual growth of industry in the postwar period was about 6 percent, quite low when considering the modest level at which it began. Even worse, the agricultural sector grew at a rate of 3.5 percent, so low that it was insufficient to meet both export requirements and domestic consumer demand. In light of the contrast between the hopefulness and rapid growth, on the one hand, with which this period began and the disappointing overall performance, on the other, it is not surprising that the period witnessed growing demand that the U.S. recognize Latin America's wartime sacrifices by assuming a greater role in its development.[5]

That demand met resistance which stemmed from disinterest in Latin American affairs that started during World War II and continued throughout the presidency of Harry S. Truman, 1945–1953, when the unfolding of the Cold War drove foreign policy formation. In summarizing U.S. policy toward Latin America five years into the postwar period, historian Gerhard Masur wrote that after 1945 "Latin America sank into oblivion. It was no longer the spoiled little brother, but rather the step-child of United States world policy planning." Crucial events in East-West relations, in Asia as well as Europe—the beginning of the Cold War, civil war in Greece and Soviet pressure on both Greece and Turkey, enunciation of the Truman Doctrine and the Marshall Plan, the Berlin Blockade, Soviet detonation of the atomic bomb, communist victory in China, and the Korean War—imposed an enormous strain on U.S. resources and its ability to attend to any region not faced with deep and prolonged crisis. At no time in this period did any part of Latin America face such a crisis. The Truman administration had to set priorities, and in the words of a student of the Truman years, "Latin America was not in great peril."[6]

5. United Nations, *The Economic Development of Latin America in the Post-War Period* (New York, 1964), 1–5, 121–25; Wagner, *U.S. Policy Toward Latin America*, 22–27.

6. Gerhard Masur, "Democracy in Eclipse," *Virginia Quarterly Review,* XXVI

Despite Latin America's low priority, the Truman administration formulated policies that became the basis for postwar U.S.–Latin American relations. Preserving and strengthening U.S. preeminence in the region was the overriding goal. As the global dimensions of the Cold War were defined in the early postwar years, anticommunism emerged as the key rationale in achieving that goal. In the absence of any real external communist threat to the hemisphere, the Truman administration linked social unrest, political instability, and nationalist tendencies to communist subversion, and under U.S. pressure most Latin American states severed relations with the Soviet Union and outlawed local Communist parties. After a protracted internal struggle, the Truman administration came to terms with Juan Domingo Perón's regime in Argentina, largely because of the Cold War imperative of hemispheric unity—but in spite of that regime's unsavory reputation.[7] Relying on the techniques of authoritarianism and nationalistic demogoguery, Perón governed Argentina for a decade following the war; under his populist leadership Argentina created a state-directed economy and launched a largely successful industrialization program. Economic problems and the needless adoption of radical measures such as anticlericalism induced the military to step in and remove him in 1955.[8] The Truman administration also moved toward closer hemispheric military cooperation, which the 1947 Inter-American Treaty of Reciprocal Assistance—the Rio Treaty—formalized through establishing a permanent defensive alliance against external or internal aggression. But effective collaboration did not become a reality until the U.S. authorized a military aid program under the 1951 Mutual Security Act and negotiated with several Latin American states bilateral mutual defense assistance pacts, the terms of which, incidentally, compelled the Latin American signatories to limit trade with Soviet bloc countries. Although support for the U.S. in the Korean War was only token—except for Colombia—by 1953 the U.S. was providing generous aid to Latin American military establishments, and

---

(1950), 340; Donald R. McCoy, *The Presidency of Harry S. Truman* (Lawrence, Kans., 1984), 135.

7. Skidmore and Smith, *Modern Latin America*, 335–37; F. Parkinson, *Latin America, the Cold War, and the World Powers, 1945–1973* (London, 1974), 13; Roger R. Trask, "The Impact of the Cold War on United States–Latin American Relations, 1945–1949," *Diplomatic History*, I (1977), 282–83; David Green, "The Cold War Comes to Latin America," 165–66, 189.

8. Baily, *The U.S. and the Development of South America*, 61–64; R. Trask, "The Impact of the Cold War on U.S.–Latin American Relations," 274–77; Burns, *Latin America*, 208–10.

they became closely linked to the U.S. through officer training, procurement of supplies, and anticommunist orientation.[9]

Reliance on private investment for development constituted an additional element of policy established during the early postwar years. Truman enunciated the U.S. position in person at the 1947 Inter-American Conference at Rio de Janeiro, where he drew a distinction between aid for Europe and aid for Latin America, declaring that for the latter "a much greater role falls to private citizens and groups than is the case in a program designed to aid European countries to recover from the destruction of war." Secretary of State George C. Marshall reiterated that position the following year at the Ninth Inter-American Conference in Bogotá, where the U.S. also opposed establishment of an inter-American bank and an inter-American development corporation. In line with this emphasis on private capital as the proper developmental vehicle, the Truman administration also favored self-help and freer trade policies, and it forcefully opposed commodity agreements, state capitalism, and economic nationalism. Although Truman advocated a technical assistance program for underdeveloped countries—Point Four—in his 1949 inaugural address, in response to complaints of unfair treatment of those countries, the program failed to achieve its potential because of modest funding by Congress, feeble support from the State Department, and lack of cooperation from business. The contrast between U.S. generosity toward Europe under the Marshall Plan and the meager dole of funds to Latin America was stunning: between 1945 and 1950 Belgium and Luxembourg received more direct aid than all of Latin America. At the end of the Truman presidency Latin America remained at the periphery of U.S. strategic interests, but the U.S. maintained preeminence there. Its policy rested on anticommunism and close military cooperation, as well as economic development through private capital, liberal trade practices, and technical cooperation.[10]

9. McCoy, The Truman Presidency, 208–209, 227–28; Baily, The U.S. and the Development of South America, 64–67, 74; Green, "The Cold War Comes to Latin America," 171–72, 177–78, 187.

10. McCoy, The Truman Presidency, 209–10; Baily, The U.S. and the Development of South America, 55, 59, 67–68; R. Trask, "The Impact of the Cold War on U.S.–Latin American Relations," 282; Truman as quoted in Trask, "The Impact of the Cold War on U.S.–Latin American Relations," 278; Green, "The Cold War Comes to Latin America," 180; Stanley E. Hilton, "The United States, Brazil, and the Cold War, 1945–1960: End of the Special Relationship," Journal of American History, LXVIII (1981), 603, 615; Wagner, U.S. Policy Toward Latin America, 129–30; Rabe, "The Elusive Conference," 283, 286; Bethall and Roxborough, "Latin America Between the Second World War and the Cold War," 182.

Inauguration of Dwight D. Eisenhower as president in 1953 offered an opportune time for reevaluating U.S.–Latin American policy, not only because he had promised such a review during his campaign but also because both the Korean War and the Marshall Plan had ended. Reviews were undertaken within the administration by the Commission on Foreign Economic Policies (the Randall Commission) and by Milton Eisenhower, the president's brother and principal Latin American adviser, who toured Latin America in 1953. The result was essentially a continuation of the Truman policies. The Eisenhower administration increased the flow of military aid to Latin America and made the great bulk of it available through outright grants. Regarding economic development, the emphasis remained on private investment, but Latin America benefited from a general trend in the 1950s that saw economic aid shift from the developed to the underdeveloped world because of the latter's perceived vulnerability to communism. Average annual aid to Latin America increased threefold from the Truman to the Eisenhower years, but Latin America remained a low-priority region to receive aid, and most of it was in the form of loans. Until late in the decade, the Eisenhower administration emphasized the same economic approach as its predecessor. In the words of a specialist on U.S. policy in this period, the U.S. pursued "limited, orthodox economic objectives in Latin America."[11] In addition, the anticommunist orientation of the Truman years was strengthened by the shift of East-West competition from Europe, as conditions there stabilized, to Third World countries, and by a crisis in Guatemala in 1954. Following the overthrow of dictator Jorge Ubico in 1944, a reformist regime came to power, and it was succeeded by the election of Jacobo Arbenz in 1950 as head of a center-left coalition whose goal was modernizing nationalism. Arbenz broadened the reform agenda to include tax reform, an expanded public works program, and land reform, which led to expropriation of large but idle acreages owned by the United Fruit Company. The Eisenhower administration was greatly alarmed by the expropriation measure, the arrival of arms from Eastern Europe following an arms cutoff by the U.S., and a perceived strategic threat to the Panama Canal and Central America. In 1954 Honduran-based Guatemalan exiles, armed and supported by the Central Intelligence Agency, mounted an attack against the Arbenz regime. Fighting was minimal and the attack easily succeeded because the military failed to come to Arbenz's defense. During the three years

11. Robert Dallek, *The American Style of Foreign Policy: Cultural Politics and Foreign Affairs* (New York, 1983), 210; Wagner, *U.S. Policy Toward Latin America*, 87–90; Baily, *The U.S. and the Development of South America*, 68–69, 73–74.

that the successor regime survived, it signaled its rejection of the reforming nationalist agenda by purging leftists from the government, reversing the expropriation of United Fruit lands, and signing a Mutual Defense Assistance Pact with the U.S.[12]

Events in Cuba in the late 1950s provided a dramatic expression of economic nationalism and energized the often-voiced warnings by U.S. officials of the menace of communism, thus sparking a lively interest in Latin American affairs. In 1957 Fidel Castro began a revolution against dictator Fulgencio Batista, who had regained power in 1952. The revolution succeeded by early 1959 because of Batista's inability to counter guerrilla attacks, the loss of public support for his increasingly repressive regime, and the U.S. decision to embargo arms shipments to both sides. During the two years following Castro's victory, Cuba came firmly under the dominance of this popular and charismatic leader, and it moved from the U.S. to the Soviet economic orbit. Castro consolidated his power by adroitly using his popular base of support and by adopting authoritarian measures while implementing sweeping reforms to improve living conditions for the island's poorest class. Those reforms included health and educational programs, radical agrarian reform, nationalization of foreign property, and state direction of the economy. In 1960 Cuba signed a trade agreement with the Soviet Union, and the Soviets also began providing military equipment. The Eisenhower administration responded with a trade embargo, then secret preparations for an invasion, and finally, in early 1961, the severance of diplomatic ties.[13]

By the mid-1950s, developments threatening to U.S. interests in Argentina and Guatemala had been contained, a revolutionary regime in Bolivia had been tempered through generous subsidies, and throughout Latin America the U.S. had largely succeeded in limiting the more-extreme expressions of economic nationalism and in keeping the region aligned as a Cold War ally. In addition, the Mexican Revolution had substantially moderated since the zealous reformism of the 1930s. It was only with Castro's advent as a major player in the Cold War that Latin American affairs could once more arouse and sustain public attention. The keen interest Latin America attracted in 1960 contrasted sharply with the inattention of the previous two decades.

During the final three years of the Eisenhower presidency, pressure mounted for a change in policy. The most-compelling argument

12. Burns, *Latin America*, 228–35; Gil, *Latin American–U.S. Relations*, 209–14; Stephen E. Ambrose, *The President* (New York, 1984), 192–94, Vol. II of Ambrose, *Eisenhower*.

13. Gil, *Latin American–U.S. Relations*, 227–32; Burns, *Latin America*, 242–47.

for reassessment arose from the leftward trend of events in Cuba. Furthermore, the contrast between Soviet aloofness from the Arbenz regime in Guatemala and its close support of Castro raised the alarming specter of Soviet movement toward a bolder and more-flexible policy in the hemisphere. Earlier, in mid-1958, additional dramatic evidence of a troubled U.S.–Latin American relationship had appeared when Vice President Richard Nixon toured eight Latin American countries while traveling to and from the inauguration of Argentina's president, Arturo Frondizi. Because of Nixon's reputation as a vigorous anticommunist and his insistence on defending U.S. policy before student groups, he became the target of escalating anti-U.S. demonstrations along his route. A threatening incident occurred in Lima, but tensions climaxed at the final stop, Caracas, where a foul-tempered, rock-throwing mob broke through security lines and seriously endangered the lives of Nixon and his wife.[14]

These incidents were broadly interpreted within the U.S. as communist-inspired, and, in fact, a widely embraced fear of communism profoundly influenced U.S. thinking about Latin America beginning about 1947. Following a tour of the region in early 1950, George F. Kennan, a State Department counselor, Soviet specialist, and an architect of the containment policy, warned in a report to the secretary of state that communist activities in the area "must be regarded as an urgent, major problem."[15] In the aftermath of Arbenz's ouster in Guatemala, one writer concluded that "the situation that made it possible for the Communists to go so far in Guatemala is duplicated all over Central and South America." In his simplistic but popular study of communism in Latin America, *Red Design for the Americas: Guatemalan Prelude* (1954), Daniel James began as follows: "The battle of the Western Hemisphere has begun. . . . We face, for the first time, the prospect of continuous struggle against Communism on a hemispheric scale. We face the possibility even of war—war on our own shores of the kind hitherto characteristic of Asia." The most-responsible and widely cited study of the communist theme was economist Robert J. Alexander's *Communism in Latin America* (1957), which argued that the threat to the region was real, that it was part of a worldwide, unified move-

14. Dallek, *The American Style of Foreign Policy,* 214; Richard M. Nixon, *Six Crises* (Garden City, N.Y., 1962), 209–225; "Hoover: Nixon Attacks Were Communist Inspired," *U.S. News and World Report,* May 23, 1958, p. 6; New York *Times,* May 11, 1958.

15. U.S. Department of State, *Foreign Relations of the United States, 1950, II: The United Nations; the Western Hemisphere* (Washington, D.C., 1976), "Memorandum by the Counselor of the Department (George F. Kennan) to the Secretary of State," March 29, 1950, p. 603 (hereinafter cited as Kennan, "Memorandum").

ment directed by the Soviet Union, and that the best hope for countering it was to support leftist democratic reformers. Despite Alexander's warning of the danger in supporting dictators, such warnings were often unheeded. For example, Congressman Overton Brooks defended dictator Rafael Trujillo and described the Dominican Republic as "that great island nation which has for so long constituted the bulwark which has protected our southeastern sea frontier from atheistic communism."[16]

This view represented a large body of opinion that accepted the strongman as the most-reliable defense against communism, a function he presumably performed by providing stability and a climate favorable for foreign investment and economic development. Praise of the dictators was particularly generous through the first term of the Eisenhower administration. For example, a journalist wrote of Nicaragua's Anastasio Somoza: "For twenty years he has been strong-arming his little country . . . into peace and prosperity." Marcos Pérez Jiménez of Venezuela received praise for setting a "breathtaking example for the rest of the hemisphere" of "internal development and modernization."[17] The exemplar of the kind of leadership frequently espoused was Manuel A. Odría of Peru, who had seized power in a military coup in 1948, suppressed the leftist opposition, and gained election without opposition in 1950 to a six-year term as president. He attempted to invigorate Peru's export-led economy by freeing exchange rates, removing import restrictions, encouraging foreign investment, and following the advice of U.S. experts on currency stabilization. Typical of the U.S. attitude toward the Odría regime was a newsmagazine article entitled "Peru: Success Story," which noted that the regime "has given Peru the most stable, progressive, and prosperous economy south of the United States."[18] The thrust of these observations about Odría and other Latin American strongmen was that they were an inevitable part of the scene, and realists must face the choice between them or communism.[19]

16. Dana Adams Schmidt, "Guatemala Highlights Latin-America's Ills," New York *Times*, June 27, 1954, Sec. 4, p. 4; Daniel James, *Red Design for the Americas* (New York, 1954), 11; Robert J. Alexander, *Communism in Latin America* (New Brunswick, N.J., 1957); remarks of Overton Brooks, *Congressional Record*, House, 85th Cong., 2nd Sess., Vol. CIV, Pt. 9, p. 11658.

17. "Nicaragua: Assassin at the Party," *Newsweek*, October 1, 1956, p. 51; remarks of Alexander Wiley, *Congressional Record*, Senate, 84th Cong., 2nd Sess., Vol. CII, Pt. 11, pp. 14367–68.

18. "Peru: Success Story," *Newsweek*, November 16, 1953, p. 54.

19. See for example Gardner R. Withrow to Howard Smith, Chairman, Committee on Rules, August 7, 1957, reprinted in remarks of Gardner Withrow, *Congressional Record*, House, 85th Cong., 1st Sess., Vol. CIII, Pt. 10, p. 14149.

In the late 1950s this tolerance for dictators began to lessen. A bitter debate over the appropriateness of providing aid to such unsavory characters as Trujillo contributed to the change.[20] The fall of several dictators during the last half of the decade encouraged the defenders of democracy to speak out against the survivors, and publication of exposés revealing some brutal and sordid practices by fallen dictators, particularly Perón and Pérez Jiménez, further discredited the surviving strongmen. Finally, some commentators charged that much of the anger directed against the U.S. in the 1958 anti-Nixon demonstrations derived from a too-cozy relationship with the dictators. In fact, the Caracas riots occurred a few months after Pérez Jiménez had been toppled and received comfortable asylum in the U.S. Also, though the successor regime to Odría in Peru generally followed his policies, praise for the Peruvian government ended in the aftermath of the demonstrations against Nixon during his visit to Lima.[21] The anti-Nixon outbursts led to the shift in attitude and contributed to the reevaluation of U.S. policy.

In the late 1950s, critics of U.S. policy, such as Christian Herter and Douglas Dillon within the administration and Senators Wayne Morse, George Smathers, and Frank Church, not only deplored the emphasis on military aid and the cordial relations with dictators but also argued that orthodox economic policy was inadequate to bring about rapid development and that social reform had to accompany economic growth. Pressure for a change in policy also came from Latin Americans who saw the U.S. attitude toward communism as obsessive and its unwillingness to provide a level of funding sufficient to promote development as niggardly. Specifically, they sought price stabilization for their export commodities through international commodity agreements or creation of a stockpile program, greater access to U.S. markets, increased lending from the Export-Import Bank, and formation of an inter-American bank. Ultimately, policy changed because of the fear of communism and because the Latin American

20. Extensive and frequent debate on U.S. support for Trujillo took place in Congress from 1957 until diplomatic relations were severed with the Dominican Republic in August, 1960. Trujillo's principal defenders were Congressmen B. Carroll Reece, George S. Long, Abraham L. Multer, John McCormack, W. J. Bryan Dorn, and Senators Olin D. Johnston and Allen J. Ellender. The attack against Trujillo was led by Congressman Charles O. Porter.

21. Geoffrey Bocca, "The Rape of Venezuela," *Coronet*, XLIV (October, 1958), 125–32; New York *Times*, September 9, 1958; "Reversing Peron's Revolution?" *Business Week*, October 1, 1955, pp. 31–32; "Peron's Legacy Is a Looted Country," *Saturday Evening Post*, February 18, 1956, p. 12; Gladys Delmas, "The Paradox of Peru," *Reporter*, September 18, 1958, pp. 30–31.

economies were simply not performing as necessary. There had been little success in fostering free trade, and the flow of private investment was disappointing, thus economic growth was slow, inflation was growing, and the export crisis was worsening.[22]

Despite the gathering consensus for change, the administration made modest adjustments. On the one hand, it responded to domestic protectionist pressures and increased import restrictions on several Latin American commodities such as lead, zinc, and petroleum. On the other hand, it reversed previous policy and in 1958 proposed establishment of an inter-American bank, supported Latin American efforts on behalf of an international coffee agreement, and favored creation of a Latin American common market system. In its final year the Eisenhower administration advocated establishing a special fund to provide loans for housing, health, literacy, and other social projects. Eisenhower obtained congressional appropriations for these projects and formally committed the U.S. to such a program in the Act of Bogotá, a document from the Inter-American Conference held September, 1960, in Bogotá that became the basis for U.S. policy in the 1960s.[23]

Official indifference to Latin America, which prevailed until the late 1950s, paralleled the attitude of the general public. The author of a bibliographical essay on books published on Latin America in 1945 noted with understatement that "the harvest was not abundant" for that year and complained of "the present state of half-knowledge between the continents"—evidence of the surprisingly fleeting legacy of the Good Neighbor era. Less surprising were the signs of ignorance and lack of interest as the Good Neighbor faded from memory, for example, a 1947 George Gallup survey of thousands of adults that revealed dismaying ignorance of basic Latin American geography. Specialist and nonspecialist noted this sharp drop in interest late in the war and during the early postwar years. Historian Lewis Hanke pronounced in 1946, "Our honeymoon with Latin America is definitely over. It was a breathtaking epoch while it lasted." And he correctly predicted a continuing decline in interest.[24] Symptomatic of the

22. W. W. Rostow, *Eisenhower, Kennedy, and Foreign Aid* (Austin, Tex., 1985), 142, 198; Wagner, *U.S. Policy Toward Latin America*, 21–26, 64, 101–103, 134.

23. Wagner, *U.S. Policy Toward Latin America*, 26–29, 55, 97, 148; Baily, *The U.S. and the Development of South America*, 76–79; Gil, *Latin American–U.S. Relations*, 238–40.

24. Mildred Adams, "This Year's Crop," *Inter-American*, IV (November, 1945), 22, 39; Harry B. Murkland, "Editor's Blind Spot," *The Americas*, I (May, 1949), 13; Lewis Hanke, "Friendship Now with Latin America," *Virginia Quarterly Review*, XXII (1946), 517.

indifference was the absence of extended discussion or analysis following such gripping events as the assassination of a popular Colombian political leader, which inflamed riotous mobs to destroy major parts of the center of Bogotá in April, 1948, while the city was hosting the Ninth Inter-American Conference. A frequent commentator on Latin America noted that "aside from the rumbas and revolutions, few North American newspaper readers have the faintest idea what is going on south of the border," and he argued that this ignorance was caused by editors who chose not to use the abundance of information provided on a daily basis. In 1949 United Press had seventeen bureaus in Latin America, Associated Press had correspondents in every South American capital, and International News Service had about twenty-five correspondents in Central and South America. Those services sent about fifteen thousand words a day from Latin America to the U.S., but little from this outpouring of information appeared in print. Two journalism professors who studied this seemingly willful ignorance attested to its persistence in the 1950s and concluded at the end of the decade that "the level of interest in and knowledge of Latin Americans among even educated United States citizens appears shockingly low."[25]

In addition to general indifference to Latin American affairs both at the official and unofficial levels, reporting on the region reflected a romantic quality occasionally bordering on the lurid in the early postwar years. A "Jungle Tale" in a 1945 newsmagazine likened homeless children encountered in the southern Venezuelan jungles to "vampires" because they allegedly disemboweled and plucked the eyes of dogs. The author of a travel column in the *Saturday Review* entitled "South America . . . Ay! Ay! Ay!" wrote: "Actually no American ever looks at South America with anything but a fleeting thought of beauty and romance, lest the glance be in the direction of the pestilencia of Perón." In a 1949 study of Hollywood characterizations of Latin America and its people, the author noted that during the 1940s the earlier, negative film stereotypes had sharply changed—under government prodding during the war but voluntarily since then: "The emphasis is now on a fairy-tale type picture, a glossy approach in which everything is sweetness and light in the country portrayed."[26] By the last half of

25. Murkland, "Editor's Blind Spot," 12–13; Edward W. Barrett and Penn T. Kimball, "The Role of the Press and Communications," in *The American Assembly, the United States and Latin America*, ed. Herbert L. Matthews (New York, 1959), 82.

26. "Jungle Tale," *Time*, October 15, 1945, p. 36; "South America . . . Ay! Ay! Ay!" *Saturday Review*, November 8, 1947, p. 39; Hernane Tavares de Sá, "Hollywood Needs Latin America," *The Americas*, I (October, 1949), 4–5.

the 1950s, however, negative stereotypes had returned, as witness the protests in Latin America against scenes in the films *Guys and Dolls* and *They Came to Cordura*.[27]

Commentary on Latin America also remained plagued with error and inaccuracy. The New York *Times* editorialist on Latin American affairs, writing in the authoritative *Foreign Policy Bulletin*, held that Brazil "was one of the last countries in Latin America to achieve independence," which, he asserted, was not gained until the expulsion of the emperor in 1889! At the end of this period when interest in Cuba was near a peak, Tad Szulc, a prolific writer on Latin American affairs, commented that during the operation of the Platt Amendment, 1902–1934, which permitted U.S. intervention in Cuba, "the amendment was never applied"—this despite a clear historical record of several interventions. An example of distorted interpretation is a newsmagazine article of the mid-1950s on Colombia's bloody guerrilla war, described by the befuddled writer as a "nearly meaningless war. Its causes," he alleged, "are rooted deep in Colombian history and temperament, a striking national indifference to death and lust for combat going back to the battles and matings of the fearless Spanish conquistadores and the warlike native Chibcha Indians."[28] Another problem with the reporting was that it often presented widely conflicting appraisals. A *Reader's Digest* article was unrelentingly optimistic about Latin America's general level of progress at midcentury and announced that "a great historical upturn has come" and that the whole region had surged forward and was "the most rapidly developing quarter of the globe." A year earlier a journalist writing in the *Nation* asserted that representative democracy was impossible in Latin America because the region's salient characteristics were "a backward economic structure, feudal mentality, poverty, malnutrition, disease, mendicancy, ignorance, illiteracy, alcoholism, and acute despair."[29]

As indicated in the above quotation, a tone of disappointment, frustration, and acerbic impatience—largely absent from the commentary for nearly two decades—had reentered it by the late 1940s. This was partly a reaction against the unrealistic expectation of a democratic

27. "Cuba. Righteous Wrath," *Time*, December 12, 1955, p. 34; New York *Times*, January 9, February 23, 1960.

28. Herbert L. Matthews, "Brazil in Travail," *Foreign Policy Bulletin*, XXXIV (December 1, 1954), 45; Tad Szulc, "Cuba: Profile of a Revolution," *New York Times Magazine*, April 24, 1960, p. 117; "Colombia: The Silent War," *Time*, December 31, 1956, p. 26.

29. Michael Scully, "Do You Know What's Been Happening South of the Border?" *Reader's Digest*, LXII (December, 1950), 143, 140; Bernard Mishkin, "'Good Neighbors'—Fast and Fancy," *Nation*, CLXIX (November 26, 1949), 512.

sweep throughout Latin America in the months immediately following the war.[30] One of the earliest expressions of this reaction appeared in 1948, when a government official asserted anonymously that we had become so accustomed to praising our southern neighbors that we often "gloss over some of the more unfavorable aspects of their character and habits." The New York *Times* averred in 1949 that the State Department had reason "to be alarmed at a number of Latin-American developments," and a few months later the same paper listed fourteen Latin American countries that had had "revolutions or the equivalent" since World War II, declaring this to be an unacceptable response to "the ferment of a new social consciousness in the masses." But any suggestion that the U.S., already heavily burdened with weighty global responsibilities, would have to attend to its disordered neighbors caused resentment. "While concerned with troubles all the way from Berlin to Shanghai and Singapore," reported one newsmagazine, "the United States is finding that it also has growing troubles nearer home, in the Western Hemisphere."[31] One writer complained that "Panama has been exposed to American influence for nearly half a century," and after all that time it is now a "police state." In a generally upbeat article on Truman's Point Four proposal, historian Henry Steele Commager suggested that a likely obstacle to its full implementation would be noncooperation from Latin America. "The benefits, for the last twenty years," noted Commager, "have been pretty much a one-way affair."[32]

At midcentury a State Department planner aptly summarized a common feeling toward Latin America in an article entitled "On a Certain Impatience with Latin America":

Public opinion in the United States has shown a sporadic impatience at the failure of many Latin American republics to achieve a greater degree of political democracy. The persistence of dictatorships in our midst throughout a war fought for democracy was a moral embarrassment. The establishment of new dictatorships after victory has seemed to some like a rejection of what we fought to achieve. While we were still fighting we put the best face on the business, just as we did with respect to our Soviet ally. The war over, opinion

30. "The Cycle of Revolt," *Newsweek*, November 12, 1945, p. 70; Roland Hall Sharp, "They Defied Dictators," *Christian Science Monitor Magazine*, May 26, 1945, p. 11.

31. Americus (pseud.), "Is the Good-Neighbor Policy Sound?" New York *Times*, March 28, 1948, as reprinted in remarks of Alexander Wiley, *Congressional Record*, Senate, 80th Cong., 2nd Sess., Vol. XCIV, Pt. 4, pp. 4284–85; New York *Times*, November 24, 1949, June 16, 1950; "Back of Spreading Revolts," *U.S. News and World Report*, December 24, 1948, p. 35.

32. New York *Times*, November 21, 1949; Henry Steele Commager, "Our Partners in Latin America," *Senior Scholastic*, April 6, 1949; p. 11.

in this country has sometimes tended to react in the manner of a stern father in the privacy of his home after his children have publicly embarrassed him.[33]

One aspect of the commentary on Latin America in this period that distinguished it from earlier times was evidence of a nagging sense of guilt about the region's problems and a growing feeling of responsibility to alleviate them. Acceptance of responsibility, though far from unanimous, derived not only from guilt but also from Cold War fears and a rekindling of the traditional American sense of mission. Many reports in the early 1950s noted Latin American complaints that they had been exploited by the U.S. during World War II and their economies seriously distorted, and that the exploitation was continuing through such U.S. practices as holding down prices of copper, tin, and sugar. Further, they were "compelled to wait for capital equipment while European countries were being rebuilt," and they had meekly acquiesced to the low priority assigned them for technical and economic assistance.[34] In the aftermath of the 1954 Guatemalan crisis, editorials in the *Commonweal* complained that following the ouster of dictator Jorge Ubico in 1944, the U.S. did little to help Guatemala's democratic forces and that "the free nations in 1954 are suffering because of the sins of the past." One writer observed that after the Guatemalan revolution people in the U.S. and Latin America suddenly realized the extent of U.S. responsibility for Central American affairs. He concluded that "U.S. government officials and businessmen ruefully agree that Central America is Uncle Sam's underdeveloped baby."[35] Through the remaining years of the decade, domestic critics of U.S. policy played on American guilt by referring to "our latent, unconfessed feeling of contempt toward Latin America," and they did not hesitate to blame the U.S. for Latin America's many ills. They also made it clear that the U.S. was the place to look for solutions.[36]

33. "On a Certain Impatience with Latin America," *Foreign Affairs*, XXVIII (July, 1950), 565; the author was identified as Louis J. Halle in "Going Forward," *Time*, July 3, 1950, p. 23.

34. "What Latins Need," *Newsweek*, January 29, 1951, p. 46; "Latin America: Poor Relations?" *U.S. News and World Report*, July 11, 1952, pp. 32–35; "Danger in Latin America," *Commonweal*, LIX (October 30, 1953), 77; "Latin America—What's Wrong?" *U.S. News and World Report*, July 17, 1953, p. 36.

35. "In the Shadow of the Volcano," *Commonweal*, LX (July 2, 1954), 308; "After Guatemala," *ibid.* (July 9, 1954), 331; "More Than Bananas and a Canal," *Business Week*, July 17, 1954, pp. 116–17.

36. George A. Smathers, "Mounting Problems of Latin America," *Vital Speeches of the Day*, XXIV (April 15, 1958), 396–97, reprinted from U.S. Senate speech of February 17, 1958; "Our Troubled Balkans," *New Republic*, CXLIII (November 28, 1960), 4–5;

The trend toward acceptance of this burden met opposition, however, ranging from mild assertions that a permanent solution to Latin America's many problems was beyond the capacities of the U.S. government, to strong arguments against foreign aid and in defense of classical economics by conservatives such as Irving Kristol and Milton Friedman. Going even further was a slashing attack by Latin American historian J. Fred Rippy against "the hucksters engaged in selling the foreign-aid programs to Congress." Another unsympathetic response came from historian Edwin Lieuwen, who noted in 1960 that Latin Americans were exerting increasing pressure on the U.S. for assistance as their economic problems became more critical and that "in many cases this pressure represents a search for a scapegoat to blame for troubles of their own making." More biting was the comment by economist Simon G. Hanson that U.S. acceptance of responsibility for Latin American development "has put the United States in a position of a man asked to protect from murder a person already engaged in committing suicide."[37]

The growing tendency during this period, despite opposition, to accept a greater role in the struggle against Latin American underdevelopment represents a throwback to the Progressive Era's confidence in the American way and enthusiasm for implanting it abroad. A prominent classical economist argued that U.S. interest in the welfare of other people extended beyond prosperity and national security, and he asserted, "We want the common man and his wife and his children to have not only Coca-Cola and chewing gum and ice cream, not only modern plumbing, automobiles, refrigerators, and electric lighting, but also good health and good diet, good education and good prospects of betterment in life."[38] A more-direct application of America's traditional sense of mission to the problems of underdeveloped nations ap-

"Catholics and the 'Have-Not' Nations," America. National Catholic Weekly Review, CI (August 8, 1959), 587; James W. Green, "Understanding the Problems in Latin America's Economy," Commercial and Financial Chronicle, October 22, 1959, pp. 1702–1703.

37. Mishkin, "'Good Neighbors'—Fast and Fancy," 514; Irving Kristol, "The Ideology of Economic Aid," Yale Review, XLVI (June, 1957), 508–509; Milton Friedman, "Foreign Economic Aid: Means and Objective," Yale Review, XLVII (June, 1958), 516; J. Fred Rippy, Globe and Hemisphere: Latin America's Place in the Postwar Foreign Relations of the United States (Chicago, 1958), 238; Edwin Lieuwen, Arms and Politics in Latin America (New York, 1960), 4; Simon G. Hanson, "Latin America Can Help Herself," in South America, ed. Lewis Hanke (Princeton, 1959), Vol. II, 115, of ed. Lewis Hanke, Modern Latin America: Continent in Ferment.

38. Jacob Viner, "America's Aims and the Progress of Underdeveloped Countries," in The Progress of Underdeveloped Areas, ed. Bert F. Hoselitz (Chicago, 1952), 176.

peared in a 1957 monograph entitled *A Proposal,* by Professors Max F. Millikan and W. W. Rostow of the Massachusetts Institute of Technology. They argued that the principal obstacles to growth were lack of capital and the inability to absorb it effectively, and they called for a substantial, long-term commitment of capital to Third World nations. Many observers concurred that the lack of capital represented the major barrier to more rapid economic development, but few so eloquently linked their analysis to the summons for a revived U.S. sense of mission. Millikan and Rostow asserted that their proposals were "designed to give fresh meaning and vitality to the historic American sense of mission—a mission to see the principles of national independence and human liberty extended to the world scene." Such an undertaking was essential, in their view, to maintain the vigor of American character, "to keep us from the stagnation of smug prosperity," and to bolster "those basic spiritual qualities which have been historically linked to the nation's sense of world mission." They held that this commitment was feasible because the U.S. possessed the necessary resources and also because "the United States is now within sight of solutions to the range of issues which have dominated its political life since 1865"—issues including racial equity, equal educational opportunity, and equitable distribution of income![39]

Debate over the appropriate response to Latin America's desire for rapid development occurred in a context in which, for the first time, the question of underdevelopment assumed a central role in the commentary on Latin America and became the subject of formal, academic study. But before looking at these efforts to formulate a theory of development, it would be well to examine observations of nonspecialists who continued to uphold traditional interpretations and to provide the core of conventional wisdom on Latin American underdevelopment.

The views of specialists and laymen most closely corresponded on the theme of Latin American character. An open airing of character deficiencies marked this period and distinguished it from the restraint of the preceding period of depression and war. The previously mentioned frustration and impatience with Latin American underdevelopment activated the discussion of character, which was often examined in the context of cultural constraints to development. Immature, emotional, destructively individualistic, and shortsighted were the most frequently mentioned among the many character defects freely assigned to Latin Americans. A State Department specialist

39. Max F. Millikan and W. W. Rostow, *A Proposal: Key to an Effective Foreign Policy* (New York, 1957), 7–8, 149–51.

on Latin America complained that in those countries with free elections the behavior of voters during an election campaign resembled "the conduct of schoolboy gangs." A journalist advised that the Latin American should be made to realize that "his emotional and explosive psychology, leading to division and revolution, are [*sic*] to blame for a large percentage of Latin political trouble."[40] Journalist Herbert Matthews attributed Colombia's political problems to the character of its people. "One must always keep in mind, " concluded Matthews, "that the hot-tempered, emotional, intense Colombian does not feel or think the way an Anglo-Saxon would in similar circumstances. Extremism is more natural than moderation in Colombia—as in many other Latin American countries." A reviewer of William L. Schurz's 1954 text on Latin American history wrote: "Perhaps the 'predominance of feeling over intelligence' which Dr. Schurz notes in the Brazilian is typical of most Latin Americans. If so, that may be a reason why Latin America has remained for so long a hinterland." Erna Fergusson, author of several Latin American travel books, compared Cuban history to "one of those novels whose tragedy depends upon the shortsightedness or complete blindness of the characters. Why, oh why, could they not have seen that they were bringing on their own destruction?"[41] The significance of these observations lies in the conviction that little development could occur as long as such traits governed Latin American conduct. These characteristics together with the often-discussed problems of corruption, sloth, and "a culturally-rooted indifference to the satisfaction of doing a job well" seemed to pose insurmountable barriers to progress.[42]

Closely related to discussion of character, though mentioned much less frequently, was evidence of the Black Legend . Major tenets of the legend were losing their hold over U.S. perceptions of the Latin American historical and cultural tradition, although its anti-Hispanic concepts were far from dead. The assault on the grand edifice of the Black

40. [Halle], "On a Certain Impatience with Latin America," 569; Peter Masten Dunne, "The Americas: Psychological Attitudes: Politics, Finance, Religion," *Bulletin of the National Catholic Educational Association*, XLV (August, 1948), 253.

41. Herbert L. Matthews, "Colombia: Political Volcano," *Nation*, CLXXV (November 8, 1952), 426; Daniel James, "The Other America: Review of *This New World: The Civilization of Latin America* by William Lytle Schurz," *New Republic*, CXXXI (September 20, 1954), 19; Erna Fergusson, *Cuba* (New York, 1946), 231.

42. David H. Shelton, "The Economic Growth of Latin America: Motivation, Prospects and Problems," *Journal of Inter-American Studies*, I (1959), 171; Herbert Cerwin, *These Are the Mexicans* (New York, 1947), 62; New York *Times*, March 11, 1952; "Why Argentina Is in Turmoil," *U.S. News and World Report*, July 6, 1959, p. 42; "Where an Empire Is Growing," *U.S. News and World Report*, December 3, 1954, p. 44.

Legend had slowly gathered momentum since the early part of the century when Edward Gaylord Bourne published his even-tempered and persuasive *Spain in America, 1450–1580*. By 1960 U.S. students of Latin America had published many studies that rehabilitated Spain's colonial record. In addition to the growing academic consensus against the Black Legend, this revisionist view was finally entering the popular mainstream. Highly favorable reviews of Salvador de Madariaga's opus, *The Rise of the Spanish American Empire* (1947), in *Newsweek* under the heading "Whitening Black Legend" and in the *Saturday Review of Literature*, contained vigorous denunciations of the myths long associated with the Black Legend. The reviewer in the latter journal wrote: "For years, North American authorities on Spanish American history have been busily hacking away at the Black Legend. There should be little or nothing left of the whacking lies about the inhuman cruelty of the Spaniard to the Indian and the Negro. But lies of this variety, especially when backed by religious hatred, die hard, and besides don't Spaniards like bullfights?"[43]

Despite formal repudiation of the Black Legend, it continued to exercise an irresistible hold over attitudes toward Latin American culture and character. Its most-evident aspect was that the Hispanic tradition had left a legacy of cruelty, greed, violence, and authoritarianism. The most-noteworthy expressions of this viewpoint appeared, ironically, in *Senior Scholastic*. An article on Mexico in a 1946 issue noted that "the colonial era was probably the darkest in Mexican history. The Spaniards proved to be cruel and corrupt masters. They robbed the country of its wealth." A decade later a *Business Week* article attributed the plight of Indians in the Andean countries to the wanton cruelty of their Spanish masters: "Slaughtered in vast numbers by the Conquistadores, then enslaved by the later Spanish colonists, the Indians have endured centuries of suffering. . . ." Elsewhere, the Portuguese were charged with "three centuries of narrow, plundering colonial exploitation" in Brazil.[44] On many occasions when observers needed to explain the Latin American turn to revolution, they tended to write despairingly that "the revolutionary urge is probably a car-

43. Benjamin Keen, Introduction to "A Reply to Bourne," in *The Colonial Origins*, ed. Benjamin Keen (3rd ed.; Boston, 1974), Vol. I, 498, of ed. Benjamin Keen, *Latin American Civilization*; "Whitening Black Legend," *Newsweek*, November 8, 1948, pp. 94–96; Herschel Brickell, "Black Legend: Review of *The Rise of the Spanish American Empire* by Salvador de Madariaga," *Saturday Review of Literature*, January 24, 1948, p. 14.

44. "Land of Revolution," *Senior Scholastic*, April 15, 1946, p. 7; "An Old Civilization Stirs Up Political Problems: Election Stakes in Peru," *Business Week*, June 9, 1956, p. 127; Matthews, "Brazil in Travail," 45.

ryover from the days under Spain," thus dismissing centuries of peace and order. In addressing the theme of violence and revolution in Latin American society, political scientist William S. Stokes argued in an article entitled "Violence: The South American Way" that belief in Latin America's rapid progress toward political democracy was the "height of political naivete." He held that force and violence were such an inherent part of Hispanic culture that they were institutionalized in Latin American politics and that the culture was characterized by authoritarianism in family and church organization, class structure, and in economic and governmental systems.[45]

In the postwar discussion of Latin American developmental problems, the role of the racial factor was also much diminished. This striking change happened in less than a generation through the impact of previously noted social science findings that repudiated scientific racism, and by the heightened value placed on democratic sentiments following the struggle against totalitarianism. Revulsion against the monstrous evils committed by the Nazis under the racial purity doctrine also helped shift attitudes. The concurrent beginning of desegregation in the U.S. suggests the sweep of this antiracist trend. Observations on Latin American race tended toward benign descriptions of racial varieties, but they also expressed occasional outright rejections of the role of race and, more rarely, positive assessments. Historian Milton I. Vanger expressed a representative judgment on race when he noted in 1958 that the explanation for disparity in development between the U.S. and Latin America—"one that still often lurks behind much American reasoning even if it is no longer openly stated—[is] the intrinsic superiority of white Anglo-Saxons to half-breed Latin Americans," but, he added, "Today this seems to be so much less satisfactory as an answer."[46]

The influence of Brazilian anthropologist Gilberto Freyre may have been a factor in the decline of the racial interpretation. Freyre, who received some of his training under Franz Boas at Columbia University, was one of the most influential Brazilian intellectuals of the century in that he profoundly changed the Brazilian sense of national identity. In essence, he argued that the decisive factor in Brazilian history

45. Milton Bracker, "Violence in Venezuela: Old Plot, New Victim," New York *Times*, November 19, 1950, Sec. 4, p. 10; William S. Stokes, "Violence: The South American Way," *United Nations World*, V (December, 1951), 51, 54. A highly Hispanophobic book, which was very favorably reviewed, is John Collier's *The Indians of the Americas* (New York, 1947).

46. Milton I. Vanger, "Latin America in Perspective," *Yale Review*, XLVIII (December, 1958), 231.

was the tendency toward ethnic and cultural fusion of Portuguese and other European immigrant groups with blacks and native Indians to form, not an inferior mongrel type, but a Brazilian who had brought forth a "dynamic and creative tropical culture" because he was ideally suited to the Brazilian climate and way of life. Prominent Latin American specialists in the U.S. such as Lewis Hanke and Frank Tannenbaum were influenced by Freyre's work in the 1930s, but in the postwar period his impact on the academic community and the educated lay public was prodigious. It derived from his occasional appearances on university campuses as a lecturer and visiting professor and from publication of his studies on Brazilian history, most particularly the English translation in 1946 of his seminal work, *The Masters and the Slaves*.[47] The ready reception of Freyre's work suggests that U.S. attitudes toward race and the interpretation of Latin American underdevelopment along racial lines had markedly changed.

Discussion of the *bracero* program in the early 1950s offers another index of the change in attitude toward race. By agreement between the U.S. and Mexico during World War II, seasonal agricultural workers from Mexico were permitted entry into the U.S. to help meet wartime labor needs, and the agreement was renewed several times until the 1960s. Discussion of renewal in the early 1950s became entangled with debate over the related problem of the growing influx of illegal immigrants from Mexico. But this debate contrasted sharply with that of twenty years earlier over Mexican immigration; it was more objective and factually based, it lacked racial reference, and it examined problems facing the undocumented entrants such as horrible living conditions. The debate of the 1950s was also somewhat alarmist, but the alarm arose from fear over the spread of contagious disease, the inability to assimilate large numbers of aliens, and the infiltration of subversive elements. This latter fear was frequently expressed in congressional debate, but a journalist summarized it as follows: "No one could guess how many Communist agents, saboteurs, and international smugglers were infiltrating the country through the mesh of holes in the border."[48]

Despite this evidence of a changing attitude, negative references to

47. Gilberto Freyre, "Brazilian Melting Pot," *Atlantic Monthly*, CXCVII (February, 1956), 105, 108; Gilberto Freyre, *The Masters and the Slaves: A Study in the Development of Brazilian Civilization*, trans. Samuel Putnam from 4th ed. of *Casa Grande e Senzala* (New York, 1946). Freyre's *Brazil, An Interpretation* (1945) was expanded, rewritten, and published in 1957 as *New World in the Tropics: The Culture of Modern Brazil*.

48. Richard Eckels, "Hungry Workers, Ripe Crops, and the Nonexistent Mexican Border," *Reporter*, April 13, 1954, p. 28.

the Latin American racial configuration were not uncommon although they lacked the strident quality of earlier times, and they were most often made indirectly or in reference to immigration. For example, the author of a travelogue on Mexico wrote, "Obviously Mexico could solve many of its more pressing problems quickly if it permitted selective immigration." Commentators also explained Costa Rica's progress relative to the rest of Central America on the basis of the elimination of Indians and the early arrival of settlers who were "an industrious Spanish middle class of artisans, farmers and shopkeepers." Latin America's Indian population evoked occasional negative comments such as the reference to El Salvador's "two million people, most of whom are sadly degenerate Indians." The traditional view of Latin American race was moderately expressed by former New Dealer Rexford G. Tugwell in his review of Dexter Perkins's highly regarded study of 1947, *The United States and the Caribbean.* Tugwell concurred with the author's conclusion that a principal cause of underdevelopment in the Caribbean nations was "a recently mixed breed in difficult tropical circumstances."[49] In the typical commentary on Latin Americans in this period, the direct, negative racial reference was replaced with less inflammatory but nevertheless very telling references to "hot-blooded Latins," "the immaturity of the people," and "the emotional (therefore unstable) quality of Latin and mestizo alike."[50]

In the triad of traditional interpretations of Latin American underdevelopment, the greatest change occurred in the assessment of climate. A few voices yet sang the old refrain of tropical debilitation, as for example a student of U.S.–Latin American relations who concluded that Brazil ranked behind Argentina in material progress because of "a certain indolence, bred by the easy existence in the tropical and semitropical climate."[51] But this became a decidedly minority view because of advances in tropical medicine, a half-decade of experience in the tropics during World War II, and a reexamination—brought on by the Cold War—of relations with underdeveloped tropical re-

49. Cerwin, *These Are the Mexicans,* 341; "Central America: Waking Nations," *Time,* May 23, 1960, p. 28; Charles Morrow Wilson, *The Tropics: World of Tomorrow* (New York, 1951), 44; Rexford Tugwell, "Enlightened Unselfishness Down South," *Saturday Review,* December 27, 1947, p. 10; this article is a review of Dexter Perkins, *The United States and the Caribbean* (Cambridge, Mass., 1947).

50. Remarks of George H. Fallon, *Congressional Record,* House, 83rd Cong., 1st Sess., Vol. XCIX, Pt. 12, Appendix, A4861; Peter Schmid, "Letter from Peru," *American Mercury,* LXXV (October, 1952), 74; Peter Masten Dunne, "Has Latin America Grown Up Politically?" *Catholic Mind,* XLVI (April, 1948), 207–18.

51. Thomas W. Palmer, Jr., *Search for a Latin American Policy* (Gainesville, Fla., 1957), 189.

gions. One advocate of such a reexamination, Charles Morrow Wilson, a representative of U.S. business interests who had spent many years in the tropics, called for an end to mindless depictions of the tropics as either "perennial green hells or palmy Utopias." He publicized recent advances in knowledge about tropical agriculture, soils, and climate and referred to the type of information found in a popular survey of Caribbean nations by a lay writer, who stated that one of the world's most-persistent myths was "the 'theory,' romanticized and perpetuated by writers from Kipling to Maugham, that people living in equatorial climes are doomed to moral and physical decay." This survey summarized results of a study of military personnel performance in tropical areas during World War II, which offered an effective rebuttal to the traditional view: "Despite prolonged stays in the humid jungles of Asia and the Pacific, often under subnormal circumstances, American, Australian and British soldiers of all races and color worked unprotected and often bareheaded, in the noonday sun. They suffered no ill effects. A result of a study by American and Canadian Army doctors and scientists showed that soldiers and civilians after five consecutive years in hot and humid areas were generally fit and efficient." The study became well known through publication in both a medical journal and in *Time* magazine.[52] Popularization of this study may have helped move the general public away from theories of tropical debilitation, but the decline in academic circles of theories long associated with Ellsworth Huntington can be traced to two events: a critique of his theories at a session of the 1938 International Congress of Geographers and publication in 1939 by the American Geographical Society of A. Grenfell Price's landmark study, *White Settlers in the Tropics*, which raised serious doubts about the validity of such theories.[53] In any case, by the postwar period specialists and increasing numbers of laymen looked askance at the notion that Latin American underdevelopment was a function of climate.

One of the most-surprising findings in a reading of the commentary on Latin America is evidence that a majority of observers continued to espouse the traditional El Dorado myth. Its firm refutation by scholars in this and previous periods had not yet carried the day by 1960.

52. Wilson, *The Tropics*, 4, 9; Albert Balink, *My Paradise Is Hell: The Story of the Caribbean* (New York, 1948), 294, 299; "The Midday Sun," *Time*, April 21, 1947, pp. 57–58.

53. Earl Parker Hanson, *New World Emerging* (New York, 1949), 54, 85–86. For other rejections of Huntington's theories see Marston Bates, *Where Winter Never Comes: A Study of Man and Nature in the Tropics* (New York, 1952), 126, 230–31; Douglas H.K. Lee, *Climate and Economic Development in the Tropics* (New York, 1957), 7–9.

On the positive side, those who still portrayed Latin America as a potential Garden of Eden were, by and large, nonspecialists, and members of Congress must be counted among the most ill informed. Senator Allen J. Ellender continued his references to "the almost limitless natural resources of the Americas to the south of us," while Senator Dennis Chavez of New Mexico, a frequent commentator on Latin American affairs, complained that its standard of living could not be raised "unless the innumerable resources of the countries of Latin America are developed. They have not been touched. . . ." Another senator noted for his interest in the region, George Smathers of Florida, asserted that Latin America was "almost the richest area on earth in mineral deposits of all kinds."[54] Countless authors of travel books, articles, essays, and editorials continued to sprinkle their work with misleading observations such as the following: "Latin America is still the new El Dorado, a vast treasure house"; Mexico has "hidden riches that can only be surmised"; Brazil is "a slumbering giant of untapped resources"; and Nicaragua is "a modern Garden of Eden." A highly regarded journalist specializing in Latin America repeated an old canard when he wrote in 1960 that the region's economic problem "is still that of the starving man with a gold mine under his feet."[55] Such frequently appearing comments by the "cornucopians," as purveyors of the El Dorado myth were labeled by one economist, overwhelmed the determined efforts of specialists to implant in the public mind a realistic assessment of Latin America's natural wealth.[56]

On the broader theme of the region's total resource base and its geographical fitness for development, the specialists were more successful in presenting the awesome natural handicaps to development. In their collective work these authorities argued that: (1) the physical barriers to transportation were formidable; (2) in contrast to the U.S., Latin America lacked good harbors, navigable rivers, and ade-

54. Remarks of Allen J. Ellender, *Congressional Record,* Senate, 82nd Cong., 1st Sess., Vol. XCVII, Pt. 8, p. 10913; remarks of Dennis Chavez, *ibid.,* 83rd Cong., 1st Sess., Vol. XCIX, Pt. 2, p. 2272; remarks of George Smathers, *ibid.,* 85th Cong., 2nd Sess., Vol. CIV, Pt. 2, p. 2237.

55. Edward Tomlinson, *Battle for the Hemisphere: Democracy Versus Totalitarianism in the Other America* (New York, 1947), 3–4; Cerwin, *These Are the Mexicans,* 48; "What Do You Know About the Green Continent?" *House and Garden,* XCII (August, 1947), 108; Balink, *My Paradise Is Hell,* 149; Tad Szulc, "Basic Questions About Latin America," *New York Times Magazine,* February 21, 1960, p. 64. See also Milton S. Eisenhower, "United States Latin American Relations: A Report to the President," *U.S. Department of State Bulletin,* XXIX (November 23, 1953), 706.

56. Simon G. Hanson, *Economic Development in Latin America: An Introduction to the Economic Problems of Latin America* (Washington, D.C., 1951), 7.

quate, well-distributed rainfall; (3) the resource base was narrow and badly distributed; (4) the region suffered from a severe shortage of quality coal; (5) only a small fraction of the total land area was arable; and (6) tropical forest soils were of very poor quality. A geology professor's pithy comment, "If Argentina had coal, it could build a steel industry, if it had iron," summarizes the frustration produced by an ungenerous Nature, which so terribly confounded development.[57] William Vogt, head of the conservation section of the Pan American Union and author of a series of articles and a well-received book, *Road to Survival* (1948), offered the most-arresting statement of this theme. He concluded that Latin America's geography, which he characterized as "the harshest and most inescapable factor limiting its human betterment," reinforced by the modern competitive economic system had created "one of the most vampirish, extractive economies existing anywhere in the world today" and that the Latin American countries, with the possible exceptions of Argentina and Brazil, "are fundamentally and inescapably so poor that a living standard approaching that of the United States is unattainable."[58] In short, Vogt argued that Latin America was facing ecological disaster. Even though the myth of vast, untapped wealth persisted, the larger picture of a region severely disadvantaged by Nature was convincingly presented beginning in the 1930s and continuing throughout this postwar period.

Vogt based his central thesis of Latin America's impending ecological disaster not only on its limited resource base but also on a newly stated argument that its rapidly growing population was undermining efforts to improve the standard of living. This sudden reversal in the traditional view that the region desperately needed immigrants to populate its immense empty spaces arose from a gradual growth in population from the turn of the century to the 1930s, the

57. George Wythe, *Brazil, An Expanding Economy* (New York, 1949), 339; Laurence Duggan, *The Americas: The Search for Hemisphere Security* (New York, 1949), 8; Nathan L. Whetten, *Rural Mexico* (Chicago, 1948), 3, 567; Bates, *Where Winter Never Comes,* 235; John P. Hogan, "The Future of American Engineers in South America," *Civil Engineering,* XV (April, 1945), 170; Abbott Payson Usher, "The Steam and Steel Complex and International Relations," in *Technology and International Relations,* ed. William Fielding Ogburn (Chicago, 1949), 70–71; Hanson, *Economic Development,* 35; Erna Fergusson, *Mexico Revisited* (New York, 1956), 8–10; Louis J. Halle, *Dream and Reality: Aspects of American Foreign Policy* (New York, 1958), 158–59; V. L. Horoth, "Economic-Political Conditions in Latin America," *Magazine of Wall Street,* June 12, 1954, p. 332; Howard A. Meyerhoff as cited in Hanson, *Economic Development,* 52.

58. William Vogt, *Road to Survival* (New York, 1948), 152–54, 157, 166–67. See also William Vogt, "A Continent Slides to Ruin," *Harper's Magazine,* CXCVI (June, 1948), 481–89.

result of a fairly constant birth rate and a sharply declining death rate, with the latter brought about by improved sanitation and public health. Vogt boldly concluded: "All Latin American countries except three or four are overpopulated. They are able to feed and shelter their citizens, and supply water for their many needs, only by a progressive and accelerating destruction of natural resources; biological bankruptcy hangs over their heads like a shaking avalanche."[59]

This new perspective on the old problem of the relationship of population base to development was not widely embraced for more than a decade, but it received strong endorsement from Frank Tannenbaum in his depressing but widely read study of Mexican history since the revolution, *Mexico: The Struggle for Peace and Bread* (1950). He argued, much as he had in the 1930s, that instead of following the U.S. model and emphasizing industrialization and creation of a national market, Mexico should strengthen its rural villages to increase agricultural and handicraft production, using Switzerland and Denmark as models. In Mexico's "rapidly increasing population and . . . rapidly eroding soil" Tannenbaum professed to see the operation of forces "that may well submerge the Mexican community and overwhelm the nation itself." In his view, "the contemporary Mexican dilemma" was an increasing population that was "hastening the threat of a seemingly inescapable doom. . . ."[60] Although Tannenbaum enjoyed a formidable reputation as a Latin Americanist, acceptance of this "population bomb" thesis was delayed, in part because of firm resistance by Latin Americans. By the late 1950s, however, the rapid increase in world population, especially in underdeveloped regions, burst forth as a matter of some urgency. Reports by the United Nations Bureau of Social Affairs (1958) and by two presidential commissions late in the decade all spoke of the critical need to bring population growth in underdeveloped countries under control. The same message was reiterated by prominent citizens who spoke of the "titanic and inexorable" force of population growth, its "skyrocketing curve," and the "catastrophic zooming of the world's population." Only a handful of writers narrowed the focus to Latin America. A professor of geochemistry declared that because of its rapid population increase, "it seems likely that we see in Latin America a vast continent-wide slum in the making."[61] But President Eisenhower stated that it would be entirely

59. Vogt, *Road to Survival,* 152.

60. Frank Tannenbaum, *Mexico: The Struggle for Peace and Bread* (New York, 1950), 242–43, 180.

61. Theodore A. Gill, "The Demographic Explosion," *Christian Century,* LXXV (August 6, 1958), 895; Jack Zlotnick, "Population Pressure and Political Indecision,"

improper for the U.S. government to assist underdeveloped countries in controlling population growth, and both presidential candidates in 1960 seemed to welcome that stance. The preference in official circles to do nothing that seemed to support birth control applied especially to Latin America because of perceived religious sensibilities and because several observers asserted that many countries there were still underpopulated.[62] Despite the rapid change in the perceived relationship between population base and development during the 1950s, by the end of the decade only a few specialists argued that Latin America's high rate of population growth was a major factor in the region's underdevelopment.

In spite of significant modification in traditional explanations for Latin American underdevelopment, most especially since the 1920s, the old themes were occasionally expressed with engaging power. Such an instance was George F. Kennan's previously cited memorandum of 1950 to the secretary of state. Simply stated, Kennan was appalled and depressed by what he observed in Latin America during his one and only tour there. "It seems to me unlikely," noted Kennan, "that there could be any other region of the earth in which nature and human behavior could have combined to produce a more unhappy and hopeless background for the conduct of human life than in Latin America." He lamented that upon a decidedly unfavorable climate and geography, "humanity superimposed a series of events unfortunate and tragic almost beyond anything ever known in human history." The Spaniards arrived, asserted Kennan, as "terrible, merciless conquerors" bearing little more than "religious fanaticism, a burning, frustrated energy, and an addiction to the most merciless cruelty." The intermarriage of Spaniards, Indians, and Negro slaves produced "unfortunate results" that weighed heavily on the "chances for human progress." Kennan concluded: "In these circumstances, the shadow of a tremendous helplessness and impotence falls today over most of the Latin

---

Foreign Affairs, XXXIX (July, 1961), 685, 687–88; New York *Times,* July 24, 1959; J. Murray Luck, "Man Against His Environment: The Next Hundred Years," *Science,* CXXVI (November 1, 1957), 903; Julian Huxley, "Are There Too Many of Us?" *Reader's Digest,* LXXIII (December, 1958), 63; Harrison Brown, "Life in the Americas During the Next Century," *Annals of the American Academy of Political and Social Science,* CCCXVI (March, 1958), 15. The entire March, 1958, issue of the latter journal was devoted to population trends in the Western Hemisphere.

62. Zlotnick, "Population Pressure and Political Indecision," 686; Theodore C. Sorensen, *Kennedy* (New York, 1965), 111–12; Ernest van den Haag, "Demographers Go to the New World," *Saturday Review,* June 20, 1959, p. 24; "'Standing Room Only' in the World?" *U.S. News and World Report,* November 23, 1959, p. 88.

world. The handicaps to progress are written in human blood and in the tracings of geography; and in neither case are they readily susceptible of obliteration. They lie heavily across the path of all human progress, and the answers which people have suggested to them thus far have been feeble and unpromising." Though self-admittedly not an expert on Latin American affairs, Kennan was a major figure in U.S. diplomatic history whose views—which a reading of his *Memoirs* suggests were prompted by his own observations and analysis—were not easily ignored. They are also a forceful reminder of the slow pace of change in the U.S. perspective on Latin America.[63]

Although the casual observations of nonspecialists reflected a broadly based public opinion that sustained the traditional interpretation of Latin American underdevelopment, those observations represented only one of the two principal levels of thought on the subject in this period. On another level, the academic specialist—typically not a Latin Americanist—attempted to incorporate the inquiry into the general question of underdevelopment, a response to rapidly growing interest in the problems of underdeveloped nations in the postwar period. The new perspective was symbolized by the sudden popularity of the terms "backward states" and "underdeveloped areas"—the former became an entry in *Reader's Guide to Periodical Literature* in 1947—to describe nations emerging as colonial empires crumbled after World War II, a war fought at least in part for democracy and self-determination. Those terms reflected a new way of thinking about the world and of categorizing nations, and because the Latin American states were classified as underdeveloped—after some initial uncertainty—they were subject to the same general analysis that all states in that category underwent. The rapid evolution of worldwide communications made the problems of Third World nations more palpable than ever, and their use of newly established international agencies such as the United Nations and the World Bank as sounding boards for their struggles made it difficult for the world's dominant power to remain passive. One economist argued that "advanced countries cannot afford to ignore economic backwardness,"and he cited the high price the world is paying for Russia's failure to emancipate its peasants and to industrialize at an early time. Gunnar Myrdal, an eminent Swedish economist who popularized the notions of vast disparities in wealth between advanced and underdeveloped nations and of the former's responsibility for this condition in his 1957 study *Rich Lands and*

63. Kennan, "Memorandum," 600–602; Roger R. Trask, "Notes and Comments: George F. Kennan's Report on Latin America (1950)," *Diplomatic History*, II (1978), 307–11; George F. Kennan, *Memoirs, 1925–1950* (Boston, 1967), 476–83.

Poor, asserted that "the misery of those far away has been brought home to the people in the richer countries and presented as a threat to their own security." More important, Myrdal's book, which was widely and favorably reviewed, called for replacing classical economic theory with a dynamic theory of development that incorporates noneconomic factors and guides underdeveloped nations in devising economic plans and developed nations in furnishing aid.[64]

Analysis of Latin American developmental problems moved in this period to a previously unoccupied plane as a result of the popularization of developmental studies within academic circles. The study of development became the academic fashion, and its faddish appeal was signaled by the launching of new journals such as *Economic Development and Cultural Change* (1952); by new courses in development offered by colleges and universities; by the appearance of popular textbooks and anthologies on development; and by the organization of multidisciplinary centers devoted to developmental analysis, such as the Research Center on Economic Development and Cultural Change at the University of Chicago. Much of this activity was fueled by an outpouring of previously unavailable data provided by vastly improved national statistical services and by the United Nations and its regional agencies such as the Economic Commission for Latin America.[65] As early as 1950, an economic specialist in development asserted that "economic development has become the economic shibboleth of our times—the watchword for every international economic discussion." During the 1950s the growth of developmental studies gathered momentum in response to several factors, including President Truman's call for a "bold new program . . . for the improvement and growth of underdeveloped areas"; the remarkable success of the Marshall Plan; uneasiness about the Soviet alternative of forced industrialization, whose achievements were symbolized by the launching of Sputnik in

64. Ivan Vallier, "Recent Theories of Development," in *Trends in Social Science Research in Latin American Studies: A Conference Report,* ed. Institute of International Studies (Berkeley, 1965), 6; "Editorial," *Economic Development and Cultural Change,* I (1952–1953), 83; Harvey Leibenstein, *Economic Backwardness and Economic Growth: Studies in the Theory of Economic Development* (New York, 1957), 1; Alexander Gerschenkron, "Economic Backwardness in Historical Perspective," in *The Progress of Underdeveloped Areas,* ed. Hoselitz, 29; Gunnar Myrdal, *Rich Lands and Poor: The Road to World Prosperity* (New York, 1957), 127.

65. Aidan Foster-Carter, "From Rostow to Gundar Frank: Conflicting Paradigms in the Analysis of Underdevelopment," *World Development,* IV (March, 1976), 171; Leibenstein, *Economic Backwardness and Economic Growth,* 2; Rostow, *Eisenhower, Kennedy and Foreign Aid,* 42; Harold Brookfield, *Interdependent Development* (London, 1975), 24–26.

1957; and the apparently successful performance of the Chinese Communist economy.[66]

An effort to formulate a theory that could explain the process of development and bring those insights to bear in a systematic assault on underdevelopment arose not only from the rapidly growing academic interest in developmental studies but also from the need to order a great outpouring of literature that increasingly emphasized the inordinate complexity of the developmental process and, in a reversal from the previous period, the noneconomic factors relevant to the process. One developmental economist complained in 1958 that despite the vast and growing literature on the subject, "the field remains ill defined" and lacks a "widely accepted set of principles." Other economists noted that the study of economic development had produced "an ever lengthening list of factors and conditions, of obstacles and prerequisites" and that historians and sociologists had identified "a number of beliefs, attitudes, value systems, climates of opinion, and propensities" favorable to development, while other specialists, including psychologists, had stressed the role of "minorities and of deviant behavior" and of "achievement motivation." A text on economic development included a three-page list of factors to be evaluated when judging prospects for development.[67] The effort to impose order on this growing disorder yielded what became known as "modernization theory."

Application of the emergent modernization theory to Latin America was the most-distinctive feature of postwar commentary on the region. This so-called modernization theory—also referred to as a paradigm or a perspective—cannot properly be called a theory, for, as noted by an economist in 1960, literature on the subject abounded with "seminal ideas, revealing insights, penetrating bits and pieces of analysis, loose ends, and unrealistic assumptions." Fourteen years later another specialist declared, "Our understanding of what modernization is remains largely intuitive; we still seem to rely on a gut feeling." Modernization theory did not gain its fullest expression until the early 1960s, but by the start of that decade it had evolved to become, at min-

66. Leroy D. Stinebower, "Discussion: U.S. Foreign Investment in Underdeveloped Areas," *American Economic Review*, XL (1950), 511; Harry S. Truman, "Inaugural Address," January 20, 1949, in U.S. Congress, *Inaugural Addresses of the Presidents of the United States from George Washington 1789 to Lyndon Baines Johnson 1965*, 89th Cong., 1st Sess., House Doc. No. 51 (Washington, D.C., 1965), 254.

67. Henry J. Bruton, "A New Text on Economic Development," *Economic Development and Cultural Change*, VII (1958), 85; Albert O. Hirschman, *The Strategy of Economic Development* (New York, 1958), 1–2; Gerald M. Meier and Robert E. Baldwin, *Economic Development: Theory, History, Policy* (New York, 1957), 443–45.

imum, a widely shared "gut feeling," and it had gained a consensus of support in the academic mainstream. One salient characteristic of the theory was that it was interdisciplinary, featuring contributions from economics, political science, sociology, psychology, and anthropology. It thus reflected the postwar vogue for interdisciplinary studies. Because developmental studies was a new field, there were no experts to set standards, but "there was enthusiasm, a missionary zeal, and a feeling of obligation."[68] Any attempt to understand the interpretation in the U.S. of Latin American underdevelopment must consider modernization theory.

In general terms modernization theory held that the path toward modernization, also referred to as "development" and early in the period as "Westernization," had been traced initially by England and followed by the U.S. and Western Europe and that other nations could follow a similar path by evolving in stages along a continuum from traditional to modern societies.[69] One economist concluded that future societies in the Third World need not be identical to Western models, but "if economic development is to proceed, value systems, attitudes and economic institutions, relations and organizations must correspond more closely to those of the West with their greater emphasis on material gain." Scholars treated modernization as an extremely broad concept involving an all-inclusive, socio-politico-economic and cultural process of replacing traditional values and institutions with modern ones, i.e., as a process requiring "nothing less than a comprehensive social transformation." Modernity was defined by such characteristics as rational, secular, urban, literate, and industrial and in politics as pluralistic and/or democratic with well-developed interest groups and large-scale participation. Traits of a modern soci-

68. Henry J. Bruton, "Contemporary Theorizing on Economic Growth," in *Theories of Economic Growth*, eds. Bert F. Hoselitz *et al.* (Glencoe, Ill., 1960), 239; Grazyna Nikonorow, "A Critique of the Modernization Paradigm," *Human Factor*, XII (1974), 98; Vallier, "Recent Theories of Development," in *Trends in Social Science Research in Latin American Studies*, 8.

69. The literature on modernization theory is abundant; the following offer useful summaries of its major tenets: Vallier, "Recent Theories of Development," in *Trends in Social Science Research in Latin American Studies*, 7–16; Foster-Carter, "From Rostow to Gundar Frank: Conflicting Paradigms in the Analysis of Underdevelopment," 170–73; Nikonorow, "A Critique of the Modernization Paradigm," 95–113; J. Samuel Valenzuela and Arturo Valenzuela, "Modernization and Dependency. Alternative Perspectives in the Study of Latin American Underdevelopment," *Comparative Politics*, X (1978), 535–43; Charles W. Bergquist, ed., *Alternative Approaches to the Problem of Development: A Selected and Annotated Bibliography* (Durham, N.C., 1979), vii–xii; Brookfield, *Interdependent Development*, 24–39.

ety also included high rates of spatial and social mobility, a complex occupational system, and self-sustaining economic growth.

Modernization assumed an evolutionary view of social change along a dichotomous traditional-modern continuum, and developmental specialists frequently referred to the position of underdeveloped societies "along the continuum of development."[70] The theory also assumed that "progress" along this continuum would be facilitated by contact with the developed world, so that modernization would occur by diffusing modern values and institutions through such vehicles as foreign aid and investment, technical aid, trade, educational exchange, and mass media influences. An example of this assumption appeared in a study of Mexican exchange students in U.S. universities; the study concluded that the student served as "an agent of culture contact, the transmitter of desired technical skills and more democratic values," and that the student returned with "new ethical concepts and notions of punctuality, cleanliness, order, and responsibility." Modernization theory was also optimistic in its assumption that once development occurred in one sphere such as the economic, it would spread to others such as the political and social, and it argued that the road to development was not all that arduous. Rostow, for example, concluded in his popular study, *The Stages of Economic Growth* (1960), that "the lesson of all this is that the tricks of growth are not all that difficult."[71] In sum, modernization theory as it had emerged by 1960 was multidisciplinary, ethnocentric, evolutionary, and optimistic.

In the economic, political, and social sectors modernization theory advocated industrialization and land reform, democracy, and a predominantly middle-class society respectively, and it referred to the emergence of Western capitalism. The move toward industrialization had made notable headway in Latin America by the 1950s, and according to economist Simon G. Hanson, the use of U.S. know-how and capital represented "the most popular prescription of our time" for development in the region, a formula particularly well suited to "the prevailing diagnosis of underdevelopment which stresses indus-

70. H. Belshaw, "Some Social Aspects of Economic Development in Underdeveloped Countries in Asia," in *Underdeveloped Areas: A Book of Readings and Research,* ed. Lyle W. Shannon (New York, 1957), 191; Douglas F. Dowd, "Two-Thirds of the World," *ibid.,* 12; Alvaro Chaparro and Ralph H. Allee, "Higher Agricultural Education and Social Change in Latin America," *Rural Sociology,* XXV (1960), 10.

71. Ralph Beals and Norman D. Humphrey, *No Frontier to Learning: The Mexican Student in the United States* (Minneapolis, 1957), 112, 105; W. W. Rostow, *The Stages of Economic Growth: A Non-Communist Manifesto* (2nd ed.; Cambridge, Mass., 1971), 166.

trialization." Its appeal grew despite disheartening obstacles such as limited markets, high unit profits, the high cost of money, and deficiencies in transportation, energy sources, and technical skills.[72] Though less prominently promoted than industrialization, land reform remained a favored program among modernizers. The complexities of the agrarian problem conjured up by the term *latifundia* had long been recognized as a major obstacle to development, and observers continued to complain of "primitive farming practices" and a "semi-feudal" agrarian economy that illustrated "allegiance to the colonial system."[73]

In the political sphere a 1949 symposium, "Pathology of Democracy in Latin America," featuring prominent area specialists, reflected the interest in exploring reasons for democracy's shortcomings south of the border. Examination of this theme seemed timely because the wartime triumph over totalitarianism was still a fresh memory, and countries long ranked as among the most democratic in Latin America, e.g., Argentina, Colombia, and Costa Rica, were in imminent danger of losing that ranking because of recent political upheavals. The symposium also offered opportunities to examine the relationship between democracy and development. Although participants were uneasy about the condescending implications of the symposium's title, they concurred that several factors hindered the achievement of Western-style democracy, such as racial and class divisions, geographic disunity, the colonial heritage, latifundia, and illiteracy. But the overarching factor, in their view, was the low standard of living of the vast majority of Latin Americans. These specialists concluded that after substantially improving the standard of living, it would be possible to move toward the conditions essential for a healthy democracy, e.g., expanding the middle class, lowering geographical barriers, and improving literacy rates. But the first step was economic growth, and to achieve it they stressed the importance of political stability, or, in the words of Professor Federico G. Gil, following the counsel of Bolívar and establishing an "'orderly society,' no matter whether founded along the lines of democratic or undemocratic structure."[74] The will-

72. Hanson, *Economic Development*, 3, 36, 183; "Debate-of-the-Month: Industrialize Latin America?" *Rotarian*, LXX (May, 1947), 28–30; Peter F. Drucker, "Frontier for This Century," *Harper's Magazine*, CCIV (March, 1952), 68; George H. Houston, "Industrializing Undeveloped Areas of the World," *Dun's Review*, LVII (March, 1949), 14–16; "Continent of the Future," *America*, XCV (May 12, 1956), 152.

73. "The Hemisphere: Ironic Requests," *Time*, February 19, 1945, p. 44; Bernard Mishkin, "Democracy in Latin America," *Nation*, CLXIX (November 26, 1949), 513; Henry William Spiegel, *The Brazilian Economy: Chronic Inflation and Sporadic Industrialization* (Philadelphia, 1949), 1.

74. "Pathology of Democracy in Latin America," *American Political Science Re-*

ingness of these political "pathologists" to give priority to stability over democracy was consistent with the desire, born of the dangers inherent in the Cold War setting, to avoid for the moment the turbulence associated with Latin American democracy.

In the social sector the one element of developed societies most frequently mentioned as a *sine qua non* for development was a substantial middle class.[75] This judgment persisted throughout the period despite demurrals by several scholars such as sociologist W. Rex Crawford, who saw in the American glorification of the middle class a tendency to see "ourselves as we like to see us" and to causally relate "things that are ours and are good."[76] This hesitation to advocate democratic, middle-class societies as important elements of development was not evident in advocating economic growth, because development was defined principally in economic terms, and the definition, in conformity with modernization theory, assumed that political and social elements would fall into place behind the locomotive of economic growth.

Academic proponents of modernization theory and nonspecialist observers who promoted traditional interpretations of Latin American underdevelopment offered distinctive perspectives on the subject, but these two approaches were not incompatible. By the late 1950s modernization theory had escaped its academic confines and had become a topic worthy of the educated layman's consideration.[77] For example, character traits were often discussed in the context of examining cultural constraints to development, and the discussion was consistent with the tenets of modernization theory. As applied to Latin America, modernization theory suggested that traditional values and

---

view, XLIV (1950), 100–49. Participants in the December, 1949 symposium were William W. Pierson, Arthur P. Whitaker, Russell H. Fitzgibbon, Sanford A. Mosk, W. Rex Crawford, Federico G. Gil, and Paul C. Bartholomew. For Gil's remarks see "Pathology of Democracy in Latin America: Comments," *ibid.,* 149.

75. The "salvation through the middle class" thesis is most notably presented in John J. Johnson, *Political Change in Latin America: The Emergence of the Middle Sectors* (Stanford, 1958).

76. W. Rex Crawford, "Pathology of Democracy in Latin America. Discussion: A Sociologist's Point of View," in "Pathology of Democracy in Latin America," 146. See also Ralph L. Beals, "Social Stratification in Latin America," *American Journal of Sociology,* LVIII (1953), 337.

77. The following are examples of discussions of modernization theory in nonacademic journals: P. T. Bauer, "Economic Growth and the New Orthodoxy," *Fortune,* LVII (May, 1958), 142–43, 194, 196, 198; Walt Rostow, "'The Stages of Growth' as a Key to Policy," *ibid.,* LX (December, 1959), 135–36, 201–202, 204, 209; Joan Robinson, "The Policy of Backward Nations," *Nation,* CLXXXIV (June 1, 1957), 485–86.

institutions posed the principal obstacles to development and that development could be brought about by changes in them. In effect, modernization theory saw in Latin America many of the same obstacles to development that observers had reported for a hundred years: the problem lay in the characteristics of the people and in their culture. By providing a pseudoscientific patina for traditional attitudes, modernization theory justified and perpetuated those ethnocentrically based attitudes. Though the Black Legend was formally repudiated, the undemocratic, semifeudal Hispanic legacy remained a favorite theme, and that heritage with its authoritarian institutional bases and conquistador mentality was still seen as a major barrier to modernization. The racial factor was less and less emphasized, but the Latin American populations were still portrayed as defective and, therefore, as impediments to progress. Descriptions of the numerous character flaws of the Latin Americans differed little from nineteenth-century portrayals except for the lack of any effort to make them humorous. The postwar descriptions revealed a willingness to criticize that recalls the smugness of predepression days. Also, the continued retelling of the El Dorado myth was a familiar refrain that strengthened the impression of a people following suicidal paths. The third in the triad of traditional explanations of underdevelopment, the tropical climate, was effectively put to rest in this period, but the disadvantages associated with the region's geographical features, such as the limited, poorly distributed resource base, remained an important though less-emphasized factor. Modernization theory concurred in this de-emphasis; it saw in the application of capital and modern technology the means for overcoming many of Nature's limitations, as illustrated by the comment that "modern science and invention have leveled the mountains that once limited the association" of the peoples of Latin America.[78]

Despite the centrality of this continuity, the interpretation of Latin American underdevelopment changed more during the postwar period than it had during the entire preceding century. The full range of the region's problems and the obstacles to its development had never before been set forth in such grim, systematic detail; from this process a picture of unanticipated complexity had begun to emerge by 1960, which left the rather simplistic traditional triad no longer sufficient to explain underdevelopment. Modernization theory attempted to formulate a more-ordered structure from increasingly complex, multi-

78. Claude C. Bowers, "The Freedoms in the Americas," in *Responsible Freedom in the Americas*, ed. Del Río, 206.

disciplinary views, but the change it symbolized was more apparent than real. Modernization theory in fact strengthened existing attitudes by disparaging Latin American institutions, traditions, and culture; even more important, it argued that they must be discarded, albeit by an evolutionary process, in order to achieve modernization. The notion that the region's development required total transformation and adherence to the U.S. economic, political, and societal model was a radical doctrine, although it was not perceived as such in that era's ethnocentric ambience. Its potential power was greater than the raucous boosterism of the 1920s because it was destined to form the basis of U.S. policy in the 1960s. Modernization theory symbolized change less in the interpretation of underdevelopment than in the attitude toward the U.S. role in the developmental process. By the end of this period many Americans had accepted the view that Latin American development required an unprecedented degree of U.S. participation. Modernization theory announced both the discovery of underdevelopment and the intention of doing something about it.

By 1960 modernization theory was sufficiently coherent to offer policymakers a sense of direction following fifteen years of inattention to Latin American affairs. World War II had dissipated the aura surrounding the Good Neighbor policy and left the U.S. with burdensome global responsibilities that focused the nation's attention on crises in Europe and Asia. The resulting neglect of Latin America changed to a growing sense of responsibility during the last years of this period as Cold War competition advanced into the region. This interest was sharpened by the educated public's quick grasp of the concept of underdevelopment and wide discussion of it, and from the classification of Latin America as underdeveloped. Consequently, Latin American underdevelopment was addressed directly, whereas in earlier periods it was addressed casually and as a matter of idle curiosity; it became a theme appropriate for academicians and policymakers in addition to travelers and laymen. It received serious attention in the postwar period not only because it was more clearly conceptualized but also because it was seen to have direct bearing on U.S. security interests. By 1960, faced with a growing threat to its interests in Latin America and a gnawing sense of some measure of responsibility for the region's underdevelopment, the United States was moving toward a policy that sought to meet leftist and nationalistic challenges to its hemispheric hegemony while expressing a characteristic sense of optimism and world mission.

7

Idealism and Disillusion in the 1960s:
The Alliance for Progress

The quest for new frontiers and the willing acceptance of challenges by the incoming administration of John F. Kennedy em-
boldened the young president to launch a new program for Latin
America, the Alliance for Progress, within weeks of his inauguration.
Implemented with confidence and optimism, this innovative program
arose from fear that communism would implacably spread throughout Latin America from its Cuban base if the U.S. continued to neglect the region and from the conviction that this menace could be
thwarted by vigorously attacking the region's underdevelopment
through a program of social and political reform and democratic modernization. The Alliance for Progress gained bipartisan backing although it was essentially a product of pragmatic liberalism. Its widespread support derived from the sense of responsibility for Latin
America's worsening plight that had been growing since the late 1950s.
Support also came from the general conviction that a cooperative hemispheric effort could succeed; this confidence rested on acceptance by
the mainstream academic community and the educated lay public
of modernization theory, which provided the program's conceptual
framework.

The history of the 1960s is a history of shattered illusions, and one
of the decade's many casualties was the Alliance for Progress. Its pu-
tative failure was less a result of Latin American events than of mo-
mentous cultural and political changes within the U.S., which sharply
curtailed the liberal agenda and also reduced the public's already no-
toriously short attention span for things Latin American. The consensus that had upheld the Alliance for Progress early in the Kennedy
administration failed primarily because of those changes, but the decade
also witnessed a growing challenge to modernization theory by a new
paradigm, which brought into doubt the theoretical underpinnings of
the Kennedy program and undermined confidence in its ultimate success.

One characteristic feature of commentary on Latin America at the
beginning of the 1960s was the frequent restatement of themes that
had been dominant for decades, such as the "beggar on a mountain

of gold" theme, as well as complaints of widespread ignorance about the region and the persistence of feudalistic traditions there. A New York *Times* editorial noted in 1960, "There is relatively little knowledge of Latin America in the United States," and it railed against the Latin American ruling class for its failure to make social and economic reforms that would move those societies "from Spanish and Portuguese colonialism and feudalism into the Nineteen Sixties." Adlai Stevenson, two-time Democratic presidential nominee in the 1950s, returned in early 1960 from an eight-week tour of Latin America "deeply concerned" because of "our ignorance about our Latin neighbors" and because of the anomaly of "a region rich in resources" in which half the people were hungry, homeless, and illiterate.[1] Senator Karl E. Mundt expressed the long-familiar ethnocentric outlook when, in an attack on Fidel Castro's distortions of Cuban history, he proclaimed in 1960: "We who in living memory rescued the island from medieval bondage; we who have given order, vitality, technical wisdom and wealth are now being damned for our civilizing and cooperative virtues!" At the same time, an editorial in the *Reporter* judged that a major past failure of the U.S. had been in not taking over Latin America following the Civil War a century earlier. "Had the United States established its empire over Latin America," claimed the writer, "it would by now either have graduated out of it, or else it might have developed the capacity to run in freedom a pluri-national society."[2]

Such remarks suggest the validity of complaints of a lack of knowledge. At the beginning of the decade Latin American studies remained poorly developed and unsophisticated but on the brink of a dynamic surge. The Joint Committee on Latin American Studies, established in 1942 by the American Council of Learned Societies and the Social Science Research Council, had disbanded in 1947, and it was not reestablished until 1959, a year that also marked the appearance of an academic journal with a fresh, interdisciplinary perspective, the *Journal of Inter-American Studies*. During that twelve-year interregnum Latin American studies stagnated in comparison with the study of other foreign areas. A substantial but uneven research foundation had nevertheless been established in some disciplines, the strongest being history, geography, and anthropology, but even here the explosion of scholarly effort lay just ahead. Woodrow Borah, a senior Latin Amer-

---

1. New York *Times*, July 12, 1960; Adlai Stevenson, "Our Plight in Latin America," *Look*, November 22, 1960, p. 104.

2. Karl E. Mundt, "How Cuban Freedom Really Was Won," *Reader's Digest*, LXXVII (August, 1960), 168; "Latin America Joins the World," *Reporter*, September 15, 1960, p. 16.

ican historian, observed retrospectively in a 1983 interview that expansion in Latin American history did not really begin until about 1960. Economics, political science, and sociology were the weakest disciplines, although each had pockets of strength such as the work done by development economists during the 1950s. But little was known of Latin America's nineteenth- and twentieth-century economic history; the first political science text on Latin America did not appear until 1949, and sociologists had done little aside from the work of a handful of rural sociologists.[3] Anthropologist Charles Wagley concluded in a 1963 survey of the state of Latin American studies, "Our present knowledge of this important area is embarrassingly poor."

Within a few short years, however, academic expansion and the proliferation of graduate students and Ph.D.'s in all disciplines touching on Latin American studies had become prodigious. The number of students in higher education more than doubled between 1955 and 1965, and federal funds flowed to those institutions in rapidly increasing amounts, particularly in the post-Sputnik era and after enactment of the National Defense Education Act in 1958. That act provided fellowships, grants, and loans to encourage science, mathematics, and foreign language study and established a graduate fellowship program that helped create new graduate programs in foreign area studies and expand existing ones.[4] By the end of the decade dozens of new Latin American studies' centers had been formed on campuses throughout the country. Shortly thereafter, the academic marketplace was glutted, a condition that was to last many years. This expansion was accompanied by the founding in 1965 of a major interdisciplinary journal, *Latin American Research Review,* which attracted contributions

3. Wagley, "Introduction," in *Social Science Research on Latin America,* ed. Wagley, 9–12, 14; James W. Wilkie and Rebecca Horn, "An Interview with Woodrow Borah, Berkeley and San Francisco, Calif., November and December, 1983," *Hispanic American Historical Review,* LXV (1985), 431; Miron Burgin, "New Fields of Research in Latin-American Studies," in *Responsible Freedom in the Americas,* ed. Del Río, 192, 194; George I. Blanksten, "The Politics of Latin America," in *The Politics of the Developing Areas,* eds. Gabriel A. Almond and James S. Coleman (Princeton, 1960), 479; Shannon, ed., *Underdeveloped Areas: A Book of Readings and Research,* ix; Merle Kling, "The State of Research on Latin America: Political Science," in *Social Science Research on Latin America,* ed. Wagley, 168, 171–72, 176.

4. Wagley, "Introduction," in *Social Science Research on Latin America,* ed. Wagley, 14; Richard R. Fagen, "Studying Latin American Politics: Some Implications of a *Dependencia* Approach," *Latin American Research Review,* XII (1977), 4; Chester E. Finn, Jr., *Scholars, Dollars, and Bureaucrats* (Washington, D.C., 1978), 20–22; Carnegie Council on Policy Studies in Higher Education, *The Carnegie Council on Policy Studies in Higher Education: A Summary of Reports and Recommendations* (San Francisco, 1980), 34.

from scholars in Latin America and occasionally published articles and research reports in Spanish and Portuguese. A year later scholars from the social sciences and humanities established the Latin American Studies Association to improve teaching and research in the relevant disciplines.

An inherent part of this growth of scholarly interest in Latin America was a grant bonanza that sent students and professors to all parts of the region for study, research, and teaching. In addition to students and scholars funded by university exchange programs, the Fulbright Commission, the Organization of American States, and private agencies such as the Ford, Tinker, and Rockefeller foundations, hundreds of Peace Corps volunteers also became well acquainted with Latin America in the 1960s. The decade thus produced new kinds of travelers who contrasted markedly with their nineteenth- and early twentieth-century counterparts in that they brought with them better academic preparation, more-acute discernment, and greater empathy for Latin American culture; they also made contact with a more-representative segment of the population. The result would be more-detailed knowledge and presentation of a much more diverse perspective.

Another indicator of the dramatic surge of interest in Latin American studies in the 1960s was the paperback revolution. The mass market paperback phenomenon began in the late 1930s, and it rode to profitability in the postwar period through publication of such favorites as mysteries, Westerns, romances, and how-to books. But the only mass market trademark with visibility in the academic market was New American Library's Mentor series, which appeared in 1948. Other mass marketers followed, and in the early 1950s two trade paperback labels, Doubleday's Anchor Books and Vintage from Knopf, led the way toward quality paperbacks for the academic audience. Because of a proliferation of paperback companies, the growth in profitability, acceptance of paperbacks by bookstores, and publication of originals, paperbacks achieved growing visibility in educational circles, and educators soon discovered the flexibility paperbacks offered in the classroom. By the early 1960s trade paperbacks had become ubiquitous on college campuses and on course reading lists. This paperback revolution made the most-recent scholarship in Latin American studies as well as classic works in the field readily available to wide audiences. The number of paperback titles on Latin America in the 1959–1964 period showed an approximate eightfold increase over the previous six-year period, and the titles for those later years included Latin American authors in the social sciences and humanities as well as several literary works in English translation. The remarkable studies of Brazilian and Mexican cultures offered respectively by Gilberto Freyre in *The Masters and the Slaves* and by Octavio Paz in *The Labyrinth of Solitude* became available in paperback in the early 1960s.[5]

Interest in Latin America in the early 1960s was high, concern was growing, and the frustration, impatience, and muted anger characterizing much of the commentary were further stirred by shocking descriptions of poverty and expressions of alarm over developments in the region. The work of anthropologist Oscar Lewis in depicting the poverty-stricken everyday lives of his Mexican subjects horrified an American public that, in the days before the "War on Poverty," remained largely innocent of the sufferings of its own sizeable underclass. In two studies, *Five Families: Mexican Case Histories in the Culture of Poverty* (1959) and *The Children of Sanchez: Autobiography of a Mexican Family* (1961), Lewis offered insightful and sympathetic portraits of his subjects whose daily lives seemed engulfed in drunkenness, disease, filth, promiscuity, and hopelessness. But Latin America's political and economic conditions attracted more attention than did its social problems. Herbert Matthews noted that even though the trend was away from dictatorships, a tour of the region left a visitor "inescapably confused, alarmed, and somewhat depressed"—a reaction to the economic crisis resulting from excessive dependence on a limited number of export items, falling export prices, and uncontrolled inflation. An editorial of early 1961 described the Latin American economic picture as "dismal and frightening." Political scientist John D. Martz predicted, in a study of the Central American nations, "the critical moments are arriving—the tide of Central American history is sweeping toward desolation, if not complete destruction."[6] In the preface to a volume of readings on South America, the editor, distinguished Latin American historian Lewis Hanke, warned of the "inroads of the Communist conspiracy in Latin America," and proclaimed

5. Kenneth C. Davis, *Two-Bit Culture: The Paperbacking of America* (Boston, 1984), 178, 208–209, 266–70, 292; John Tebbel, *The Great Change, 1940–1980* (New York, 1981), 350, Vol. IV of Tebbel, *A History of Book Publishing in the United States*; Georgette Magassy Dorn, comp., *Latin America, Spain and Portugal: An Annotated Bibliography of Paperback Books* (Rev. ed.; Washington, D.C., 1976); Freyre, *The Masters and the Slaves*; Octavio Paz, *The Labyrinth of Solitude: Life and Thought in Mexico*, trans. Lysander Kemp (New York, 1963).

6. Oscar Lewis, *Five Families* (New York, 1959); Oscar Lewis, *The Children of Sanchez* (New York, 1961); Herbert Matthews, "A New Chapter Opens in Latin America," *New York Times Magazine*, January 11, 1959, pp. 13, 72; New York *Times*, January 12, 1961; John D. Martz as quoted in Harold Ballous, "A Study of Central America: Review of *Central America, the Crisis and the Challenge* by John D. Martz," *New Republic*, CXL (April 6, 1959), 19.

that "the continent is in social ferment." Another specialist declared that Latin America's current social revolution had "explosive potentialities beside which the usual political and military revolutions pale into insignificance."

In late 1960 a popular book with an angry message authored by a "radical gadfly" among sociologists, C. Wright Mills, appeared under the arresting title *Listen, Yankee*. Written in the first person and presented as a composite view of the Cuban revolutionary, it was based on interviews conducted in Cuba with leaders, soldiers, and intellectuals identified with the revolution. Above all, it expressed anger against Yankee exploitation. In his introduction Mills stated that it was a voice speaking for "the hungry-nation bloc," and he cautioned that the people behind this voice "are becoming strong in a kind of fury they've never known before." If we do not listen, he added, "other powerful nations are listening—certainly the Russians."[7] After a tour of South America, the venerable Senator George Aiken proclaimed, "Latin America is in a race between evolution and revolution"—a common aphorism of the day—and Adlai Stevenson quoted a well-known Latin American political leader who warned, "There is now only a 50-50 chance of saving South America." In this alarmist context more and more commentators called for a program resembling the Marshall Plan to rescue Latin America from stagnation, backwardness, communism, and—it should be added—from itself.[8]

Movement toward a new Latin American policy took place within an unfamiliar ambiance of foreboding not only about trends within the hemisphere but also about the U.S. position in the world at large; this unsettling vision was most notably promoted by John F. Kennedy, whose central message during the year preceding his January, 1961, inauguration was a summons to the nation to intensify its Cold War efforts throughout the world.[9] In an inaugural address devoted to foreign affairs, Kennedy referred to that moment as freedom's "hour of maximum danger," and he summoned the nation "to bear

7. Hanke, ed., *South America*, 97, 4; John P. Gillin, "Some Signposts for Policy," in *Social Change in Latin America Today*, eds. Richard N. Adams *et al.*, (New York, 1960), 14; C. Wright Mills, *Listen, Yankee: The Revolution in Cuba* (New York, 1960), 7.

8. Remarks of George Aiken, *Congressional Record*, Senate, 86th Cong., 2nd Sess., Vol. CVI, Pt. 12, p. 15963; Stevenson, "Our Plight in Latin America," 104–105. Albert O. Hirschman reported in his popular book *Journeys Toward Progress* (Garden City, N.Y., 1963), 333, that a common view in Latin America was that change could come about only through revolution.

9. Bruce Miroff, *Pragmatic Illusions: The Presidential Politics of John F. Kennedy* (New York, 1976), 41.

the burden of a long twilight struggle . . . against the common enemies of man: tyranny, poverty, disease and war itself." The address was rooted in Cold War dogma, and reaction to it was highly favorable largely because of the strength of the Cold War consensus.[10] Kennedy's warnings became more ominous in his first State of the Union message when he referred to the "rapidly deteriorating situations at home and abroad" and asserted: "Our problems are critical. The tide is unfavorable. The news will be worse before it is better." After summarizing the nation's domestic problems, he addressed the several crisis points abroad and the "harsh enormity of the trials through which we must pass in the next four years. Each day the crises multiply," he warned. "Each day we draw nearer the hour of maximum danger, as weapons spread and hostile forces grow stronger. . . ." Several months later in an address to the United Nations Kennedy forcefully restated his sense of dark foreboding: "The events and decisions of the next ten months may well decide the fate of man for the next ten thousand years."[11]

In Kennedy's view Latin America stood out as a region of rapidly emerging crisis requiring urgent attention. Like the rest of the nation, his interest in Latin America had been quickened by the 1958 anti-Nixon riots and the Eisenhower administration's move toward a confrontational stance with Cuba. U.S.–Latin American policy became an important issue in the 1960 campaign, addressed in speeches, press conferences, and the famous televised debates between Kennedy and Nixon. Though Kennedy's personal experience in and knowledge of Latin America were limited, "No continent was more constantly in the President's mind . . . than Latin America," according to his chief speech writer, Theodore C. Sorensen.[12] Kennedy's deep concern about Latin America was revealed in his remark, "Next to Berlin it's the most critical area, and will be for a long time. The whole place could blow up on us." Kennedy placed Latin America toward the top of his agenda for several reasons, including his desire to focus on foreign policy and the positive influence of Democratic predecessor Franklin D. Roo-

10. *Public Papers of the Presidents of the United States: John F. Kennedy, Containing the Public Messages, Speeches, and Statements of the President, January 20 to December 31, 1961* (Washington, D.C., 1962), 2; Jim F. Heath, *Decade of Disillusionment: The Kennedy-Johnson Years* (Bloomington, Ind., 1975), 62; Herbert S. Parmet, *JFK: The Presidency of John F. Kennedy* (New York, 1983), 6; Louise FitzSimons, *The Kennedy Doctrine* (New York, 1972), 8, 12.

11. John F. Kennedy, "State of the Union Address," January 30, 1961, in *Public Papers of President Kennedy*, 22–23, 27; "Address in New York City Before the General Assembly of the United Nations," September 25, 1961, *ibid.*, 625.

12. Theodore C. Sorensen, *Kennedy*, 533.

sevelt's Good Neighbor policy. Also, pressure from Latin America for a change in policy had been building during the 1950s and was voiced by influential figures such as Brazil's president, Juscelino Kubitschek. Indeed, key elements of the forthcoming Kennedy program had their origin in Latin America; it also had roots in the Eisenhower administration, which had slowly responded to pleas from critics during its last three years to end the neglect of Latin America, stop the cozy relationship with dictators, and begin supporting democratic forces. But the central reason for change was the challenge to the hemisphere posed by the Cuban revolution.[13]

During the early months of 1961, Latin American policy formulation rested largely in the hands of Adolf Berle, former assistant secretary of state for inter-American affairs, whose diplomatic experience went back to the days of the Good Neighbor policy, and two White House advisers with no significant experience in Latin America, Richard Goodwin and Arthur M. Schlesinger, Jr. Before his inauguration, Kennedy appointed a Latin American task force, chaired by Berle and including government and academic specialists and two Puerto Ricans with developmental experience on that island, to formulate new policy suggestions. Goodwin, a recent Harvard Law School graduate and talented speech writer for Kennedy, was "Kennedy's man on Latin America," though his qualifications, in his own words, were limited to "a layman's interest in the area, preparation of the candidate's speeches, a short Berlitz course in Spanish." His sole venture in Latin America consisted of "one orgiastic night just beyond the Texas border during the campaign."[14] His influence derived from Kennedy's request that he set up the Berle-chaired Latin American task force and because he was the only member with whom the president regularly conferred about the group's progress. On general Latin American topics Kennedy probably consulted most frequently with Goodwin and Schlesinger, the latter a distinguished Harvard historian; both advisers shared the president's forebodings and sense of urgency about the

13. Richard N. Goodwin, *Remembering America: A Voice from the Sixties* (Boston, 1988), 147, 150; Arthur M. Schlesinger, Jr., "Myth and Reality," in *The Alliance for Progress: A Retrospective*, ed. L. Ronald Scheman (New York, 1988), 67; Howard J. Wiarda, "Did the Alliance 'Lose Its Way,' or Were Its Assumptions All Wrong from the Beginning and Are Those Assumptions Still with Us?" in *The Alliance for Progress*, ed. Scheman, 96.

14. Jerome Levinson and Juan de Onís, *The Alliance That Lost Its Way: A Critical Report on the Alliance for Progress* (Chicago, 1970), 52–54; DeLesseps S. Morrison, *Latin American Mission* (New York, 1965), 28; Arthur M. Schlesinger, Jr., *A Thousand Days: John F. Kennedy in the White House* (Boston, 1965), 192; Goodwin, *Remembering America*, 134, 162.

region. In February Kennedy sent Schlesinger on a quick tour of Latin America; he returned convinced that the struggle of the region's masses to join the twentieth century "was confronting the United States with a crisis—one which, if ignored, might end by transforming the southern half of the hemisphere into a boiling and angry China. . . ." Unless the U.S. acted affirmatively, Schlesinger foresaw that "new Castros would undoubtedly rise across the continent."[15]

The Alliance for Progress quickly emerged in the buoyant early months of the Kennedy administration in response to the rapidly growing consensus for fundamental reorientation in the nation's posture toward its hemispheric neighbors. Suggestions from the Latin American task force together with input from a group of Latin Americans provided the basis for the president's White House address of March 13, 1961, announcing the Alliance for Progress to the Latin American diplomatic corps and a congressional representation. Details of the proposed program were set forth in an agreement negotiated between the U.S. and the Latin American states, which met as the Inter-American Economic and Social Council at Punta del Este, Uruguay, in August.[16]

The Charter of Punta del Este establishing the Alliance for Progress contained unusually specific and highly ambitious economic and social development goals. Its economic goals called for formulation of a national development plan for each country; an annual per capita growth rate of "not less than 2.5 percent"; reduced dependence on primary exports; price stability for those exports; accelerated industrialization and agricultural productivity; and economic integration leading toward a Latin American common market. The social goals included comprehensive agrarian reform; tax reform; elimination of illiteracy; improved programs of health, nutrition, and sanitation; an increase in life expectancy at birth of at least five years; and increased construction of low-cost housing. Though these economic and social goals were uppermost in the charter, the signatory nations also pledged to "improve and strengthen democratic institutions." The Alliance for Progress thus undertook a program of economic and social modernization through democratic reform as a middle course between the status quo upheld by the oligarchy and revolutionary change promoted by Cuba. The resources necessary to carry out this decade-long program were to come from tax and fiscal reforms, greater and more-efficient development of natural resources, and increased capital flows from abroad

15. Goodwin, *Remembering America,* 151; Schlesinger, A *Thousand Days,* 195, 186–87.

16. Levinson and Onís, *The Alliance,* 54–63.

through private investment and long-term development loans. Up to $20 billion was to come from the U.S., principally from public funds.[17]

Throughout 1961 Kennedy sought to garner public support for the Alliance for Progress through a barrage of publicity accompanying his initial presentation at the gala White House fete in March, a special message to Congress the following day, the meeting at Punta del Este in August, and a trip to Venezuela and Colombia at the end of the year. He also attempted to keep attention focused on Latin America by issuing periodic warnings of the dire consequences of drift and inaction. In his March message to Congress he warned: "Latin America is seething with discontent and unrest. We must act to relieve large-scale distress immediately if free institutions are to be given a chance to work out long-term solutions." Two weeks later a spokesman for the United States Information Agency testified before the House Appropriations Subcommittee that the "efforts of Castro and his Communist allies to export their subversive revolution to the entire hemisphere have rendered critical the explosive conditions in many American Republics." In a December address in Bogotá, Kennedy declared that unless the fundamental reforms envisioned under the Alliance were quickly undertaken by Latin American leaders acting in cooperation with the U.S., "the heritage of centuries of Western civilization will be consumed in a few months of violence."[18]

Presentation and promotion of the Alliance by the Kennedy administration were dramatic not only because the program emerged from a perceived imminent hemispheric crisis set within the larger framework of Cold War confrontation but also because of the unaccustomed bold scope of its goals and the expectations they aroused. In the words of DeLesseps S. Morrison, the ever-optimistic mayor of New Orleans named by Kennedy as U.S. ambassador to the Organization of American States, the Alliance for Progress was nothing less than "an over-all blueprint to build Latin America from the ground up."[19]

17. "Charter of Punta del Este" *ibid.*, Appendix B, 349–71; Miroff, *Pragmatic Illusions*, 117; Martin C. Needler, *The United States and the Latin American Revolution* (Boston, 1972), 47–48.
18. "Special Message to the Congress Requesting Appropriations for the Inter-American Fund for Social Progress and for Reconstruction in Chile," March 14, 1961, in *Public Papers of President Kennedy*, 180; "United States Information Agency's Estimate of the Latin American Situation March 28, 1961," *Hearings Before the House Appropriations Subcommittee*, "Departments of State, and Justice, the Judiciary and Related Agencies Appropriations for 1962," reprinted in "Government Documents," *Inter-American Economic Affairs*, XV (1961), 89; "Address at a Dinner at the San Carlos Palace in Bogotá," December 17, 1961, in *Public Papers of President Kennedy*, 814.
19. Morrison, *Latin American Mission*, 83.

The Alliance exhibited the spirit of daring adventure, supreme confidence, and exuberance so characteristic of the Kennedy administration during its first year. It was the same spirit that created the Peace Corps, pledged to defend democracy in South Vietnam, and set as a national goal landing a man on the moon by the end of the decade. Kennedy forthrightly communicated this attitude of unlimited possibilities, most notably in his oft-quoted inaugural address, but also in a campaign speech of October, 1960, in which he declared: "You share the same view that I do, that this country's potential is unlimited. There is no responsibility, no burden, no hazard that the United States cannot meet. . . ." One Kennedy-appointed ambassador to Latin America succinctly explained the youthful exuberance of the early 1960s by noting, "We were young beyond our years." Schlesinger described the aura of self-confidence that predominated during the early months of the Kennedy administration as follows: "The currents of vitality radiated out of the White House, flowed through the government and created a sense of vast possibility. . . . Euphoria reigned; we thought for a moment that the world was plastic and the future unlimited."[20] It was, of course, a world of illusion, and by the early 1970s the word often used to characterize many of Kennedy's men was "hubris."[21]

Public response to the call for an innovative Latin American policy was highly favorable. Commentators concurred that a state of crisis existed in Latin America and that the U.S. bore some responsibility for solving the region's many problems. The crisis theme served as a standard introduction to discussion and analysis of Latin American topics throughout 1961. Following Kennedy's March address proposing the Alliance, the New York *Times* noted editorially that "just as the Marshall Plan was the United States answer to Josef Stalin, so the Kennedy Plan is the United States answer to Fidel Castro." On the occasion of the Punta del Este meeting the same paper concluded that "because of Cuba the cold war has spread to Latin America. The magnitude, complexity and urgency of the problems are frightening." A year-end article in a newsmagazine recalled Kennedy's observation that his program represented the "Western Hemisphere's chance to

20. Kennedy speech at Sunnyside Gardens, Queens, New York, October 27, 1960, quoted in Thomas E. Cronin, "John F. Kennedy: President and Politician," in *John F. Kennedy: The Promise Revisited*, eds. Paul Harper and Joann P. Krieg (New York, 1988), 10; John Bartlow Martin, *Overtaken by Events: The Dominican Crisis from the Fall of Trujillo to the Civil War* (Garden City, N.Y., 1966), 15; Schlesinger, *A Thousand Days*, 213–14.

21. Heath, *Decade of Disillusionment*, 60–62; Thomas G. Paterson, "Introduction: John F. Kennedy's Quest for Victory and Global Crisis," in *Kennedy's Quest for Victory: American Foreign Policy, 1961–1963*, ed. Thomas G. Paterson (New York, 1989), 15–16.

cast off 'the chains of poverty,'" and the article concluded, "It could be the last chance." Despite frequent comments that the Alliance for Progress could succeed only if the Latin Americans assumed major responsibility for instituting drastic reforms, commentators explicitly conveyed the notion of U.S. responsibility. Tad Szulc, a journalist specializing in Latin America, wrote in an article entitled, "Now It Is Up to Latin America": "Like a good parent—though the comparison may be odious to some Latins, despite its accuracy—the United States can provide education for its Latin-American offspring and give them a start."[22]

Despite a few scattered demurrals, observers also endorsed the grandiose goals of the Alliance.[23] A *Business Week* article characterized the Alliance goals as spelled out by Treasury Secretary Douglas Dillon at Punta del Este as "a controlled revolution leading to a Latin American social order with political and economic values close to our own." According to *Newsweek*, the purpose of the Alliance was "to rescue its southern neighbors from poverty and discontent." An article in *Christian Century* suggested that, if properly set up and supported both by the U.S. and Latin America, the Alliance could achieve wondrous results. "Such a plan," it argued, "could set, and attain, the stirring goal of doubling literacy, food supply and national income within a decade." The subheading of a newsmagazine article stated: "Private enterprise and U.S. investors are counted on for a key role in ambitious plans for remaking Latin America."[24]

The consensus of support for the Alliance during the early months of the new administration was striking, particularly in view of Kennedy's difficulty in gaining enactment of his domestic program. Since 1958, public opinion had been moving toward the view that something was seriously amiss in Latin America, so the administration's task in persuading the public that a crisis existed and of the need for a program to meet it was not difficult. Latin American leaders happily lent themselves to this propagandistic endeavor, and their endorsement of the

22. New York *Times*, March 15, 1961; *ibid.*, August 5, 1961; H. Lavine, "Alliance for Progress: What Chance of Success Does It Really Have?" *Newsweek*, December 25, 1961, p. 36; Tad Szulc, "Now It Is Up to Latin America," *New York Times Magazine*, August 13, 1961, p. 11.

23. For examples of such reservations see James Burnham, "Rising Expectations of What?" *National Review*, September 9, 1961, p. 156; Albert O. Hirschman, "Second Thoughts on the 'Alliance for Progress'" *Reporter*, May 25, 1961, pp. 20–23.

24. "International Outlook," *Business Week*, August 12, 1961, p. 79; "Alliance Progresses," *Newsweek*, August 21, 1961, p. 44; "Partnership Offers Way to New Era," *Christian Century*, July 26, 1961, p. 894; "How Aid Plans Look to U.S. Business in Latin America," *U.S. News and World Report*, August 28, 1961, p. 55.

Alliance helped persuade the reluctant. Given the widespread agreement on the need for a new policy, the lack of any well-considered alternative to the Alliance also muted opposition. While acknowledging the complexity of the underdevelopment issue, most commentators optimistically concluded that substantial headway could be made toward Latin American development during the 1960s' "Decade of Development." Convergence of the Alliance's reform and modernizing goals with U.S. strategic goals proved a winning combination in 1961. Not even the debacle of the Bay of Pigs—the failed invasion of Cuba in April by exiles under Central Intelligence Agency sponsorship—caused any noticeable slowdown in the drive toward implementing the Alliance. In fact, it may have spurred it by fomenting a sense of Cold War urgency and by heightening the crisis atmosphere. But all in all, self-confidence and optimism, which were so much a part of the era, characterized discussion of the Alliance, as evidenced in comments about plans for "remaking Latin America" and blueprints "to build Latin America from the ground up."

While the Alliance for Progress was being formulated and promoted, commentary on it offered opportunities to discuss the problems the program was designed to overcome, that is, the causes for Latin American underdevelopment. Despite extensive academic examination of the theoretical aspects of underdevelopment in the years preceding the Alliance, discussion in the early 1960s of the causes of Latin American underdevelopment was superficial, standardized, and replete with social science jargon. The discussion was also notable for its slight attention to prominent factors in the past such as race, climate, topography, and resource base. The racial factor had been out of vogue for two decades, and Americans had become further sensitized to the issue by the growing momentum of the civil rights movement. Commentary on the role of climate, topography, and resource base in hindering development assumed that those limitations could be overcome through the application of U.S. technical know-how. They, therefore, were scarcely mentioned. Also intriguing was the silence of the Charter of Punta del Este and its proponents on the relationship between population growth rates in Latin America and development. Those growth rates, among the world's highest, directly impacted problems targeted by the Alliance, such as housing, education, health, and sanitation, but almost no one seemed to notice. One of the few who objected was the outspoken president of the Population Reference Bureau, Robert C. Cook, who wrote in 1962: "The problem of economic development which now looms so large cannot be divorced from the problem of rapid population growth. Yet there has been no effective recognition of this, either north or south of the Rio Grande."[25] The undisputed population trends, their impact on Alliance goals, and expression of their significance by specialists who had grown ever more insistent since broaching the subject in the late 1950s produced a shift in official policy during the last half of the 1960s, when several Latin American nations adopted population control as public policy and the U.S. government began providing aid for family planning and population studies.[26] Nevertheless, very little commentary on the Alliance in the early 1960s mentioned the connection between population growth and Latin American underdevelopment.

One major cause of underdevelopment according to the commentary was a powerful, entrenched oligarchy that blocked reform and upheld the status quo. Critics attacked the traditional elite not only for its corruption, mismanagement, and theft of national wealth but also for its active opposition to substantive reform. One journalist blamed "the tiny but powerful economic elite" for the failure of previous development plans under which "uncounted millions of dollars were lost through graft and corruption or just plain maladministration." Another observer concluded: "In the past these 'oligarchs' have closed ranks with petty dictators and local 'grandees' to form an alliance of privilege that has milked Latin America dry."[27] The entrenched elites who upheld traditional values and institutions were targets of the modernization effort; at minimum, they had to be persuaded to accept a reform agenda that would, in the long run, bring their own salvation. This attitude represented a noteworthy change from earlier times when the elites were often seen as cultured, sophisticated representatives of the grand cultural heritage of Western civilization. In the early 1960s Americans more and more looked to the so-called middle sectors—people presumably like themselves, led by members of a reforming elite such as President Rómulo Betancourt of Venezuela— to generate and sustain the modernizing impulse.[28]

Another major cause of underdevelopment repeatedly advanced by commentators was the inherited, long-standing inertia, corruption, and careless inattention to economic and social problems. Such criticism was usually couched in inoffensive language, but at its core the

25. Robert C. Cook, "Where Is Science Taking Us?" *Saturday Review,* November 3, 1962, p. 64.

26. Levinson and Onís, *The Alliance,* 220–23; Enrique Lerdau, "The Alliance for Progress: The Learning Experience," in *The Alliance for Progress,* ed. Scheman, 172–73.

27. Tad Szulc, "Selling a Revolution to Latin America," *New York Times Magazine,* December 17, 1961, p. 60; Lavine, "Alliance for Progress: What Chance of Success Does It Really Have?" 34.

28. Miroff, *Pragmatic Illusions,* 122–23.

message differed little from the Black Legend of decades past, which saw in the inherited culture a pattern of flawed character traits, medieval cultural traditions, and defective institutions that posed the essential obstacles to progress. One journalist declared that Latin American poverty was caused by "the curse of human mismanagement," and another asserted, "There is no magic wand which can wave away the hodge-podge of troubles Latin America has been piling up over the last 469 years. . . ." According to Tad Szulc, progress would come to Latin America only if its leaders could overcome the "languorous neglect and irresponsibility of the past." A management consultant with extensive experience in the region argued that demands for more rapid economic development arose primarily from "a protest against age-old social injustices, injustices inherited in large part from conquistador and colonial viceroy, if not from Inca and Aztec."[29]

A thought-provoking study by economics professor Everett E. Hagen, *On the Theory of Social Change: How Economic Growth Begins* (1962), indirectly lent support to the argument that the Hispanic heritage had retarded development. In a case study of Antioquia, a region in north-central Colombia well known throughout Latin America for its economic dynamism, Hagen argued that development had occurred there because of the enterprise of the Antioqueños and not because of economic advantages such as a larger market, better natural resources, or greater availability of capital. He asserted that Antioqueños were different from other Colombians in that they were more creative, hardworking, materialistic, and more likely to exhibit a "Puritan ethic." In examining social conditions characteristic of the region and their influence on personality formation, Hagen concluded that the entrepreneurial spirit arose from several factors, but he argued that most important was the struggle by Antioqueños "to prove their worth" through economic prowess, a behavior aroused by the disparagement and disrespect they had long endured from other Colombians because of their isolation, purported backwardness, and personality distinctiveness. The significance of Hagen's study lies in the attention this economist gave to cultural as opposed to economic factors and in his attribution of Antioquia's economic development to character traits associated more commonly with Yankees than Latin Americans.[30] The

29. Lavine, "Alliance for Progress: What Chance of Success Does It Really Have?" 36; David Smyth, "Kennedy's Gamble on Latin America," *Nation,* CXCIII (September 16, 1961), 162; Szulc, "Now It Is Up to Latin America," 11; Peter F. Drucker, "A Plan for Revolution in Latin America," *Harper's Magazine,* CCXXIII (July, 1961), 31.

30. Everett E. Hagen, *On the Theory of Social Change: How Economic Growth Begins* (Homewood, Ill., 1962), 367–79. For a vigorous critique of Hagen's thesis see Frank

Antioquia case highlighted the Hispanic legacy's encumbrance to development by suggesting that Antioqueños had succeeded because they overcame it.

Hagen's Antioquia case study also illustrates growing specialization and sophistication in the study of Latin America, and it offers evidence that clear distinctions were being made among regions within Latin American nations in terms of their levels of development, as well as among the nations themselves. For many decades the relative progress of Argentina, Chile, and Costa Rica had been reported by specialists, and it was often explained by the absence or limited impact of racial, climatic, and cultural factors. Distinctions based on stages of development were refined in the 1960s. For example, W. W. Rostow, in his popular book *The Stages of Economic Growth* (1960), gave his imprimatur to Argentina and Mexico for having completed the "take-off" stage of economic growth, and he noted that other Latin American countries such as Brazil and Venezuela were successfully moving through that same stage.[31] Though the differences from one Latin American country to another had long been blurred in the American imagination by the tendency to lump them all into a category of stagnation, by the 1960s the progress of the more-developed and more rapidly advancing nations was being credited and documented.

The Alliance for Progress was intellectually sustainable because of notable changes in interpreting Latin American underdevelopment in the postwar period. The shift in emphasis from racial, climatic, and cultural factors to what were essentially cultural factors occurred as modernization theory evolved. In fact, its emergence was made possible by this shift. And modernization theory, in turn, was expressed as policy in the Alliance for Progress. Both the policy and the theory foresaw development as a process of rapid evolution along the traditional-modern continuum, that is, as a nonviolent middle path between stagnation and Cuban-style revolutionary violence. Commentary on policy and theory was richest and fullest in its insistence on extirpating "medieval" and "feudalistic" Hispanic traditions and replacing them with modern ones. Theoreticians and policy architects assumed that the U.S. was the source of what was modern and advanced and that the closer the ties between the U.S. and Latin America, the more rapidly modernization would occur through the "transmission of demonstration effects." Those modern values and institutions

Safford, "Significación de los antioqueños en el desarrollo económico colombiano: Un examen crítico de la tesis de Everett Hagen," *Anuario Colombiano de Historia Social y de la Cultura*, II (1965), 18–27.

31. Rostow, *The Stages of Economic Growth*, 127.

so highly esteemed in modernization theory would be transmitted to Latin America under the Alliance, through technical aid missions, cultural and educational exchanges, and foreign aid and investment. Both policy and theory also assumed that underdevelopment was an internal problem with no significant external component. Few observers even mentioned the need for unprotected markets for Latin American exports. The Alliance for Progress became U.S. policy largely because it was upheld by a theory widely accepted in the academic world and popularized among the educated public. In addition, its inherent optimism captured the mood of the time and expressed the traditional American sense of mission. Fundamentally, that mission remained what it had been throughout the postwar period: defense of the noncommunist world. Under the Alliance the U.S. was to carry out that mission by serving as a model for Latin American development and by transmitting to those nations modernizing methodology, values, and institutions that would propel them toward development, thus rendering them less vulnerable to the communist menace. Although the military aspect of the Alliance's anticommunist thrust—counterinsurgency and support for anticommunist military regimes—gradually emerged as a major component of the policy, in 1961 the more heavily publicized reform and modernizing agenda held the spotlight.[32]

The Peace Corps provides another indication of the power and scope of modernization theory when linked to a Cold War rationale. Launched by the Kennedy administration in the same month as the Alliance for Progress, the Peace Corps shared with it a spirit of optimism, enthusiasm, and innovation. Created as a semiautonomous government agency in 1961 under the directorship of Kennedy's energetic brother-in-law, R. Sargent Shriver, the Peace Corps recruited, trained, and dispatched thousands of two-year volunteers to Latin American and other underdeveloped countries around the world to carry out a three-fold mission: to teach needed skills, to increase Third World understanding of Americans, and to increase American understanding of other peoples. Most observers rated the Peace Corps a noteworthy success, and Kennedy took great pride in the spirit of youthful service it came to symbolize. By 1964 approximately ten thousand volunteers were at work in forty-six countries. The majority were recent college graduates, generalists lacking technical skills but full of idealism and imbued with a mission of imparting American values to under-

---

32. Miroff, *Pragmatic Illusions*, 131–34; Baily, *The U.S. and the Development of South America*, 88–91, 95–96.

developed peoples, thereby helping to reduce their "cultural lag."[33]

Midway through the decade-long commitment to the Alliance for Progress, as U.S. attention was shifting from Latin America to Southeast Asia, that attention was briefly but dramatically refocused south of the border by the sudden dispatch of U.S. Marines to the Dominican Republic—the first such intervention in Latin America in more than three decades. Ordered by President Lyndon B. Johnson in 1965, the military intervention in the Dominican Republic, whose annexation had been championed by Ulysses S. Grant nearly one hundred years earlier, provided a body of commentary as revealing of U.S. perspectives on Latin American underdevelopment as was that of 1870.

Rafael Trujillo, brutal but efficient Dominican dictator since 1930, was assassinated in 1961, and under internal and U.S. pressure the successor regime moved toward constitutional democracy by sponsoring free elections late in 1962. Juan Bosch, a liberal, reform-minded intellectual, won the presidency and the support of official Washington, which expected him to convert his country into a showcase for the Alliance for Progress. But his inefficient administration and his tolerance for political participation by all groups, including increasingly active communist elements, led a coalition of forces headed by the Dominican army and air force to overthrow him seven months after his inauguration. The anti-Bosch regime, a military-dominated triumvirate, promised future elections, but it quickly lost support because of worsening economic conditions, evidence of rampant corruption among senior military officers, fear that it would cancel elections scheduled for September, 1965, and successful organization of a diverse, pro-Bosch coalition demanding a return to "constitutionalism." In April, 1965, the pro-Bosch alliance, with the support of several military units, attempted a coup. Bloody fighting erupted in the capital and continued sporadically for several days as revolutionary forces appeared to gain the upper hand. Alarming reports about the number and influence of communists within the "constitutionalists" caused President Johnson to respond to the beleaguered regime's pleas and to dispatch U.S. Marines, eventually numbering nearly twenty-three thousand, to protect American citizens and prevent a "second Cuba." The Organization of American States subsequently authorized the intervention, and military forces from a few other hemispheric nations later supplemented U.S. units. Under these stabilized conditions, a ceasefire was imposed and a moderate interim regime selected; in 1966 elections were held and foreign forces withdrew.[34]

33. Gerald T. Rice, *The Bold Experiment: JFK's Peace Corps* (Notre Dame, 1985), 172, 270; Sorensen, *Kennedy*, 531–32.

34. The most-detailed accounts of the Dominican crisis and U.S. intervention

Reportage of the Dominican intervention was extensive. It included television specials, radio and television interviews of key participants, description and analysis in newspapers and periodicals, editorial commentary, congressional debate, and books on the crisis published within months of the crisis. The bulk of commentary centered on the merits of U.S. action and, more specifically, on the question of the seriousness of the communist threat. The emphasis on communism and the danger of "another Cuba" was more intense and pervasive than the preoccupations that gave rise to the Alliance for Progress early in the decade. The concerns of 1965 were exemplified by the headline of a weekly newsmagazine account: "Full Story of Caribbean War: How Reds Plotted a Take-Over" and by the attention given to a Dominican revolutionary's declaration that "Santo Domingo is a volcano that is going to envelop all Latin America in flames!" Also, the sense of responsibility for developments in Latin America early in the decade remained a fixed guide for U.S. policy, as shown both by the intervention itself and by commentary during the crisis, such as Senator James O. Eastland's assertion that "the islands in the Caribbean are the soft underbelly of the United States." Complaints in the early 1960s of ignorance about Latin America also seemed borne out by the commentary surrounding the Dominican crisis. Despite abundant coverage, it was marked by a glaring absence of background information. Observers who attempted to place the episode in historical context did so most often by simply declaring that the revolution was a legacy of the Trujillo era. This lack of background knowledge is exemplified—and justified—by the conclusion of the U.S. ambassador to the Dominican Republic that "The history of the Republic is really non-history. It shows no development of social or political institutions. It shows no growth of a nation. . . . Dominican history . . . comes to nothing. The Dominicans have ended where they began."[35]

A survey of the proffered explanations for Dominican underdevelopment and its prospects for development contained in the commentary on the crisis yields several relevant conclusions. Observers rarely

are: Abraham F. Lowenthal, *The Dominican Intervention* (Cambridge, Mass., 1972); Jerome Slater, *Intervention and Negotiation: The United States and the Dominican Revolution* (New York, 1970); Bruce Palmer, Jr., *Intervention in the Caribbean: The Dominican Crisis of 1965* (Lexington, Ky., 1989); Martin, *Overtaken by Events*.

35. "Full Story of Caribbean War: How Reds Plotted a Take-Over," *U.S. News and World Report*, May 10, 1965, p. 32; "Dominican Republic: The Fighting Resumes," *Time*, June 25, 1965, p. 49; remarks of James O. Eastland, *Congressional Record*, Senate, 89th Cong., 1st Sess., Vol. CXI, Pt. 7, p. 9005; Martin, *Overtaken by Events*, 31–32.

mentioned race, climate, or resource base as factors hindering development but judged the fundamental problems to be the people, their institutions, and their culture. One article noted, "Wonders could be performed with the land, if it were properly used. The key would be to change the way almost everything is done." The author further declared that many of the problems were due to "the idiosyncrasies of Dominicans themselves." A U.S. official responsible for overseeing technical assistance felt optimistic about constructing an infrastructure and modernizing agriculture and education, but he argued that the real problem was to "find some way to make these people decide to solve their own problems. . . ." Another writer asserted that Latin America's problem generally was with fundamental matters such as "political attitudes and institutions" and "its own state of mind" going back three centuries to the Spaniards, who came not as colonists but as exploiters. The occasional references to historical background invariably reminded readers of a tradition of corruption, an inherited "lopsided social structure," and a legacy of violence and brutality dating from early colonial beginnings when "the captains from Castile thought nothing of shearing an ear from a disobedient Indian or letting their dogs disembowel him."[36] Several commentators declared the need to "overhaul" the economy, undertake fundamental land reform, break "the stranglehold of absentee landlordism," and encourage growth of a middle class. One observer concluded that the Alliance for Progress could stop communism only over the long haul and then only if it were successful in creating "a dominant middle class." As in the past, commentators also contrasted the considerable potential wealth with the needless poverty. One visitor complained that the fighting has made this "forlorn, hate-filled little Caribbean island" more like hell on earth than "the warm, jasmine-scented paradise it might be."[37]

Discussion of Dominican underdevelopment at mid-decade little resembled that of a century earlier. The major change was the omis-

36. "It Could Be a Great Little Country, If . . ." U.S. News and World Report, May 24, 1965, p. 39; "U.S. Aid While the Bullets Fly—the Real Dominican Story," ibid., July 19, 1965, p. 50; "What's Wrong in Latin America," ibid., May 24, 1965, pp. 40–41; "The Roots of Revolt," Newsweek, June 7, 1965, p. 30; "Hispaniola: A History of Hate," Time, May 7, 1965, p. 30.

37. John Goshko, "Economic Collapse Aggravates Island Crisis," Washington Post, June 7, 1965, reprinted in remarks of Wayne Morse, Congressional Record, Senate, 89th Cong., 1st Sess., Vol. CXI, Pt. 9, p. 12771; remarks of Stephen M. Young, ibid., Pt. 18, p. 24733; John Paton Davies, Jr., "Yankee Go Home? Stay Home? Intervene?" New York Times Magazine, May 23, 1965, p. 78; "Hispaniola: A History of Hate," Time, May 7, 1965, p. 30.

sion of racial and climatic factors, although, as previously noted, both factors had persisted in discussions of Latin American underdevelopment until nearly the mid-twentieth century. In evaluating the obstacles to Dominican development in 1965, however, commentators remained convinced of the importance of cultural factors and were certain the nation possessed great natural potential but that progress would come only as traditional values, institutions, and social structures were modernized. Dominican underdevelopment was thus seen as an internal phenomenon, lacking any noteworthy external causes. Numerous commentators were also determined to promote the modernization process—a sharp contrast to the laissez-faire attitude of a century earlier—through technical assistance programs, educational exchanges, and the efforts of Peace Corps volunteers. An increasingly exaggerated communist threat gave urgency to the task. In 1965 modernization theory undergirded analysis of Latin American underdevelopment, as seen in the Dominican case, though it was less and less expressed with the high idealism of a few years earlier. This decline in idealism, evident in the complaint that there was "no foreseeable end to the chronic turmoil that besets much of the Caribbean," presaged failure of the Alliance for Progress.[38]

Intervention in the Dominican Republic together with military coups in Brazil in 1964 and Argentina in 1966 darkened the assessments of the Alliance for Progress during the remainder of the decade and infused them with a sense of disillusionment. An economics professor visiting from Mexico wrote despairingly at mid-decade: "The passwords now are military aid, counter-insurgency, civic action and armed intervention. The Brazilian coup and the occupation of Santo Domingo are the two better known—but by no means the only—incidents of this hard stage." At the same time, a former Alliance official wrote about the "Spiritless Alliance" and complained that "the Alliance is losing the people" because of hard-nosed and shortsighted diplomacy and the growing influence of economists and technicians. Another critic reported the following Brazilian joke in 1967: "The Alliance for Progress must be succeeding; we're getting a better class of dictator."[39] Other observers judged that the Alliance's objectives were "too ambitious," that the Johnson administration had stripped the Alliance of its "crusading mystique" and reduced it to

38. "Power—and the Ticking of the Clock," *Newsweek*, May 10, 1965, p. 35.

39. Edmundo Flores, "Latin America: Alliance for Reaction," *Nation*, CC (June 21, 1965), 659; Robert B. Goldman, "Spiritless Alliance," *New Republic*, CLIII (October 30, 1965), 15; Nathan Miller, "Alliance Without Progress," *New Republic*, CLVII (September 9, 1967), 8.

"just another aid program," and that the Alliance should be renamed "the Alliance for Procrastination." A retrospective article assessing the Alliance on its fifth anniversary captured the general disillusion of the last half of the decade as follows: "The real question now is whether even an effort as big and ambitious as the Alliance for Progress can cope with Latin America's fundamental ills."[40]

By the end of the decade the Alliance's failure to meet its impossibly high reformist goals and economic targets was generally acknowledged. Senator Edward M. Kennedy wrote in 1970: "For the vast majority of Latin Americans, the alliance has failed. . . . The alliance has been a major economic disappointment. . . . a social failure. . . . a political failure." One of its most sympathetic evaluators concluded that in almost all respects there had been progress but that probably only a minority of the Alliance's specific economic and social targets had been reached. Despite the validity of arguments supporting the Alliance's accomplishments—that, for example, it laid a foundation for future progress, unleashed forces of creativity, and improved development planning—its tangible accomplishments were disappointing, especially in relation to the "devastating population growth rates which left increased unemployment, housing shortages, illiteracy, and landless peasants." The average population growth rate for Latin America during the 1960s was 2.9 percent compared with 2.4 percent for Africa, 2.5 percent for Southern Asia, and 1 percent for the industrialized countries.[41] Central to the dozens of specific goals set for the Alliance was achievement of an annual per capita growth rate in gross domestic product of 2.5 percent. As shown in Table 1, the rate of growth varied substantially from country to country, ranging from a decline of 0.7 percent in Haiti to a 4.6 percent gain in Panama, but the growth rate for Latin America as a whole was 2.4 percent, a rather modest improvement over the 2.1 percent gain of the previ-

40. John M. Hunter, "Latin American Integration and the Alliance," *Current History,* LIII (November, 1967), 257; William V. Shannon, "The Marines Have Landed," *Commonweal,* LXXXII (May 21, 1965), 279; "The Alliance After Six Years: Progress or Not?" *Senior Scholastic,* April 14, 1967, p. 16; "Alliance for Progress: How It Looks After 5 Years," *U.S. News and World Report,* August 29, 1966, p. 68.

41. Edward M. Kennedy, "Beginning Anew In Latin America: The Alianza in Trouble," *Saturday Review,* October 17, 1970, pp. 18–19; Needler, *The U.S. and the Latin American Revolution,* 51; L. Ronald Scheman, "The Alliance for Progress: Concept and Creativity," in *The Alliance for Progress,* ed. Scheman, 12, 6, 14. The earliest and mostthorough evaluation of the Alliance, written in 1970, is Levinson and Onís, *The Alliance;* for evaluations written during the 1960s see Harvey S. Perloff, *The Alliance for Progress* (Baltimore, 1969), and William D. Rogers, *The Twilight Struggle: The Alliance for Progress and the Politics of Development in Latin America* (New York, 1967).

Table 1

Average Annual Growth Rates of Per Capita Gross Domestic Product in
Latin American Countries, 1951–1970 (Percentages)

Country	1951–60	1961–65	1966–70	1961–70
Argentina	1.0	2.1	2.1	2.1
Bolivia	-1.7	2.8	3.7	3.2
Brazil	3.7	1.6	4.3	2.9
Chile	1.1	2.4	1.3	1.9
Colombia	1.4	1.3	2.3	1.7
Costa Rica	3.3	1.8	3.3	2.6
Dominican Rep.	2.6	-2.2	2.8	0.3
Ecuador	1.8	1.1	2.3	1.7
El Salvador	1.8	3.7	1.6	2.6
Guatemala	0.8	2.1	2.4	2.3
Haiti	-0.1	-1.2	-0.2	-0.7
Honduras	0.4	1.9	1.5	1.7
Mexico	2.7	3.6	3.6	3.6
Nicaragua	2.2	5.7	2.2	3.9
Panama	1.9	4.7	4.6	4.6
Paraguay	-0.2	1.5	0.7	1.0
Peru	2.9	3.4	1.0	2.1
Uruguay	0.6	-0.4	0.3	-0.1
Venezuela	3.6	1.6	0.9	1.3
Latin America	2.1	2.1	2.7	2.4

Source: L. Ronald Scheman, "The Alliance for Progress: Concept and Creativity,"
Table 1.4, p. 15, in Scheman, ed., *The Alliance for Progress: A Retrospective.* Data for
Cuba not available.

ous decade. Furthermore, the 2.5 percent goal was met in only seven
countries, and the most-impressive gains for the entire region came
in the final years of the decade, by which time disillusionment with
the Alliance had set in. One major cause of that disillusionment was
the failure to break through stubborn, traditional resistance to land
reform, a goal highlighted by reformers at the beginning of the decade.

Added to this, the gap between rich and poor nations, e.g., between the U.S. and the Latin Americans nations, continued to widen, even though the target of $20 billion in capital inflow was met. Latin America's share of world trade declined, and economic dependence on the advanced nations increased. At the same time, political democracy retrogressed while government became more authoritarian and subject to military influence. As Senator Kennedy noted in his critique of the Alliance: "[T]hirteen constitutional governments have been overthrown in nine years."[42]

The failure of the Alliance for Progress derived from many factors in addition to rapid population growth, resistance to change, and excessively ambitious goals. Factors not directly related to the Alliance included the distraction of war in Vietnam, the fading of the Cuban "threat," balance of payments problems, and the decline of liberal reformism as the decade advanced. The heady optimism, supreme confidence, and reformist spirit that had infused the formulation of U.S. policy toward Latin America at the beginning of the decade were spent well before its end. During the last half of the decade the loss of consensus on a wide range of issues became the norm. Those years were distinguished by consensus-shattering events such as black protest in the inner cities; protest against the Vietnam War; growth of the counterculture, student movement, and feminist movement; and general demand for "the transformation of systems of domination."[43] As has been seen so often in the past, the interpretation of Latin American underdevelopment was profoundly shaped by events in the United States. The smug confidence of the early 1960s had nourished a perspective that saw Latin America's developmental problems as essentially of internal origin and external solution, but the turbulent events of the decade dissipated that confidence while the growing protest movement placed the onus for Latin America's problems on a U.S. political and economic system portrayed as exploitative.

What is significant here is not an analysis of the Alliance's failure but rather that that failure was beginning to be perceived by mid-decade. That perception inevitably led specialists to reexamine the premises underlying the Alliance, that is, to reexamine the intellec-

42. Norman Girvan, "Economic Nationalism," *Daedalus*, CIV (1975), 149; Scheman, "The Alliance for Progress: Concept and Creativity," in *The Alliance for Progress*, ed. Scheman, 8–9; Kennedy, "Beginning Anew in Latin America: The Alianza in Trouble," 19; Foster-Carter, "From Rostow to Gundar Frank: Conflicting Paradigms in the Analysis of Underdevelopment," 173.

43. Fernando Henrique Cardoso, "The Consumption of Dependency Theory in the United States," *Latin American Research Review*, XII (1977), 17.

tual foundation provided by modernization theory. As one theorist noted, "The major anomaly of development theory was the continuing lack of development."[44] The shortcomings of both the Alliance for Progress and development theory stimulated the emergence in the U.S. during the last half of the decade of a theoretical viewpoint on Latin American underdevelopment antithetical to the major tenets of modernization theory. Popularly known as "dependency theory," this new perspective, by its rather sudden appearance as a competitive paradigm, ruptured the near-consensus that had upheld modernization theory in the early 1960s. The crisis in liberal thinking on development represented by the emergence of dependency theory was a natural complement to the many other discordant events of the period. This challenge highlighted a growing tension between the U.S. perspective on underdevelopment and that of large numbers of Latin Americans, who had come to embrace dependency theory by the mid-1960s. Their analysis would subsequently claim significant numbers of adherents within the U.S. academic community.

U.S. interest in Latin America and its developmental problems reached a peak of intensity in the early 1960s through the convergence of heightened concern about the problems of the underdeveloped world in general and the growing threat of a communist sweep in the hemisphere. U.S. leadership in the drive for development conformed to the nation's anticommunist mission of the postwar period, and it was thoroughly compatible with the American notion of steady, nonviolent progress. By the time the Alliance for Progress was launched, the academic community was increasingly engaged in examining many issues surrounding Latin American underdevelopment and had the beginnings, noted one specialist, "at least of something like real acquaintance" with the region. But a genuine depth of knowledge was still lacking; there still existed "an imbalance between Latin American reality and research." Interpreting that reality and formulating development theory for the region remained ethnocentric; the theoretical constructs were "infested with Anglo-American assumptions," suggested one economist.[45] Demeaning, racially based comments about

44. Federico G. Gil, "The Kennedy-Johnson Years," in *United States Policy in Latin America: A Quarter Century of Crisis and Challenge, 1961–1986*, ed. John D. Martz (Lincoln, Nebr., 1988), 14–19.

45. Lyman Bryson, "Introduction," in *Social Change in Latin America Today*, eds. Adams *et al.*, 1; Miron Burgin, "New Fields of Research in Latin-American Studies," in *Responsible Freedom*, ed. Del Río, 189; David F. Ross, "Economic Theory and Economic Development: Reflections Derived from a Study of Honduras," *Inter-American Economic Affairs*, XIII (1959), 32.

Latin Americans had largely disappeared, but even at the time of the Dominican intervention the region's inhabitants were still seen as seriously flawed individuals, victims of a pathological cultural tradition that severely impeded their ability to follow the U.S. example. Launching the Alliance for Progress in the face of such widely held assessments was a measure of American optimism as well as of the incongruity between underlying beliefs and policy.

8

Conclusions

By the late 1960s the concordance that had characterized U.S. views on Latin American underdevelopment early in the decade had disappeared. It was replaced by conflict, which still continues, between modernization theory and dependency theory and by a sense of disillusionment among development economists. Lauchlin Currie, an economist who spent decades giving advice to governments in underdeveloped countries in Latin America and other regions, wrote in 1981 that "there is no agreement on the nature of the problem of development and its solution. The diagnoses and prescriptions differ widely, rather more than less as time has passed, and there have been few attempts to appraise the overall effort."[1] The conflict between modernization theory and dependency theory was fundamentally a conflict between a cultural interpretation and a recrudescent economic interpretation whose original effort in the 1930s had been derailed by postwar prosperity. The postwar period saw racial and climatic interpretations discarded, while the economic interpretation of the depression era was deemphasized despite the growing interest of economists in underdevelopment. The consensus of the early 1960s was therefore unidimensional—culturally based and ethnocentric. It was a durable survival from past generations of American thought on Latin American underdevelopment. The collapse of such a consensus must be rated a major plus because of its constricted intellectual base and because its collapse occurred largely in response to the gradual infiltration of Latin American views into U.S. academic circles.

Dependency theory is beyond the scope of this study, but a brief discussion of it offers an appropriate epilogue to past themes and a suggestion of trends beyond the 1960s. Although dependency theory was not accepted by a significant segment of the U.S. academic community until the late 1960s, its radical critique of the U.S. economic relationship with Latin America had been put forth earlier in the century by such writers as Lincoln Steffens, Margaret Alexander

---

1. Lauchlin Currie, *The Role of Economic Advisers in Developing Countries* (Westport, Conn., 1981), 3.

Marsh, and Carleton Beals. At its core, dependency theory revived imperialist analysis, and its rise was spurred by postwar movements for national liberation in Third World countries. The term itself is rooted in the writings of Lenin, though many of its advocates were non-Marxist. Major components of its critique were advanced during the 1940s and 1950s by a handful of economists and neo-Marxist analysts—Hans Singer, Paul A. Baran, and Gunnar Myrdal—and by historians and social scientists from Latin America.[2]

The clearest and most-persistent voice articulating the Latin American perspective was that of Raúl Prebisch, an Argentine professor of political economy, government economic adviser, and general manager of the Central Bank of Argentina, who was appointed executive secretary of the United Nations Economic Commission for Latin America (ECLA) upon its creation in 1948. Under the firm guidance of Prebisch until 1962, ECLA distinguished itself from the more technically oriented Economic Commission for Asia and the Far East and the Economic Commission for Africa by its more-active advocacy of specific programs. It articulated a Latin American point of view on development through extensive publication of economic data, studies of the economies of several Latin American countries, and analysis of underdevelopment. That analysis externalized the causes of underdevelopment to the prevailing system of international trade between developed and underdeveloped countries, that is, between the center and the periphery. Prebisch's major contributions to this analysis were his arguments that the economies of the periphery were fundamentally different from those of the center, that countries in the periphery were held in an underdeveloped position through an enduring, hegemonic relationship with the center, and that the center obtained some of its wealth from the periphery through "unequal exchange." Prebisch's work was highly influential throughout Latin America; he earned respect because his writing was technical and thoughtful, and it lacked the accusatory polemic so evident in the work of many who followed in his footsteps.[3] ECLA advocated spe-

2. Steve J. Stern, "Feudalism, Capitalism, and the World System in the Perspective of Latin America and the Caribbean," *American Historical Review*, XCIII (1988), 833; Ronald H. Chilcote, "A Question of Dependency," *Latin American Research Review*, XIII (1978), 59.

3. Albert O. Hirschman, "Ideologies of Economic Development in Latin America," in *Latin American Issues: Essays and Comments*, ed. Hirschman (New York, 1961), 12–16; Hirschman, "Appendix: United States Views on Latin American Economic Development," in *ibid.*, 37; Werner Baer, "The Economics of Prebisch and ECLA," *Economic Development and Cultural Change*, X (1962), 169–70; Armando Di Filippo, "Prebisch's Ideas on the World Economy," *CEPAL Review*, No. 34 (1988), 153–57; Joseph L.

cific programs for Latin American development including state intervention to achieve import-substituting industrialization, agrarian reform, income redistribution, and regional economic integration. ECLA's analysis contributed to the formulation of dependency theory, and its analysis together with its programmatic advocacy were important factors leading to the theory's consideration by U.S. Latin Americanists.

Briefly stated, dependency theory held that development and underdevelopment were aspects of the same historical process of worldwide European colonization that led to regional economic specialization and an international division of labor, in which underdeveloped nations became producers and exporters of primary goods to the advanced nations and importers of their manufactured products. Underdeveloped nations were disadvantaged by long-term worsening terms of trade as they were integrated into the world capitalist system, and thus they became fixed in a condition of dependency. This process not only governed the evolution of Latin American economies but also shaped their internal political and social structures so that those structures upheld the primary export system. The "traditional" characteristics of Latin American society were thus introduced or strengthened. In looking for the causes of underdevelopment, dependency theorists examined the nature of relationships with the advanced external world and within the structure of society instead of looking at its cultural and institutional features. In their view progress could come by breaking the ties that had incorporated underdeveloped nations into the global system and not through efforts to recapitulate the advanced nations' experience of gradual evolution from traditional to modern societies. Through their analysis of underdevelopment while using Marxist language, advocating socialism, and calling for a revolutionary break in the existing global political-economic structure, dependency theorists caused great commotion in the academic world and disrupted the general theoretical consensus that had underlain the Alliance for Progress. The ensuing debate also reinforced the growing awareness of the inordinate complexity of Latin American underdevelopment.[4]

Love, "Raúl Prebisch and the Origins of the Doctrine of Unequal Exchange," *Latin American Research Review*, XV (1980), 45–46, 57.

4. For succinct summaries of dependency theory as it emerged in the late 1960s see: Peter F. Klarén, "Lost Promise: Explaining Latin American Underdevelopment," in *Promise of Development: Theories of Change in Latin America*, eds. Peter F. Klarén and Thomas J. Bossert (Boulder, Colo., 1986), 14–26; Bergquist, ed., *Alternative Approaches to the Problem of Development*, ix–xii; Valenzuela and Valenzuela, "Mod-

Dependency theory gained currency during the 1960s not only because of the perceived failure of the Alliance for Progress and the inadequacies of modernization theory but also because it exhibited a certain cogency of argument. If it had been only Marxist it could have been readily dismissed, but it was also grandly historical and was supported by prominent Latin American thinkers whose views were no longer confined to a select group of academic specialists. Its emergence was also advanced by the spread of liberation theology in Latin America following Vatican II and the 1968 general conference of the Latin American episcopacy of the Catholic church in Medellín, Colombia. Proponents of dependency theory and liberation theology shared a common analytical framework that saw in Latin America's dependent condition the origin of oppressive political, economic, and social structures operating for the benefit of the privileged few. Significantly, many members of the U.S. Catholic hierarchy adopted these views. Dependency theorists effectively promoted their cause by founding new academic journals and organizations to institutionalize their school of thought and to challenge modernization theory. The appearance in 1970 of the much-read study by Stanley J. and Barbara H. Stein, *The Colonial Heritage of Latin America: Essays on Economic Dependence in Perspective,* may be taken as a mark of the growing respectability of dependency ideas because of its sympathetic consideration of the new paradigm.[5]

By the late 1960s it was evident that the reformulation of a new consensus on Latin American development among academic specialists would prove troublesome because contenders for modernization and dependency theories were driven by ideology and because of an increasingly insistent exposition of the Latin American view both in that region and within the U.S. The American public at large, however, seemed content with a policy of benign neglect at the end of the decade and reverted to its historical lack of attention to Latin America. Interestingly, by the early 1990s a general concordance of

ernization and Dependency: Alternative Perspectives in the Study of Latin American Underdevelopment," 543–52; Cardoso, "The Consumption of Dependency Theory in the United States," 7–21; Foster-Carter, "From Rostow to Gundar Frank: Conflicting Paradigms in the Analysis of Underdevelopment," 173–76.

5. Deane William Ferm, *Third World Liberation Theologies: An Introductory Survey* (Maryknoll, N.Y., 1986), 6–12; Foster-Carter, "From Rostow to Gundar Frank: Conflicting Paradigms in the Analysis of Underdevelopment," 173–74; Stern, "Feudalism, Capitalism, and the World System in the Perspective of Latin America and the Caribbean," 836.

views on development had emerged among U.S. policymakers, international lending agencies, key Latin American leaders such as Mexican president Carlos Salinas de Gortari, and the American public. This consensus outside of the academic community sprang from the growing globalization of economic activity and the sudden end of the Cold War. The developmental model advocated by this new consensus was the market model, and its favored policies were those promoting free trade, privatization of state-owned enterprises, reduced regulations, and private investment. In its essential points, the market model conformed to modernization theory, which seemed closer to implementation in the 1990s than at any time since the demise of the Alliance for Progress. Although Latin American thinkers had strongly influenced evolution of development theory in U.S. academic circles, it appears that the debt crisis, the globalization of trade and investment, and the end of the Cold War exerted an even-stronger influence on policymakers within Latin America.

For much of the period examined here, Latin American writers most familiar to Americans—Sarmiento, Martí, García Calderón—held views on development that were thoroughly compatible with American notions. Latin Americans hardly seemed to possess a distinctive perspective, with a few exceptions such as José Enrique Rodó's "Arielism" at the turn of the century, because they shared with Americans a Western heritage that provided common general assumptions about race, culture, and environment and the influence of those factors on historical development. The confidence-shattering experience of World War I invited reexamination of those common assumptions, and the Mexican Revolution offered both a testing ground and forum for a Latin American approach to development and its own vision of the future. The Great Depression further encouraged alternative perspectives and additional experimentation. By the post–World War II period, distinctive Latin American perspectives on development had emerged, although Americans generally ignored them. But by the 1960s any discussion of Latin American underdevelopment that did not seriously consider what Latin Americans themselves were saying lacked authenticity. Prebisch is the most-obvious, though certainly not the only example of growing intellectual maturity and assertion, which did not, however, guarantee that Latin Americans were any less confused, frustrated, and divided than Americans in their efforts to spur development; this they certainly were, even into the 1960s when large numbers of Latin American intellectuals embraced dependency theory. As the Latin American voice became more audible in the U.S. through visiting professorships, lecture tours, translated works, publications in scholarly journals, and research collaboration with U.S. scholars, changes occurred in the American perspective. It became more fragmented, losing its aura of certainty, and it registered a heightened awareness of Latin America's diversity and the complexity of the development issue. Those changes arose not only from the growing Latin American influence but also from simultaneous disenchantment with the Alliance for Progress.

Attitudes toward Latin America and explanations for its underdevelopment have been remarkably consistent and enduring in the course of the century covered by this study. The inherited images of the distant past have shaped U.S. perceptions even into the last half of the twentieth century. Cultural explanations for the region's developmental problems have been the most lasting, and they still flourish in the guise of modernization theory. The racial factor, though under attack beginning in the 1920s, survived until after World War II, when it faded, in part, through a process of self-censorship. The role of Latin America's tropical climate in retarding progress was largely discounted by midcentury because of advances in sanitation and tropical medicine and the realization that the majority of Latin Americans do not live in the tropics. The notion that Latin America is a veritable cornucopia of untapped natural abundance has also shown remarkable staying power despite clear evidence presented by specialists before World War II of the many natural deficits, maldistributions, and obstacles to full development of existing resources. These views shaped U.S. interpretation of Latin American underdevelopment for such a long time because few specialists were available to challenge them until the 1920s and 1930s. Until then the principal source of firsthand information about the region came from travelers who usually did not speak Spanish or Portuguese, visited only the peripheral population centers, and conversed primarily with resident aliens and educated Latin Americans. The resulting sketches typically described quaint, charming societies steeped in medieval traditionalism and destined to remain stagnant producers of raw materials for the indefinite future. Explanations for this backward state were usually offered incidentally, but they received strong confirmation from Latin American intellectuals at least through the 1920s.

That decade has a distinctly modern feel about it, although it is inexact to call it a turning point in a history marked by gradual evolution of ideas and perceptions. It was distinguished by the emergence of area specialists who began challenging traditional views, especially on race; by a growing diversity of opinions about the region; by direct presentation of Latin American views; and by a radical critique that saw in foreign capitalist exploitation the root of Latin American developmental problems. These characteristics of the commentary on development, which were only discernible in the 1920s, became pronounced in the 1960s. By then, academic specialization had reached maturity, and interpretation of Latin American underdevelopment was more diverse and complex than ever before. At the same time, Latin Americans' perceptions of their developmental problems were receiving full coverage in the U.S., as was the economic theme, the latter through debate surrounding dependency theory. Unlike the casual reports of amateur observers written for homebound readers during the early decades studied here, much information reported in the 1950s and 1960s focused directly on issues surrounding development. It expressed an urgency to understand the region's underdevelopment, accept some responsibility for it, and help overcome it. Latin American underdevelopment had never before been approached with as strong a sense of mission as that which came out of the Cold War era.

Many Americans have long believed that economic, political, and social development was the natural outcome of the historical process, because in their experience it seemed to be so. Rapid progression from raw materials producer and exporter, while relying on foreign capital investments, to industrial superpower created an optimistic outlook. The path to development seemed so easy that failure to achieve it was often explained as a consequence of racial incapacity, failure of will, or perversity of character. The sharp contrast between the material well-being of Americans and the poverty of the Latin American masses exaggerated an always-present ethnocentric outlook. Ethnocentrism has been a constant factor in shaping the U.S. interpretation of Latin American underdevelopment, although by the 1960s it no longer exercised the pervasive influence of a century earlier. For generations it hindered a fair-minded assessment of the peoples and cultures of Latin America. In the nineteenth and early twentieth centuries it was racially and culturally based, but since approximately the mid-twentieth century ethnocentrism has largely rested on a cultural foundation. That more-restricted base has been further limited by the erosion of its religious and linguistic components. For example, it has been many decades since Latin American Catholicism was linked to a weak work ethic or the Spanish language was considered a barrier to the introduction of efficient business techniques. The gradual spread, since its rise in the 1960s, of a multicultural perspective may further constrain the ethnocentric influence on U.S. attitudes toward foreign cultures. In fairness, it must be kept in mind that ethnocentrism is not unique to American culture; the

Latin American interpretation of life in the United States is also burdened with its own ethnocentric limitations.

Development throughout Latin America during the past century has been substantial—impressive in some countries. A century ago Latin America was considered a backward region, and today, despite its progress, it is still labeled underdeveloped and Third World. Its progress has often gone unnoticed, or more commonly, it has been masked by such frequently reported problems as political turmoil, guerrilla insurgencies, drug trafficking, and hyperinflation. As another example of masking good news with bad, Mexico's remarkable progress since the turbulence of the revolution has received less attention than the influx into the U.S. of large numbers of undocumented workers whose plight highlights Mexico's poverty. In addition, a fair-minded assessment of Mexican and Latin American development has been made difficult by the propinquity of the U.S. example of democratic stability, social mobility within a middle-class framework, and economic advance propelled by scientific invention and technological innovation.

Despite signs of change, disparagement of Latin America's peoples and cultures has been a long-standing, deeply engrained characteristic of the U.S. perspective, and it seems destined to last well into the future, as suggested by the following remark by Irving Kristol, originally made in the mid-1970s and recalled a decade later: "Who really thinks that poverty in South America would endure if for instance tomorrow you were to drop 50 million Swiss in Brazil?" In 1949 noted Latin American specialists participated in a symposium entitled "Pathology of Democracy in Latin America." The title was an apt summary of U.S. attitudes for not only that year but for a century earlier and today as well. It reflected a culturally rooted conviction that a diseased Latin American politics was the product of a diseased culture, hence the drive to administer the medicine of U.S. modernization techniques. Together with disparagement there is also a timeless bafflement felt by many Americans when confronting Latin American reality. "Latin America is a bewildering place," concluded John Bartlow Martin, U.S. ambassador to the Dominican Republic in the mid-1960s. "Confronted with the tangle of Latin American politics, most people in the United States throw up their hands. Some laugh. And some say, 'Send the fleet.'"[6] Such attitudes of derogation and bewilderment are no longer dominant, but enduring historical tradition

6. William F. Buckley, Jr., transcript of *Firing Line* television program, "What About Liberation Theology?" taped in New York City, December 6, 1984, p. 16; Martin, *Overtaken by Events*, 724. See also Lawrence E. Harrison, "The Cultural Component," in *The Alliance for Progress*, ed. Scheman, 237.

makes their survival certain. After all, the legends, images, and perceptions studied herein were not based on transitory sentiments reflecting fickle public opinion. They grew from cherished beliefs stubbornly held, generation after generation.

Bibliography

I. Primary Sources

A. Articles, editorials, and book reviews from the
following academic and popular journals and magazines

These sources were consulted and/or cited for the years indicated. A single, well-recognized title is listed in lieu of all variations, e.g., *Harper's Magazine* in lieu of *Harper's, Harper's Magazine, Harper's New Monthly Magazine,* and *Harper's Weekly.*

Advertising and Selling, 1929.
America, 1944–1956.
America. National Catholic Weekly Review, 1959.
American Economic Review, 1950.
American Historical Review, 1895–1965.
American Journal of Sociology, 1953.
American Mercury, 1924–1953.
American Monthly Review of Reviews, 1897–1907.
American Political Science Review, 1950.
American Review of Reviews, 1907–1928.
American Scholar, 1937.
Americas, 1949.
The Americas, 1944–1965.
Annals of the American Academy of Political and Social Science, 1890–1965.
Annual Proceedings, National Education Association, 1929.
Annual Report of the American Historical Association, 1907.
Arena, 1894.
Atlantic Monthly, 1868–1966.
Barron's, 1921–1965.
Bulletin of the National Catholic Educational Association, 1948.
Bulletin of the Pan American Union, 1893–1948.
Business Week, 1929–1965.

Catholic Mind, 1948.
Catholic School Journal, 1944.
Catholic World, 1933.
Century Magazine, 1906.
Chautauquan, 1902–1904.
Christian Century, 1908–1965.
Christian Science Monitor Magazine, 1934–1951.
Civil Engineering, 1945.
Collier's, 1905–1957.
Commercial and Financial Chronicle, 1896–1965.
Commonweal, 1924–1965.
Contemporary Review, 1927.
Coronet, 1958.
Current History, 1914–1965.
Current Opinion, 1915.
Dial, 1912.
Dun's Review, 1949.
Economic Development and Cultural Change, 1952–1965.
Education, 1933.
Elementary School Journal, 1944.
Focus, 1965.
Foreign Affairs, 1922–1965.
Foreign Policy Bulletin, 1931–1961.
Foreign Policy Reports, 1931–1951.
Fortune Magazine, 1930–1965.
Forum, 1919–1932.
Harper's Magazine, 1870–1965.
Harvard Business Review, 1928.
Hispanic American Historical Review, 1918–1922, 1926–1965.
House and Garden, 1947.
Independent, 1900–1928.
Inter-American, 1943–1946.
Inter-American Economic Affairs, 1947–1965.
Journal of American History, 1964–1965.
Journal of Development Studies, 1964–1965.
Journal of Economic History, 1941–1965.
Journal of Heredity, 1919.
Journal of Inter-American Studies, 1959–1965.
Journal of International Relations, 1922.
Journal of Political Economy, 1935.
Latin American Research Review, 1965.
Life, 1936–1965.

Literary Digest, 1924–1936.
Living Age, 1910–1928.
Look, 1937–1965.
Magazine of American History, 1890.
Magazine of Wall Street, 1954.
Mentor, 1925.
Missionary Review of the World, 1934.
Mississippi Valley Historical Review, 1914–1964.
Modern Language Journal, 1938.
Nation, 1870–1965.
National Geographic Magazine, 1899–1959.
National Republic, 1931.
National Review, 1961.
Nation's Business, 1929.
New Leader, 1958.
New Republic, 1914–1965.
Newsweek, 1933–1965.
New Yorker, 1953.
New York Times Magazine, 1931–1965.
North American Review, 1849, 1870–1940.
Outlook, 1899–1914.
Overland Monthly, 1905.
Pacific Historical Review, 1939.
Political Science Quarterly, 1920–1921.
Popular Science Monthly, 1904, 1910.
Proceedings, National Conference of Social Work, 1928.
Publications of the American Sociological Society, 1924.
Public Opinion, 1895.
Publishers Weekly, 1940–1944.
Reader's Digest, 1922–1965.
Reporter, 1949–1965.
Review of Reviews, 1890–1897, 1929–1936.
Rotarian, 1947.
Rural Sociology, 1960.
Saturday Evening Post, 1927–1965.
Saturday Review of Literature, 1924–1970.
Scholastic, 1936.
School and Society, 1923–1932.
Science, 1957.
Scientific American, 1896.
Scribner's Magazine, 1938.
Senior Scholastic, 1946–1956.

Sunset, 1920.
Survey, 1924–1932.
Time, 1923–1965.
Travel, 1938.
United Nations World, 1951.
U.S. Department of State Bulletin, 1953.
U.S. News and World Report, 1948–1965.
Virginia Quarterly Review, 1943–1950.
Vital Speeches, 1944–1958.
World Outlook, 1916.
World Today, 1908–1909.
World's Work, 1903–1932.
Yale Review, 1892–1965.

B. Articles from the following anthologies:

Adams, Richard N., *et al.*, eds. *Social Change in Latin America Today*. New York, 1960.
Almond, Gabriel A., and James S. Coleman, eds. *The Politics of the Developing Areas*. Princeton, 1960.
Blakeslee, George H., ed. *Latin America: Clark University Addresses, November, 1913*. New York, 1914.
Cowdry, Edmund V., ed. *Human Biology and Racial Welfare*. New York, 1930.
Del Río, Angel, ed. *Responsible Freedom in the Americas*. Garden City, N.Y., 1955.
Gersovitz, Mark, *et al.*, eds. *The Theory and Experience of Economic Development*. London, 1982.
Hanke, Lewis, ed. *South America*. Princeton, 1959. Vol. II of Hanke, ed., *Modern Latin America: Continent in Ferment*. 2 vols.
Herring, Hubert, and Herbert Weinstock, eds. *Renascent Mexico*. New York, 1935.
Hoselitz, Bert F., ed. *The Progress of Underdeveloped Areas*. Chicago, 1952.
———, *et al.*, eds. *Theories of Economic Growth*. Glencoe, Ill., 1960.
Ogburn, William Fielding, ed. *Technology and International Relations*. Chicago, 1949.
Pike, Fredrick B., ed. *Freedom and Reform in Latin America*. Notre Dame, 1959.
Saenz, Moises, and Herbert I. Priestley, eds. *Some Mexican Problems (Lectures on the Harris Foundation 1926)*. Chicago, 1926.
Shannon, Lyle W., ed. *Underdeveloped Areas: A Book of Readings and Research*. New York, 1957.

C. Books

Acheson, Dean. *Present at the Creation: My Years in the State Department.* New York, 1969.

Adams, Frederick Upham. *Conquest of the Tropics.* 1914; rpr. New York, 1976.

Adams, Richard N., and Charles C. Cumberland. *United States University Cooperation in Latin America.* East Lansing, Mich., 1960.

Agassiz, Louis, and Elizabeth Cabot Agassiz. *A Journey in Brazil.* Boston, 1895.

Alexander, Robert J. *Communism in Latin America.* New Brunswick, N.J., 1957.

American Council on Education. *Latin America in School and College Teaching Materials.* Washington, D.C., 1944.

Andrews, Christopher C. *Brazil: Its Condition and Prospects.* New York, 1887.

Bain, H. Foster, and Thomas Thornton Read. *Ores and Industry.* New York, 1934.

Balink, Albert. *My Paradise Is Hell: The Story of the Caribbean.* New York, 1948.

Bancroft, Frederic, ed. *Speeches, Correspondence and Political Papers of Carl Schurz.* 6 vols. New York, 1913.

Barron, Clarence W. *The Mexican Problem.* Boston, 1917.

Bates, Marston. *Where Winter Never Comes: A Study of Man and Nature in the Tropics.* New York, 1952.

Beals, Carleton. *America South.* New York, 1937.

Beals, Ralph, and Norman D. Humphrey. *No Frontier to Learning: The Mexican Student in the United States.* Minneapolis, 1957.

Beard, Charles A., and Mary R. Beard. *The Rise of American Civilization.* New York, 1927.

Bell, Daniel. *The End of Ideology.* Glencoe, Ill., 1960.

Bemis, Samuel Flagg. *The Latin American Policy of the United States: An Historical Interpretation.* New York, 1943.

Bingham, Hiram. *Across South America: An Account of a Journey from Buenos Aires to Lima by Way of Potosí, with Notes on Brazil, Argentina, Bolivia, Chile, and Peru.* Boston, 1911.

———. *The Journal of an Expedition Across Venezuela and Colombia, 1906–1907.* New Haven, 1909.

Blake, Mary Elizabeth, and Margaret F. Sullivan. *Mexico: Picturesque, Political, Progressive.* Boston, 1888.

Blanshard, Paul. *Democracy and Empire in the Caribbean.* New York, 1947.

Blum, John Morton. *Years of War, 1941–1945*. Boston, 1967. Vol. III of Blum, *From the Morgenthau Diaries*. 3 vols.

Bonsal, Stephen. *The American Mediterranean*. New York, 1912.

Bourne, Edward Gaylord. *Spain in America, 1450–1580*. New York, 1904.

Bowers, Fredson, ed. *Tales of Adventure*. Charlottesville, Va., 1970. Vol. V of Bowers, ed., *The Works of Stephen Crane*. 10 vols.

Brown, Hubert W. *Latin America*. New York, 1901.

Bryce, James. *South America: Observations and Impressions*. New York, 1914.

Butler, William. *Mexico in Transition from the Power of Political Romanism to Civil and Religious Liberty*. New York, 1892.

Carpenter, Frank G. *Lands of the Andes and the Desert*. Garden City, N.Y., 1924.

———. *South America*. New York, 1900.

Carr, Katherine. *South American Primer*. New York, 1939.

Carson, W. E. *Mexico: The Wonderland of the South*. New York, 1909.

Cerwin, Herbert. *These Are the Mexicans*. New York, 1947.

Chamberlain, George Agnew. *Is Mexico Worth Saving?* Indianapolis, 1920.

Chapman, Charles E. *A History of the Cuban Republic*. New York, 1927.

———. *Republican Hispanic America: A History*. New York, 1937.

Chase, Stuart, and Marian Tyler. *Mexico: A Study of Two Americas*. New York, 1931.

Church, George Earl. *Mexico, Its Revolutions: Are They Evidence of Retrogression or of Progress?* New York, 1866.

Codman, John. *The Round Trip by Way of Panama Through California, Oregon, Nevada, Utah, Idaho, and Colorado, with Notes on Railroads, Commerce, Agriculture, Mining, Scenery, and People*. New York, 1879.

———. *Ten Months in Brazil, with Incidents of Voyages and Travels, Descriptions of Scenery and Characters, Notices of Commerce and Productions, etc.* Boston, 1867.

Collier, John. *The Indians of the Americas*. New York, 1947.

Conkling, Alfred R. *Appletons' Guide to Mexico Including a Chapter on Guatemala, and a Complete English-Spanish Vocabulary*. New York, 1884.

Conkling, Howard. *Mexico and the Mexicans; or, Notes of Travel in the Winter and Spring of 1883*. New York, 1883.

Cooke, Morris Llewellyn. *Brazil on the March: A Study in International Cooperation. Reflections on the Report of the American Technical Mission to Brazil*. New York, 1944.

Coolidge, Archibald Cary. *The United States as a World Power.* New York, 1908.

Cooper, Clayton Sedgwick. *The Brazilians and Their Country.* New York, 1917.

————. *Latin America: Men and Markets.* Boston, 1927.

Creel, George. *The People Next Door.* New York, 1926.

Croly, Herbert. *The Promise of American Life.* Cambridge, Mass., 1909.

Crowther, Samuel. *The Romance and Rise of the American Tropics.* Garden City, N.Y., 1929.

Curtis, William Eleroy. *Between the Andes and the Ocean: An Account of an Interesting Journey Down the West Coast of South America from the Isthmus of Panama to the Straits of Magellan.* Chicago, 1900.

————. *The Capitals of Spanish America.* New York, 1888.

Dana, Richard Henry. *Two Years Before the Mast.* 1841; rpr. New York, 1946.

Davis, Charles Belmont, ed. *Adventures and Letters of Richard Harding Davis.* New York, 1917.

Davis, Richard Harding. *Three Gringos in Venezuela and Central America.* New York, 1896.

Duggan, Laurence. *The Americas: The Search for Hemisphere Security.* New York, 1949.

Duggan, Stephen. *The Two Americas: An Interpretation.* New York, 1934.

Dunn, Wallace. *From Harrison to Harding: A Personal Narrative, Covering a Third of a Century, 1888–1921.* 2 vols. New York, 1922.

Eder, Phanor James. *Colombia.* London, 1913.

Edwards, William Seymour. *On the Mexican Highlands with a Passing Glimpse of Cuba.* Cincinnati, 1906.

Ellsworth, P. T. *Chile: An Economy in Transition.* New York, 1945.

Ewbank, Thomas. *Life in Brazil, or a Journal of a Visit to the Land of the Coca and the Palm with an Appendix, Containing Illustrations of Ancient South American Arts in Recently Discovered Implements and Products of Domestic Industry, and Works in Stone, Pottery, Gold, Silver, Bronze, etc.* New York, 1856.

Fergusson, Erna. *Chile.* New York, 1943.

————. *Cuba.* New York, 1946.

————. *Mexico Revisited.* New York, 1956.

Fiske, John. *The Discovery of America with Some Account of Ancient America and the Spanish Conquest.* 2 vols. Boston, 1899.

Flandrau, Charles Macomb. *Viva Mexico!* New York, 1908.

Fletcher, James C., and D. P. Kidder. *Brazil and the Brazilians Portrayed in Historical and Descriptive Sketches.* Boston, 1879.

Forbes-Lindsay, Charles Harcourt Ainslie, and Nevin O. Winter. *Cuba and Her People of Today.* Rev. ed. Boston, 1928.

Ford, Isaac N. *Tropical America.* New York, 1893.

Franck, Harry A. *Rediscovering South America.* Philadelphia, 1943.

———. *Roaming Through the West Indies.* New York, 1920.

———. *Tramping Through Mexico, Guatemala and Honduras.* New York, 1916.

———. *Vagabonding Down the Andes: Being the Narrative of a Journey, Chiefly Afoot, from Panama to Buenos Aires.* Garden City, N.Y., 1917.

———. *Working North from Patagonia: Being the Narrative of a Journey, Earned on the Way, Through Southern and Eastern South America.* New York, 1921.

Franck, Harry A., and Herbert C. Lanks. *The Pan American Highway, from the Rio Grande to the Canal Zone.* New York, 1940.

Frank, Waldo. *America Hispana: A Portrait and a Prospect.* New York, 1931.

Freyre, Gilberto. *Brazil: An Interpretation.* New York, 1945.

———. *The Masters and the Slaves: A Study in the Development of Brazilian Civilization.* Translated by Samuel Putnam from 4th ed. of *Casa Grande e Senzala.* New York, 1946.

———. *New World in the Tropics: The Culture of Modern Brazil.* New York, 1957.

García Calderón, Francisco. *Latin America: Its Rise and Progress.* Translated by Bernard Miall. London, 1913.

Gibbon, Thomas Edward. *Mexico Under Carranza: A Lawyer's Indictment of the Crowning Infamy of Four Hundred Years of Misrule.* Garden City, N.Y., 1919.

Goodwin, Richard N. *Remembering America: A Voice from the Sixties.* Boston, 1988.

Gorgas, William Crawford. *Sanitation in Panama.* New York, 1915.

Grant, Madison. *The Passing of the Great Race, or the Racial Basis of European History.* New York, 1916.

Grant, Ulysses S. *Personal Memoirs of U.S. Grant.* 2 vols. New York, 1885–1886.

Gray, Albert Zabriskie. *Mexico As It Is, Being Notes of a Recent Tour in That Country.* New York, 1878.

Gruening, Ernest. *Mexico and Its Heritage.* New York, 1928.

Gunther, John. *Inside Latin America.* New York, 1941.

Hagen, Everett E. *On the Theory of Social Change: How Economic Growth Begins.* Homewood, Ill., 1962.

Hale, Albert. *The South Americans.* Indianapolis, 1907.

Halle, Louis J. *Dream and Reality: Aspects of American Foreign Policy.* New York, 1958.

Hanson, Earl Parker. *Journey to Manaos.* New York, 1938.

———. *New World Emerging.* New York, 1949.

Hanson, Simon G. *Economic Development in Latin America: An Introduction to the Economic Problems of Latin America.* Washington, D.C., 1951.

Haring, C. H. *South American Progress.* Cambridge, Mass., 1934.

Harper's Pictorial History of the War with Spain. New York, 1899.

Harris, Seymour E., ed. *Economic Problems of Latin America.* New York, 1944.

Harrison, Lawrence E. *Underdevelopment Is a State of Mind: The Latin American Case.* Cambridge, Mass., 1985.

Herndon, William Lewis, and Lardner Gibbon. *Exploration of the Valley of the Amazon, Made Under Direction of the Navy Department.* 2 vols. Washington, D.C., 1853.

Herring, Hubert. *Good Neighbors: Argentina, Brazil, Chile, and Seventeen Other Countries.* New Haven, 1941.

Huntington, Ellsworth. *Civilization and Climate.* New Haven, 1915.

Huxley, Aldous. *Beyond the Mexique Bay: A Traveller's Journal.* London, 1934.

Inman, Samuel Guy. *Latin America: Its Place in World Life.* Chicago, 1937.

———. *Problems in Pan Americanism.* New York, 1921.

James, Daniel. *Red Design for the Americas.* New York, 1954.

James, Herman G., and Percy A. Martin. *The Republics of Latin America: Their History, Government, and Economic Conditions.* New York, 1923.

James, Preston E. *Latin America.* New York, 1942.

Jennings, Herbert S. *The Biological Basis of Human Nature.* New York, 1930.

Johnson, John J. *Political Change in Latin America: The Emergence of the Middle Sectors.* Stanford, 1958.

Jones, Chester Lloyd. *Caribbean Backgrounds and Prospects.* New York, 1931.

———. *Costa Rica and Civilization in the Caribbean.* New York, 1935.

———. *Mexico and Its Reconstruction.* New York, 1922.

Jones, Clarence F. *South America.* New York, 1930.

Keller, Albert Galloway. *Colonization: A Study of the Founding of New Societies.* Boston, 1908.

Kennan, George F. *Memoirs, 1925–1950.* Boston, 1967.

Kidd, Benjamin. *The Control of the Tropics.* New York, 1898.

Kirkham, Stanton Davis. *Mexican Trails.* New York, 1909.

Knight, Melvin M. *The Americans in Santo Domingo.* New York, 1928.

Lee, Douglas H.K. *Climate and Economic Development in the Tropics.* New York, 1957.

Leibenstein, Harvey. *Economic Backwardness and Economic Growth: Studies in the Theory of Economic Development.* New York, 1957.

Lerner, Daniel. *The Passing of Traditional Society: Modernizing the Middle East.* Glencoe, Ill., 1958.

Lewis, Oscar. *The Children of Sanchez.* New York, 1961.

——. *Five Families.* New York, 1959.

Lieuwen, Edwin. *Arms and Politics in Latin America.* New York, 1960.

Link, Arthur S., ed. *The Papers of Woodrow Wilson.* 55 vols. Princeton, 1966–1986.

Lippmann, Walter. *Public Opinion.* New York, 1922.

Lodge, Henry Cabot, ed. *Selections from the Correspondence of Theodore Roosevelt and Henry Cabot Lodge.* 2 vols. New York, 1925.

Lossing, Benson John. *A Pictorial History of the United States: From the Earliest Period to the Present Time.* Rev. ed. New York, 1867.

Lummis, Charles F. *The Spanish Pioneers.* Chicago, 1893.

Marsh, Margaret Alexander. *The Bankers in Bolivia: A Study in American Foreign Investment.* New York, 1928.

Martin, John Bartlow. *Overtaken by Events: The Dominican Crisis from the Fall of Trujillo to the Civil War.* Garden City, N.Y., 1966.

McBride, George McCutchen. *The Land System of Mexico.* New York, 1923.

McCarty, J. Hendrickson. *Two Thousand Miles Through the Heart of Mexico.* New York, 1886.

Meier, Gerald M., and Robert E. Baldwin. *Economic Development: Theory, History, Policy.* New York, 1957.

Merwin, Mrs. George B. *Three Years in Chile.* Edited by C. Harvey Gardner. Carbondale, Ill., 1966.

Miller, Benjamin L., and Joseph T. Singewald, Jr. *The Mineral Deposits of South America.* New York, 1919.

Millikan, Max F., and W. W. Rostow. *A Proposal: Key to an Effective Foreign Policy.* New York, 1957.

Mills, C. Wright. *Listen, Yankee: The Revolution in Cuba.* New York, 1960.

Mills, Charles A. *Climate Makes the Man.* New York, 1942.

Montgomery, D. H. *The Student's American History.* Boston, 1897.

Morison, Elting E., ed. *The Letters of Theodore Roosevelt.* 8 vols. Cambridge, Mass., 1951–1954.

Morrill, G. L. *Rotten Republics: A Tropical Tramp in Central America*. Chicago, 1916.

Morris, Ira Nelson. *With the Trade-Winds: A Jaunt in Venezuela and the West Indies*. New York, 1896.

Morrison, DeLesseps S. *Latin American Mission*. New York, 1965.

Moses, Jasper T. *Today in the Land of Tomorrow*. Indianapolis, 1909.

Muzzey, David Saville. *The American Adventure*. New York, 1922.

Myrdal, Gunnar. *Rich Lands and Poor: The Road to World Prosperity*. New York, 1957.

Nash, Roy. *The Conquest of Brazil*. New York, 1926.

Niles, Blair. *Casual Wanderings in Ecuador*. New York, 1923.

Nixon, Richard M. *Six Crises*. Garden City, N.Y., 1962.

Nordhoff, Charles. *Nine Years a Sailor: Being Sketches of Personal Experience in the United States Naval Service, the American and British Merchant Marine, and the Whaling Service*. Cincinnati, 1857.

Normano, J. F. *The Struggle for South America: Economy and Ideology*. Boston, 1931.

Olson, Paul R., and C. Addison Hickman. *Pan American Economics*. New York, 1943.

O'Shaughnessy, Edith. *A Diplomat's Wife in Mexico*. New York, 1916.

———. *Intimate Pages of Mexican History*. New York, 1920.

Palmer, Thomas W., Jr. *Search for a Latin American Policy*. Gainesville, Fla., 1957.

Parker, John H. *History of the Gatling Gun Detachment Fifth Army Corps at Santiago*. Kansas City, Mo., 1898.

Paz, Octavio. *The Labyrinth of Solitude: Life and Thought in Mexico*. Translated by Lysander Kemp. New York, 1963.

Peck, Annie S. *The South American Tour*. New York, 1913.

Perkins, Dexter. *The United States and the Caribbean*. Cambridge, Mass., 1947.

Pierson, William W., and Federico G. Gil. *Governments of Latin America*. New York, 1957.

Pomfret, John E., ed. *California Gold Rush Voyages, 1848–1849: Three Original Narratives*. San Marino, Calif., 1954.

Porter, Katherine Anne. *The Collected Essays and Occasional Writings of Katherine Anne Porter*. New York, 1970.

Porter, William Sidney [O. Henry]. *The Complete Works of O. Henry*. Garden City, N.Y., 1953.

Prescott, William H. *History of the Conquest of Mexico and History of the Conquest of Peru*. Modern Library ed. New York, n.d.

Prewett, Virginia. *Reportage on Mexico*. New York, 1941.

Price, A. Grenfell. *White Settlers in the Tropics*. New York, 1939.

Priestley, Herbert I. *The Mexican Nation: A History.* New York, 1923.

Quackenbos, George Payn. *Elementary History of the United States.* 1884 ed. New York, c. 1860.

Rea, George Bronson. *Facts and Fakes About Cuba: A Review of the Various Stories Circulated in the United States Concerning the Present Insurrection.* New York, 1897.

Redfield, Robert. *Tepoztlán, A Mexican Village.* Chicago, 1930.

Rippy, J. Fred. *The Capitalists and Colombia.* New York, 1931.

———. *Globe and Hemisphere: Latin America's Place in the Postwar Foreign Relations of the United States.* Chicago, 1958.

———. *Latin America: A Modern History.* Ann Arbor, 1958.

Robertson, William Spence. *History of the Latin American Nations.* New York, 1922.

Rogers, William D. *The Twilight Struggle: The Alliance for Progress and the Politics of Development in Latin America.* New York, 1967.

Romoli, Kathleen. *Colombia, Gateway to South America.* Garden City, N.Y., 1941.

Roosevelt, Theodore. *The Works of Theodore Roosevelt.* 24 vols. New York, 1923.

Ross, Edward Alsworth. *The Social Revolution in Mexico.* New York, 1923.

———. *South of Panama.* New York, 1914–1915.

Rostow, W. W. *The Stages of Economic Growth: A Non-Communist Manifesto.* 2nd ed. Cambridge, Mass., 1971.

Ruhl, Arthur. *The Central Americans.* New York, 1928.

Ruiz, Ramón Eduardo, ed. *An American in Maximilian's Mexico, 1865–1866: The Diaries of William Marshall Anderson.* San Marino, Calif., 1959.

Salinger, Pierre. *With Kennedy.* Garden City, N.Y., 1966.

Sanborn, Helen J. *A Winter in Central America and Mexico.* Boston, 1886.

Sands, William Franklin. *Our Jungle Diplomacy.* Chapel Hill, N.C., 1944.

Sarmiento, Domingo F. *Life in the Argentine Republic in the Days of the Tyrants; or, Civilization and Barbarism.* Translated by Mary Mann. 1868; rpr. of 1st American ed. from 3rd Spanish ed., New York, 1971.

Schlesinger, Arthur M., Jr. *A Thousand Days: John F. Kennedy in the White House.* Boston, 1965.

Schurz, William Lytle. *Latin America: A Descriptive Survey.* New York, 1941.

Scruggs, William L. *The Colombian and Venezuelan Republics, with*

Notes on Other Parts of Central and South America. Boston, 1900.

Sharp, Roland Hall. *South America Uncensored.* New York, 1945.

Simpson, Eyler N. *The Ejido: Mexico's Way Out.* Chapel Hill, N.C., 1937.

Simpson, Lesley Byrd. *Many Mexicos.* Berkeley, 1941.

Smith, Herbert H. *Brazil: The Amazon and the Coast.* New York, 1879.

Smith, Randolph Wellford. *Benighted Mexico.* London, 1916.

Sorensen, Theodore C. *Kennedy.* New York, 1965.

Sorokin, Pitirim. *Contemporary Sociological Theories.* New York, 1928.

Soule, George, David Efron, and Norman T. Ness. *Latin America in the Future World.* New York, 1945.

Speer, Robert E. *Missions and Modern History.* 2 vols. New York, 1904.

Spiegel, Henry William. *The Brazilian Economy: Chronic Inflation and Sporadic Industrialization.* Philadelphia, 1949.

Squier, Ephraim George. *Notes on Central America.* New York, 1855.

———. *Peru: Incidents of Travel and Exploration in the Land of the Incas.* New York, 1877.

Stark, Harry. *Modern Latin America.* Coral Gables, Fla., 1957.

Steffens, Lincoln. *The Autobiography of Lincoln Steffens.* New York, 1931.

Stimson, Henry L. *American Policy in Nicaragua.* New York, 1927.

Stoddard, T. Lothrop. *Clashing Tides of Colour.* New York, 1935.

———. *The Rising Tide of Color Against White World-Supremacy.* New York, 1920.

Stokes, William S. *Latin American Politics.* New York, 1959.

Strong, Josiah. *Expansion Under New World-Conditions.* New York, 1900.

———. *The New Era or the Coming Kingdom.* New York, 1893.

———. *Our Country.* 1885; rpr. Cambridge, Mass., 1891.

Sweet, William Warren. *A History of Latin America.* New York, 1919.

Tannenbaum, Frank. *The Mexican Agrarian Revolution.* New York, 1929.

———. *Mexico: The Struggle for Peace and Bread.* New York, 1950.

———. *Ten Keys to Latin America.* 2nd ed. New York, 1962.

———. *Whither Latin America: An Introduction to Its Economic and Social Problems.* New York, 1934.

Tarr, Ralph S., and Frank M. McMurry. *Tarr and McMurry Geographies. Second Book: North America.* New York, 1900.

Thompson, Wallace. *The Mexican Mind: A Study of National Psychology.* Boston, 1922.

———. *The People of Mexico: Who They Are and How They Live.* New York, 1921.

————. *Rainbow Countries of Central America.* New York, 1926.

Tomlinson, Edward. *Battle for the Hemisphere: Democracy Versus Totalitarianism in the Other America.* New York, 1947.

Trowbridge, E. D. *Mexico Today and Tomorrow.* New York, 1919.

Turner, John Kenneth. *Barbarous Mexico.* Chicago, 1910.

Van Dyke, Harry Weston. *Through South America.* New York, 1912.

Van Loon, Hendrik. *America.* New York, 1927.

Viner, Jacob. *International Trade and Economic Development.* Glencoe, Ill., 1952.

Vogt, William. *Road to Survival.* New York, 1948.

Walker, William. *The War in Nicaragua.* 1860; rpr. Tucson, Ariz., 1985.

Wallace, Dillon. *Beyond the Mexican Sierras.* Chicago, 1910.

Walling, William English. *The Mexican Question.* New York, 1927.

Warshaw, Jacob. *The New Latin America.* New York, 1922.

Wells, David A. *A Study of Mexico.* New York, 1886.

West, Willis Mason. *The Story of American Democracy: Political and Industrial.* Boston, 1922.

Weyl, Nathaniel, and Sylvia Weyl. *The Reconquest of Mexico: The Years of Lázaro Cárdenas.* London, 1939.

Whetten, Nathan L. *Rural Mexico.* Chicago, 1948.

Whitaker, John W. *Americas to the South.* New York, 1939.

Whitney, Caspar. *What's the Matter with Mexico?* New York, 1916.

Wilcox, Earley Vernon. *Tropical Agriculture.* New York, 1916.

Wilgus, A. Curtis. *The Development of Hispanic America.* New York, 1941.

Williams, Henry Lionel. *Fantastic South America: Continent of the Future.* New York, 1958.

Wilson, Charles Morrow. *Ambassadors in White.* New York, 1942.

————. *Challenge and Opportunity: Central America.* New York, 1941.

————. *The Tropics: World of Tomorrow.* New York, 1951.

Winter, Nevin O. *Brazil and Her People of To-Day.* Boston, 1910.

————. *Mexico and Her People of Today.* Rev. ed. Boston, 1918.

Winton, George B. *Mexico Today: Social, Political and Religious Conditions.* New York, 1913.

Wright, Irene A. *Cuba.* New York, 1910.

Wythe, George. *Brazil, An Expanding Economy.* New York, 1949.

————. *Industry in Latin America.* New York, 1945.

Ybarra, T. R. *America Faces South.* New York, 1939.

Zahm, John Augustine [H. J. Mozans]. *Along the Andes and Down the Amazon.* New York, 1911.

D. News reports, book reviews, and editorials from the
New York *Times*, 1868–1965.

E. Remarks by members of Congress reported in *Congressional
Globe*, 1870–1871, and *Congressional Record*, 1900–1965.

F. Other primary sources

Buckley, William F., Jr. "What About Liberation Theology?" Transcript
of *Firing Line* television program taped in New York City, December 6, 1984.

Parrish, Samuel L. "Self-Government in the Tropics." U.S. Congress.
Senate Documents. 64th Cong., 1st Sess., No. 364, December 20,
1915.

*Public Papers of the Presidents of the United States. John F. Kennedy,
Containing the Public Messages, Speeches, and Statements of the
President, January 20 to December 31, 1961*. Washington, D.C.,
1962.

Richardson, James D., comp. *A Compilation of the Messages and Papers of the Presidents, 1789–1905*. 11 vols. Washington, D.C.,
1897–1907.

U.S. Congress. *House Reports*. 48th Cong., 1st Sess., No. 1445.

U.S. Congress. *House Executive Documents*. 49th Cong., 1st Sess.,
No. 50.

U.S. Congress. *Inaugural Addresses of the Presidents of the United
States from George Washington, 1789, to Lyndon Baines Johnson,
1965*. 89th Cong., 1st Sess., House Doc. No. 51. Washington, D.C.,
1965.

U.S. Department of State. Diplomatic Dispatches from U.S. Ministers
to Argentina, Brazil, Central America, Mexico, Peru, and Venezuela,
1870–1930.

U.S. Department of State. *Foreign Relations of the United States, 1950,
II: The United Nations; the Western Hemisphere*. Washington, D.C.,
1976. "Memorandum by the Counselor of the Department (George
F. Kennan) to the Secretary of State," March 29, 1950.

II. Secondary Sources

A. Books

Adas, Michael. *Machines as the Measure of Men: Science, Technology, and Ideologies of Western Dominance*. Ithaca, 1989.

Ambrose, Stephen E. *The President*. New York, 1984. Vol. II of Ambrose, *Eisenhower*. 2 vols.

Baily, Samuel L. *The United States and the Development of South America, 1945–1975.* New York, 1976.

Beezley, William H. *Judas at the Jockey Club and Other Episodes of Porfirian Mexico.* Lincoln, Nebr., 1987.

Bergquist, Charles W., ed. *Alternative Approaches to the Problem of Development: A Selected and Annotated Bibliography.* Durham, N.C., 1979.

Berkhofer, Robert F., Jr., *The White Man's Indian: Images of the American Indian from Columbus to the Present.* New York, 1978.

Britton, John A. *Carleton Beals: A Radical Journalist in Latin America.* Albuquerque, N.M., 1987.

Brookfield, Harold. *Interdependent Development.* London, 1975.

Bryant, Keith L., Jr., *Alfalfa Bill Murray.* Norman, Okla., 1968.

Burns, E. Bradford. *Latin America: A Concise Interpretive History.* Rev. ed. Englewood Cliffs, N.J., 1977.

Burton, David Henry. *Theodore Roosevelt: Confident Imperialist.* Philadelphia, 1968.

Carnegie Council on Policy Studies in Higher Education. *The Carnegie Council on Policy Studies in Higher Education: A Summary of Reports and Recommendations.* San Francisco, 1980.

Carr, Albert Z. *The World and William Walker.* New York, 1963.

Caughey, John Walton. *Hubert Howe Bancroft: Historian of the West.* Berkeley, 1946.

Cline, Howard F. *The United States and Mexico.* Rev. ed. New York, 1971.

―――, ed. *Latin American History: Essays on Its Study and Teaching, 1898–1965.* 2 vols. Austin, Tex., 1967.

Cole, Garold. *American Travelers to Mexico, 1821–1972: A Descriptive Bibliography.* Troy, N.Y., 1978.

Crawford, William Rex. *A Century of Latin-American Thought.* Rev. ed. Cambridge, Mass., 1961.

Currie, Lauchlin. *The Role of Economic Advisers in Developing Countries.* Westport, Conn., 1981.

Curti, Merle, and Kendall Birr. *Prelude to Point Four: American Technical Missions Overseas, 1838–1938.* Madison, Wis., 1954.

Cutright, Paul Russell. *The Great Naturalists Explore South America.* 1940; rpr. Freeport, N.Y., 1968.

Dallek, Robert. *The American Style of Foreign Policy: Cultural Politics and Foreign Affairs.* New York, 1983.

Davis, Harold Eugene. *Latin American Social Thought: The History of Its Development Since Independence, with Selected Readings.* Washington, D.C., 1961.

Davis, Kenneth C. *Two-Bit Culture: The Paperbacking of America.* Boston, 1984.

DeConde, Alexander. *Herbert Hoover's Latin-American Policy.* Stanford, 1951.

De León, Arnoldo. *They Called Them Greasers: Anglo Attitudes Toward Mexicans in Texas, 1821–1900.* Austin, Tex., 1983.

Doenecke, Justus D. *The Presidencies of James A. Garfield and Chester A. Arthur.* Lawrence, Kans., 1981.

Dorn, Georgette Magassy, comp. *Latin America, Spain, and Portugal: An Annotated Bibliography of Paperback Books.* Washington, D.C., 1976.

Drake, Paul W. *The Money Doctor in the Andes: The Kemmerer Missions, 1923–1933.* Durham, N.C., 1989.

Dyer, Thomas G. *Theodore Roosevelt and the Idea of Race.* Baton Rouge, 1980.

Ellis, L. Ethan. *Republican Foreign Policy, 1921–1933.* New Brunswick, N.J., 1968.

Elson, Ruth Miller. *Guardians of Tradition: American Schoolbooks of the Nineteenth Century.* Lincoln, Nebr., 1964.

———. *Myths and Mores in American Best Sellers, 1865–1965.* New York, 1985.

Estes, Thomas S., and E. Allan Lightner, Jr. *The Department of State.* New York, 1976.

Fausold, Martin L. *The Presidency of Herbert C. Hoover.* Lawrence, Kans., 1985.

Ferm, Deane William. *Third World Liberation Theologies: An Introductory Survey.* Maryknoll, N.Y., 1986.

Fifer, J. Valerie. *United States Perceptions of Latin America, 1850–1930: A 'New West' South of Capricorn?* Manchester, Engl., 1991.

Finn, Chester E., Jr. *Scholars, Dollars, and Bureaucrats.* Washington, D.C., 1978.

FitzSimons, Louise. *The Kennedy Doctrine.* New York, 1972.

Foner, Philip S. *The Spanish-Cuban-American War and the Birth of American Imperialism, 1895–1902.* 2 vols. New York, 1972.

Fosdick, Raymond B. *The Story of the Rockefeller Foundation.* 1952; rpr. New Brunswick, N.J., 1989.

Garraty, John A. *Henry Cabot Lodge: A Biography.* New York, 1965.

Gellman, Irwin F. *Good Neighbor Diplomacy: United States Policies in Latin America, 1933–1945.* Baltimore, 1979.

Gibson, Charles, ed. *The Black Legend: Anti-Spanish Attitudes in the Old World and the New.* New York, 1971.

Gil, Federico G. *Latin American–United States Relations.* New York, 1971.

Gossett, Thomas F. *Race: The History of an Idea in America.* Dallas, 1963.

Green, David. *The Containment of Latin America: A History of the Myths and Realities of the Good Neighbor Policy.* Chicago, 1971.

Grenville, John A.S., and George Berkeley Young. *Politics, Strategy, and American Diplomacy: Studies in Foreign Policy, 1873–1917.* New Haven, 1966.

Grieb, Kenneth J. *The Latin American Policy of Warren G. Harding.* Fort Worth, Tex., 1977.

Haines, Gerald K. *The Americanization of Brazil: A Study of U.S. Cold War Diplomacy in the Third World, 1945–1954.* Wilmington, Del., 1989.

Hakuta, Kenji. *Mirror of a Language: The Debate on Bilingualism.* New York, 1986.

Hanke, Lewis. *The Spanish Struggle for Justice in the Conquest of America.* Boston, 1965.

————. ed. *Do the Americas Have a Common History? A Critique of the Bolton Theory.* New York, 1964.

Healy, David F. *The United States in Cuba, 1898–1902: Generals, Politicians, and the Search for Policy.* Madison, Wis., 1963.

Heath, Jim F. *Decade of Disillusionment: The Kennedy-Johnson Years.* Bloomington, Ind., 1975.

Henderson, James D. *Conservative Thought in Twentieth Century Latin America: The Ideas of Laureano Gómez.* Athens, Ohio, 1988.

Hicks, John D. *Republican Ascendancy, 1921–1933.* New York, 1960.

Hirschman, Albert O. *Journeys Toward Progress.* Garden City, N.Y., 1963.

————. *The Strategy of Economic Development.* New York, 1958.

Horn, Paul V., and Hubert E. Bice. *Latin-American Trade and Economics.* New York, 1949.

Horsman, Reginald. *Race and Manifest Destiny: The Origins of American Racial Anglo-Saxonism.* Cambridge, Mass., 1981.

Johannsen, Robert W. *To the Halls of the Montezumas: The Mexican War in the American Imagination.* New York, 1985.

Johnson, Allen, and Dumas Malone, eds. *Dictionary of American Biography.* 22 vols. New York, 1928–1958.

Johnson, John J. *A Hemisphere Apart: The Foundations of United States Policy Toward Latin America.* Baltimore, 1990.

————. *Latin America in Caricature.* Austin, Tex., 1980.

Kevles, Daniel J. *In the Name of Eugenics: Genetics and the Uses of Human Heredity.* New York, 1985.

Kirk, John M. *José Martí, Mentor of the Cuban Nation.* Tampa, Fla., 1983.

Klarén, Peter F., and Thomas J. Bossert, eds. *Promise of Development: Theories of Change in Latin America.* Boulder, Colo., 1986.

LaFeber, Walter. *The New Empire: An Interpretation of American Expansion, 1860–1898.* Ithaca, 1963.

Langley, Lester D. *The United States and the Caribbean in the Twentieth Century.* Rev. ed. Athens, Ga., 1985.

Leuchtenburg, William E. *Franklin D. Roosevelt and the New Deal, 1932–1940.* New York, 1963.

Levin, David. *History as Romantic Art: Bancroft, Prescott, Motley, and Parkman.* Stanford, 1959.

Levinson, Jerome, and Juan de Onís. *The Alliance That Lost Its Way: A Critical Report on the Alliance for Progress.* Chicago, 1970.

Lewis, Oscar. *Sea Routes to the Gold Fields: The Migration by Water to California in 1849–1852.* New York, 1949.

Linderman, Gerald F. *The Mirror of War: American Society and the Spanish-American War.* Ann Arbor, 1974.

Link, Arthur S. *Wilson: The New Freedom.* Princeton, 1956.

Lowenthal, Abraham F. *The Dominican Intervention.* Cambridge, Mass., 1972.

Manthorne, Katherine Emma. *Tropical Renaissance: North American Artists Exploring Latin America, 1839–1879.* Washington, D.C., 1989.

May, Ernest R. *American Imperialism: A Speculative Essay.* New York, 1967–1968.

———. *Imperial Democracy: The Emergence of America as a Great Power.* New York, 1961.

May, Stacy, and Galo Plaza. *The United Fruit Company in Latin America.* 1958; rpr. New York, 1976.

McCann, Frank D., Jr. *The Brazilian-American Alliance, 1937–1945.* Princeton, 1973.

McCoy, Donald R. *Calvin Coolidge: The Quiet President.* 1967; rpr. Lawrence, Kans., 1988.

———. *The Presidency of Harry S. Truman.* Lawrence, Kans., 1984.

McCullough, David. *The Path Between the Seas: The Creation of the Panama Canal, 1870–1914.* New York, 1977.

McFeely, William S. *Grant: A Biography.* New York, 1981.

Mecham, J. Lloyd. *The United States and Inter-American Security, 1889–1960.* Austin, Tex., 1961.

Merk, Frederick. *Manifest Destiny and Mission in American History: A Reinterpretation.* New York, 1963.

Miroff, Bruce. *Pragmatic Illusions: The Presidential Politics of John F. Kennedy.* New York, 1976.

Morison, Samuel Eliot. *The Maritime History of Massachusetts, 1783–1860*. Rev. ed. Cambridge, Mass., 1961.

Morse, Richard M. *New World Soundings: Culture and Ideology in the Americas*. Baltimore, 1989.

Mosk, Sanford A. *Industrial Revolution in Mexico*. Berkeley, 1950.

Munro, Dana G. *Intervention and Dollar Diplomacy in the Caribbean, 1900–1921*. Princeton, 1964.

Needler, Martin C. *The United States and the Latin American Revolution*. Boston, 1972.

Nevins, Allan. *Grover Cleveland: A Study in Courage*. New York, 1932.

———. *Hamilton Fish: The Inner History of the Grant Administration*. New York, 1936.

Nisbet, Robert. *History of the Idea of Progress*. New York, 1980.

O'Flaherty, Daniel. *General Jo Shelby, Undefeated Rebel*. Chapel Hill, N.C., 1954.

Osborn, Scott Compton, and Robert L. Phillips, Jr. *Richard Harding Davis*. Boston, 1978.

Palmer, Bruce, Jr. *Intervention in the Caribbean: The Dominican Crisis of 1965*. Lexington, Ky., 1989.

Parkinson, F. *Latin America, the Cold War, and the World Powers, 1945–1973*. London, 1974.

Parmet, Herbert S. *JFK: The Presidency of John F. Kennedy*. New York, 1983.

Perloff, Harvey S. *The Alliance for Progress*. Baltimore, 1969.

Perrett, Geoffrey. *America in the Twenties: A History*. New York, 1982.

Pettit, Arthur G. *Images of the Mexican American in Fiction and Film*. College Station, Tex., 1980.

Pike, Fredrick B. *Chile and the United States, 1880–1962: The Emergence of Chile's Social Crisis and the Challenge to United States Diplomacy*. Notre Dame, 1963.

———. *The United States and Latin America: Myths and Stereotypes of Civilization and Nature*. Austin, Tex., 1992.

Plesur, Milton. *America's Outward Thrust: Approaches to Foreign Affairs, 1865–1890*. DeKalb, Ill., 1971.

Pletcher, David M. *The Awkward Years: American Foreign Relations Under Garfield and Arthur*. Columbia, Mo., 1962.

———. *Rails, Mines, and Progress: Seven American Promoters in Mexico, 1867–1911*. Ithaca, 1958.

Ponko, Vincent, Jr. *Ships, Seas, and Scientists: U.S. Naval Explorations and Discovery in the Nineteenth Century*. Annapolis, 1974.

Powell, Philip Wayne. *Tree of Hate: Propaganda and Prejudices Af-*

fecting United States Relations with the Hispanic World. New York, 1971.

Reeves, Thomas C. *Gentleman Boss: The Life of Chester Alan Arthur.* New York, 1975.

Rice, Gerard T. *The Bold Experiment: JFK's Peace Corps.* Notre Dame, 1985.

Robinson, Cecil. *Mexico and the Hispanic Southwest in American Literature.* Tucson, Ariz., 1977.

Ronning, C. Neal. *José Martí and the Emigre Colony in Key West: Leadership and State Formation.* New York, 1990.

Rosenberg, Emily S. *Spreading the American Dream: American Economic and Cultural Expansion. 1890–1945.* New York, 1982.

Rostow, W. W. *Eisenhower, Kennedy, and Foreign Aid.* Austin, Tex., 1985.

Scholes, Walter V., and Marie V. Scholes. *The Foreign Policies of the Taft Administration.* Columbia, Mo., 1970.

Schoonover, Thomas D. *The United States in Central America, 1860–1911: Episodes of Social Imperialism and Imperial Rivalry in the World System.* Durham, N.C., 1991.

Sievers, Harry J. *Benjamin Harrison, Hoosier President.* 3 vols. Indianapolis, 1960–1968.

Skidmore, Thomas E., and Peter H. Smith. *Modern Latin America.* New York, 1984.

Slater, Jerome. *Intervention and Negotiation: The United States and the Dominican Revolution.* New York, 1970.

Smith, Robert Freeman. *The United States and Revolutionary Nationalism in Mexico, 1916–1932.* Chicago, 1972.

Stabb, Martin S. *In Quest of Identity: Patterns in the Spanish American Essay of Ideas, 1890–1960.* Chapel Hill, N.C., 1967.

Steigerwalt, Albert K. *The National Association of Manufacturers, 1895–1914: A Study in Business Leadership.* Grand Rapids, Mich., 1964.

Stein, Stanley J., and Barbara H. Stein. *The Colonial Heritage of Latin America: Essays on Economic Dependence in Perspective.* New York, 1970.

Steward, Dick. *Trade and Hemisphere: The Good Neighbor Policy and Reciprocal Trade.* Columbia, Mo., 1975.

Stewart, Watt. *Henry Meiggs, Yankee Pizarro.* 1946; rpr. New York, 1968.

———. *Keith and Costa Rica: A Biographical Study of Minor Cooper Keith.* Albuquerque, N.M., 1964.

Stocking, George W., Jr. *Race, Culture, and Evolution: Essays in the History of Anthropology.* Chicago, 1982.

Stout, Joseph Allen, Jr. *The Liberators: Filibustering Expeditions into Mexico, 1848–1862, and the Last Thrust of Manifest Destiny.* Los Angeles, 1973.

Tansill, Charles Callan. *The United States and Santo Domingo, 1789–1873: A Chapter in Caribbean Diplomacy.* Baltimore, 1938.

Tebbel, John. *The Great Change, 1940–1980.* New York, 1981. Vol. IV of Tebbel, *A History of Book Publishing in the United States.* 4 vols.

Trask, David F. *The War with Spain in 1898.* New York, 1981.

Tulchin, Joseph S. *The Aftermath of War: World War I and U.S. Policy Toward Latin America.* New York, 1971.

Tullis, F. LaMond. *Mormons in Mexico: The Dynamics of Faith and Culture.* Logan, Utah, 1987.

Turton, Peter. *José Martí: Architect of Cuba's Freedom.* London, 1986.

Tuveson, Ernest Lee. *Redeemer Nation: The Idea of America's Millennial Role.* Chicago, 1968.

United Nations. *The Economic Development of Latin America in the Post-War Period.* New York, 1964.

Wagner, R. Harrison. *United States Policy Toward Latin America: A Study in Domestic and International Politics.* Stanford, 1970.

Weinberg, Albert K. *Manifest Destiny: A Study of Nationalist Expansionism in American History.* Baltimore, 1935.

Welles, Sumner. *Naboth's Vineyard: The Dominican Republic, 1844–1924.* 2 vols. New York, 1928.

———. *The Time for Decision.* New York, 1944.

———. *Where Are We Heading?* New York, 1946.

Weston, Rubin Francis. *Racism in U.S. Imperialism.* Columbia, S.C., 1972.

Wilgus, A. Curtis. *Latin America in the Nineteenth Century: A Selected Bibliography of Books of Travel and Description Published in English.* Metuchen, N.J., 1973.

Williams, Frances Leigh. *Matthew Fontaine Maury, Scientist of the Sea.* New Brunswick, N.J., 1963.

Williams, Stanley T. *The Spanish Background of American Literature.* 2 vols. New Haven, 1955.

Wirth, John D. *The Politics of Brazilian Development, 1930–1954.* Stanford, 1970.

Wood, Bryce. *The Making of the Good Neighbor Policy.* New York, 1961.

B. Articles

Ameringer, Charles D. "Philippe Bunau-Varilla: New Light on the Panama Canal Treaty." *Hispanic American Historical Review,* XLVI (1966), 28–52.

Baer, Werner. "The Economics of Prebisch and ECLA." *Economic Development and Cultural Change*, X (1962), 169–82.

Barrett, Edward W., and Penn T. Kimball. "The Role of the Press and Communications." In *The American Assembly, the United States and Latin America*, edited by Herbert L. Matthews. New York, 1959.

Basadre, Jorge. "Introduction" to *Latin American Courses in the United States* by Pan American Union (Washington, D.C., 1949), as reprinted in *Latin American History: Essays on Its Study and Teaching, 1898–1965*, edited by Howard F. Cline. 2 vols. Austin, Tex., 1967.

Bastert, Russell H. "Diplomatic Reversal: Frelinghuysen's Opposition to Blaine's Pan-American Policy in 1882." *Mississippi Valley Historical Review*, XLII (1956), 653–71.

———. "A New Approach to the Origins of Blaine's Pan-American Policy." *Hispanic American Historical Review*, XXXIX (1959), 375–412.

Bernstein, Harry. "Free Minds in the Americas." In *Responsible Freedom in the Americas*, edited by Angel Del Río. Garden City, N.Y., 1955.

Bernstein, Marvin D. "Introduction." In *Foreign Investment in Latin America: Cases and Attitudes*, edited by Marvin D. Bernstein. New York, 1966.

Bethall, Leslie, and Ian Roxborough. "Latin America Between the Second World War and the Cold War: Some Reflections on the 1945–8 Conjuncture." *Journal of Latin American Studies*, XX (1988), 167–89.

Blassingame, John W. "The Press and the American Intervention in Haiti and the Dominican Republic, 1904–1920." *Caribbean Studies*, IX (1969), 27–43.

Britton, John A. "In Defense of Revolution: American Journalists in Mexico, 1920–1929." *Journalism History*, V (1978–1979), 124–30.

Brown, Stephen Dechman. "The Yankees of South America or the Apaches? Nineteenth Century United States Perceptions of Chile." *SECOLAS Annals*, XVI (1985), 5–20.

Burgin, Miron. "New Fields of Research in Latin-American Studies." In *Responsible Freedom in the Americas*, edited by Angel Del Río. Garden City, N.Y., 1955.

Cardoso, Fernando Henrique. "The Consumption of Dependency Theory in the United States." *Latin American Research Review*, XII (1977), 7–24.

Chilcote, Ronald H. "A Question of Dependency." *Latin American Research Review*, XIII (1978), 55–68.

Cline, Howard F. "Latin American History: Development of Its Study and Teaching in the United States Since 1898." In *Latin American History: Essays on Its Study and Teaching, 1898–1965*, edited by Howard F. Cline. 2 vols. Austin, Tex., 1967.

Coatsworth, John H. "Obstacles to Economic Growth in Nineteenth Century Mexico." *American Historical Review,* LXXXIII (1978), 80–100.

Cronin, Thomas E. "John F. Kennedy: President and Politician." In *John F. Kennedy: The Promise Revisited,* edited by Paul Harper and Joann P. Krieg. New York, 1988.

Dávila, Carlos. "The Press in Inter-American Relations." In *Responsible Freedom in the Americas,* edited by Angel Del Río. Garden City, N.Y., 1955.

Di Filippo, Armando. "Prebisch's Ideas on the World Economy." *CEPAL Review,* No. 34 (April, 1988), 153–63.

Fagen, Richard R. "Studying Latin American Politics: Some Implications of a *Dependencia* Approach." *Latin American Research Review,* XII (1977), 3–26.

Foster-Carter, Aidan. "From Rostow to Gundar Frank: Conflicting Paradigms in the Analysis of Underdevelopment." *World Development,* IV (1976), 167–80.

Gardiner, Clinton Harvey. "Foreign Travelers' Accounts of Mexico, 1810–1910." *The Americas,* VIII (1952), 321–51.

Gil, Federico G. "The Kennedy-Johnson Years." In *United States Policy in Latin America: A Quarter Century of Crisis and Challenge, 1961–1986,* edited by John D. Martz. Lincoln, Nebr., 1988.

Girvan, Norman. "Economic Nationalism." *Daedalus,* CIV (1975), 145–58.

Green, David. "The Cold War Comes to Latin America." In *Politics and Policies of the Truman Administration,* edited by Barton J. Bernstein. Chicago, 1970.

Harmon, George D. "Confederate Migration to Mexico." *Hispanic American Historical Review,* XVII (1937), 458–87.

Harrison, Lawrence E. "The Cultural Component." In *The Alliance for Progress: A Retrospective,* edited by L. Ronald Scheman. New York, 1988.

Hill, Lawrence F. "Confederate Exiles to Brazil." *Hispanic American Historical Review,* VII (1927), 192–210.

———. "The Confederate Exodus to Latin America." *Southwestern Historical Quarterly,* XXXIX (1935), 100–34.

Hilton, Stanley E. "The United States, Brazil, and the Cold War, 1945–1960: End of the Special Relationship." *Journal of American History,* LXVIII (1981), 599–624.

Hirschman, Albert O. "Ideologies of Economic Development in Latin America." In *Latin American Issues: Essays and Comments,* edited by Albert O. Hirschman. New York, 1961.

Hutchins, John G.B. "The American Shipping Industry Since 1914." *Business History Review*, XXVIII (1954), 105–27.

Kaufman, Burton I. "United States Trade and Latin America: The Wilson Years." *Journal of American History*, LVIII (1971), 342–63.

Keen, Benjamin. Introduction to "A Reply to Bourne." In *The Colonial Origins.* 3rd ed. Boston, 1974. Vol. I of *Latin American Civilization,* edited by Benjamin Keen.

————. "The Black Legend Revisited: Assumptions and Realities." *Hispanic American Historical Review*, XLIX (1969), 703–19.

————. "Main Currents in United States Writings on Colonial Spanish America, 1884–1984." *Hispanic American Historical Review*, LXV (1985), 657–82.

Klarén, Peter F. "Lost Promise: Explaining Latin American Underdevelopment." In *Promise of Development: Theories of Change in Latin America,* edited by Peter F. Klarén and Thomas J. Bossert. Boulder, Colo., 1986.

Kling, Merle. "The State of Research on Latin America: Political Science." In *Social Science Research on Latin America,* edited by Charles Wagley. New York, 1964.

Koppes, Clayton R. "The Good Neighbor Policy and the Nationalization of Mexican Oil: A Reinterpretation." *Journal of American History,* LXIX (1982), 62–81.

Leuchtenburg, William E. "Progressivism and Imperialism: The Progressive Movement and American Foreign Policy, 1898–1916." *Mississippi Valley Historical Review*, XXXIX (1952), 483–504.

Lockey, Joseph B. "Diplomatic Futility." *Hispanic American Historical Review*, X (1930), 265–94.

Love, Joseph L. "Raúl Prebisch and the Origins of the Doctrine of Unequal Exchange." *Latin American Research Review*, XV (1980), 45–72.

Muller, Dorothea R. "Josiah Strong and American Nationalism: A Reevaluation." *Journal of American History*, LIII (1966), 487–503.

Nikonorow, Grazyna. "A Critique of the Modernization Paradigm." *Human Factor*, XII (1974), 95–127.

O'Brien, Donal Cruise. "Modernization, Order, and the Erosion of a Democratic Ideal: American Political Science 1960–70." *Journal of Development Studies*, VIII (1972), 351–78.

Paterson, Thomas G. "Introduction: John F. Kennedy's Quest for Victory and Global Crisis." In *Kennedy's Quest for Victory: American Foreign Policy, 1961–1963,* edited by Thomas G. Paterson. New York, 1989.

Peskin, Allan. "Blaine, Garfield and Latin America: A New Look." *The Americas*, XXXVI (1979), 79–89.

Pierson, W. W. "Pathology of Democracy in Latin America." *American Political Science Review*, XLIV (1950), 100–49.

Pike, Fredrick B. "Latin America and the Inversion of United States Stereotypes in the 1920s and 1930s." *The Americas*, XLII (1985), 131–62.

Pletcher, David M. "Inter-American Shipping in the 1880's: A Loosening Tie." *Inter-American Economic Affairs*, X (1956), 14–41.

Rabe, Stephen G. "The Elusive Conference. U.S. Economic Relations with Latin America, 1945–1952." *Diplomatic History*, II (1978), 279–94.

Rezneck, Samuel. "Patterns of Thought and Action in an American Depression, 1882–1886." *American Historical Review*, LXI (1956), 284–307.

Robertson, William Spence. "Introduction" to *Guide to the Hispanic American Historical Review*, compiled by Ruth Lapham Butler (Durham, N.C., 1950), as reprinted in *Latin American History: Essays on Its Study and Teaching, 1898–1965*, edited by Howard F. Cline. 2 vols. Austin, Tex., 1967.

Robertson, William Spence *et al.* "Report of a Committee of the Pan American Union on the Teaching of Latin-American History in Colleges, Normal Schools, and Universities of the United States." *Hispanic American Historical Review*, VII (1927), 352–61.

Safford, Frank. "Significación de los antioqueños en el desarrollo económico colombiano: Un examen crítico de la tesis de Everett Hagen." *Anuario Colombiano de Historia Social y de la Cultura*, II (1965), 18–27.

Scheman, L. Ronald. "The Alliance for Progress: Concept and Creativity." In *The Alliance for Progress: A Retrospective*, edited by L. Ronald Scheman. New York, 1988.

Schlesinger, Arthur M., Jr. "Myth and Reality." In *The Alliance for Progress: A Retrospective*, edited by L. Ronald Scheman. New York, 1988.

Seidel, Robert N. "American Reformers Abroad: The Kemmerer Missions in South America, 1923–1931." *Journal of Economic History*, XXXII (1972), 520–45.

Stansifer, Charles L. "Application of the Tobar Doctrine to Central America." *The Americas*, XXIII (1967), 252–69.

———. "José Santos Zelaya: A New Look at Nicaragua's 'Liberal' Dictator." *Revista/Review Interamericana*, VII (1977), 468–85.

Stern, Steve J. "Feudalism, Capitalism, and the World System in the Perspective of Latin America and the Caribbean." *American Historical Review*, XCIII (1988), 829–72.

Trask, Roger R. "The Impact of the Cold War on United States–Latin American Relations, 1945–1949." *Diplomatic History*, I (1977), 271–84.

———. "Notes and Comments. George F. Kennan's Report on Latin America (1950)." *Diplomatic History*, II (1978), 307–11.

United Nations Department of Economic and Social Affairs. "The Growth of Foreign Investments in Latin America." In *Foreign Investment in Latin America: Cases and Attitudes*, edited by Marvin D. Bernstein. New York, 1966.

Valenzuela, J. Samuel, and Arturo Valenzuela. "Modernization and Dependency. Alternative Perspectives in the Study of Latin American Underdevelopment." *Comparative Politics*, X (1978), 535–57.

Vallier, Ivan. "Recent Theories of Development." In *Trends in Social Science Research in Latin American Studies: A Conference Report*, edited by Institute of International Studies. Berkeley, 1965.

Wagley, Charles. "Introduction." In *Social Science Research on Latin America*, edited by Charles Wagley. New York, 1964.

Wiarda, Howard J. "Did the Alliance 'Lose Its Way,' or Were Its Assumptions All Wrong from the Beginning and Are Those Assumptions Still with Us?" In *The Alliance for Progress: A Retrospective*, edited by L. Ronald Scheman. New York, 1988.

Wilgus, A. Curtis. "James G. Blaine and the Pan American Movement." *Hispanic American Historical Review*, V (1922), 662–708.

Wilkie, James W., and Rebecca Horn. "An Interview with Woodrow Borah, Berkeley and San Francisco, Calif., November and December, 1983." *Hispanic American Historical Review*, LXV (1985), 401–41.

Woll, Allen L. "Hollywood's Good Neighbor Policy: The Latin Image in American Film, 1939–1945." *Journal of Popular Film*, III (1974), 278–93.

C. Dissertations

Bald, Ralph Dewar, Jr. "The Development of Expansionist Sentiment in the United States, 1885–1895, as Reflected in Periodical Literature." Ph.D. dissertation, University of Pittsburgh, 1953.

Grier, Douglas Audenreid. "Confederate Emigration to Brazil, 1865–1870." Ph.D. dissertation, University of Michigan, 1968.

Leary, David Thomas. "The Attitudes of Certain United States Citizens Toward Mexico, 1821–1846." Ph.D. dissertation, University of Southern California, 1970.

Seidel, Robert Neal. "Progressive Pan Americanism: Development and United States Policy Toward South America, 1906–1931." Ph.D. dissertation, Cornell University, 1973.

Vivian, James Floyd. "The South American Commission to the Three Americas Movement: The Politics of Pan Americanism, 1884–1890." Ph.D. dissertation, American University, 1971.

Weinland, Thomas P. "A History of the I.Q. in America, 1890–1941." Ph.D. dissertation, Columbia University, 1970.

Zelman, Donald Lewis. "American Intellectual Attitudes Toward Mexico, 1908–1940." Ph.D. dissertation, Ohio State University, 1969.

INDEX